RED CROSS

THE INCORPORATION OF OUR TOWN

RAY QUICK

Copyright © 2015 Raeford C. Quick.

All rights reserved. No part of this book may be reproduced, stored, or transmitted by any means—whether auditory, graphic, mechanical, or electronic—without written permission of both publisher and author, except in the case of brief excerpts used in critical articles and reviews. Unauthorized reproduction of any part of this work is illegal and is punishable by law.

ISBN: 978-1-4834-3709-5 (sc)
ISBN: 978-1-4834-3710-1 (hc)
ISBN: 978-1-4834-3708-8 (e)

Because of the dynamic nature of the Internet, any web addresses or links contained in this book may have changed since publication and may no longer be valid. The views expressed in this work are solely those of the author and do not necessarily reflect the views of the publisher, and the publisher hereby disclaims any responsibility for them.

Any people depicted in stock imagery provided by Thinkstock are models, and such images are being used for illustrative purposes only.
Certain stock imagery © Thinkstock.

Lulu Publishing Services rev. date: 12/17/2015

CONTENTS

Fears on the Horizon ---------- 1
Starting Things into Motion ---------- 5
Community Meetings ----------7
The People's Mandate ----------35
The Petition to Incorporate ----------37
Red Cross is Declared a Town ----------66
What does it mean to become a Town? ----------74
The Interim Council (2002/2003) ----------77
The First Election (2004/2005) ----------91
The Second Election (2006/2007) ----------162
The Third Election (2008/2009) ----------192
The Fourth Election (2010/2011)----------210
The Fifth Election (2012-2013) ----------219
The Sixth Election (2014-2015) ----------227
Planning & Zoning ----------232
Business Recruitment ----------251
Annexations ----------264
The Widening of Highway 24/27 ----------271
Making Highway 24/27 an Expressway----------279
Sales & Use Tax ----------288
Red Cross Works to get Zip Code----------296
Sewer Needs ----------300
Grant Opportunities ----------340
A Town Hall ----------349
How Will Growth Affect Red Cross?---------- 361
My Personal Thoughts ---------- 382
Epilogue ---------- 406

"We don't want to live in a town, but if we're going to live in a town we'd like for it to be our town."

J. D. Hinson

Wisdom consists of the ability to understand the long-term consequences of decisions, the ability to seek council and the ability to draw from available resources.

Raeford Quick

ACKNOWLEDGEMENTS

During the incorporation process I developed a great deal of respect for County and State employees. I found them to be extremely competent and helpful. It seemed to be the norm that these people were more than willing to help us in meeting our needs and frequently offered valuable suggestions.

I learned that, yes, the system moves slowly but it does so for a reason. There are so many checks and balances in the system that it can't move fast. However, it is also these same checks and balances that keep errors down and make it difficult for someone to deliberately circumvent the system.

I would like to recognize the following people for their contributions in helping get Red Cross incorporated and setup.

Representative Bobbie Harold Barbee: Representative Barbee was the person that carried our petition to Raleigh and championed it through the Legislature. I don't know all that he did, or how he did it, but I do know he was the major factor in our getting incorporated. Although our petition did meet the minimum criteria for incorporation, we were so marginal that our petition could have just as easily been rejected. Had he not given it such strong support I question whether we would have succeeded?

Senator William Purcell, Senator Arron W. Plyler, Senator Fletcher L. Hartsell, Jr. and Representative Wayne Goodwin: For their support of Representative Bobbie Harold Barbee and for sponsoring our incorporation petition through the House and Senate. Without these people there would have been no one to present and/or champion our petition through both chambers of the Legislature.

Dan Short (Midland): Dan was one of the leaders that led Midland through its incorporation process. Even though he only met with us once, I called him a number of times for advice and guidance. He was the one that got our incorporation process started on the right track.

Dan Baucom (Stanly County Tax Assessor): Dan was a lifesaver. He was very easy to work with and offered a lot of very good advice. He guided us through the first draft of our paper survey. This relieved us from having to use the services of a surveyor and probably saved us a few thousand dollars.

Paul Reynolds (Stanly County GIS): Every time I went into mapping Paul was always ready to help. His knowledge of GIS (Graphical Information Systems) and his willingness to explain things were invaluable. I have no idea of the number of times I asked him to redraw our town map and he never expressed any reluctance. He always acted like he was enthusiastic and ready to get started.

Jerry Myers (Stanly County Manager): Jerry was an excellent source of information and wisdom. He told me up front that he would do what he could to help but that I should understand that his first loyalty was to the County. I considered Jerry to be like one of those proverbial wise men that sat on top of a mountain and dispensed wisdom. He had the ability to break a problem down into simple terms and give advice that was easy to follow.

Michael Sandy (Stanly County Planning & Zoning Director) - Michael was a wealth of information and gave us a lot of guidance on our zoning adoption and during the establishment of our zoning, land use, and vision plans, etc. He wrote our first zoning ordinance (adopted from the County zoning ordinance) and came out to Red Cross numerous times to provide instruction to our Planning Board.

Dr. David Lawrence (Professor, Institute of Government): Dr. Lawrence was the one of those people that everyone goes to for advice, even Legislators and Judges. I called him numerous times with questions and he seemed to have all the time in the world to explain things. He always had answers to my questions.

Josh Morton (Attorney): Josh allowed us to use him as our attorney of record during the incorporation process. He served as our town attorney for several years. He worked with us in procuring the land for the town hall. We owe him a great deal for his assistance.

Wilson Barbee (Mayor of Locust): Wilson was a man with a good heart and a lot of common sense. In the early days, after incorporation, I often talked to him about getting the town organized. I didn't trust the advice of many local people but Wilson was honest and straightforward. His philosophy of what a town should be was different from mine but his advice was invaluable. He always gave me something to think about.

Representative David Almond: Although not a part of the incorporation process, Representative Almond worked with the Town on several occasions and was invaluable in helping with legal issues (see the chapter on "Sales & Use Tax").

Carol Rhea (Rhea Consulting): Although Ms. Rhea was a contracted planning consultant, she was probably the best person we could have found to guide our Planning Board through the development of our zoning codes, land use plan, growth plan, and vision plan. Her skills at working with different, and strong-willed, personalities to create relevant, applicable, and viable codes were extremely impressive. Her ability to understand, adapt and reflect our desire for the protection of our lifestyle into our zoning codes was equally impressive.

Stanly County, NC, government: The entire body did everything they could to help us get organized and get the town set up. I was very impressed with their competence, willingness to help and the level at which they extended their helping hand. I know I mentioned several County employees specifically but that was because of the extended interaction we had with them as individuals. We owe the entire body a great debt of thanks.

I would also like to express my appreciation to the "Carolina Planning Journal", the "Stanly News & Press" and "The Weekly Post" for giving permission for their material to be used in this book.

For those that I left out, please accept my apology and my thanks. It's been 14-years and names fade with time.

For many of the people I have noted above, most would say that they were just doing their job; they probably were, but from my perspective, they went well beyond their job requirements. These people went the extra mile to help. This speaks well, not only for them but for the administrators above them, both in philosophy and in work ethics. To me, it implies the administration's commitment of service to the people. These are people that make for great State and County employees.

INTRODUCTION

This book is being written as a historical account of Red Cross's founding as having been told through my participation in the process. Since Heath Hahn and I initiated the incorporation process and since I served as chairman of the incorporation committee and as first mayor, it should be fairly comprehensive.

Many topics have been expanded so that the reader will have an understanding of the issues being discussed, reasons why decisions were made and actions taken, and of what we were trying to achieve.

I would have preferred to tell the story in chronological order but some of the events occurred over an extended period of time and often overlap other events. Because of this I have broken many of these events out into their own chapter.

When covering the Council meetings I only reference those meetings where something interesting happened. The other "omitted" meetings were still necessary so that routine business could be taken care of. It should be noted that minor/uninteresting topics within meetings have often been omitted.

Some of the more interesting facts about the incorporation of the Town of Red Cross are as follows:

- Heath Hahn and Ray Quick initiated the incorporation process. We called the first community meeting and presented the idea to the community on August 14, 2001.

- The five incorporation committee members that led the community into incorporation were C. J. Barbee, Heath Hahn, J. D. Hinson, Ray Quick and Larry Wayne Smith. Representative Bobby Harold Barbee was the State Legislator that carried our petition to Raleigh and championed it through the Legislature.

- Although we were told to expect it to cost us between $8,000 and $10,000 to complete the incorporation process, it was done at a cost of slightly less than $500.

- We met all the incorporation requirements as laid out by the Joint Legislative Commission on Municipal Incorporations and were issued a "positive" recommendation from them.

- The percentage of registered voters signing our petition in favor of incorporation was so high (92.1%) that the North Carolina State Legislature declared us a Town in the Legislative Session without our having to come back for a referendum.

- It was accomplished in less than a year - with the idea first presented to the community on August 14, 2001, the incorporation committee formed on August 28, 2001, and the town declared incorporated on August 1, 2002 during a regular session on the NC State Legislature.

We must have done a good job getting incorporated because, for several years afterwards, I received calls for advice from people wanting to incorporate their communities into a town. Misenheimer was a successful local community that I assisted. I eventually made up a checklist, or guideline, for people calling me requesting information on how to get incorporate (can be found in Appendix-8).

Surprisingly, it would appear that most incorporation ideas never succeed. I say "ideas" because there are a lot more people that think about incorporating than actually start the process. A lot of communities that do pursue incorporation are unable to meet the requirements for incorporation, most often as a result of proximity to another municipality. I remember one community that had become frightened by the aggressive annexations of a large municipality; unfortunately, they had waited until its encroachment was within their 10-mile radius, thus, excluding them from pursuing incorporation. There were even communities that couldn't get their people organized enough to follow through with their incorporation process. The community from which I obtained my initial information failed because two opposing groups were struggling for control of their incorporation efforts. It is probably realistic to assume that over 95% of incorporation "ideas" never mature into incorporations.

Book Cover Photo:

The dust jacket photo is of the first paving of Highway 27 through the crossroads in Red Cross in 1925. The photo was taken by some unknown person looking towards the crossroads from east to west on Highway 27. Looking at the pavement closely, a 12-inch apron can be observed running along each edge. Although the main part of the road was asphalt, concrete was laid along the edges to keep the asphalt from being pushed out.

The store on the left side of the picture was a general store, the owner is unknown. The man to the far left walking away, is Lo-Dockus Hahn, great-grandfather of Heath Hahn. The store on the right side of the picture was a service station owned by Dan Hinson, father of J. D. Hinson. The woman standing in front of the store is Bell Hinson, wife of Dan Hinson. She is holding her son, J. D. Hinson, and her daughter, Joyce Hinson, is standing by her side.

By the late twenties Dan Hinson had replaced the original gas station with a block gas station. During this same time period he also built a large brick store across the highway (south east corner of the intersection) to sell various products. From that store he also sold Case tractors and Oldsmobile cars. It is reported that the first car from his store is still in the possession of a local resident. The store is today known as "The Red Cross Store" and is owned by his grandson, Mike Hinson.

The book cover photo was supplied by the J. D. and Violet Hinson Family.

RED CROSS

THE INCORPORATION OF OUR TOWN

FEARS ON THE HORIZON

In 2000, I started becoming concerned about the future of our community. Nearly every day I could look out the window and see an Oakboro police car sitting at the Variety Pick-up next door. I became increasingly uneasy about this and started getting the feeling that Oakboro might be extending its sphere into our community.

I knew that Oakboro was required to provide police protection to the Oakboro annexed developments of Stony Run and Arbor Heights, so there was a legitimate reason for their police cars being in our community. However, I had heard rumors of Oakboro police setting up speed checks on Highway 205 at Hatley-Burris Road, and of making at least one traffic stop at the intersection of Highway 24/27/Highway 205. Since both of these locations were well outside the Oakboro city limit and deep within the Red Cross community, it only added to my suspicions that Oakboro may be extending its influence into our community and probably was already considering our community to be a part of the Oakboro sphere.

I started thinking of other things which might give indications of Oakboro's wanting to extend its influence into the Red Cross Community. Sewer lines were being run up Ridgecrest Road to Ridgecrest School. Oakboro was in the process of installing water lines in the southern part of our community. Oakboro had annexed the developments of Stony Run and Arbor Heights deep within our community. With the widening of Highway 24/27 we were probably beginning to look a lot more attractive to them - both as a gateway into Oakboro and as a profit center. Further fueling myfears/assumptions that Oakboro was starting to develop too much interest in our community.

Although the Stanly County School Board had funded the instillation of sewer lines for the schools in the Red Cross community, the County was turning over ownership of those lines to the Town of Oakboro. This coupled with the fact that Oakboro was in the process of installing waterlines within the Red Cross community started me wondering, why was Oakboro willing to invest so heavily in our community?

Just a few years ago the Town of Oakboro had extended its northern town limit to include the Big Lick community. Was there going to be another expansion by Oakboro? It would be a logical assumption because, with the addition of a four-lane, there would be growth in Red Cross. This would be an excellent opportunity for Oakboro to increase its geographical footprint, tax base, and to gain access to a major travel corridor.

After thinking all this through I was really beginning to believe that our Red Cross community was a prime candidate for annexation, if not already being targeted. Even if my fears were wrong, the people in Red Cross should be concerned that the conditions were right and the opportunity and motivation very much real. I started asking questions and trying to figure out what to do should an annexation attempt be made by Oakboro.

Call it paranoia, but I was afraid to ask the question directly to either Locust or Oakboro. I was afraid that if people did start asking then it might prompt either Oakboro or Locust to initiate an annexation attempt. Later, during the incorporation process, I did find out that (allegedly) some of the Oakboro Council Members had previously made inquiries about annexing parts of the Red Cross community. My understanding is that they wanted to extend the Oakboro city limits up Highway 205 (250 ft. on each side of the highway) to the intersection of Highway 205/Highway 24/27 and then turn east on Highway 24/27 and take in West Stanly High School.

As my concerns grew I started talking to some of the people in the community about Oakboro's presence in our community and it seemed that everyone felt some level of concern about being annexed. Based on some of the conversations, I found that both Oakboro and Locust had, at some point in the past, expressed an interest in being able to extend their city limits to encompass the center of the Red Cross community. I also got the impression that there was some contention between Locust and Oakboro as to which would be able to annex us first.

One prominent fear was that Locust would annex east along Highway 24/27 and Oakboro would annex north along Highway 205. As to which would annex the intersection of Highway 205/Highway 24/27 and West Stanly High School, it seemed opinions were fairly evenly split. Very few people in Red Cross wanted the Red Cross community split into two separate communities.

I started checking and found that there was no way we could block an involuntary annexation should either of them decide to annex us. In fact, should either town pursue annexation of the Red Cross community, the people of the Red Cross community would have no control in the outcome of that annexation? It would be decided in the Councils of Oakboro and/or Locust and in the North Carolina State Legislature.

I found that there were two basic types of annexations; voluntary and involuntary.

In a voluntary annexation the people in the outlying area petition the Town to accept them into the Town. Everything can be handled locally, within the Town Council, so long as annexation laws arc met. No State legislative approval is required - only a petition by the people of the outlying area requesting annexation, a public hearing and a positive vote of acceptance by the Town Council approving the annexation is required. This is how Oakboro was able to voluntarily annex Stony Run and Arbor Heights. It is not unusual for new developments to request annexation as a means of obtaining services such as water, sewer, waste collection, police protection, etc.

Surprisingly, voluntarily annexed properties do not have to be contiguous to the existing Town limits. They can be several miles from the existing Town limits - just as was done with Arbor Heights (3.5-miles) and Stony Run (5-miles). Annexations such as these are called satellite annexations. Although not connected directly to the Town proper, these satellites enjoy all the services, benefits and taxes as the rest of the town.

The major restriction in a town's being able to satellite property is that the potential satellite area must be closer to the town doing the annexation than to any other town and the annexation must be voluntary.

However, an involuntary annexation differs substantially in that approval is required by the State Legislature. In an involuntary annexation the Town does not have to ask permission of the people in the targeted area. In fact, the annexing town doesn't even have to tell the targeted people that they are going to be annexed. One major limitation is that the targeted area must be adjacent to, and attached to, the existing Town limits. All the annexing town has to do is make a conscious decision to annex the area and submit a petition to one of their State Legislative Representatives. If that Representative chooses to sponsor it, then it is presented to the State Legislature for a vote and approval. Today, annexation laws covering involuntary annexation have changed substantially (ref. North Carolina Session Law 2011-11).

The surprising thing that I found was that the people living in the targeted involuntary annexation area have no legal input into the annexation process. They can call their legislators and/or appeal to the annexing town, but other than that there is almost nothing they can do to control the outcome of the annexation.

I did find that there was only one way to be sure a potential annexation could be blocked - and that was for the people to incorporate themselves. If we in the Red Cross community could form ourselves into a town then we would have control over our community and no other town could ever annex us.

STARTING THINGS INTO MOTION

I knew someone in another community that was starting their incorporation process and called them - I believe it was in the fall of 2000. Unfortunately, they were still in the early stages of their process and didn't have a lot of useful information, however, I did get enough information from them to cement the idea in my mind and give me a starting point for gathering more information.

It is unfortunate, but apparently because of internal power struggles (two groups fighting for control of their incorporation process) they were never able to advance in their incorporation process and I was not able to continue using them for guidance - they did not incorporate.

I continued talking to both Heath Hahn and J. D. Hinson for the rest of the year and well into 2001 about the possibility of incorporating Red Cross. J. D. Hinson felt it would be a good thing but didn't think our community would go for it. Heath Hahn also felt we needed to do it but had some of the same reservations as J. D. Hinson. Although we continued to talk about it we didn't take any action.

While waiting for preaching to start on Sunday morning, August 12, 2001, Robert Thompson came to me and said he had heard I was talking about wanting to incorporate Red Cross into a town. He said that Locust had made past attempts to annex out in his direction and he was afraid that they would succeed in taking him in at some point. He wanted to stay a part of Red Cross. I told him to give me a week to check on it and I would get back to him.

After lunch that afternoon I called Heath Hahn and told him about my conversation with Robert Thompson. Heath Hahn said the only thing he knew to do was to call a community meeting, put it to the people, and see what they thought about it. It would have been nice to have also talked with J. D. Hinson but he was away on a trip and wouldn't be back for a couple weeks.

Heath Hahn and I started making a list of everyone we could think of to call and divided it up between us. Heath suggested we go ahead and set a meeting for Tuesday night August 14, 2001, to be held in the basement of Red Cross Baptist Church.

I can't say as to whether it was Robert Thompson or Heath Hahn that lit the match that actually started things moving, but it could be said that one held the fuse while the other lit the match. They both made the call for action and both were responsible for getting the process moved from the talking stage to the action stage. For historical purposes, Heath Hahn should be credited with calling that first meeting of the community for incorporation.

As a side note, it should also be noted for historical purposes that Heath Hahn was also instrumental in getting the first stop light installed in Red Cross at the intersection of Highway 24/27/Highway 205.

COMMUNITY MEETINGS

Please note that I am including information and/or agendas for both community meetings and committee meetings, intermixed, but in chronological order. This may at first seem a little confusing but it will, hopefully, allow for a greater understanding of events as they occurred. The community meetings were where everyone in the community met and the committee meetings are where just the incorporation committee met. I will say that the incorporation committee didn't keep very good notes. Part of the reason was that the incorporation committee was running around trying to get things done. There was a lot of communication, just not in formal meetings.

The First Community Meeting (08-14-2001):

Heath Hahn and I had called as many people as we could think of and set up a community meeting for Tuesday night, August 14, 2001, to be held in the basement of Red Cross Baptist Church. We had no idea of how many would attend or of what their reaction would be.

Although the people had only a two day notice it seemed to work well because there were 47 people there in addition to the two of us.

One of the things we hadn't thought of was to have someone keep a record of the meeting. We were fortunate that Linda Yow volunteered to take minutes of the meeting. She continued to do so throughout the incorporation process. We really didn't know what to expect going into this meeting.

The issue put forth was that there were strong indications that Oakboro was moving towards Red Cross. They had already annexed the Big Lick community, had two developments annexed deep within our community, and were becoming the provider of water and sewer for much of the Red Cross community. And, as everyone had observed there was a strong presence of the Oakboro police within our community. All this implies that, at some point, Oakboro intends to annex us.

We told the group that by meeting that night we would be making a conscious decision on our future. That we had four options:

(1) We could make a decision to do nothing and let whatever happens happen.

(2) We could ask Oakboro to annex us.

(3) We could ask Locust to annex us.

(4) We could incorporate Red Cross into a town.

The bottom line is that "either way, even if we choose to do nothing, by meeting tonight, we will have made a conscious decision on our future and will not have to look back with regret saying 'I wish we had done something'".

We took a poll of what the people wanted to do and it was in the direction of incorporating. The vote by the 47 people present was 100% in favor of exploring our options regarding incorporation. This decision was not to start the incorporation process but to gather more information about incorporating and report back to the people in the community.

It was decided by vote that the exploratory committee should consist of five people. Three people were chosen that night to serve on the exploratory committee; they were C. J. Barbee, Heath Hahn and me (Ray Quick). It was decided to wait until more people from the community were present before choosing the last two people to serve on the committee. It was also decided that we would hold a community meeting at least once a week to keep the people informed of our findings.

We will find out later that it wasn't practical to hold meetings on a weekly basis. Things just didn't move that rapidly - not with all the work required for each qualifying item on the petition. I believe everyone understood this because the issue of holding weekly meetings was never brought up again.

I was surprised that everyone was so interested and ready to entertain the idea of incorporation. Apparently, all that was needed was someone to get everyone together and get it started. As previously stated, it was Heath Hahn that called for that first meeting.

I've heard stories about the men sitting around Bill Hill's gas station talking about Red Cross one day becoming a town. Joyce Hill talked about it in the "Our State" magazine when the magazine did their article on Red Cross in January 2002. These men would speculate on who would be Mayor, who would be the Police Chief, where the Town Hall would be, etc. - in short, just blue-sky talking. Unfortunately, by the time the Town of Red Cross became a reality most of these people had already passed on. I wonder what they would have to say about Red Cross today.

I think J. D. Hinson summed up everyone's feelings best when, in a January 2002 interview with Channel-14 News, he said "We don't want to live in a town, but if we're going to live in a town, we'd like for it to be our town." Mr. Hinson always did seem to have a way of saying so much with just a few words.

Since those present at that first meeting had expressed such a strong interest in incorporating Red Cross, we immediately began trying to get information sources lined up. The next day, after the first meeting, I went to the Stanly County GIS office (Graphical Information Systems) and requested maps of the Red Cross community and a database of addresses of people within area. This would give us a better idea of the people we should call for the next meeting. We still didn't know where the town boundaries would be but we knew we wanted everyone that may be affected to be aware of what we were doing so that they could be involved in the decision process should we decide to incorporate.

On August 16, I made my first contact with Dr. David Lawrence of the Institute of Government in Chapel Hill. He said we needed to:

1. Contact our representatives and let them know what we are doing. They are Bobby Harold Barbee, Aaron Plyler, and Bill Purcell.

2. Contact and get information from an agency of the General Assembly called the Joint Legislative Commission on Municipal Incorporations.

We were still gathering information and not actually pursuing incorporation, so we were not yet ready to let anyone outside of our community know about our interest in incorporating. Nor were we ready to approach our local State Legislator, Representative Bobby Harold Barbee. We still had to make a decision on whether we wanted to incorporate or not. And if we did, where the town limits would go, who would be in the town, etc.?

One of the things we didn't do, but I wish we had, was contact the Joint Legislative Commission on Municipal Incorporations. They had a wealth of information. At the time we didn't know enough to realize the value of some of the available resources.

The agenda that Heath Hahn and I used for this first meeting can be found in Appendix-3.

The Second Community Meeting (08-28-2001):

The second community meeting was held on August 28, 2001 in the basement of Red Cross Baptist Church. Because there were only 47 people, plus Heath Hahn and me, at the first meeting, it had been decided to wait and select the last two people for the five person exploratory committee at the second meeting when more people would be present.

For the second meeting there was a larger turnout from the community, a total of 167 people. Since a lot of these people had not been at the first meeting we reviewed the material that we covered in the first meeting so that everyone would be brought up to speed before presenting the new information we had obtained.

The final two members of the exploratory committee were chosen; they were J. D. Hinson and Larry Wayne Smith. This completed the committee and now we were ready to get to work gathering information.

One catalytic thing did happen towards the end of this second meeting; someone raised an objection to our incorporating the Red Cross community. I believe they felt that we would be much better off to allow Oakboro to annex us. This proved to be the catalyst for cognizing the people. It seemed that at that point everyone made a conscious decision on what they wanted to do: incorporate.

Realizing this, we took a vote of the people. There were 169 people present; 165 voted in favor of incorporating, two people opposed incorporation and two people abstained from voting. This was done by a standing vote so that there was no chance that anyone's vote was misread. This meant that 97.6% of those present were in favor of pursuing incorporation. That was a very clear directive from the people to go ahead and start the incorporation process.

It was at that point we decided to roll-over the exploratory committee into an incorporation committee. This was done by a vote of the people. Linda Yow agreed to continue to serve as the secretary for the committee throughout the remainder of the incorporation process. Effectively, Red Cross began its incorporation process on the night of August 28, 2001.

The next day after the second incorporation meeting I got a call from Douglas Sams of the Stanly News & Press, wanting to come out and talk with us on the following Monday morning. Word really got around fast once the people decided to pursue incorporation.

The agenda used for the second community meeting can be found in Appendix-4.

The First Incorporation Committee Meeting (08-30-2001):

Our first step was to elect a chairman to head up the incorporation committee. This would be the first official meeting of the incorporation committee. The five of us (C. J. Barbee, Heath Hahn, J. D. Hinson, Ray Quick and Larry Wayne Smith) met at my house. It was decided to select a chairman for the committee by secret ballot. The result of that vote was that there were two votes for C. J. Barbee, two votes for me and one vote for Heath Hahn. With such a small group it was easy to determine how each person voted. I believe it went like this; I voted for Heath Hahn, Heath Hahn and J. D. Hinson voted for me, and C. J. Barbee and Larry Wayne Smith voted for C. J. Barbee.

It was decided that the only way to break the tie between me and C. J. Barbee was to flip a coin. I flipped the coin and C. J. Barbee made the call. I won the toss and was placed in as chairman.

We went through an overview of what we thought we would need to do for the incorporation process. Basically it was an organizational meeting to get started. The following is the outline of the things we discussed.

1. Discuss problem(s) with taking pledges and responding to questions from floor. Talked to David Lawrence with Institute of Government and he said he had never heard of the requirement of being incorporated prior to taking pledges or money. Said most communities never incorporated their committees. Actually felt it was unnecessary.

2. Discuss appointing a committee chairman. Need to establish voting procedures before choosing one. Example: will the chairman have a vote other than breaking a tie vote? Hand out slips for secret ballot.

3. Need to have a secretary and treasurer (outside the committee) elected at the next meeting.

4. When will we need an attorney?

5. Does committee really need to be incorporated?

6. We need to set some form of agenda for the different stages of our progress where the people will vote their acceptance on it.

    6.1. Town limits
    6.2. Zoning
    6.3. Petitioning
    6.4. Submitting to Legislature
    6.5. Etc.

7. Set up guidelines for meeting outlines. Suggest having an established format – following through on that format with as little deviation as possible and ending the meeting.

    7.1. Review last meeting.
    7.2. Outline what the committee has done to-date
    7.3. Have a vote on acceptance of work done to-date (gives people sense of control and participation – should relieve anxiety).
    7.4. Outline actions planned for next meeting.
    7.5. Set next meeting date
    7.6. Adjourn meeting.

8. Responding to questions during meetings:

    8.1 Should answer questions as accurately as possible and will not interject any information not relevant to that question.
    8.2 If we don't know the answer we will let the people know we do not know but will find out.
    8.3 If question is premature to our stage of work we let people know that we haven't reached that point yet and will not give them a bogus answer.
    8.4 Discuss grandfather clause?

The Second Incorporation Committee Meeting:

The first priority set by the committee was to determine the boundaries for our new town. If I remember correctly it only took a couple hours to draw the first map. For this task we met at the home of Heath Hahn. Once we had what we thought would be a good outlay for the town we were feeling pretty good. This is a case where I can truly say ignorance is bliss. We didn't yet have any idea of the real work that would be required to put a functional map together.

The Third Incorporation Committee Meeting (September 3, 2001):

The day after the community voted to pursue incorporation (August 28, 2001) I received a call from Douglas Sams, with the "Stanly News and Press". He said he would like to meet with us on Monday, September 3, 2001, to do an article on our incorporation process. He said they wanted to run it in Tuesday's paper.

This was probably the best way to make it public, it would be announced to the whole County at one time. It would also eliminate the potential for a lot of rumors and misinformation. Still, we were really early in the process and didn't have a lot of useful information to offer, only our hopes and intent.

During this time the incorporation committee had gotten together and drawn up a map of where we thought the town should be. We then contacted our State Legislator, Representative Bobby Harold Barbee, and met with him. We showed him what we hoped would be a map of the town. I remember him saying "Well fella's, I can't really say I'm surprised. I kind'a thought something like this might happen." In my mind I can still hear him saying it in an almost humorous tone.

Representative Bobby Harold Barbee looked over the map and listened to what we had to say. To our relief, he seemed to be in favor of it. He offered us some suggestions and gave us his assurance that he would help us when the time came. Had Representative Barbee not been willing to support us then I don't think there would have been any reason to continue pursuit of incorporation. If a bill doesn't have the support of the local Legislators then it doesn't stand a chance in the House and Senate.

Monday came and we met with both Douglas Sams of the "Stanly News and Press" and John Long of the "Weekly Post" in the basement of Red Cross Baptist Church on Monday, September 3, 2001. This was our official "public" declaration that the Red Cross community was pursuing incorporation.

We made an outline of discussion items so that we would be prepared for any questions they might ask. Hopefully, regardless of who on the committee the papers asked, our answers would be almost the same. Below is a copy of that outline:

1. "We have had two meetings with a tremendous response (almost unanimous) in favor of incorporating.

2. We have obtained maps and property owner listings (Access database format) for all properties within a three-mile radius of the center of Red Cross and are presently in the process of determining our town boundaries. It should be noted that the maximum distance in any direction for our town limit would be no more than two miles at most and less in most cases from the center of Red Cross.

3. We are fortunate in having access to two local towns that have been through the process in recent years. Badin went through it in 1990 and Midland incorporated last year. This gives us the perspective of one town (Midland) that has just completed the process and has good first hand information, and the second (Badin) that has had time to review what they did and offer suggestions for improvements in the process. We have been talking with the Mayor's of Midland and Badin, Dan Short and Tom Garrison respectively, and they have been very helpful in giving us guidance.

4. We have also been getting guidance from the Institute of Government in Chapel Hill.

5. We have talked with our state representative and have received assurance we will get the support in both the House and Senate. That they will be willing to submit our request to the legislature in February if we have everything ready.

6. We have talked to the mayors both adjacent towns (within four-miles of Red Cross) and have verbal assurances we will obtain favorable resolutions from them baring anything unexpected at their next town council meetings. We are planning to wait till we have a proposed town limit before approaching the County Commissioners/County Manager for their resolution.

7. At the last meeting (second meeting) we asked for pledges and received a little over $3,000 in pledges.

   Note: Actual pledges ended up totaling $3,700 and actual donations totaled $2,425.

8. At the last meeting we had two people that were very vocal in their opposition to the process. As a result we took a vote of confidence and had 165 in favor, 2 abstained-votes, and two opposed to our process of incorporation.

9. We are presently in the process of getting a tax number.

10. Next week we will be laying out the potential town limits and working out the people per square mile ratios. We anticipate some difficulties in this area since there are several large tracts of land that will infringe on our population density.

11. We have received quite a few questions about zoning and have told the people we could not address the zoning issue until we have established a proposed town boundary.

12. Highway 24/27 is in the process of being expanded from two-lane to four-lane and we have observed tremendous growth in Mint Hill, Midland, Locust, and Stanfield as sections of the project were completed out of Charlotte. Highway 24/27 bisects our community and is a crossroads for highways going to Ridgecrest in the north and Oakboro in the south. **We have to be organized, have our city infrastructure in place, and be ready for the growth once the highway expansion reaches us.**

Points to emphasize:

1. We recognize that, due to expected growth, we no longer have the option of remaining a rural community. We have to make a choice of being annexed by Oakboro or Locust, or create our own town.

2. Anticipation of the expected growth as a result of highway construction and of our desire to be prepared to handle it when it arrives in 2003.

3. A desire to preserve the quality and integrity of our community.

4. A desire for self-determination.

5. Both Oakboro and Locust are good towns with good people and our desire to incorporate is not a reflection on either town. Note: Both towns would like to annex us. To do so would, in all probability; put about 40% of our community in Locust and 60% in Oakboro (these are unqualified estimates). We do not want to be split up.

6. We have received tremendous support for pursuing the incorporation of Red Cross by the people that have attended the meetings so far.

Items 2, 3, and 4 are of primary interest to us and have been a focal point of our meeting's to-date.

> Items 2 and 3 should be stressed that we are expecting growth and want to plan for it so that it will fit well into our community. We should not make any references to growth that will be considered negative."

This public disclosure opened the door for us to be able to openly go out and gather information. One of the first things we did was to contact Dan Short of Midland, NC, and set up a meeting with him. He was one of the architects that helped put Midland's incorporation together. For that meeting he brought a lot of the incorporation material that had been used in the Midland incorporation and explained each piece to us. It was Dan Short's information the put us on the right track and gave us a general roadmap to follow. He gave us a digital copy of some of that information so that we would be able to refer back to it whenever needed.

From that point on we were free to contact anyone we wanted to. The exception to this was that we still didn't want to have dialogue with either Oakboro or Locust. We were afraid of them. We felt that both of them had, at some level, a desire to annex us and may try to block our incorporation effort. This fear later proved to have some foundation because (allegedly) Locust did send a letter to our State Legislators expressing their concerns about our incorporation attempt. We were not aware of any attempt by Oakboro to oppose our incorporation.

We had a problem in that we still didn't have a clear roadmap on how to become incorporated. Dan Short, and the information he provided, had been a lot of help but it still was not like following a cookbook. We had to find the right people to communicate with on various issues; what and when for different agencies in both State and County government and how to format the material we submitted. However, wc were given sources that provided excellent information. Still, there were times when it felt as if we were blindly feeling our way along.

What really made it difficult was that the new laws concerning incorporations were being brought into full implementation during this time and it appeared we were in the first batch of new incorporations that had to fully comply with these new laws. There just didn't seem to be any recently incorporated towns that had followed this route.

The following two articles are from the Stanly News & Press and the Weekly Post announcing our incorporation attempt:

Red Cross: a town in the making

"If we don't do something, we are going to regret it"

Community seeks self-determination
By Douglas Sams, News Editor
The Stanly News & Press

To many, Red Cross is just an intersection with a caution light on the way down NC 24/27 to Charlotte.

To Ray Quick and other who live in this old farming community, Red Cross is a place where people still think about the past. Some families have lived here for eight generations.

Still, plans for wider highways and new subdivisions could just sweep the past away.

So Smith and other residents have started meeting At Red Cross Baptist Church to consider a way to preserve the community's identity. Their idea is to make Red Cross a town with its own government. It's a process known as incorporation.

Quick said a town government can help manage growth before it gets out of control.

"If we don't do something, we are going to regret it later," Quick said.

"It's about self-determination."

Midland, a community in Cabarrus County about 15 miles down the highway from Red Cross, incorporated last year. Many state and local planners say the stretch of 24-27 through western Stanly will be a future focal point for rapid development.

To become a town, a community such as Red Cross has to show interest in the idea, then its residents eventually vote to go ahead with it. The N.C. legislature would have the final approval.

Red Cross residents seem interested in at least talking about their community of roughly 1,500 one day becoming incorporated. About 50 came to the first meeting. By the last meeting, the turnout had more than tripled.

Another community meeting at the church is set for 7 p.m., Tuesday, Sept. 25.

Meanwhile, Quick and others on a five-member incorporation committee will think about how far the proposed town limits should stretch and how many residents Red Cross should include.

"We want to keep Red Cross on the map," said Heath Hahn, who is also a committee member.

Red Cross was established sometime in the early 1800s, its long-time residents say. It owes its name to its red soil - an obstacle to travelers years ago when heavy rains turned the crossroads into slick, red mud.

Years later, Red Cross is still the junction of major state and county roads.

To the south, N.C. 205 runs about four miles to Oakboro. To the north, Ridgecrest Road winds through farmland all the way to Richfield. To the west, it's about 30 miles down 24-27 to Charlotte.

J. D. Hinson, another committee member, knows all about the change that's coming to Red Cross.

From the Baptist church, he can look over the highway and see his father's old farming equipment store.

His son now uses the store to display regional memorabilia - old signs, car parts, even a giant Coble milk carton.

Before long, though, the old store he knew as a boy will be torn down so that N.C. 24-27 can add two more lanes. That's going to make a faster route from the rural Piedmont to Charlotte.

"I grew up in that building," Hinson said. "It's still the best know landmark in the community."

There are other signs that growth is already affecting Red Cross.

New housing developments are springing up along 205 and Ridgecrest Road. Meanwhile the county is building a new EMS station in Red Cross to meet the need for more emergency services in fast-growing west Stanly.

At one time, even Oakboro had considered expanding its town limits up 205 toward Red Cross.

Towns such as Oakboro typically annex nearby communities to expand their populations and tax base.

Oakboro Mayor Joyce Little said she has no problem with Red Cross becoming a town, if that's what the community wants.

"They're really nice people up there,' she said.

"Whatever decision they make, I'm sure it will be the right decision."

If nothing else, just talking about incorporation reinforces what most in Red Cross already know.

Said Quick: "We've got to accept change - and try to deal with it."[1]

---

[1] The Stanly News & Press, by Douglas Sams, September 2001

Red Cross Plans New Town

Residents begin incorporation steps

The Weekly Post
September 5, 2001

The town of Red Cross. Get use to the idea. The community may, sometime next year, become the ninth municipality in Stanly County.

There has been casual talk about incorporating for a year, and last month two meetings were held for residents of Red Cross. There was near unanimous support for becoming a town.

"There has been an overwhelmingly positive response," says Ray Quick, one of the leaders in the incorporation drive. "This is a good community. We want to keep it intact." And C.J. Barbee says he "would like to preserve Red Cross as it is, keep our identity."

The widening of Highway 24/27 is a major impetus behind incorporation. The state will take two historic buildings at the intersection of 24/27 and 205/Ridgecrest Road. The brick building, now owned by mike Hinson, is on the state's list of historic buildings. It was built by his grandfather, D.A. Hinson, in the early part of the last century as a general store and dealerships for Oldsmobile and Case farm machinery. His father, J.D. Hinson, grew up in living quarters on the second floor and later operated a nursery and vegetable business across the highway in the white building. Today, J.D. is active in creating the town of Red Cross and saddened that both of these buildings will be taken by the state Department of Transportation to create turning lanes. He also will lose his mother and father's house on 24/27.

"Our community will change forever," says Hinson at the loss of the two stores.

Thus he and others want to exercise greater control over how Red

Cross grows in the coming years. They don't oppose growth, but they want to shape it.

The boundaries of the new town have not been determined. They will extend south on 205 to Hilltop Road. Heath Hahn lives at the corner and he is one of the leaders working for incorporation. A fifth leader in the effort is Larry Wayne Smith.

Quick says work has begun on locating the homes in the area and the number of residents. The state requires a density of at least 250 persons per square mile. The boundaries of the town will be set to meet this rule.

In general, the Red Cross community extends down Hilltop Road to Pless Mill, Crossing 24/27 and extends north on Running Creek to Bethel Church Road. It then picks up Austin Road over to Ridgecrest. The highway east of 205 toward the high school also is Red Cross, but some of that area may not meet the density requirements for annexation.

The process of incorporation is not easy. State law was changed a couple of years ago and it is much more difficult. A bill for incorporation must be submitted in the General Assembly next year by local legislators. Those whose support is crucial are state Reps. Bobby Harold Barbee and Pryor Gibson and Sens. Aaron Plyler and Bill Purcell.

The town also will seek letters of support from nearby towns, probably from Oakboro and Locust, perhaps Stanfield and Albemarle.

The petition for incorporation must include a map of the town, list of proposed services to be provided, names of three persons to serve as an interim council, the estimated population, assessed valuation of property, degree of development, a budget for the first year, and the proposed property tax.

Barbee says that this is a lot to do in the coming months but says it can be done. He wants the bill to be ready for the legislature soon after it convenes next February.

The first Public meeting was held August 14 and 47 residents attended. These were individuals who were contacted by phone or in person by Hahn, Quick, Barbee, Hinson, and Smith. There was total agreement on incorporation.

A second meeting was held August 28 with 173 persons attending. Again there was, with two exceptions, total support.

Residents have been told that every effort will be made to keep the new tax rate at 20 cents or less per $100 valuation. The state requires a 5-cent tax, but without much business, the tax burden in the first years will fall on homeowners. "The support is very strong," says Quick.

A third meeting will be held on Tuesday, September 25. It is open to the public. It will be held in the basement of Red Cross Baptist Church at 7 pm.

Quick has talked with Dan Short, mayor of Midland, and with officials in Badin. Badin incorporated in the early Nineties. Midland became a town earlier this year. It was an immense struggle for Midland because of fierce opposition from a very few, some of whom did not live in the town. Opposition also came from Corning, Concord city government, the Cabarrus Chamber of Commerce, Cabarrus county commissioners, State Legislators, and state Department of Commerce.

Still, Midland prevailed after agreeing that Corning and adjacent industrial park would not be incorporated for at least 10 years. The General Assembly passed legislation to that effect. With this in place, Sen. Fletcher Hartsell of Concord threw his support behind incorporation of Midland.

Red Cross does not face this kind of suffocating opposition and there is confidence that the legislature will give its approval sometime next year.

Contact also has been made with the Institute of Government in Chapel Hill. The Institute is a state agency which gives guidance to local government. He was told that initial work toward incorporation looks good.

Red Cross is a very old community. It began as a crossroads when 24/27 was about two-tenths of a mile south and 205 was a ways east. J.D. Hinson's father had a general store at the old intersection and later built again when the roads were moved to their present location and later paved around 1935.

He says the community got its name because of the red clay at the old crossroads, thus Red Cross.[2]

The Fourth Incorporation Committee Meeting:

Our next step was to contact Midland, and Dan Short came and met with us in the basement of Red Cross Baptist Church. He went over the material they had used during their incorporation process and gave us a fairly good understanding of what we needed to do.

The information he provided would become our guide going forward for putting our information together and in the creation of our petition to incorporate.

The Third Community Meeting (09-25-2001):

The third community meeting was held on September 25, 2001 in the basement of Red Cross Baptist Church.

We were told to expect it to cost between $8,000 and $10,000 to complete the incorporation process. We had a major problem in that we didn't have any money to hire a lawyer. There was no way we could afford it. We hoped that we could do it for under $5,000.

---

[2] The Weekly Post, September 2001

It should also be noted that a normal part of the incorporation process is for a referendum to be called before the incorporation can be passed into law. If we had to pay for a referendum then that alone could cost $1,500. The reason for a referendum is that there are not usually a large enough percentage of the voting people in the requesting community signing the petition in favor of incorporation for it to carry through without a referendum.

A petition to incorporate requires only 15% of the voting residents to sign the petition. However, and somewhat unusual, if at least 85% of the voting residents sign the petition then there is a good probability that the Legislature will pass the petition during session and declare the community a town without having to hold a referendum. We had 92.1% signing in favor of incorporation, so we were declared a town in session and didn't have to go back for a referendum.

Surprisingly, of the 7.9% that refused to sign our petition, the greatest majority was not opposed to the incorporation; they just didn't want to get involved.

We put it to the community and it was decided to take up a collection to finance the incorporation process. Although we received pledges totaling $3,850 we actually collected $2,425, way short of what we thought we would need if we were going to hire a lawyer.

I found out that, although incorporation processes are usually done through a lawyer, it is not required that a lawyer be used. If we could do the work ourselves then we might be able to pull it off. I had experience writing budgets, project justifications, technical and training manuals, SPS's, etc. and was computer literate so I was going to give it a try. After all, how different would it be in writing an incorporation justification than in writing a project justification?

By doing our own legal work we ended up going through the whole incorporation process for slightly less than $500. That money was spent on paper, ink cartridges, mailings, legal postings,

I would like to point out that Josh Morton allowed us to use him as our attorney of record. We will always owe him our gratitude for that.

If we spent less than $500 during the incorporation process then I imagine people are wondering what happened to the rest of the $2,425 that was donated for the incorporation process. Well here is the answer. Because we had not made prior arrangements to separate the remaining money from the incorporation process prior to being declared a town, the money automatically transferred into the town treasury at the point the Legislature declared us a town.

Under State law we were not, as a town, allowed to reimburse the people out of town funds. However, we were very fortunate to have that money in the treasury because without it we would not have had any money to start the town up. We could have gone out and tried to borrow the money, but that would not have been a good footing to start out on. Think about the obstacles of trying to start a town up on just $2,000?

It should be noted that C. J. Barbee said he had told everyone that they would get their money back after the incorporation process was over. I was not aware of this at the time. He felt strongly enough about it that he sent everyone a personal check to cover the amount of their donation. I think most people returned their check to him stating that it was a donation and they didn't expect to get it back.

At this third meeting we let the people know that we had addressed the following:

- We had obtained an Attorney of Record in that Josh Morton had agreed to serve as our attorney during the incorporation process.

- We had received pledges totaling $3,700.00.

- We had the preliminary town map drawn up for the people to see.

- We had contacted our State Legislative Representative, Bobby Harold Barbee, and he was agreeable to help us.

- We gave the people a copy of the section of NCGS 120-163 concerning incorporation requirements

Since this was the first meeting after the community had voted to pursue incorporation we had to make decisions of several things. All of the following items were voted on by the community:

- Make a formal decision on the town name (Town of Red Cross).

- Specifying our form of government. We recommended having a traditional mayor and council (four council members).
- Specify the people that would serve on the town council once we were declared a town.

- To take a vote on the acceptance of our proposed town boundaries.

As per the above, the community participated in and made the final decisions on what courses of action the incorporation committee took.

The agenda used for this third community meeting can be found in Appendix-5

The Fourth Community Meeting (10-25-2001):

The fourth community meeting was held on October 25, 2001, in the basement of Red Cross Baptist Church. Again, there was again a large turnout of people from the Red Cross community. However, this time there were additional dignitaries present, Dan Baucom (Stanly County Tax Assessor), Paul Reynolds (Stanly County GIS Office), Ken Furr (Chairman of the Stanly County Commissioners), John Long (Editor of the "Weekly Post"), and Douglas Sams (Reporter for the "Stanly News & Press").

We reviewed the actions taken in previous meetings in case there were people that had not been at the last meeting. This may seem a little redundant and time consuming but we wanted everyone to be fully informed of what was going on and knew that they had full involvement in, and control over, whatever actions were taken. Also, we wanted to be sure that no one became uncomfortable with the process and that there would not be any opportunity for unfounded rumors to get started.

The business for the night was to set a tax rate, present a budget, and have the people vote on acceptance of these items. We also informed the people that we would need to create a petition by the people of Red Cross for showing community support in incorporating our community and someone would be going to each person's house with a petition to incorporate and asking them to sigh it. All of these items were approved by the community.

The agenda used for this fourth community meeting can be found in Appendix-6

The Fifth Community Meeting (01-10-2002):

By this time we felt we had the petition ready to be given to our State Legislator, Bobby Harold Barbee. We brought it back before the people for their approval to submit it. Because of the size of the petition, and some fear of copies being distributed in the community, we didn't hand out copies of the petition. We did go through each of the items in the petition and had a projector to display each section as we covered it. We had already voted on each element, so we didn't have to revote anything other than get the approval of the community, by vote, to submit the petition. Little did we know that we still had a lot of work to do in tweaking our petition to make it acceptable to the Local Government Commission?

Since this was probably the final community meeting, we also did a full review of each of the previous meetings. A copy of the agenda used for this fifth meeting can be found in Appendix-7.

Incorporation Committee Meeting (04-08-2002):

The following is the handout from which we worked for this meeting:

Committee Meeting (04-08-02)

1. **C.J. Barbee to tell us about upcoming meeting we need to attend.**

2. **Update on events to-date**

Bobby Harold Barbee carried petition to Raleigh Monday, two weeks ago.

Got call from Ms. [name omitted] (attorney in Bill Drafting Office) that we had to get dates on our petition signatures. We have done that.

Bobby Harold Barbee hand delivered them to that office this past Friday.

Received call from Mr. [name omitted] (North Carolina Division of Community Assistance) this past Monday. He asked for another map – Sent him one of the full-sized maps with our boundaries marked in red (including right-of-ways). He said he would be the one doing the verifications of our petition – he would verify the survey, number of houses, number of residents, number of businesses, budget, and would end up physically standing in front of each piece of property within our town boundaries and evaluating it. Said he would probably start in the next couple weeks and it would take him a couple weeks to complete his survey. He would then report back to the Joint Commission on Municipal Incorporations.

Mr. [name omitted] had some questions as to how we did our survey. He said that, although it is technically correct, it is overly complicated and there may be some problems when it gets to bill-drafting. He said he would be able to work with it as it is now and we wouldn't have to re-do it for him but might for the bill-drafting. Said it would have been better if we had used pin numbers rather than property deeds as reference.

Names to Know:

[Name list omitted]

Emails to date are as follows:

From: [name omitted]
To: "'R. Quick'" <[omitted]>
Subject: RE: Red Cross Incorporation
Date: Mon, 1 Apr 2002 10:27:02 -0500

Mr. Quick, Thanks for the update. When I get the certification from Rep. Barbee, I'll add it to your petition. I believe [name omitted] has completed the review of your petition, and we only found the Board certificate missing. So, I think you guys are okay now that the certificate is forthcoming. I haven't received John's report yet but I expect to get it in the next day or so. If there're any other problems, I'll let you know immediately. GM

To: Ms. [name omitted]
Subject: Red Cross Incorporation
Ms. [omitted]:

Just to let you know we have completed updating all the petitions with date-of-birth for each petition signer and will turn them over to the Stanly County Board of Elections Monday morning at 8:30 am.

I've also called Rep. Bobby Harold Barbee and updated him on our progress. Barring any other information from you, he is planning to be at your office with the results on Friday morning at 10:00 am.

Please let us know if there is anything else we can do from

our end.

Thanks,
Ray Quick
Red Cross Incorporation Committee

Mr. [name omitted]:
Ms. [name omitted]:

[Omitted]

Ms. [name omitted] - The Stanly County Board of Elections completed our petition certification today (04-02-02) and we will turn the results over to Rep. Bobby Harold Barbee tomorrow. He is still planning to be at your office Friday morning (04-05-02) at 10:00 a.m. to give it to you. The final count was 381 registered signers with 438 registered voters within the proposed town limits. This comes out to 87.0% of the community signing in favor of incorporation. Not as good as we hoped but better than expected without the purging.

Mr. [Name omitted] - I will have the map you requested in the mail in the morning - you should have it by Friday. It's a 42" map from the Stanly County GIS Office with the proposed town of Red Cross highlighted in yellow and with a pin number on each property. I've also marked the boundaries as per your request. This map should be a lot easier to read.

If there is anything else we can/need to be doing please let us know?

Ray Quick
Red Cross Incorporation Committee

3. Zoning

We will need to start work on zoning for our town sometime soon. There will probably be as much work in it as there was in the survey.

4. Highway

Bobby Harold Barbee said he has done all he can do to get the highway changed but it doesn't look as if he is going to be able to get it done. Said we should get involved at this point. The first place to start will be the Albemarle office and we should talk to a Wilson man (I think the name was Wilson). Said we shouldn't go as a whole committee but only a couple of us should be there.

5. Oakboro's request to talk with Red Cross:

Members of the committee have been contacted several times by Oakboro Council Members wanting to talk with us about long-range growth plans. Terry Whitley has initiated most of these contacts.

At the West Stanly High School presentation of the Stanly County Growth Plan Terry Whitley approached us again on the subject. Items discussed (that might be on the agenda) were:

- Oakboro would send only two councilmen to meet with us since this would be an unofficial meeting. The two people would probably be Terry Whitley and David Love.

- Oakboro would like to provide police protection for Red Cross.

- Oakboro wants Oakboro, Red Cross, and other towns to get together as a group to develop a growth plan for the western part of Stanly County.

- Implied that Oakboro would like our blessing/help in Oakboro's obtaining an ETJ to the north that would extend to Hilltop Road. At present the County will not let them extend their ETJ north past Big Lick/Liberty Hill Roads.

- Sphere-of-influence agreement was not discussed but would probably be one of the topics of discussion should we meet with Oakboro.

- Water and Sewer – Terry Whitley said Oakboro was close to capacity in its ability to handle sewer needs in this part of the County. He did not give a direction as to how Oakboro is leaning/thinking on this but said Oakboro was contracting with both Locust and Stanfield.

Side-Note: I (Ray Quick) took a tour of Oakboro's waste treatment facility last fall and obtained the following facts.

- Sewage capacity is 1.2-million gallons per day.

- Oakboro had just completed an expansion – doubling their capacity to accommodate Stanly Knitting Mills (prior to the mill's closing). As a result they were using only one-eighth of their capacity (including sewage from Locust). At the time they were still negotiating a contract with Stanfield.

- Monies obtained for the expansion were from a grant.

- Unknowns are how much sewage volume Locust and Stanfield has contracted for, does each town contract for a specific volume, and if so how much is each town contracting for?

THE PEOPLE'S MADATE

The most overwhelming directive given by the people during the incorporation process was that they liked their community; they liked the lifestyle and they wanted it protected. This was clearly the primary objective, or mandate, for our incorporation.

Everyone would say we incorporated to keep from being annexed by another town. That is true and is consistent with the above statement of protecting our lifestyle. If we were to be annexed by another town then the other town's zoning codes, local laws, growth plans, vision plans, etc. would be applied to us. If that happened then we would lose both our identity and our lifestyle. Our identity would be lost because we would become a part of the annexing town and our lifestyle would be lost because the annexing towns zoning codes, ordinances, etc., would be imposed on us, which would remold our community's "personality" into that of the annexing town.

During one of the incorporation meetings Mrs. Grantham made the statement that we should pass an ordinance that no one be allowed to sell their property. This would keep people from coming in and changing our lifestyle. She was being facetious, but it clearly demonstrated that our people liked our community and wanted it protected. Everyone was afraid that the central part of Red Cross would quickly grow into a business district. Remember, this was before the economic collapse and there was a real possibility that growth would come fairly quickly.

The second major issue, really a part of our lifestyle, was the desire by a large percentage of our people for the town not to pass any ordinance(s) restricting hunting or the firing of firearms. This was because many of our residents had large tracts of land that were well suited for hunting.

The above two issues were the only real "mandates" that came from our people during the incorporation process. Nothing was ever said about making us look like a town and/or recruiting businesses. Of course it goes without saying that everyone wanted low taxes.

We will later come to the understanding that we, as a town, would have the ability to protect our people's mandate. We could do it through zoning codes, designing them to reflect and support those values which we wanted to retain. We could set standards and manage incoming development so that it respected our lifestyle and meshed well within our community.

To do this we would need to create a completely new and unique set of zoning codes specifically tailored to our community's needs. We would need those codes to reflect and protect those values that we cherished. We would also need to establish a vision of what we wanted and of how we wanted our community to grow and we needed everyone to accept that common vision as their own.

THE PETITION TO INCORPORATE

At the core of our incorporation process was the creation of our "Petition to Incorporate" that we would present to our State Legislator, in our case Representative Bobby Harold Barbee (see Appendix-1).

We found the creation of the petition and in meeting all the requirements necessary for compliance to be an extremely difficult task. A new commission had been created in the State Legislature to oversee municipal incorporations. This commission was the Joint Legislative Commission on Municipal Incorporations and it had a daunting list of rules and regulations covering incorporation processes. This appeared to be the first year that all the incorporation criteria was being fully applied and enforced. Any petition to incorporate had to receive their approval before going to the Legislature. So our task was going to be even harder.

Our understanding is that this commission was created by a State Legislator from High Point, NC, to control and reduce the number of ad-hock incorporations that were occurring across the State. It seems that an increasing number of communities were seeking incorporation for the sole purpose of keeping other municipalities from annexing them. Once incorporated they never did anything else to set up their town structure. By making these rules the Commission was trying to ensure that any community wanting to incorporate had to form a municipal structure and function as a town.

We established the following guideline using the North Carolina General Statutes on incorporations to create our petition to incorporate:

- The Community requesting incorporation must have a petition signed by at least 15% of the registered voters in the incorporation area.
- The petition signatures must be verified by the county board of elections.
- The petition must include:

    a. The purposed name for the city.
    b. A map of the city.
    c. A paper survey of the city.
    d. A list of services to be provided. Four of the following eight must be provided:
        i. Police protection
        ii. Fire protection
        iii. Solid waste collection or disposal
        iv. Water distribution
        v. Street maintenance
        vi. Street construction or right-of-way acquisition
        vii. Street lighting
        viii. Zoning
    e. A list of at least three people that will be serving on the interim government.
    f. A provisional charter for the town.
    g. The following statistical information must be included:
        i. estimated population
        ii. Assessed valuation
        iii. Degree of development
        iv. Population density
        v. Recommended form of government
        vi. Manner of elections
    h. A statement that the proposed municipality will have a budget ordinance with an ad valorem tax levy of at least five cents (5¢) on the one hundred dollar ($100.00) must be included.
    i. Include a statement of intent that the proposed municipality will offer four of the following services no later than the first day of the third fiscal year following

the effective date of the incorporation:

i. police protection
ii. fire protection
iii. solid waste collection or disposal
iv. water distribution
v. street maintenance
vi. street construction or right-of-way acquisition
vii. street lighting
viii. zoning

Although it was not specified in the general statutes, we did have to declare an attorney of record for the Town.

We used the above checklist for creating our petition. Although it doesn't look that difficult, each of the components required a great deal of time. Just supplying the "map of the city" along with the paper survey probably required a couple hundred labor hours. Just about all the work was done by the five appointed committee members. This is not counting all the work that Paul Reynolds of the Stanly County GIS office did or the work that Dan Baucom, Stanly County Tax Assessor, did when helping us create our first paper survey. That time J. D. Hinson, Heath Hahn and I spent two tedious nights and one Saturday working on it under his guidance.

Deciding on a Name for the Town:

This may seem a little trivial because if we were deciding to become a town then the name of our town should be "Red Cross". Well, that part didn't require a lot of thought but when considering whether to be classified, as a city, town, village, hamlet or parish, it became very important.

Today there is little difference between a town, a city, and in some places a village. However, the term "city" usually denotes extensive services, government structure, and of being primarily commerce oriented. A town is usually considered a mixture of moderate government and services and a mixture of commerce, residential and possibly agricultural activities for the primary purpose of serving its local community.

Although not always true, a city is usually considered as being larger than a town and a town is usually larger than a village, etc. A lot depends on the evolution of the municipality and/or the connotation the people of that community wish to convey about their identity to the world.

Misenheimer decided to call itself the Village of Misenheimer, Oakboro called itself the Town of Oakboro and Locust called itself the City of Locust. When a town is requesting incorporation it has to determine if it wants to be called a town, city, village, etc. For Red Cross, once we became incorporated our legal name could have been the "Town of Red Cross", the "City of Red Cross" or one of the other designations. However, once we made our declaration then we would officially become know by that name.

Because of our rural and agricultural base we decided that we wanted to be called a town.

Think of the implied interpretation of saying "I'm going to town" vs. "I'm going to the city". Saying "I'm going to town" implies a local trip whereas "I'm going to the city" implies a more substantial trip.

Remember the story of how Endy got its name. It use to be called "Eudy", but a mistake occurred in the spelling and it ended up being officially called "Endy" - probably as a result of a typing error. That is why we made very sure that our town name was exactly as we wanted it.

As a side note, Red Cross use to be called "Red Crossing". No one remembers when it was shortened to just "Red Cross" but it seems that it was in the early 1800's. Red Crossing use to be a major crossroads for traffic going north to south and east to west. The name "Red Crossing" came from the road conditions at the crossroads. It seems that when it rained the slick red clay mud made it difficult to get through Red Crossing.

Creating a Town Map:

Creating the town map was the most time consuming part of the incorporation process. We, the incorporation committee, invested numerous labor hours in developing a map that allowed us to comply with all the other statistical requirements of the petition.

The first map we created identified all the areas where people felt they were a part of the Red Cross Community. We used the main arteries of Highway 24/27 for east and west, and Highway 205 and Ridgecrest Road for north and south to give the first dimensions of the community. Our first assumption went something like this: Using the crossroads of Highway 205/Highway 24/27 as a center point, we felt our town should extend to Austin Road to the north, Brattain Road to the west, Big Lick to the south and Lakewood road the east. For the outlying areas (off the main arteries) we used the dimensions defined by the main arteries to create a sphere, or radius, to encompass the rest of the boundaries using the intersection of Highway 24/27/Highway 205 crossroads as a center point for the town. However, it wasn't like drawing a circle because we tended to follow property lines.

As we began trying to meet the requirements of population density and percent development we began to understand that this map would not work. We had to meet population density and percent development requirements if we wanted our petition to make it through the Joint Commission. This meant we would have to go back and remove some of the larger properties from our proposed town map. It ended up with the map serving as the foundation for the statistical data we would later be required to include in our petition to incorporate.

Surprisingly, population density ended up being the defining factor for our town map. Under the incorporation requirements, as defined by the Joint Legislative Commission on Municipal Incorporations, we had to achieve a minimum population density of 250 people per square mile. We had to go back and start excluding and/or including selected properties in order to bring the population density up to the minimum level. This was one of the most difficult parts to achieve since Red Cross was composed of mostly large land plots. With each piece of property added or removed we would recalculate to see what the new population density would be.

Fortunately, Stanly County's GIS department had supplied us with a database of the Red Cross area and, since I knew databases/SQL, I wrote a procedure that would recalculate our percentages almost instantly after each property inclusion/exclusion. We would plug each change in and see what the outcome would be. We kept doing this until we had the numbers we needed to meet the Joint Commission's requirements. Our proposed town boundary wasn't pretty but it was functional and met the incorporation requirements.

We're not sure how many nights we worked on the map but it took several nights with the whole committee working to finally get a population density that would allow us to go forward. Once we had the map we were ready to start tackling the other items on the list.

Creating a Survey of the Town:

A second part of the mapping process was to create a paper survey of the proposed town boundaries. Although this is usually done by a surveyor it is not required that a surveyor has to do the work. We did it ourselves to save money.

> **"NCGS § 160A-22. Map of corporate limits.**
> The current city boundaries shall at all times be drawn on a map, or set out in a written description, or shown by a combination of these techniques. This delineation shall be retained permanently in the office of the city clerk.
> Alterations in these established boundaries shall be indicated by appropriate entries upon or additions to the map or description made by or under the direction of the officer charged with that duty by the city charter or by the council.
> Copies of the map or description reproduced by any method of reproduction that gives legible and permanent copies, when certified by the city clerk, shall be admissible in evidence in all courts and shall

> have the same force and effect as would the original map or description. The council may provide for revisions in any map or other description of the city boundaries. A revised map or description shall supersede for all purposes the earlier map or description that it is designated to replace. (1971, c. 698, s. 1; 1973, c. 426, s. 10.)"

NCGS 160A-22 can be interpreted to read that we didn't have to do the paper survey, but the information we had at the time indicated that it was necessary. For us it was not an option. We had to be sure we met the requirements and approval of the Joint Commission on Municipal Incorporations, so we supplied both a map and a paper survey of the Town. We were required to redo the paper survey two additional times to make it acceptable for the Joint Commission on Municipal Incorporations. The first time was to convert from pin numbers to tax record numbers and remove exceptioned properties so that we had a single contiguous town boundary. The second time was to correct errors in our paper survey.

One of the things that surprised me was that when I later pulled up the Red Cross incorporation bill on the N.C. Legislative website I found that it appears to contain the first paper survey we submitted instead of the last survey we sent in. I do not know why this happened.

Part of our collection of information included talking with the Stanly County Tax Assessor, Dan Baucom. This was one of the best things that could have happened for us. During our conversation with him he asked about our paper survey. He said that he had helped on a recent paper survey for New London and could show us how it was supposed to be done.

We owe Dan Baucom (Stanly County Tax Assessor) a great deal of thanks for his help on the paper survey. Dan Baucom, J. D. Hinson, Heath Hahn and I (Ray Quick) spent two long tedious nights and one Saturday putting our first paper survey together. He probably saved us a couple thousand dollars.

Dan Baucom would call out the coordinates, Heath Hahn or J. D.

Hinson would follow on a second map verifying the coordinates, and I used my laptop to type in the coordinates. Although it was slow tedious work it went well. We ended up with a seven page, single-spaced survey. We had it ready by November 19, 2001.

Another part of the process was for our paper survey to be reviewed by the North Carolina State Demographics Office. After their first review I received a call from them stating that our method of property identification would not work, that they needed the tax record numbers instead of the pin numbers we had used and we couldn't have any exceptioned properties in our survey - our town boundary had to be one continuous line. This was our first submitted paper survey.

Fortunately, by this time Stanly County was in the process of converting from pin numbers to tax record numbers. The unfortunate part was that it was easier to just create another survey than to try and cross-reference all the old pin numbers to the new tax record numbers.

I didn't want to bother Dan Baucom any further so I took it upon myself to create the new survey. I think it took me a couple days to do it. As I said earlier, Stanly County's GIS Department was very up-to-date (I had heard that they had one of the better GIS Departments in the State). I was able to access their GIS maps over the Internet and work from home. This worked out well because it gave me the privacy to do this tedious work without any distractions.

Later we would have to completely redo the survey one more time due to errors in the second survey. We worked all night on this one because I got a call around 4:00 PM on Monday afternoon concerning errors in the survey. This was a catastrophic setback because our petition, with boundary description, was to be presented to the Joint Commission on Municipal Incorporations at 10:00 AM the next morning. We had less than eighteen hours to correct our survey and get it to them.

In reviewing the errors I found it easier to again completely redo the survey than to try and correct the errors. Yea, practice makes perfect. I called the other committee members and we began working. I stayed at my house so I could work from my computer accessing the Stanly County GIS system and C. J. Barbee, Heath Hahn, J. D. Hinson and Larry Wayne Smith met at Heath Hahn's house. I would type up the boundary description, send it to them, and they would go through and verify those descriptions against the map. When they found errors they would call me to make the changes. I think they finished around 2:00 AM and I finalized and emailed the final draft around 5:00 AM. We made it in time and this survey was accepted.

In talking with Representative Barbee later, he said Raleigh thought we were using an attorney to do our work because they commented to him that they didn't see how we got our attorney to work through the night to get it done. He said that he felt it was better to just let the comment ride because, if they believed we were using an attorney then they would be less critical of our work. This was a compliment to us and it indicated that we were doing our paperwork correctly - and professionally. And, hopefully, it would keep Raleigh from being overly critical of our submitted information.

Establishing Contracts for Services:

One of the requirements for incorporation was that the petition must include a statement of intent for the services to be provided.

The NCGS statute covering incorporations required the adoption of four of eight specified services: police protection, fire protection, solid waste collection or disposal, water distribution, street maintenance, street construction or right-of-way acquisition, street lighting, and zoning.

Although we had to declare these services (police protection, fire protection, solid waste collection and zoning) in our petition we were not required to implement them until January 1, of the third year of incorporation, for Red Cross that would be on January 1, 2004. Not only did we have to declare them but we also had to show that our proposed budget would support them.

Police Protection:

In looking at police protection we knew we couldn't afford to have our own police department. To have one police officer would require a salary, payroll, retirement, taxes, insurance, a car, operating expenses, and an office to work from. We estimated this cost to be, at a minimum, $60,000 to $70,000 per year for one officer. Knowing that that a single officer couldn't work or be on call 24 hours a day, 7 days a week, 365 days a year, meant that a second officer would be required. That second officer would cost at least another $40,000 per year, including insurance, retirement, etc. With a total cost of over $100,000 per year there was just no way that we could afford it.

C. J. Barbee assumed responsibility of exploring this service and for contacting the Sheriff's Department. We found that both New London and Richfield contracted with the Sheriff's Department for their police protection. C. J. Barbee set up a meeting with the Stanly County Sheriff and we discussed our problem with him. Sheriff Tony Frick was more than willing to work with us and showed us copies of the contracts with they had with New London and Richfield. We found that we could contract with the Sheriff's Department for about $12,000 per year. This would give us 40 hours of dedicated service each month. It was within our budget and was allowable under the NCGS requirements. So we decided to list police protection as one of our proposed services.

It should be noted that C. J. Barbee initiated the idea that, if possible, Red Cross should provide space for a satellite Sheriff's Office to serve western Stanly County. This became a reality when the Town purchased property for a Town Hall in 2007.

Fire Protection:

Providing fire protection opened up a whole can of worms. For us to provide our own fire protection, we felt it would cost us between one million and two million dollars. The Red Cross community was already being served by three different fire departments: Oakboro, Locust and Ridgecrest. There is a general statute which states that if we were to assume responsibility/ownership for those areas covered by other fire departments then we would also have to assume a portion of their outstanding debt. In short, we would have to do a buyout for the right to provide our own fire protection. This may sound a little harsh but there is good reason for it.

C. J. Barbee was charged with working out the details of our fire protection coverage. In talking with emergency services we found that we could assume responsibility with no change in fire district mapping or coverage. It would only be a paper change in that we would assume responsibility for collecting the fire tax and then paying that tax to the respective fire departments - basically, we would make the fire tax a part of our tax rate. The Stanly County Tax Office would calculate how much each fire department was to be paid by us.

We decided to follow this route and include fire protection as one of our services. We also decided to embed it in our tax rate so that all Red Cross citizens would be charged the same rate regardless of which fire district they were in. This was different from the way the County had been collecting fire tax. For them, they had been charging an add-on tax that was billed at the same time as the property tax.

The North Carolina General Statute allowing us to contract with local fire departments is as follows:

"69-25.14. Contract with city or town to which all or part of district annexed concerning property of district and furnishing of fire protection.

Whenever all or any part of the area included within the territorial limits of a fire protection district is annexed to or becomes a part of a city or town, the governing body of such district may contract with the governing body of such city or town to give, grant or convey to such city or town, with or without consideration, in such manner and on such terms and conditions as the governing body of such district shall deem to be in the best interests of the inhabitants of the district, all or any part of its property, including, but without limitation, any fire-fighting equipment or facilities, and may provide in such contract for the furnishing of fire protection by the city or town or by the district. (1957, c. 526.)"

Waste Pickup:

The third service we looked at was solid waste collection. Larry Wayne Smith took responsibility for getting quotes for this service.

For people living outside of the towns in Stanly County, the County added a waste collection tax of $25 per year per house. Under this plan the people had to carry their garbage to collection centers set up throughout the County. Some people wanted garbage pickup at their house and had already established individual contracts with waste collection services such as Waste Management or BFI. Even though these people were contracting with a separate service, they still had to pay the County's waste collection tax.

Stanly County was not agreeable to let us collect this tax and then pay them the $25 per year per household for the use of their service centers - so this meant that we either had to provide the service ourselves or pass up on using solid waste collection as one of our services.

After lengthy discussions among the incorporation committee it was decided that the Town would assume responsibility for waste collection. However, in agreement with North Carolina General Statutes we did not have to start providing this service until January 1, of the third year after incorporation.

It should be noted that we considered two options for waste collection. The first was to have a central location for everyone to bring their waste to, much as the County was doing. The second option was to have curbside pickup. We chose to go with the second option.

We talked with the waste companies of Waste Management and BFI and chose to go with Waste Management. Unfortunately, because we were not ready to sign a contract at this time we could not get a firm price but we did get a general target price of around $9 per month per household. With about 250 houses in Red Cross this would mean an annual cost of about $27,000. It made for a really difficult decision. It should be noted that, since incorporating, there have been about 150 additional properties that have voluntarily annexed into Red Cross. As a result, waste collection costs today have substantially increased.

Street Maintenance and Street Construction:
Street maintenance and street construction were totally out of the question for us. If we did assume responsibility for a road then at some point it would need resurfacing and the cost would be well beyond our means. In short, it would be a reoccurring cost that we didn't want to assume.

Our request for information on street maintenance showed that to resurface a standard secondary road was prohibitively expensive as is illustrated by the response to my inquiry to DOT:

Dear Sir:
I have been asked to respond to your request for statewide, average construction and maintenance costs for a secondary road. The costs are outlined below:

1. Maintenance of unpaved road = $2,816/center-line mile/year

2. Maintenance of paved road = $3,695/center-line mile/year

3. Pave an unpaved road = approx. $400,000/center-line mile

(this cost include curb & gutter which is normally not installed)

> The cost for snow and ice removal varies from year to year and different geographical regions of the state.
>
> I hope this information is helpful. If you have any questions about the numbers above or any additional questions, I may be reached at 919.733.XXXX.
>
> (Name Removed), P.E.
> Maintenance Systems Engineer
> NCDOT-State Road Maintenance Unit

We were not in any position to assume responsibility for any street maintenance and we all agreed that we needed to pass up on this option.

Street Lighting:
Heath Hahn took responsibility for exploring this possibility. Street lighting was one of the services we gave serious consideration but eventually decided not to adopt as one of our services. There were several factors causing us to pass up on this. One was cost; it would cost us over $9 per light per month to contract with the power company to provide lighting. Think how many lights it would take to put a light on every other power pole in Red Cross. If we were to provide this service to any part of the Town then we would have to provide it to the whole Town. The second reason was that we were primarily a rural area and there were a fairly large number of people indicating that they didn't care about or want street lighting.

Zoning:
I took the lead, with the assistance of C. J. Barbee, in exploring our taking ownership of Zoning. Zoning was one of the services we definitely wanted to have control over. It would allow us self-determination on how our community would develop. We didn't know what the long-term cost would be, but the immediate cost was minimal.

Another compelling factor for going ahead and including zoning was that under North Carolina General Statutes we would have 60 days from the date of incorporation to assume ownership of zoning or we would permanently loose that right. If that happened then the County would retain ownership and control of our zoning and we would have to go to them for any zoning request/changes. For these reasons we did choose to include zoning as one of our services.

Tax Collection:

Heath Hahn and I took responsibility for exploring this requirement. One of the specified requirements of incorporation was that the incorporated municipality must levy a tax of no less than five-cents per one hundred dollars valuation. We had no choice but to levy a tax on the residents of Red Cross.

We ran budget projections out several years to see what our operating cost would be once we put all services into full implementation. Once in full operation we believed we would need the 16-cent tax rate. Remember, we were folding the two big expenses of waste collection and fire protection into our base tax rate.

In looking at what other towns in Stanly County were doing during this time, Richfield had the lowest tax rate at fifteen-cents; however, their tax rate did not include their fire tax. We do include our fire tax as a part of our tax rate so that would immediately be seven-cents coming right off the top. In short, this would effectively give Red Cross the lowest tax rate of any town in the County as can be seen from the following table:

Town	Tax Rate	
Albemarle	.54	
Baden	.23	
Locust	.36	plus .08 Fire Tax
New London	.16	plus .05 Fire Tax
Oakboro	.44	
Red Cross	.16	
Richfield	.15	plus .07 Fire Tax
Stanfield	.38	

Based on our initial findings we could have initially gotten by with a ten-cent tax levy and then increased the tax rate once we were ready to implement our services. However, we decided to go ahead and set the tax rate to at least sixteen-cents. Two reasons for this: (1) we didn't want to have to raise taxes later because that would be psychologically worse than setting an initial tax rate of sixteen-cents and (2) we needed to quickly build up some funds in the town treasury.

We also needed a way to collect taxes. To do it ourselves would require a staff to maintain property listings, valuations, issue tax statements and for collecting taxes. We found that the County handled tax collection for most of the towns in the County. We talked with the County and they were willing to do it for us. It would cost us 1-1/2% of the collected revenues. That would come to about $750 per year - a whole lot cheaper than we could do it ourselves. This became one of our proposed services.

Once we had evaluated our options we decided our four declared services would be zoning, fire protection, waste collection and police protection.

Required Statistical Information:

We were starting to feel pretty good because it seemed everything was beginning to fall in place. Our biggest problem still remained in that we had to meet the statistical requirements of population density and percent development. Our inability to meet either of these would generate an "unfavorable" response from the Joint Commission on Municipal Incorporations. An "unfavorable" recommendation would kill our petition. It would not be allowed to go to the Legislature.

Population Density:

Both population density and percent development were very difficult for us to obtain because most people in our community owned large tracks of land. Under the Joint Commission on Municipal Incorporation's guidelines we were required to achieve a minimum population density of 250 people per square mile.

The way we found our population density is as follows: based off the County tax records we were able to obtain an accurate number of houses and acreage for each property included in our proposed town boundary. Statistically, there was an average of 2.53 people per household in Stanly County based on the last US Census. We would then multiply the number of occupied houses (92% occupancy rate) by the average occupancy per household and then divide by the total acreage. We kept adding or deleting property to/from our database until we were able to reach the required 250 people per square mile.

It sounds simple, but it wasn't. Our problem was that we didn't have enough people per square mile. We had to figure out a way to remove larger tracts of land area while retaining those with the highest concentration of people. This was very difficult because we had to retain the integrity of the town boundary while doing this.

This wasn't just technical; it also had an emotional aspect to it. We knew just about all the people we were going to have to leave out and knew that they wanted to be in the town at the time of incorporation. We knew that a lot of them would be hurt if they were not allowed to be in the original incorporation.

Fortunately, we were eventually able to work out a viable solution and when we went around and talked to those people we were going to have to leave out, they understood and were not offended. In fact, the biggest question asked by them was, would they be allowed to annex in after incorporation?

Degree of Development:

We though population density was our biggest problem, when we got to the percent development we almost hit a wall. It wasn't that it was hard to calculate - it was that we just didn't have enough.

Percent development meant that a house counted for 6.48 acres of development regardless of the actual amount of land the person had.

There were a lot of people that only had an acre or less but there were a whole lot more with larger tracts of land, regardless, each counted as 6.48 acres. On the other hand commercial property counted for the actual acres developed. We scraped together every commercial acre we could find, from the daycare to the computer shop. Had it not been for the large land area of West Stanly High School we would have fallen short of the minimum requirement,

We still almost didn't make it. I got a call from State Demographics informing me that our degree of development was not enough meet the requirements. I knew I had done the calculations correctly and that we did meet the requirement. The State Demographer and I started going over the figures and found that there was a discrepancy on the developed land being allowed for West Stanly High School. State Demographics had not allowed credit for the recently purchased back 20-acres of the school. The land was under development for athletic fields but the State was not aware of this. I advised them that the school was clearing the land for athletic fields and it should be considered as developed. They agreed to allow it and it was enough to allow us to meet our percentage of development.

If State Demographics had denied the 20 acres credit we did have one last-ditch backup plan and that was to take in Running Creek School. We didn't want to do that because we felt it was too politically volatile. We didn't want to chance creating problems with either the County or Locust, because an objection coming from either would just make it that more difficult for us to get our petition passed by the Legislature.

It felt kind of like we were in a boat that was barely afloat, with water up to the gunnels, and if anything rocked our boat then it would sink. We were doing everything we could to keep the boat from rocking while still trying to make our way to safety.

Recommend Form of Government:

For our recommended form of government we chose to have a mayor and council structure. This may sound like a given, but because we were starting a new town up we wanted to think everything through and be sure the town was as well set up as possible.

At the time we submitted our petition we didn't think about planning for staggered terms of office for the council. Due to this, our Charter came back for a rewrite to build in staggered terms.

We felt the most effective size for our council would be to have four members and a mayor. The council would vote and the mayor would only vote in the event of a tie vote of the council.

We also wanted our mayor to be an elected mayor of the people. Some towns elect a council and then the council elects the mayor from within the council.

All of this was subjective, but we felt it would provide the best form of government for our town.

Who Would Serve on the Interim Town Council?

We were required to include in our petition the names of at least three people who would serve on the interim Town Council once we incorporated.

Although other people could have been chosen to serve on the first Town Council it was decided during one of the incorporation meetings, by vote, to roll over the incorporation committee into the Interim Town Council. This was because the committee was more familiar with getting the town set up and it would make it a much easier transition than trying to get new people up to speed. After all, the Interim Council would only be serving until the first election.

We submitted our names with a brief description about ourselves:

> **C.J. Barbee** – C.J. Barbee is a life-long resident of Red Cross with family history dating back several generations in the Red Cross

community. He served in the European Theater during WWII and is a retired elevator mechanic from Otis Elevator Company. He is active in community affairs.

Heath Hahn – Heath Hahn is a life-long resident of Red Cross with a family history dating back several generations in the Red Cross community. He is a veteran of WWII and is active in community affairs. Charter member of Red Cross Baptist Church. Retired lineman for Union Electric. Worked for Flame Refractors for 15 years before retiring. Heath and Kathleen Hahn (married 56-years) have three children, six grandchildren, and two great-grandchildren.

J.D. Hinson – J.D Hinson is a life-long resident of Red Cross with a family history dating back several generations in the Red Cross community. Served in the US Marine Corp and is active in community affairs. Active member of Red Cross Baptist Church. Received Governor's Award for Community Service in 2001. Grew greenhouse vegetables at Red Cross for 25-years before retiring in 1991.

Raeford Quick – Raeford "Ray" Quick graduated from West Stanly High School, UNCC with a BA in Business and BS in Management Information Systems. He is a member of Red Cross Baptist Church. He teaches computer information systems/computer engineering technology for Stanly Community College.

Larry Wayne Smith – Larry Wayne Smith is a life-long resident of Red Cross with a family history dating back several generations in the Red Cross community. He is a local businessman owning several investment/business properties in the Red Cross community. He and his wife, Larcenia, are members of Big Lick Baptist Church.

Creating a Budget for Our New Town:

A part of the requirement of incorporation was that the new town must have a tax rate of not less than 5-cents and must provide at least four of the eight specified services as listed under NCGS 120-163. These had to be specified in the petition to incorporate.

The inclusion of a budget was a required part of the submitted petition. We had to have some reasonable idea of what our tax rate, revenues, and expenses would be and put it to paper. We also had to project our budget out to where all expenses were included once all services were fully implemented. That meant that we needed a three year budget projection.

Our first step was to determine the categories for our budget. We knew we had to adopt four of eight specified services and had already identified them. We also had a fairly good estimate of what the cost would be once we put them into operation. What we really didn't know was what other cost towns would incur as a normal part of their operation. For this we just had to guess at it.

Fortunately, there was enough information on the Internet to give a good idea of how a municipal budget should be structured and to allow us to create a basic outline for our budget. The nice thing was that, since we were a new town, we would have a very simple budget.

The first thing we needed to know was what our expected expenses would be. We, as an incorporation committee, had already obtained estimates for the cost of the services we would be providing. The exception was that we still didn't have any real idea of what the cost of zoning service would be once we did start work on modifying them. We just knew that we had only 60-day window in which to take possession of it. So we decided to just take control of it and worry about the cost once we had some money built up in the town treasury. We did, however, plug $2,500 into our budget as anticipated zoning cost. Little did we know that the creation of our zoning codes, vision plan, land-use/growth plan, and transportation plan would eventually exceed $80,000?

The cost estimates we received for waste collection was $9.50 per household per month. With 212 identified houses this would come out to about $24,168 per year. We also plugged in a 20% buffer for the potential of any price increase that may occur before we began actual implementation. This meant we would need to plan for an annual waste collection cost of at least $29,000.

Police protection, based on information received from Sheriff Tony Frick indicated we could expect our annual police protection to be around $12,000 per year. This was based on the minimum required protection of 40-hours per month at a rate of $25 per hour. This would be dedicated hours where deputies, on an overtime basis, would patrol our community exclusively. Richfield and New London had similar agreements and both were satisfied with their service.

Fire protection was a more difficult problem to solve. The County had been collecting fire taxes as an add-on tax, with the fire tax being based on property valuation. This made it easier for them to break out and calculate the cost of fire protection. Unfortunately it would also mean that Red Cross would be served by three different fire districts and with each having a different tax rate.

We chose to fold the fire tax into our base tax rate and eliminate the problem of trying to maintain three different fire tax rates within the proposed town of Red Cross. It was our opinion that: (1) all residents within our town should be paying the same tax rate, (2) it greatly simplified our fire tax collection, and (3) our fire tax needed to be a part of our base tax rate.

Once we received the numbers from the County Tax Office we found that we would initially have to budget $18,550 dollar for fire protection. It should be noted that the County would provide this information at no additional cost to Red Cross.

Once we had a fairly good estimate of our operating cost the next step was to calculate our revenues. There were two primary sources of revenue for us. The first was from taxes collected from residents and the second was from Sales & Use Tax disbursements. We were able to collect a few utility taxes but those were very minor.

Property tax collection was basically a fixed revenue with a collection rate of about 97%. The County would handle all billing and collection of taxes and would charge us a 1.5% collection fee for all property taxes collected. This collection fee amounted to about $750 per year.

By knowing our population count we were able to get a fairly good idea of what the Sales & Use Tax disbursements would be. We had been told to expect somewhere between $110 and $120 dollar for each individual living within our corporate limit. With a statistical 536 people living in Red Cross we could expect to receive somewhere around $61,640 per year. We actually ended up receiving less.

Once we had determined our expenses and the revenue received from the Sales & Use Tax we were then able to figure a tax rate based on how much money we would need once we were at full operation, presumably in 2004. Based on the numbers derived, we felt we should have a tax rate, once fully operational, of 16-cents per one hundred dollars valuation. This yielded a property tax revenue to the town of $48,888. This would give us a combined revenue of about $110,528 per year. Actual Sales & Use Tax revenue was actually lower, giving us a more realistic combined revenue of about $102,500 per year.

Petition Signatures:

An important part of our petition was the collection of petition signatures of all registered voters within our proposed town limits. Surprisingly, only registered voters could sign the petition and would be the only people recognized as being for or against the incorporation process.

We went to the Board of Elections and obtained a list of voters in our area. We also obtained a stack of voter registration forms so that when we ran across someone that wasn't registered to vote, we could get them registered. Although it may sound unusual, there were a number of people that mistakenly thought they were registered. Many had been purged from voter list for not having voted in recent elections.

The list was divided up, by road, among the incorporation committee members and each of went to their assigned area and got people to sign the petition. Please note that we did include all required material with the petition. However, issues such as fire protection, waste collection and zoning were issues that we felt would require additional explanation. For this reason we created a guideline, or talking notes, to carry along so that we would all be giving the same concise answer. The following is a copy of that guideline:

Guidelines for People Carrying Petitions

Fire Protection:

1. Neither the residents nor the fire departments will realize any change in their area of coverage. The 911 mapping service will continue to issue emergency calls just as if nothing has changed.
2. Each fire department will continue to receive the same amount of funds it received prior to the Red Cross incorporation.
3. There is a change in the amount of fire tax residents in each of the fire districts will have to pay. The fire tax has been set to a standard six-cents for all the residents of the Town of Red Cross, regardless of which fire district they are in. Some people have been paying eight-cents and others have been paying four-cents – now all residents will pay six-cents.

Police Protection:

1. We are planning to contract with the Stanly County Sheriff's Department to cover our police service needs.
2. We have set down with Sheriff Tony Frick and received verbal assurance from him that we will continue to receive the standard coverage and, if we enter into contract with his department, we will receive additional (dedicated) coverage.
3. This dedicated coverage will be dedicated coverage in addition to the standard coverage we are now receiving from the Sheriff's Department.
4. Deputies will provide this additional coverage on an overtime basis where they will patrol our Town exclusively. They will also patrol roads in the town not normally patrolled by the Sheriff's Department.
5. We are planning to contract for 40-hours per month additional

coverage at a cost of $25.00 per hour. This equates to $1,000.00 per month or $12,000.00 per year.

Taxes:

1. Taxes for the Town of Red Cross have been set at sixteen-cents per one hundred dollars by vote of the community.
2. Included in the tax is six-cents that will go to the fire departments. In reality, the residents of Red Cross will realize a ten-cent tax because they will no longer pay County Fire Taxes.
3. Will taxes go up? The tax rate is dependent on the needs of the town to meet its expense (budget) requirements. If the residents start requesting additional services of the town then the money to provide these services will have to come from somewhere – most likely from a tax increase.
4. The bottom line is that the people control the tax rate.

Waste Collection:

1. We have received estimates from both Waste Management and BFI.
2. Waste Management quoted us at $9.50 per household and BFI quoted us $12.00 per household. These are projected figures for waste collection starting in January 2004. Actual figures may vary.
3. We were advised to add a 20% buffer to our cost of waste service by Waste Management. The reason for this is that there could be an increase in fuel cost, landfill cost, or additional houses in our town. Should any of these increase the cost of service then that cost will be added to the next months bill to the town.
4. The collection service will provide trash carts for people to put their waste in.
5. Collection will probably be on a Monday or Tuesday of each week. This will not be firmed up until we are ready to sign a contract.
6. The service we have requested does not include annual cleanup days. That is, if you have appliances or large items not traditionally associated as being standard household garbage, you will have to carry this type waste to the landfill.

7. We are hopeful we can negotiate more favorable terms once we are ready to sign a contract.

Zoning:

1. The Incorporation Committee cannot, by law, address zoning issues. The Interim Council must do this once Red Cross is incorporated. However, once the Town of Red Cross is incorporated, it will want to manage its own zoning.
2. The Interim Council will have 60-days from the date of incorporation to assume responsibility for Zoning or the Town will have to yield services to the County.
3. Initially, the Town of Red Cross will adopt the Counties zoning ordinances.
4. Later, zoning will be done under contract with the County, however, the Town of Red Cross will lay out its own zoning.
5. Long-range hopes are that the Red Cross Town Council will contract with the state to review, advise, and provide qualified assistance in establishing a viable zoning plan for Red Cross.

Electing the Town Council:

1. Initially, the town council will be the interim council. That is, they will be the people that were elected in one of the community meetings during the incorporation process. These people are C.J. Barbee, Heath Hahn, J.D. Hinson, Ray Quick, and Larry Wayne Smith.
2. In 2003 there will be the first public election of town officials, on a nonpartisan basis, in which the mayor and four council members will be elected. These people will take office with the first council meeting in 2004.
3. All terms are to be four-year terms. However, in order to stager the terms of the council members, the two council members receiving the highest number of votes in the general election will serve four-year terms and the other two will serve two year terms. This is specified in the town charter.

What will happen after we sign the petition:

1. Once the petition is signed it will go to the Stanly County Board of Elections for certification.
2. The Incorporation Committee will then complete the package, or Request for Incorporation, and give it to our State Representative, Bobby Harold Barbee.
3. He will then give it to the Joint Commission on Municipal Incorporations and they will verify our material. If there are problems they will return it to us as incomplete. If there are no problems they will issue a positive recommendation and return it to Bobby Harold Barbee.
4. Bobby Harold Barbee will present it to the House of Representatives and Arron Plyler will present it to the State Senate.
5. It will then be voted on by the Legislature.
6. If it passes it will come back to the people of Red Cross for a public vote. If it fails – then it is over.
7. It is very rare, but if the petition for incorporation is signed by a significant margin of the voting residents of Red Cross there is a chance that the Legislature will not require a public vote.

There was one frustrating thing that did happen during the petition signing, which was we didn't know that each person's date of birth was required to be included along with their signature. When we submitted our petition signatures to the Board of Elections for verification they were rejected and we had to go back and get a date of birth for each person. Once the dates of birth were included then they were accepted and verified.

Required Notifications:

We were required to notify the County and all Towns within the County prior to our sending in our petition to incorporate. We sent certified letters to each requesting a positive response. We weren't really surprised that we didn't get any endorsements but everyone did acknowledge receipt of our letter and we were not aware of anyone filling objections. However, we will find later that Locust did have some objections.

The key thing was that we sent certified letters requesting signed receipts so that we had documentation of notification from each municipality, which we included in our "Petition to Incorporate". Below is a listing of notifications:

Town	Signer	Position	Date Acknowledged
Oakboro	Ms. Joyce Little	Mayor	November 16, 2001
Richfield	Mr. Floyd Wilson	Mayor	November 16, 2001
Albemarle	Mr. Roger Snyder	Mayor	November 16, 2001
Badin	Mr. John Garrison	Mayor	November 20, 2001
Locust	Mr. Wilson Barbee	Mayor	November 29, 2001
Norwood	Mr. Darrell Almond	Mayor	November 20, 2001
New London	Mr. Calvin Gaddy	Mayor	December 4, 2001
Stanfield	Mr. Mark Alberghini	Mayor	December 6, 2001

County Commissioners:

Mr. Kenneth Furr November 27, 2001
(Chairman of Stanly County Commissioners)

Another thing that was required prior to our sending our petition to the Legislature was that we put a public notice in the paper at least two weeks prior to our sending in our petition and that it must be posted twice. The following is what we posted in the "Stanly News & Press":

Public Notice

In accordance with North Carolina General Statute 120-164 – public notice is hereby given that the community of Red Cross will present to the Legislature a petition for the incorporation of the Town of Red Cross.

In our petition to incorporate we also included a copy of the petition signatures, the Board of Elections certification of the signatures, copies of signed receipts of our certified letters to the County and Towns within the County, copies of all our public notice postings, etc. so that there would be a clear track record of our having followed all the guidelines of incorporation. Our bound petition ended up being a little over a 1/2-inch thick.

Once we had completed all our notification requirements the incorporation committee, as a group, went to see Representative Bobby Harold Barbee and presented our petition to him. This was a proud moment for us. We had worked hard and had completed our work. He looked through it and felt confident that we would succeed in becoming a town. He did however caution that our petition would first have to pass the Joint Commission on Municipal Incorporations. He said that he could do his part but if we couldn't get it past that commission then he wouldn't be able to present it to the Legislature.

Representative Bobby Harold Barbee did do a good job of keeping us informed of the petition's status. For my part, I would call him anytime I thought something might be happening with the petition or if I thought it might be moving too slow. I called him weekly and on occasion daily. He never seemed to mind and always seemed to know what was going on with our petition.

RED CROSS IS DECLARED A TOWN

The following are the dates our bill for incorporation traveled through the North Carolina State Legislature per the North Carolina Legislative website for Session Law 2002-56. The "Action" descriptions are as represented on the Legislative website[3].

Date	Chamber	Action
06-04-2002	House	Filed
06-05-2002	House	Ref to the Com on Local Government ll and, if favorable, to the Com on Finance
06-25-2002	House	Reported Fav Com Substitute
06-25-2002	House	Re-ref Com On Finance
07-08-2002	House	Reptd Fav Com Substitute
07-08-2002	House	Cal Pursuant Rule 36(b)
07-09-2005	House	Placed On Cal For 07-10-2002
07-10-2002	House	Passed 2nd Reading
07-11-2002	House	Passed 3rd Reading
07-15-2002	Senate	Rec From House
07-15-2002	Senate	Ref To State and Local Government. If fav, re-ref to Finance
07-17-2002	Senate	Reptd Fav
07-17-2002	Senate	Re-ref Com on Finance
07-23-2002	Senate	Repted Fav as Amended
07-23-2002	Senate	Com Amend Adopted #1
07-25-2002	Senate	Passed 2nd Reading

[3] http://www.ncga.state.nc.us/gascripts/BillLookUp/BillLookUp.pl?Session=2001&Bil lID=H1525

07-25-2002	Senate	Withdarawn from Cal
07-25-2002	Senate	Placed On Cal For 07-30-2002
07-30-2002	Senate	Passed 3rd Reading
07-30-2002	House	Red To Concur in S Amend
07-30-2002	House	Cal Pursuant Rule 36(b)
07-30-2002	House	Placed On Cal For 07-31-2002
07-31-2002	House	Concurred In S Amend
08-01-2002		Ratified
08-01-2002		Ch. SL 2002-56

At 10:55 AM on August 1, 2002 I received a call from Representative Bobby Harold Barbee informing me that our bill had just cleared both the House and Senate and we were now officially the Town of Red Cross. I immediately called the other members of the incorporation committee to let them know. It still had to be signed by the Speakers of the House and Senate but that was just a formality. As a local bill it didn't require signing by the Governor. I am not sure at just what time the speakers actually signed it but it was done that same day. It took us eleven and a half months, from the time Heath Hahn and I first presented the idea to the community, to be declared a town. We were now a town!

We found out later that it was highly unusual to be declared at town in less than one year. It was also unusual to be declared a town during Legislative Session without having to return for a vote of the people. However, 92.1% of the registered voters signed in favor of incorporation, so it sent a clear message that a vote was not necessary.

We held our first meeting on August 14, 2001 and became a town on August 1, 2012. In reality August 14, was not the official start of the incorporation because we spent the first couple weeks as an exploratory committee and did not become an incorporation committee until the night of August 28, 2001. So, in reality we can claim we did it in eleven months.

One unique thing that did happen was that at the moment we were declared a town, the incorporation committee ceased to exist and the Red Cross Town Council came into existence. We had previously declared our Council Members in our petition and, as a part of the Legislative process; these people would function as the appointed Town Council until the first election.

However, until we took the oath of office we would have no power to act on the town's behalf. Until an elected or appointed official takes the oath of office that official has no power to represent themselves as a public official or to act as a public official. In fact there is a general statute prohibiting this and making it a Class-1 misdemeanor to do so.

For us this was good because it allowed us to continue to meet as a group without having to worry about quorum rules. We were able to make plans for the swearing-in ceremony and discuss some things for the town. We still weren't able to take any official action. Now we had to shift mental gears and start thinking like a Town Council.

We had to have a Town Clerk. Linda Yow had done a great job as the secretary of the incorporation committee but, regrettably, she chose not to become our Town Clerk. Fortunately, Bobbie Kay Thompson had retired and agreed to serve as the new Town Clerk.

We were very fortunate that she was willing to assume the job considering the fact that it was not a paid position. We didn't have any money to pay a salary and, considering the expected volume of work to be done, not many people would have been willing to accept the job.

It was tough because we were starting up a new town and beginning with nothing; no structure, no documentation, had a lot filings to do, and information to get out, etc. This work couldn't be done until after we became incorporated. Basically, during that first year we had to create the town and it put a heavy load on the new Town Clerk.

None of us had ever been on a Town Council before. Having served on a Town Council would have helped but it would not have given any real insight into setting up a town. There were a lot of laws, rules and regulations to be followed and we had to do them correctly. Because of this I frequently called the League of Municipalities and the Institute of Government for guidance. They were a fantastic source of knowledge and extremely impressive in their willingness to help.

I know that for me it was a tremendous strain. I remember I was taking graduate classes at UNCC when the 120 property owners made their voluntary request to come into the town during our first Council meeting. I ended up having to drop out so that I could do the certifications, paper survey and filings for accepting the properties into the town (see chapter on "Red Cross Doubles in Size).

For Bobbie Kay Thompson it was equally hard. She had so much paperwork I was amazed at how she managed to do it. The people of Red Cross owe her a great deal for her contribution towards getting the Town started. Again, the people should be aware that she was doing this without any pay.

It should note that, as a new town, we shouldn't have had a penny in the treasury until tax revenues started coming in - and there wouldn't be for several months. Fortunately, we had collected $2,425 to fund the incorporation process. Because we hadn't made prior arrangements to have that money separated from the incorporation process prior to our being declared a town the remaining $2,000 automatically became a part of the town treasury.

This became a catch-22 for us. It was great to have money in the treasury but until we were sworn in as town officials we had no power to spend that money. We couldn't even use what we had to pay for the swearing-in ceremony. We couldn't even act on behalf of the town to borrow money for our start-up.

The people gave this money to the incorporation process to help fund the incorporation effort and it was not known if anyone expected to get their money back should we not use it all? The returning of the unused portion of the incorporation money became a moot point because State law did not allow the Town to return this money. In reality, this money could, and should, be considered as going towards getting the town incorporated and start-up. Almost immediately after incorporation we had documents to file and zoning that had to be dealt with within the first 60-days of our incorporation date. This money proved to be a lifesaver for the town's beginning.

On Sunday afternoon, August 18, 2002, we held our swearing-in ceremony in the front yard of Red Cross Baptist Church. This was the official inauguration of our new town. We had contacted our State Representatives, Representative Bobby Harold Barbee, Representative Wayne Goodwin and Senator William Purcell. All attended and spoke at the ceremony. We asked David Price, Clerk of Court for Stanly County, to conduct the swearing-in of the Council. Outside of the August heat it turned out to be an ideal afternoon.

It was a fairly large ceremony with well over a hundred people filling the front church yard. Most people brought lawn chairs and were able to sit in the shade - it was a hot August afternoon. It was in some ways a lot like social gathering. Way Side Restaurant from Oakboro, Food Lion from Locust and Oakboro and some of the ladies of the community donated tables of refreshments and ice tea. Lowes of Albemarle donated the patriotic decoration and Mike Hinson of Red Cross supplied a large trailer to serve as a stage. Jim and Jane Whitley of Albemarle commissioned a photographer to take pictures. The community support was fantastic!

Below is a copy of the speech I gave at that ceremony:

Mayor urges citizens to take responsibility for Red Cross

The Weekly Post
August 21, 2002

Here are Mayor Ray Quick's remarks during the celebration Sunday of the incorporation of Red Cross. He and the council were sworn into office by Clerk of Court David Fisher. Quick spoke atop a flat bed truck on the front lawn of Red Cross Baptist Church.

I would like to start off by saying thanks to a whole lot of people. Having worked on the incorporation committee, I have had the opportunity to see the best in people. It seems everyone we came in contact with was willing to help - even to go the extra mile and offered assistance and suggestions, even though they were not asked.

Our Rep. Bobby Harold Barbee worked hard in Raleigh helping us get incorporated. Others jumped in to help - Aaron Plyler, Fletcher Hartsell, Pryor Gibson, Wayne Goodwin, and William Purcell all helped make this endeavor a success. And we thank them.

At the county level - no offense to anyone - I never expected the level of competence and willingness to help that our county people displayed. I even heard complements out of Raleigh.

Regardless of whom we went to, be it the tax office or the county manager, their door was always open and they were always willing to help.

To use Dan Baucom as an example, he even helped us on our survey. This had nothing to do with his job. On his own time, he spent two nights, and one Saturday working with us. Jerry Myers, the county manager, is a busy man but he always had time to sit down with us.

Even the local businesses chipped in to help on this celebration. Take Pepsi, Food Lion (of both Locust and Oakboro), Wayside, Lowes, and others. The common thread was what do you need, we will help. Our businesses have a sense of belonging and of community responsibility.

As for the people in the community, look around you. A lot of these people helping set up tables, brought food, and are still working managing the food. They don't expect special recognition or gain from doing it. They are simply doing it because it needed doing for the community.

People in the community and county care about each other and are willing to help each other whenever they can. This is a common attitude for the people of Stanly County. This is a precious thing to have. We're going to see a lot more people coming out of Charlotte who want to live in and be a part of a community such as ours.

Last year, this community saw a need to further strengthen the community to preserve these qualities and (its citizens) banded together and worked for the common goal of making Red Cross a town.

Their primary concern was in wanting to preserve the community and the qualities that it possesses. At one of the meetings, 169 people stood up as one to be counted for continuing the incorporation process. There was no indecision or waiting to see what someone else was going to do. People made up their minds and took charge, and worked together as one.

The bottom line is that the people of the Red Cross community care about the community, like living in it, feel ownership of it, and want to preserve the qualities that our community possesses.

People, a historic event for this area occurred on August 1. Red Cross became a town. There are a lot of people in this community who are no longer with us who had dreams of this happening. I've heard people talking of being at Bill Hill's station and listening to some of those standing around talking about Red Cross someday becoming a town.

It would be nice for them to be here today to see those dreams finally happen.

Red Cross' becoming a town is not something that popped up on the spur of the moment, but was a gradual maturation of the community. As much as we would have liked to stay rural, we had the foresight to realize the necessity of incorporation. The necessity is that we must be in a position to absorb and manage future growth and still retain the qualities that make our community special to us.

Another thing to be proud of is the decisiveness of the people of this community. We look ahead, decide what is necessary, and do what we must to make it happen. We did this in incorporating Red Cross.

Unfortunately, Red Cross' becoming a town is like a double-edged sword. It can cut both ways. The town can serve the people or the people can serve the town. This is an important distinction.

The people can sit back doing nothing and let the town take control to the point where they start serving it.

Were it possible, I would like to have had the people of Red Cross take an oath similar to what we have just done. You, the people, made this town by voting on it and signing a petition.

You now have a responsibility for and ownership of it, to each other, to your children, and to future generations to insure that it remains a town that belongs to the people.

You must stay active in the town management, know what is being voted on by our town council, and you have the responsibility of putting people on the council who are capable and willing to serve the needs of the people of the town.

I can't repeat too strongly, the town council is here to serve the people of the town and not to serve the town. Pay attention and stay involved in the town government. Make sure this town doesn't fall into a trap and take on a life of its own and try to take control of the people.

We will have an election next year to install a new town council in January 2004. A lot of you are good capable people who have the needed skills and can offer a lot to this town.

Don't hold back, Stand up and be willing to serve on the town council, guide the growth of the town, and guard the interest of the people.

Set a good, honest example for your children to follow. They'll be the ones filling these positions before you know it. You'll be helping not only yourself, but your friends and neighbors as well.[4]

---

[4] "The Weekly Post", "Mayor urges citizens to take responsibility for Red Cross", August 21, 2002

WHAT DOES IT MEAN TO BECOME A TOWN?

The most important thing for us is that now no one can annex us.

Red Cross didn't look any different after it became a town, but by being declared a town by the State of North Carolina, it made a substantial difference to the people of our community. It became the entity "Town of Red Cross", much as a small business becomes an independent entity when it incorporates.

A good example is that of a person starting up a business. When that person first starts out they negotiate and enter into contracts, borrow money, sell products and/or services based on their personal recognizance and finances. However, once they incorporate their business, then the business assumes all responsibility and liability during contract and financial negotiations. At the point of incorporation the owner has separated his personal assets from that of the incorporated business and the corporation starts operating under its own recognizance and finances.

The people's role in a newly incorporated town can be viewed as being much like that of voting stockholders in a corporation, however, in this case each person can have no more than one vote and they must be registered to vote in the State's general elections. As such, the people have control of the entity "Town" by whom they choose to put on their board, much as a corporation does when electing officers for its board. Just as the corporate board is accountable to its stockholders for its actions and the performance of the corporation the town's council is equally accountable to its voters for its actions and the performance of the town.

It is often difficult to grasp the full significance, or the full impact, incorporating can have on the future of a community. However, by having incorporated, the people have obtained self-governance, the ability to bargain for and enter into contracts for services, the ability to pass laws in the form of ordinances and even to borrow money as a collective entity while keeping the residents safe from individual liability. The community has even obtained the right to choose its own future path.

With respect to laws, many towns have laws governing the use of bicycles and skateboards on sidewalks, the firing of guns within the town limits, the sale of alcohol, etc.; however, the most prominent law of a town is its zoning ordinance. A town's zoning ordinance is the most comprehensive, extensive and binding ordinance a town can pass. However, a town cannot pass any ordinances, or laws, that violate county and state laws and is restricted from passing any law, or conveying power, that is not granted by the state in which the town resides. Still, this gives the people of the town their best assurance for self-governing and self-determination.

As previously stated, a town does not have any powers other than those granted by the state in which it resides. The State of North Carolina has created two commissions governing incorporations and municipal management. The first is the Joint Legislative Commission on Municipal Incorporations, which provides oversight and governs incorporation process; the second is the Local Government Commission, which maintains oversight of town operations.

The Joint Legislative Commission on Municipal Incorporations has set standards, through general statutes, governing the incorporation process of a town. It specifies the requirements and verifies all qualifications for incorporation. No community may submit a petition to incorporate to the Legislature without first meeting the requirements set forth by this body. Basically, this body insures that if a community wants to incorporate into a town then it must become a town in both structure and function.

The Local Government Commission is an oversight commission that monitors the operations of all towns within the State of North Carolina. The size doesn't matter, the town may be as small as the Town of Red

Cross or as large as the City of Charlotte, the rules are the same.

This is a very valuable commission to both the people of the town and to the State of North Carolina. Not only does it verify that the town's operations are within acceptable standards, but it verifies that the town's administration operates within the parameters of the rights granted by the State. This commission is the strongest ally the people have for insuring the future of their town.

Having said all this, what does it "really" mean for Red Cross to become a town? Probably the best answer is that Red Cross, as a newly incorporated town, now has self-determination and has the tools necessary to bring that self-determination to reality. What it chooses to do with it, good or bad, is now up to its people.

THE INTERIM COUNCIL (2002/2003)

The First Meeting of the Town Council (August 26, 2002):

Interim Town Council:

Mayor	Ray Quick
Council Member	C. J. Barbee
Council Member	Heath Hahn
Council Member	J. D. Hinson
Council Member	Larry Wayne Smith
Town Clerk	Bobbie Kay Thompson

Officers appointed:

Treasurer	C. J. Barbee
Waste Collection	J. D. Hinson
Police Protection	Larry Wayne Smith
Zoning	Ray Quick
Fire Protection	C. J. Barbee
Finance	Heath Hahn
Street Maintenance	Heath Hahn

This was the first meeting of the Red Cross Town Council. It was a momentous occasion for us because it meant we were really a town. It also meant that we had a lot of things to get done, and were under a lot of pressure to accomplish them very quickly. It should be noted that we had already held our swearing in ceremony on August 18, 2002, where the Council and Town Clerk were all sworn in.

1. The first action of the new Town Council was to read the Charter for the Town of Red Cross into the town records.

2. We set a fixed date for our town meetings and authorized it to be published in the local papers. This may sound a little trivial but it is an important aspect of holding Town Council meetings. However, it also meant that if a Council meeting were to be held at any other date or time then that meeting would have to be posted.

3. Officers were appointed. C. J. Barbee would be treasurer and would be responsible for fire Protection, J. D. Hinson would be responsible for waste collection, Larry Wayne Smith would be responsible for Police Protection, Ray Quick would be responsible for Zoning, and Heath Hahn would serve as our finance officer and would be responsible for street maintenance.

4. Another very important issue to be dealt with was the adoption of our zoning. We had 60-days from the date of incorporation to assume control of our zoning or that control would forever revert back to the County. A public hearing would be required before we could vote to accept control of the County's portion of zoning covering our town, which we did set.

   Since public hearings have to be set in a session of regular council, and public notices of that hearing must be ran in a local paper no less than ten days before the hearing, we were limited to only scheduling the public hearing at this meeting.

5. We had to set a tax rate for our town. This also required a public hearing before we could adopt a tax rate. The same rules applied to this as did the adoption of zoning codes.

   We had already determined our tax rate to be sixteen cents and had stated that rate in our petition to incorporate, but it was more complicated now. Because we didn't get incorporated by the start of the fiscal tax year on July 1, we were forced to prorate our taxes for the remainder of the fiscal year. This meant that our residents would be effectively paying a prorated, or an eleven cents tax, for the tax year ending June 30, 2003. To allow for this, after a public hearing, we had to vote on an eleven cents tax rate for the first fiscal year with an automatic reversion to a sixteen cents tax rate beginning July 1, 2003.

6. We had to vote to set the Stanly County Tax office as our tax administrator. This did not require a public hearing.

Stanly County agreed to handle our tax collection for 1-1/2% of the collected taxes - that came out to be around $750. They were doing it for most of the Towns in the County. This was good for us because we didn't have, nor could we have afforded, the staff necessary to handle this function.

7. We voted to set the Stanly County Planning and Zoning Department as our zoning authority.

We needed someone to administer our zoning for us. We had no way of doing it ourselves so we voted to enter into a contract agreement with the County of Stanly to serve as our zoning administrator once our public hearing was cleared.

Most people don't realize it but there is a lot of work associated with managing a town's zoning. Zoning codes have to be maintained and administered, permits have to be handled, and zoning compliance issues have to be dealt with. Stanly County was already set up to do this and was serving as the zoning authority for some of the other towns in the County. We were grateful to them for doing it for us.

8. We received request for the voluntary annexation of 120 properties (tracts of land) to come into Red Cross. These would require verification and, upon verification, a public hearing prior to voting acceptance into the town. The following are the people that requested voluntary annexation at this first meeting:

C. J. Barbee Kathleen H. Brooks

Jerry I. Haggler & Mannie L. Haggler
Bernie W. Plyler
Johnnie D. Burris
Stephanie Morgan
Bruce Dorsey & Velvane Dorsey
Red Cross Baptist Church
Tessie Hartsell
Dorthy Helms
J. D. Hinson
James Hudson
Tracie Ann Tomberland
Jerry Jordan
Roselle Hunt
Brenda Lambert
James R. Murray & Pauline Murray
Harold J. Plyler & Dorothy J. Plyler
Ray Von Hunneycutt
Vernnie Smith
Larry Wayne & Larcenna Smith
Theron C. Smith & Myrtle N. Smith
Wayne H. Smith
Mel Cooper
Artis Tucker
Russell E. Davis
Ronald J. Williams
Jimmy & Esther Smith
K. T. Hatley Foster
Harland Brattain
Bobby G. Love
Lillian B. Love
Danny Huneycutt
Barbara Huneycutt
Chad Huneycutt
Joel Smith
Willie Smith
Ronald Stancil
Charlene Stancil
Jerry Brattain
Rebecca Brattain
Donald Ray Barbee
Loretta Barbee
Nancy Eudy
Danny A. Barbee
David L. Mullis & Nancy H. Mullis
Bryth B. Flake
Oscar M. Evans & Jo Ellen Evans
Clarence Dean Huneycutt
Charles Tucker
Loyd Austin
Gene Grantham

As Council Member C. J. Barbee pointed out, these were people that had originally wanted to be included at the time of incorporation but were asked to wait until after the town became incorporated due to their large property sizes. For historical purposes, these people should be considered as original/charter members of the Town of Red Cross at the time of incorporation. These people worked to help get the town incorporated.

Because of the size of these tracts we had gone to the people during the incorporation process and asked them to allow us to omit them from the original incorporation petition so that we could meet the incorporation requirements as has been stipulated by the Joint Commission on Municipal Incorporations. All of these people were agreeable so long as they would be allowed to come into the town as soon as we incorporated.

Most of these people owned large tracks of land and/or multiple parcels having individual deed titles. Some of them were able to have their home included during the incorporation petition, but not all of their property. Some of these tracts were over a hundred acres and the acceptance of these properties literally caused the Town of Red Cross to more than double in geographical size within the first few months after incorporation.

The cohesiveness of the people of the Red Cross community is both amazing and incredibly impressive. These people were now protected from the threat of annexation, yet their sense of being a part of the Red Cross community was strong enough that they still wanted to be included as a part of the town proper. This is an excellent example of why our community is so great.

Town Council Meeting (September 2002):

1. After the public hearing the Council voted to:

    - Set the tax rate for fiscal year 2002/2003 to eleven-cents with an automatic revision to the Town Charter's stated sixteen-cents beginning with fiscal year 2003/2004.

    - Accept/transfer zoning control from the County to the town.

2. Council voted to accept an Inter-local Cooperation Agreement between the County of Stanly and the Town of Red Cross for the County to administer permitting according to the town's zoning.

The agreement would still need to go before the County Commissioners for their approval.

3. Received voluntary annexation request:

   - Bob Love presented fourteen requests of properties owners for voluntary annexation.

   - J. D. Hinson presented two requests of property owners for voluntary annexation.

   - Ned Austin presented two requests of property owners for voluntary annexation.

   A public hearing was scheduled and the above properties were later brought into the town.

Town Council Meeting (October 2002):

1. It was at this meeting that Red Cross began addressing the issue of the highway expansion that was being planned through our community. Present Department of Transportation plans were to put a four-lane highway with divided median through Red Cross. Looking at Midland and Locust, just to our west, both municipalities had five-lane highways being put through their towns. If both of them could have five-lanes then why shouldn't we. It was our belief that a five-lane highway would make us look more like a town and encourage more business development. (See the chapter on "The Widening of Highway 24/27").

Town Council Meeting/Public Hearing (November 2002):

1. Voted to accept the voluntary annexation of 120 properties into the Town of Red Cross. I had done the certifications on these properties and all were in compliance. The Council voted unanimously to accept them into the Town.

   As stated earlier, these were people that wanted to be in the Town when we incorporated but couldn't because of either property size or location. The constraint imposed on us in having to meet a population density of 40% required that these people wait until after incorporation and then request voluntary annexation into the Town of Red Cross.

Since these requests were for voluntary annexation we weren't required to go through the State Legislature, we could do it from within our own Town Council by vote. Under the process of voluntary annexation we were required to provide a verification of survey, verification of signatures against deed titles, and to hold a public hearing before we could vote to accept them in. Only after all the above criteria had been met could we vote to accept them into Red Cross.

Final work was done and the properties were accepted into Red Cross in the November 2002 Council Meeting. Once we did accept them in there was still a lot of paperwork to be done. We had to file the appropriate papers with various State agencies and file a paper survey with the Stanly County Register of Deeds.

2. We were approached by the people on Barbee's Road requesting annexation into the Town of Red Cross. Since this occurred over a three month period it probably should be broken out into its own chapter (see the Chapter "Annexations", "Barbee's Road Annexation").

Town Council Meeting (December 2002):

1. The main topic of this meeting was on working towards getting a five-lane highway through Red Cross instead of the proposed four-lane. It was decided that the first action would be for us to talk with Representative Bobby Harold Barbee. We would also need to call Representative Wayne Goodwin and Senator William Purcell and get them involved. See the Chapter on "Widening of Highway 24/27" for details.

2. C. J. Barbee suggested we consider purchasing Doris Whitley's house for use as a town hall. Since the Council needed to look at the property we set up a workshop so that the entire Council could go out as a single group to look at the property. Under North Carolina State Law a Council cannot meet in a quorum (majority) without first calling and posting a meeting. (See the chapter on "A Town Hall").

3. Approved sending three people to a two day class on town elected officials training sponsored by the Institute of Government and the League of Municipalities to be held in Fayetteville, NC. Town Clerk Bobbie Kay Thompson, Mayor Ray Quick and Council Member Larry Wayne Smith agreed to go while Council Members Chip Speight and Heath Hahn chose not to go.

Town Council Meeting (January 2003):

1. Voted to not accept the annexation request from the people on Barbee's Road. Although we had received a substantial number of requests for voluntary annexations we were now starting to receive request from some individuals wanting to withdraw their petition for voluntary annexation. Since we recognized that there were some irregularities and probable false information that initially drove their request we felt it would be best not to accept the properties at this time (see the Chapter "Annexations", "Barbee's Road Annexation").

2. David Love and Terry Whitley of Oakboro came to our meeting and did presentations:

   David Love talked about what Oakboro was doing, grants applications and community services.

   Terry Whitley talked about some of the things Red Cross should be looking at doing, such as vision and growth plans, etc., towards getting the town set up.

   He and David also talked about strengths that Oakboro had that would enhance our town. This information and support coming from Oakboro at so soon after our incorporation was well-timed, applicable, and much appreciated.

I was very impressed with the information these two Oakboro representatives provided. However, Terry Whitley's special emphasis on us not dwelling on the daily activities and for the need to start addressing our long-term needs such as our zoning, growth plan, and vision plan and of how it would affect us in years to come was some of the best local advice we could have received at this time.

For me, the advice from Terry Whitley about long-term planning was an epiphany, or an awakening to awareness, of what we, as a town council, really needed to be doing in preserving our community's values.

Town Council Meeting (March 2003):

Tom Thrower of DOT came and did a presentation on the intended DOT construction plans for the section of highway coming through Red Cross. Surprisingly, there were only 53 residents in attendance; a much lower turnout than would have been expected for an issue that would have this much impact on the future of our community.

Of those present, there was a strong voice in favor of installing a four-lane with center turning lane instead of the four-lane with grassy median as was being proposed by DOT.

Tom Thrower of DOT made his presentation based, primarily, on the safety aspect of a four-lane with grassy median over that of a four-lane with center turning-lane.

On the Red Cross side there appeared to be four main thrust related to having a four-lane with center turning-lane over four-lane with grassy median:

1. We will develop businesses along Highway 24/27 only if we have

a four-lane with center turning-lane (five-lane).

2. The speed limits on Highway 24/27 should be set at 35 mph.

3. A four-lane with grassy median will cause more accidents because people will be making more U-turns.

4. We will have our own police force to control traffic.

Town Council Meeting (April 2003):

It was at this meeting that we established a Zoning Committee. Appointed, and sworn in to that Committee were Ray Von Burleson, Barbara Carpenter, Lou Eubanks, Blane Hathcock, Jerry Jordan, and Tom Staples. It was voted that the Town Council would serve as the Board of Adjustment. The charge given to the Zoning Committee was to develop a zoning plan customized to our town.

Town Council Meeting (May 2003):

1. Centralina Council of Government made their presentation to the Red Cross community about the value of a four-lane highway over that of a five-lane highway. This is covered in more detail in the chapter of "Widening Highway 24/27". This study was commissioned by DOT.

2. We discussed a letter we had received from the Department of Transportation requesting that we adopt a resolution accepting the modified speed limits that DOT had established for selected roads within the Red Cross town Limits. Those speed limit recommendations are as follows:

Speed Limit	Description
45	Ridgecrest Road
55	NC 205
55	Peach Tree Road
55	NC 24/27

Although we voted to accept the speed limit recommendations there was considerable discussion because some of our people wanted us to set a maximum speed limit for all roads within the Red Cross town limits, including Highway 24/27, to be no more than 45 MPH.

It should be noted that towns cannot dictate speed limits for State roads, even within the town limits. A town can make a request to the State that the speed limit be set to some limit, but it is a request only and the State has no obligation to act on the request. If a town wants to control the speeds on roads then that town must adopt, or either build, the roads.

3. J. D. Hinson told the Council that he and his wife, Violet Hinson, would donate enough land on Highway 24/27 for the Town to build a town hall. That the Hinson family had been a part of Red Cross for many years and wanted to continue their support of this community.

   This was the first awareness of this that the Council had. No action was taken at this meeting because it surprised everyone so much that it seemed no one knew what to say. It wasn't until January 2004 that all survey and paperwork was completed so that we were able to formally accept the property.

   It should be noted that after the land transfer Mr. Hinson took it upon himself to change the fencing around the property - at no cost to the Town.

Town Council Meeting/Public Hearing (June 2003):

1. 2003/2004 budget approved

2. The major issue in this meeting was the amount of Sales & Use Tax we were receiving. It appeared we were being given credit for having fewer people within our town than we really had. The only way to correct the problem was to commission a new survey to be conducted by the U.S. Census Bureau. If we could get it corrected it would

mean an additional $25,000 per year Sales & Use Tax revenue for the town. See the Chapter on "Sales & Use Tax".

I presented my findings to the Council and requested permission to commission the survey. One Council Member strongly opposed our commissioning the survey; however, the Council majority gave their support and passed it on a three-to-one vote.

The actual cost of the survey ended up being $1,530.

3. Marion and Judy Gayle Hubbard requested annexation into the Town of Red Cross.

Town Council Meeting (August 2003):

1. Approved and entered into contract with Waste Management to do our waste collection.

2. Approved expenses associated with the transfer of land donated by J. D. and Violet Hinson. The town agreed to assume all expenses associated with title transfer and survey. Council Member Heath Hahn volunteered to handle the survey title transfer, etc., from the town's side.

3. We received a formal response from the Secretary of Transportation on their position to our request for a five-lane highway through Red Cross. They did not agree with our request and intended to continue with a four-lane.

4. Voted to commission the US Census Bureau to do a census of the Town of Red Cross.

   This is a continuation of the June 2003 discussion of our work on having a new census done for our town (see Chapter on "Sales & Use Tax"). This was a vote to approve and enter into contract with them.

5. Made decision on how to handle the purchase and installation of the

new road signs as required by the County. Council Member Larry Wayne Smith took responsibility for purchasing and installing of these signs. It should be noted that resident James Speight assisted in the instillation of these signs.

Town Council Meeting (September 2003):

In this meeting we had to correct an annexation problem (this is a carryover of the June 2003 Council actions). We had to vote to make a request to the State Legislature to de-annex the property of James Ballard.

Previously Marion and Judy Gayle Hubbard had requested voluntary annexation into the Town of Red Cross. During my verification of the property I accidently transcribed the tax record number of the adjacent property, belonging to James Ballard, and used that tax record number for accepting Mr. and Mrs. Hubbard into the Town?

This caused Mr. Ballard's property to be annexed into the town. We were able to voluntarily annex the correct Hubbard property without any problems; however, it was a different story with the Ballard property. De-annexing property is a major issue and is extremely rare. A town cannot do it. We had to make a request to the State Legislature to de-annex the Ballard property. Fortunately, our Representative, Bobby Harold Barbee, was able to carry it through the Legislature without any problems and everything was corrected.

I should not have made this error but, of the estimated 150 voluntary annexation request I did verifications on, this was the only one that I messed up on.

Town Council Meeting (October 2003):

1. Approved the supplemental law enforcement contract with the Stanly County Sheriff's Department to begin providing supplemental coverage with our town. This was our fourth and final required service to be provided. Services to begin January 1, 2004.

2. Set Public Hearing on annexation of properties of Judy Gayle Hubbard (record number 12349).

3. Discuss possibility and/or method of erecting “Welcome to Red Cross” signs – Robert Thompson presenting.

THE FIRST ELECTION (2004/2005)

In accordance with the Town Charter, the Interim Council was appointed to serve only until the first election. With the election of November 2003, the first elected Town Council would take office in January 2004.

Because we didn't want every seat on the Council to come up for election at the same time we had stipulated in our charter that the two Council Members with the most votes would serve four years and the remaining two Council Members would serve two year terms. The two year terms would exist only for this one election and in all future elections all Council members would be elected to four year terms.

C. J. Barbee, J. D. Hinson, Heath Hahn, Larry Wayne Smith and Ray Quick had been on the Interim Council. However, J. D. Hinson and C. J. Barbee decided not to run for Council again. Five people ran for the four Council positions. They were Barbara Carpenter, Heath Hahn, Larry Wayne Smith, Chip Speight and Tom Staples. Two people ran for the position of Mayor. They were C. J. Barbee and Ray Quick.

Once the election was over Barbara Carpenter, Heath Hahn, Larry Wayne Smith and Chip Speight were elected to serve on the first elected Town Council. Ray Quick was elected to serve as mayor. Larry Wayne Smith and Chip Speight received the highest number of votes and would serve four year terms. This meant that Barbara Carpenter and Heath Hahn would serve two year terms.

The changeover from the old Council to the new Council has a prescribed process. At the last meeting in December of the retiring Council, the outgoing Council will adjourn and the newly elected Council will be sworn in. The new Council will then set in brief session. The primary functions for this is to vote acceptance of all contracts and obligations of the old Council, to set a date and time for the next year's Council meetings and, if the new Council chooses, to appoint officers.

It may seem a little odd that the new Council has to vote to accept the contracts of the old Council but it is a standard procedural process that removes any gray areas concerning the legality of contracts entered into by the previous Council.

Town Council Meeting (January 2004):

Town Council Members:

Mayor	Ray Quick
Council Member	Barbara Carpenter
Council Member	Heath Hahn
Council Member	Larry Wayne Smith
Council Member	Chip Speight
Town Clerk	Bobbie Kay Thompson

Officers were appointed:

Finance	Heath Hahn
Fire Protection	Barbara Carpenter
Police Protection	Larry Wayne Smith
Street Maintenance	Larry Wayne Smith
Town Improvement	Barbara Carpenter
Utilities	Heath Hahn
Waste Collection	Chip Speight
Zoning	Chip Speight

1. The Zoning Committee notified the Town Council that they would be bringing their 20-year growth plan before the Council in the February meeting.

2. "Discuss tabled issue concerning problem of firing guns within the

Town limits of Red Cross. Ray Quick presenting."[5]

"Diane Tribble requested the item be placed on the November 2003 agenda but was not present when it came before the Council. C. J. Barbee made motion to table item until January 2004 meeting. Diane Tribble called Ray Quick late in November [should be December] 2003 asking that the item be removed from the agenda - stating that she and the other party had reached an agreement. For Liability reason need to bring off table and have formally withdrawn. No action required by Council other than acknowledge that the item is being withdrawn by request."[6]

Although the issue of firearms originally came up in the December 2003 meeting it was decided to table the issue until more facts could be obtained and to let the on-coming "elected" Town Council make the final decision in the January 2004, meeting. If we did have to take action on this issue it would be done in the form of an ordinance.

An ordinance differs from a resolution in that an ordinance is an enforceable town law, where a resolution is only a statement of position with no enforceable qualities. Also, the passing of an ordinance requires a public hearing whereas a resolution does not.

This issue came up because someone was doing target practice on their own property and one of their neighbors became concerned that there may be a safety problem.

This presented a unique problem for the Town in that when we incorporated the people said that they didn't want their lifestyle altered. A high priority on that lifestyle list was that, should we incorporate, the town would not pass any ordinances restricting hunting or firearms within our community. After all we were primarily rural and there were a lot of large property owners (hunting areas) within our corporate limits, areas where the land owners didn't

[5] From the agenda of the January 12, 2004, Red Cross Town Council meeting

[6] From the minutes of the January 12, 2004, Red Cross Town Council meeting

want their right to hunt their property interfered with.

Because the Town Council had received a formal complaint it was now required to address it. This put the Town Council in a bind. It had to reach a satisfactory solution with the complainant while yet respecting the desires of a large percentage of the community.

Fortunately, one of the town residents, James Speight, interceded by getting both parties together. This occurred after the December 2003 Council meeting and prior to the January 2004, Council meeting. Once the concerned person found that safety precautions were in place and there was no danger of a stray shot, they withdrew their complaint. It is my understanding that the two parties reached an agreement to respect each other's rights and the party with the personal shooting range agreed to not shoot at times that may be inconvenient to the concerned party. As a result the complaint was withdrawn and the Town didn't have to take any action.

This would have become a major issue within the community had the Town Council been forced to take action. One of the concerns with this issue, and probably considered a part of the overall issue of protecting our lifestyle, was that it was made very clear by a substantial number of our residents during the incorporation process that they didn't want their right to hunt their property or the right to shoot their firearms on their property restricted in any way. Basically, the town was not going to pass any law keeping them from hunting their land! If it had been said during the incorporation process that there would be no firing of firearms within the town limits then, in all probability, a large number of people would have fought against the incorporation - enough that the incorporation process would probably not have passed.

For those people not familiar with our community it might sound like we are a bunch of wild rednecks. We're not. We're good people where nearly everyone knows everyone else and we enjoy a very low crime rate. We are a good rural community with many of our property owners having large tracks of land.

In studying the issue of shooting, there appears to be a great deal of difference in perception of gun ownership and hunting between rural areas and larger towns and cities. People in rural areas seem to be acceptant of gun ownership and hunting whereas people in cities seem much less likely to see a need for either.

Many of our people view a gun as a tool for harvesting meat just as a rod & reel is for catching fish. They do not easily grasp the negative connotation that a lot of urban people, and Hollywood, attach to guns. In today's world, where meat prices have risen nearly 500% over the past few years, it is not hard to imagine that more people will be hunting to supplement their dietary need for meat.

To further exemplify the progressive changes in perception, I have heard my older relatives talking about when they were boys in school. The boys would take their 22-rifles to school and stand them in the corner of the classroom until school let out. After school they would get together and go squirrel hunting. This was probably prior to 1935.

When I was in school (not West Stanly High School) I can remember a lot of the high school boys drove their pickups to school. It was a common practice to have a gun rack in the back glass of the pickup with a rifle or shotgun and a homemade walking stick (snake killer) hanging in it. The pickup would be parked in the school parking lot all day and no one seemed to have a problem with it. I don't think anyone even locked their vehicle. I can even remember some of the boys bringing long-gun parts into the vocational agriculture shop to make a custom stock or forearm. Time changes perception, especially with the shift in population from low density agriculture to high density urban.

It should be noted that a few years later the Town of Red Cross did have to enact an ordinance limiting shooting to between the hours beginning one-half hour prior to sunrise and ending one-half hour after sunset and with no shooting at all on Sunday. This enactment should be considered as to have been driven by people (nonresidents) using their guns as toys instead of working tools. As of December

2011, this is the only ordinance of this type the Town has had to enact.

The above issue came up because some nonresident commercial renters were using a bank of dirt behind their rented property (at the edge of town) as a shooting range. They were shooting at night and practically all day on Sunday with high powered and black powder firearms. There was a housing development only a few hundred yards from the shooting site and the people in the development started complaining about the noise.

In order to reach a satisfactory solution to all parties (residents and hunters) the Town Council decided to limit the hours of discharging firearms to those of legal hunting hours. The residents of that development weren't opposed to the renters shooting but were opposed to the hours that they were shooting. They even commented that they didn't want to interfere with people's right to hunt.

Based on discussions with the development's residents, had it not been for the Sunday shooting (all day), they probably would not have filed a complaint. The decision reached by the Council was satisfactory to both the development's homeowners and other property owners/hunters within the community. We never heard anything from the shooters; however, it was not long afterward that the renters moved away.

3. "J. D. Hinson presented a deed for 0.77 acres of land on Highway 24-27 for a Town Hall. Mayor Quick stated that the Town was most grateful for his and Violet's generous donation."[7]

   The land was a gift from J. D. and Violet Hinson for the purpose of building a town hall on it. The town would pay all cost associated with the land transfer and should the town not use the land for a town hall or should the land ever be abandoned by the town then the land would revert back to the original property owners, or their heirs.

[7] From minutes of the January 12, 2004 Red Cross Town Council meeting

The town eventually purchased a larger tract of land and the property was deeded back to the Hinson family. All transfer cost was assumed by the town.

4. Discussion on pursuing grants for the town hall. Ray Quick presenting.

   "Mayor Quick contacted USDA about grant availability for a town hall. He and Council Member Heath Hahn will pursue this matter for more information."[8]

   We will later find out that it was not a grant opportunity but an opportunity for loan support for when we did pursue a loan for purchasing property for a town hall.

5. "Motion #110 Councilman Speight made motion that the Zoning Committee be [renamed] the Zoning Board. Seconded by Councilwoman Carpenter. Motion carried. The Five members will take their oath of office at their monthly meeting on January 24, 2004 in the home of Lou Eubanks."[9]

Town Council Meeting (February 2004):

1. Accept zoning report from Zoning Board. Chip Speight presenting.

2. Submission of comprehensive growth plan.

3. Discuss changing zoning board to six members and do away with alternates. If change passes, look at approving C. J. Barbee as sixth member of zoning board.

4. Discuss making term limits for the Zoning Board. Recommend two years term with three people serving two years and three people serving three years. Thereafter all members would serve two year

[8] From minutes of the January 12, 2004 Red Cross Town Council meeting

[9] From minutes of the January 12, 2004 Red Cross Town Council meeting

terms. This allows roll-off of only three members at a time.

5. "Councilman Smith stated that the three digit house numbers will be assigned to houses and business in the near future. However we do have a problem with EMS since Oakboro also has a North and South Main Street. Because of this maybe we can get a different zip code for Red Cross."[10]

6. "Councilwoman Carpenter has contacted Larry Branch in Oakboro concerning applying for Grants for Town Improvements. Once a need is determined, then the town can pursue a grant. She also wants to petition for a lower speed limits on the main streets and at the schools"[11]

7. "Councilman Speight made motion that another person is added to the Zoning Board, therefore having a six-person board and eliminating the alternates. Seconded by Councilman Hahn, Motion Carried. Councilman Speight recommended that C. J. Barbee be added as the sixth person."[12]

   "Councilwoman Carpenter made motion that C. J. Barbee is added as the sixth person on the Zoning Board. Seconded by Councilman Smith. Motion carried."[13]

8. "Discuss possibility of needing to put moratorium on building/subdivisions until the Town has a zoning/subdivision ordinance? If so, will need to notify County not to issue any permits?" Chip Speight presenting.

   "Councilman Smith made motion to put a moratorium on subdivision until Zoning Board and Town Council can approve an ordinance that meets their approval. Seconded by Councilman Hahn. Motion carried."[14]

---

[10] From the Minutes of the February 9, 2004 Red Cross Town Council Meeting

[11] From the Minutes of the February 9, 2004 Red Cross Town Council Meeting

[12] From the Minutes of the February 9, 2004 Red Cross Town Council Meeting

[13] From the Minutes of the February 9, 2004 Red Cross Town Council Meeting

[14] From the Minutes of the February 9, 2004 Red Cross Town Council Meeting

Although our intentions were good, we didn't realize at the time that we couldn't put an indefinite moratorium on subdivisions. This was the first time we had addressed a moratorium issue. We later found that standard practice is not to exceed 90-days. If needed, the moratorium can be renewed.

Town Council Public Hearing (February 24, 2004):

A public hearing was requested by Highway Commissioner Larry Helms to address the issue of a five-lane vs. four-lane section of Highway 24/27 through the Town of Red Cross. I don't think many of our people understood that this public hearing was being held as a means for seeking closure to the issue. The following are the minutes of that meeting:

"Present: Mayor Quick, the Council - Larry Wayne Smith, Heath Hahn, Chip Speight and Barbara Carpenter and 85 Citizens

Guest: Larry Helms, Highway Commissioner, and Mrs. Helms, Benton Payne, District 10 Engineer, and Tom Thrower, Division 10

Mayor Quick called the meeting to order and had the invocation. He welcomed everyone and recognized our guest.

Mayor Quick explained how the meeting would be conducted and explained that only subject to be discussed would be the widening of Highway 24-27, and he would serve as the moderated.

The Highway Officials will present their presentation first. Once they have finished members of the Town Council will be allowed to address the Highway Officials, and then the discussion will be open to the floor for the citizens to ask questions and express their concerns.

Mr. Helms said every month for the past two years the Highway Department meets and the subject of the these meetings is to improve safety, save lives, and route traffic through the community. After all these meetings, he said that four lanes are safer. Goal is to build a good road that does not require a by-pass at a later date. Five lane roads are more dangerous because people do not know how to use them. Mr. Helms supports Tom Thrower and respects his knowledge and 38 years of experience in planning roads. Main concerns in building a road are make sure we have a safe community, accessibility to community roads and that the roads are safe for a long period of time. Accessibility and feasibility are essential for the development of Red Cross. Mr. Helms said if they had the chance to redesign the plan for Locust there would be a divided highway through that town. It takes eight to ten years to design and build a road.

Mr. Thrower emphasized five lanes are more dangerous because a lot of people don't know how to use them, and a lot of head on collisions is a result of these roads. His primary responsibility is to build highways that are safer. It is not always the bad people who cause accidents, but good Christian people are involved. DOT investigates the site of every accident when there is a fatality to try to prevent this from happening again and deter[mine] if the road was the problem. He said divided highways control the number of left turns therefore cutting down on the number of accidents. He thinks Locust and Albemarle will regret having a five-lane highway. The four lanes were approved through Red Cross before we were incorporated, and strongly feel that a four-lane highway is the best choice for our Town. There will be a cross over and traffic lights at Bethel Church Road, and a cross over and a signalized light at West Stanly High School. There will also be a cross over at Lakewood and Liberty Hill Church Road.

Mr. Helms said that he is aware of the petitions and a visit to the Governor's Office, and gotten input from them. He mentioned Rock River RPO and the report that COG did. It was recommended to keep Highway 24-27 a four-lane road. Contracts have been issued and any changes would be expensive and require time to process. It would be impossible for a pedestrian to cross a five-lane road. Design Engineers have added three back to back left turn between Smith Grove Road and Lakewood Road. David Diggs is the Resident

Engineer for this project. Residents having problems with driveways during the construction should contact him.

Mr. Payne said the five-lane road between Albemarle and Richfield has caused a lot of problems. There are more accidents in front of North Stanly High School than any other school in the County. DOT makes annual visits to address the PTA and School Board concerning this problem. There are eight conflict points in front of the school.

Mayor Quick asked for questions from the Council.

Councilwoman Carpenter asked Mr. Helms how can a divide highway make a town closer. She met with Mr. Franklin, an assistant to Governor Easley, he said he could understand not building five-lanes through Red Cross if they were not building them in Locust and other parts of the State. The Bible says a house divided will not stand. Councilwoman Carpenter says a Town divided will not stand. She feels the Four-lane is to move traffic through Red Cross at 70 MPH.

Councilman Smith said the Town cannot develop on a four-lane road, and business will not locate here. He states a problem with EMS and Fire Departments when responding to an emergency. Four lanes will kill our growth as well as his business on Gaddis Road. The town needs taxes that businesses will generate.

Following are the comments from the floor.

One lady said we couldn't develop a town on a four-lane road. Cannot plan a good town with a 40-foot medium.

Operator of the West Stanly Variety said his business will decrease by 40% and may be forced to close.

Since contract has already approved, one person asked if this meeting is in vain, but wants the safest highway. Also wants to benefit the economy.

One citizen, a lifetime resident, was adamant about five-lanes. He has seen more accidents on four-lane roads than five-lane, and traffic moves faster on four-lanes. Red Cross is as good as anyone in the County. If Locust and Midland have five lanes so should Red Cross.

With Five-lanes the town would have accessibility and feasibility, which are the keys for success and growth for Red Cross. If extra policemen are needed to enforce the speed limits, they will earn their salary from revenue from tickets issued.

One citizen supported DOT for four-lanes and median, because the town was incorporated so we could basically stay the way we are.

Safety is the main concern said one lady. She has seen too many accidents in front of West Stanly High School.

One lady said her husband is more cautious on a five-lane road. Also concerned about business on a four-lane road.

One lady asked to see static's of accidents on a four-lane road compared to a five-lane road.

Mr. Helms said it is important how we grow, and we have a wonderful opportunity for growth on the outskirts of the main road. Highway 205 is a great opportunity for this purpose. Town needs to design and overall Master Plan for the Town we will be proud of. There is no support to make Highway 24-27 a five-lane highway through Red Cross.

Mayor Quick thanked the people from DOT and the citizens for attending the meeting. The Highway is not the most important thing, the people are. We incorporated [not] because we wanted to live in a town, but [to] preserve this community and the friendship of the people."[15]

---

[15] From the minutes of the February 24, 2004, Red Cross Public Hearing

In looking back at the issues it would appear there were several reasons for DOT's resistance to a five-lane:

- When the original design for Highway 24/27 was drawn up Red Cross was under the Oakboro Transportation Plan and was not recognized as an independent entity. Therefore no consideration had been given for making allowances for a five-lane through Red Cross. As such, a redesign of that section of highway would take about a year.

- In the view of DOT there was just not enough development along Highway 24/27 within the Red Cross community to justify installing a five-lane highway.

- DOT's stated objective was to efficiently move traffic from one location to another. The instillation of a five-lane would necessitate a reduction in speed limit through Red Cross and create additional safety hazards, creating a conflict in DOT's objective of efficiently moving traffic.

- Substantial pressure was being applied by the County and nearly all towns within the County for DOT to continue with the planned four-lane. Nearly all municipalities had sent resolutions requesting DOT continue with its present plan of a four-lane.

From the side of the people of Red Cross the primary reasons given for needing a five-lane were:

- A five-lane highway with center turning lane is safer than a four-lane with divided medium.

- It would harm existing businesses

- It would harm businesses recruitment

- It would harm the ability to gain needed tax money

- It would divide the town

Most people using the "five-lane is safer" argument were using it as an unqualified counter argument against DOT's statement that five-lane highways are inherently less safe than four-lane highways. Had the section of Highway 24/27 through Red Cross not been a major transportation corridor, and were the speed limit to be reduced to 35 MPH, then there may have been grounds for a five-lane. The key element in this argument is the reduction in speed limit. Unfortunately, Red Cross just didn't have enough existing development along Highway 24/27 to make a reduction in speed limit a viable justification.

Although several people from Red Cross put forth that we could enforce a 35 MPH speed limit, DOT remained highly skeptical of our able to enforce such a speed limit? Our people countered that we could have our own police department to enforce it. Even back in the March 2003 Town Council meeting during a DOT presentation Council Member Smith, apparently speaking for the Council, affirmed that "we will have our own police force, we will!"[16] During this meeting a number of other residents supported the creation of a Red Cross police department with one unidentified person making the justifying statement that "if extra policemen are needed to enforce the speed limits, they will earn their salary from revenue from tickets issued."[17]

The concern of harming existing businesses is a legitimate concern of any business owner and any governmental agency should take this into consideration when making changes. There was only one notable occurrence of a business suffering harm from the four-lane - that was the Variety Pick-Up across from West Stanly High School. According to its proprietor, he anticipated losses in revenue of about 40%.

With respect to the desire for business recruitment and the harming of tax revenues that would have resulted from recruited businesses, all indications were that this was being promoted by only a select and

[16] From audio of the March 2003, Red Cross Town Council meeting

[17] From the minutes of the February 24, 2004, Red Cross Public Hearing

very vocal few from the community.

Town Council Meeting (March 2004):

1. "Councilman Speight reporting for the Zoning Board that C. J. Barbee was sworn as the sixth member on February 17, 2004. Newly elected officers are C. J. Barbee as chairman and Lou Eubanks as secretary. The Zoning Board recommends term limits for two, three and four year first term limits for the present board. A second term of four years allowed with approval of Zoning Board and Town Council. Thereafter, no more than two terms, eight years to serve consecutively. The present board limits will be as follows: two year term Jerry Jordan and Ray Burleson, Three year term Tom Staples and Marion Hubbard and four year term C. J. Barbee and Lou Eubanks."[18]

2. "Request for change of street names. Lou Eubanks presenting.

    "Wants to change names of the following roads as was designated in Motion-62 by the Town Council:

    - Highway 205 from South Main to as yet unspecified name.

    - Ridgecrest Road from North Main to as yet unspecified name.

    - Highway 24/27 from East/West Main to as yet unspecified name(s).

    NOTE: With the passage of motion-62, it was agreed during the discussion that no road would/will be named after an individual. However, the Council does have the right to change both this and the road names."[19]

---

[18] From the Minutes of the March 8 2004, Red Cross Town Council meeting

[19] From the agenda of the March 2004 Red Cross Town Council meeting

"Councilman Speight [made motion] at the recommendation of Lou Eubanks that the following roads names be changed:

North Main Street changed to Oak Ridge Road North

South Main Street changed to Oak Ridge Road South

West Main Street changed to Red Cross Road West

East Main Street changed to Red Cross Road East

Councilwoman Carpenter seconded the motion. Motion carried. Councilman Hahn voted no to the motion."[20]

In the February Council Meeting it had been made clear how the conflict in street names would allow us to obtain our own zip code. The introduction of this request at the very next meeting was both surprising and disappointing. This action completely blocked our opportunity for obtaining a unique zip code for Red Cross (see Chapter on "Red Cross works to get Zip Code").

For Red Cross, having our own zip code was important, it would be a strong reinforcement to our being an independent town and would remove us from being under the umbrella of another town.

3. Council Member Chip Speight brought the Zoning Committee's 20-year growth plan before the Town Council for their review and making a request to retain an Oakboro planner to provide guidance on the creation of the Red Cross zoning codes.

Below is an excerpt from the Council discussion on that issue during the March 2004, Council meeting exemplifying the opposing views with respect to the design of our zoning codes:

Chip Speight: "We had a lengthy discussion today and the will of

[20] From the minutes of the March 8 2004, Red Cross Town Council meeting

the Zoning Board is to go out and, uh, the name come up of, well I could say one name but, well the one name we talked about was to bring in somebody to help us, answer some questions, give us some guidance, uh, not sure we're spread out in left field.

So, ah, do I need to bring it before the Council before I go and approach somebody? After the meeting today I'm planning to talk to David Love from Oakboro, seeing if he would be willing to work for us on an hourly basis. If we need a question answered, have him come to a meeting, give us some guidance, show us the way to go, just to make sure we're not staring off into right field.

So, if I need to bring that before the Council for their approval before I do that. Um, the last time I asked about that I was told I didn't need to come back before the Board before I brought help in so it's whatever you'll want to do.

But, we definitely think it would be a big help. If'n he might not even be willing to do it. Michael Sandy's name was mentioned. This lady..."

Lou Eubanks: "Evans."

Chip Speight; "Evans, said they would work on an hourly basis. So those three names we talked about today, and get some guidance, approach them and see if they will help us.

Do I need to make that a request to go out and get it or I just do it on my own and get em?"

Larry Wayne Smith: "I say you go and get em. That's what you've got the money allotted for."

Ray Quick: "David Love is a knowledgeable man and he can be of help to you, but I would temper that, he has used consultants before. And, I wouldn't go to deep with it just off of his..."

Chip Speight: "Well, no, we're just wanting to get, we've got... I see it, and the Board sees it, we talked about this today that they feel like they don't need to go out here and spend, because they have had several people come in and say, you know, this is what we want. How much, you know, will you help us, and they want to know how much money we've got to spend. And, we don't need nobody like that to get us off the ground and running.

You know, I feel like if we can keep it local, keep the money local. You bring somebody in, like somebody said today, Chicago, they don't know how we live here in Red Cross. The people that live here in this community, Stanly County, know how we live and I think they will relate better to the people, and it will be cheaper too.

We're not saying that David draw out our whole zoning plan. He can get us to a point where we are comfortable with it and then we can take it to an agency that's professional and get their blessing on it. We think we'll save money by doing that.

Ray Quick: "Well, you're looking at me. I'll say my two cents worth. You all vote, I don't..."

Chip Speight: "I'll make it a motion; I don't mind making that..."

Ray Quick: "Let me say my piece. The zoning and land use are the two most important things this town will ever do - at least once it became a town. Becoming a town, yea, that was the biggest step but this is the most important thing, and yea, get local people, it's good, they're easier to work with and we're more comfortable with them. But, they're not as knowledgeable. Now, I respect David Love, he is knowledgeable within limits, and he is a nice guy, and he's going to do the best he can, and I'll put, personally...

I mean we budgeted $20,000. It shouldn't take that, but, if it did it would still be worth it to make sure we had the best setup we could get. Because what we lay down now, it's going to be with us forever. As zoning is developed, it's going to be a living document; it's going to be changing. But, it's going to have a common root. It will all spring from this and what we set down will be how the town starts out and it's going to influence it from now on.

For my part, I'd rather see a professional that has an objective viewpoint that's not tailored to 'their' town. David Love has worked hard to tailor it for Oakboro, and, uh, Locust has got theirs, Albemarle has got theirs, but they all look at it from their perspective, and they would, I believe, do their best but, they would, based on their knowledge of their local community. And, we're a clean slate right now.

Chip Speight: "Like we talked today. We can make it look like whatever we want to. Most towns don't have that opportunity right now. We have the opportunity to make the town like we want it and, there's still, unless somebody shows me different... There's still a basic guideline package that's zonings based on. There's going to be name changes here paragraph here but there's a basic format. If we go and hire someone out of Charlotte, they're going to use the same thing that Michael Sandy could give us at probably half the price.

I'm not saying let's not use a professional to finish it up. I can't see how we can we can justify spending that extra money to get this company to do the same thing we can do for half the price.

And, then once we're happy with it then we can turn it over to them and we haven't paid them twice the amount of money. That's the way I look at it. I mean, I just feel like the best interest of the town is... These people work here, live here, I mean they going, I mean we got the option that David Love has never had down there in Oakboro. Cause, when he become zoning officer, the town was already formed and they had their zoning and he basically filled in and carried on where (could not understand name) left off. Now he can, he may have some ideas we haven't even thought about. And, I think, I worked with David. I think he's a very knowledgeable person and I don't think he would try to it throw in, throw something in here, you know, cause he's only going to be on consultant he's not writing our stuff. We got the Zoning Board to do that. And, they're, in my opinion sharp people on there. That's got good ideas and got a lot of experience on that Board. And, that's my opinion. I mean, everybody's got an opinion. I'd like to hear from the Board. It's not my money; it's the town's money we're going to spend. I'd like to get the most amount of money, the most bucks for what we can get.

Heath, you got any comments?"

Heath Hahn: "No, not at the moment. I'd like to see what the other people's got to say."

Larry Wayne Smith: "[could not understand first part of comment] ...I feel like Michael and probably Mr. Love can help a lot and, ah, I really think we, myself, we should let Zoning handle that."

Chip Speight: "That was one of the things that, you know, that come, I brought the idea up, I give the example when I was on zoning board at Oakboro how the zoning officer worked down there. I told the Board today, if there was ever in the future that need, we do have the money to go out and get that person and they took it from there and after talking for some time, you know, those three names come up.

I was asked to approach those three people and see if we can get at least one of them and come in and, you know, it may not be we ever need em, but like if we have a question and, you know, we don't know what to do with it. We can go to these people and get some guidance.

This is not my idea. This is coming from the Zoning Board."

Barbara Carpenter: "We trusted him with our Zoning Board, on this Board, and I think we should trust his intelligence on spending it."

Larry Wayne Smith: "What about, what about the zoning if you did all that work, spend all this money to do it, like Locust tells us, they keep changing theirs all the time. You know, you don't know what's going to be changed down the road."

Chip Speight: "If we could see in the future, it'd be the main thing, but we can't do that."

Larry Wayne Smith: "We'd live better wouldn't we."

Chip Speight: "Right!"

Ray Quick: "Do you have a dollar amount you are thinking of for David Love?"

Chip Speight: "No, I don't."

Ray Quick: "Do you want to list a dollar amount for a cap if you're going to put a motion out?"

Chip Speight: "I don't want, I mean I know, I'd like to talk to David and Michael and see, uh, I mean... If we want to set $5,000, $4,000, uh, 300..."

Tom Staples (Zoning Board) "$30 dollars an hour."

Chip Speight: "$30 dollars an hour."

Tom Staples (Zoning Board): "That's what I've heard some of them say, as a consultant."

Chip Speight: "Right."

Tom Staples: "I don't know if that's cast in stone or not, but I've heard that number."

Chip Speight: "He may not even be in it, I mean interested in it, but when Bill was doing it he was working with the Town of Stanfield too. And that, you know, that kept him busy. They worked as a filtering system the same way the Zoning Board is going to work through a filtering system for us.

It'd be ideal; I mean there's no way I could have served in the majority of the people served on the town of Oakboro Board if we didn't have Bill (could not understand last name) there. We didn't know, I didn't know what I was doing. I was, I knew my, had my book I could go turn to. If I had questions on a developer, questioning me right there on the spot, I wouldn't have had a clue. It would have took me a lot of thumbing in the book, but Bill was sitting there and he'd say turn to page 300, this is covered right here.

It's well worth, in my opinion, well worth Bill... [inaudible] ...salary for Oakboro and have him sitting there on that Zoning Board.

In that matter, well we're going to grow and I think everybody will agree to that. But, om, it's going to be, I think that will be something we will need to look at in the future, having a, um, part-time zoning officer, maybe a full-time eventually. Down the road, he really helped; I mean he took a load off the Zoning Board. And he knew what to do and what was correct and what not and, you know, he's the filtering system.

I'm not saying let's go and hire one part-time right now, I just think on an hourly basis. But, um, in the future I really see we can have a part-time zoning officer.

Want to set a cap at $30 per hour and see if, might not get em. I think whatever they charge, you know, I've never heard nothing but good things about all three of em.

If you want to make a motion I'll make a motion."

Heath Hahn: "What's the Zoning Board planning on doing? Are you going to write the thing out like you think might, might work and use him for correction? Will this work or will it not work, or are you going to follow someone else's zoning?"

Chip Speight: "Well, basically, if you look at our zoning book, it's going to have subdivision, it's going to have..."

Heath Hahn: "Yea, yea, I..."

Chip Speight: "It's going to have your commercial and what goes in here. Basically, you're going... You're going to have to follow somebody's unless you're going to sit down and..."

Heath Hahn: "There's a lot in there that we don't need to cover at this time. Now I'm sure you're aware of that."

Chip Speight: "But, om, it's been a push and, you know, to get some type of zoning and everybody's got to remember we're covered under Stanly County Zoning. Right now!

We're work on, and, uh, you know, we don't have any type of zoning, we do. But there's going to be some stuff in there and we're wise to look for the future. And try to think, it's... We could ask everyone on this panel, on this Council, right now what it's going to look like in 10-years. We come up with five different answers.

And, for this Board to sit down right now and try to say this is what we're going, it's going to take them a while to do it. I think it's something we want to... We need to do it in a hurry but we need to do it slow, that makes any sense and get it right.

I don't want to rush into something and then a year from now I wish we hadn't done that. But, you know, we always have the option to change and, um, but, you know, I really think, you know, we're going to have to deal with probably some commercial items right now. You know, some of the stuff we don't really see, but, you know, um, I think our zoning, I mean our subdivision, highway business needs to be touched on pretty quick.

They're fixing to start on construction on the road and in two and a half years it'll be completed, maybe. That's when everybody thinks it's going to happen. But I do know, I don't..."

Ray Quick; "Well, I'll offer a suggestion. If you make it in the form of a motion, ah, can you put a cap on how much you're going to spend with individuals like David Love, etc.?"

Chip Speight: "It's hard to sit here and say Ray, and give you a figure. I mean what we want to spend We can..."

Ray Quick: "I mean, how much are you asking for?"

Lou Eubanks (Zoning Board): "Excuse me, may I say something? What we're thinking about is using David, or Sandy, or Ms. Evans for, it's like when a developer comes in and wants to do 'this". They are going to be the ones that look at it to see if it meets all specifications that we've asked for. They're not going to be writing our policy, or anything of the sort. We're getting that together, then we want a 'somebody' to tweak it, to do it that way. But we want David, or Michael Sandy, or Ms. Evans to case-by-case thing if somebody comes in and wants to rezone or build, or whatever, to be sure all the "T's" are crossed or the "I's" are dotted. That's what we want to use them for. So it's kind'a hard to say we need $50,000 or we need $10. It depends on..."

Ray Quick: "Wait a minute, Chip's... If I understand you, you're talking about helping them develop..."

Chip Speight: "No, no, not develop it, if they have questions. Or I mean there's going to be some times when their coming up with these books when they say well they can't, well, you know, we don't really know what to do, what's legal to do. I mean, you know, if, plus what their talking about is having them there to look at it too. Once, he uses like, I made a comment to what Bill was doing in Oakboro.

In my opinion, I may be, I mean they may be a lot smarter than I'm giving them credit for. I think they're going to need some help somewhere in this time of writing this stuff up. But, if they can call, alright, David we're going to have a meeting, or I'm just using this as an example because I know him better than the rest of em. Can you come to this meeting for an hour and we got'a talk here and we don't know quite how to go about doing it.

So, I mean it's, uh, you know, we may not use him at all. But then, definitely, down the road when we have a developer come in or, um, it's going to be an hourly consultant. He's going to consult, he's not going to be telling us, you know, you got to do this and this, you know. He's not going to actually write our zoning. These people are going to write the zoning.

Just in case we need, we may not need him on the first part. What I'm thinking we're going to need..."

Ray Quick: "Are you saying we should get somebody at $30 an hour for an unspecified amount of time?

Larry Wayne Smith: "Well, we've already voted to allot $20,000. Why do we have to go back and do it again?"

Ray Quick: "We don't. All we have to do is approve the expenditures."

Tom Staples (Zoning Board): "Can I just make one comment, I would, first of all, David Love has been a lot of help, as far as I'm concerned, to the town of Red Cross. He's done a lot of things for free. I don't know what his hourly rate is. I've heard the number of $30 per hour bantered about but I think I speak for the members of the Zoning Board here, I hate to see our hands tied over $30 an hour.

First of all, we may not need him for a long time. But, if we do need somebody, I'd rather pay them $50 an hour rather than be hamstrung with a $30 an hour budget and then get a slipshod job.

So, I personally, as a member of that Zoning Board, I hate to see us bound by a $30 an hour number. We've got a budget the town's already approved, and I think most of us are, even though we think we may not know a lot about zoning, we know how to control money. We know we aren't going to spend it too fast. And we'll spend it wisely because we pay the taxes too. Om, but I'd hate to think we were, that we were locked into a $30 an hour. I rather use him less and pay him good money to do the job right.

Chip Speight: "Each time we use somebody, you know, the next month I can bring it and let you know we used so much money."

Heath Hahn: (Unintelligible) "...something in writing. Something to look at."

Ray Quick: "Put it down as a motion then."

Chip Speight: "I make a motion that we go out and approach an individual to give us guidance on an hourly basis to help the Zoning Board." And report back when we use, how much we used, and, you know, keep a close eye on it. That's the motion."

Ray Quick: "Ok, motions on the floor. I think everybody's heard it. Is there a second or any comment before the second?"

Larry Wayne Smith: "I second."

Ray Quick: "Ok, have a second. Those in favor?"

[Passed unanimously]

Ray Quick: "So carries."[21]

The above dialogue gives a good representation of how many felt about designing our zoning codes. It appears that at least two of the six Zoning Board members and three of the four voting Town Council Members were in favor of the in-house approach to creating our own zoning codes.

Our Zoning Committee was looking to Oakboro to help us build our zoning codes. This is understandable because Oakboro has done well. It is a nice town, its council has managed it well and there is little fault to be found.

If we were to adopt, or at least model, our zoning codes from Oakboro's zoning codes then we would be adopting their "personality" and not retaining our own. This is because zoning codes have a great deal of influence on the personality of a town. Did we want to change our personality, or lifestyle, to mirror that of Oakboro? If we did want to be like Oakboro,

[21] From the audio of the March 8, 2004, Red Cross Town Council Meeting (00:13:38)

then why didn't we allow Oakboro to annex us instead of incorporating ourselves?

In looking back at the incorporation meetings, the overriding "mandate" from our people, it was that we like our community, we didn't want it changed and we wanted it protected.

Still, there was a great deal of fear that we would end up with generically cloned zoning codes from another town. It seemed that there was nothing that could be done in convincing our people to retain a competent consultant.

There was also considerable concern in the manner in which approval of expenditure of funds were being handled. The reader is encouraged to review the previous dialogue with respect to approval of expenditures.

Town Council Meeting (April 2004):

1. "Motion #134 Councilwoman Carpenter made motion to send a resolution for a five-lane road through Red Cross to Raleigh, N.C. before accepting the maps from the Highway Department. Motion was not seconded; therefore Mayor Quick exercised the option for individual vote with the Town Clerk recording each Council members vote. Councilman Speight asked to be removed from the Council during this vote, due to conflict of interest.

   Motion #135... Councilman Hahn voted nay, Councilman Smith voted nay, and Councilwoman Carpenter voted yea. Motion was defeated. Councilwoman Carpenter wants it recorded in the history of Red Cross that she fought for and supported a five-lane road.

   Motion #136 Councilman Smith made a motion to send a resolution to accept the maps from the Highway Department with the addition of another cross over between Smith Grove Road and Bethel Church Road. Motion seconded by Councilman Hahn. Councilman Hahn voted yea, Councilman Smith voted yea and Councilwoman Carpenter voted nay. Motion Carried. Councilman Speight returned to the Council."[22]

2. "Councilman Hahn suggested that we have access to on-line banking. Mayor Quick does not recommend this because of the [weak] security and protection on the Town Clerk's personal computer."

3. "Councilman Smith asked about the website. [Quick responded] The town received the grant, but turned it down."[23]

Town Council Meeting (May 2004):

1. The Planning Board presented the Council with first draft of the twenty-year growth plan. Chip Speight presenting.

2. Motion to put crossover in front of the future site of Town Hall (land donated by J. D. and Violet Hinson).

   J. D. and Violet Hinson had donated 0.78-acres of land on Highway 24/27 for building a town hall and the town was voting a resolution requesting DOT to consider putting a crossover in front of this land. As a result of this action a crossover was built into the highway design.

3. First reading of the 2004/2005 budget.

Public hearing/ Special Council Meeting (June 2004):

1. "Mayor Quick called the meeting to order and stated the Public hearing was to rezone approximately 1.95 acres of a 43.041 acre tract of property on Highway 24-24 at the intersection of Brattain Road belonging to Lillian B. Love from R/A to Highway Business."

   "...Barbara Huneycutt, daughter of Lillian and Bobby Love spoke on their behalf. She said the business opened in the 1940's as a grocery store, before Stanly County had a Zoning Board. They are paying

---

[22] From the minutes of the April 5, 2004, Red Cross Town Council meeting

[23] From the minutes of the April 5, 2004, Red Cross Town Council meeting

commercial taxes on this property, and no additional structure is being added. They were encouraged by the Town of Red Cross and County of Stanly to rezone the property from R/A to Highway Business. If the rezoning is not approved it will delay the opening of the business.

Planning Board Chairman Barbee asked the Town Council not to approve the rezoning, but present the permit to the Zoning Board for their approval and then present it to the Council. He doesn't agree with the way this is being handled.

Mayor Quick said in this case contractors were on the job site and could not wait until the next Town Council meeting. He asked Ms. Evans (Stanly County Zoning Office) to clarify the handling of this matter. She said they could not operate until this matter is corrected. She said the County had revoked the zoning permit [construction permit] because it was issued in error. According to our Town's Ordinance any legal nonconforming use or structure can be changed to another nonconforming use, which this is and was in place before the County had a Zoning Board. When Mr. Love applied for the permit, he should have been told to go before the Board of Adjustment to get a Special Use Permit. After getting the permit, contractors were hired and they began the work. When the County Zoning realized that they had issued the permit in error, they stopped the work and revoked the permit. That is the reason for the urgency for this meeting to get this problem solved."[24]

In the Special Council meeting "Council Member Smith made motion to accept the rezoning of the Love property from R/A to Highway Business. Seconded by Councilwoman Carpenter. Motion carried with all members voting in favor of the motion."

As indicated from the above minutes, the problem had arisen due to a conflict between the actual use and zoned use of the property. It was one of those properties that fell through the cracks during the initial adoption of the zoning codes. Although it had been used as a business for over 60-

[24] From the June 1, 2004 Red Cross Town Council Public Hearing minutes

years, it was still zoned as residential/agricultural. No one noticed this discrepancy until after the Loves' obtained their permit to renovate the building.

Once brought to light, the permit was pulled. As a result, it potentially became a very volatile issue that needed to be resolved quickly. There were several irregularities that had occurred which would leave the town in a vulnerable situation should the property owners file with the court. The issue had to be settled before it reached that level. Consider the following:

- The property had been used as businesses for over 60-years.
- A permit had been approved and issued for work to begin.
- The permit was pulled after the renovations started causing problems with the contractor, renter, and potential loss of rental revenue on the owner's part.
- Allegedly, one of the Red Cross Zoning Board Members called Mr. Love telling him that he would have to stop work and remove modifications to the structure.

It should be noted that concerns were raised by Council Members Carpenter and Speight and Zoning Board Chairman, Barbee, about not allowing the Planning Board to review the zoning change request prior to the public hearing,[25] as had been standard practice. However, the Council did vote to approve the zoning change request.

Town Council Meeting (June 2004):

1. "Mayor Quick said that in January the Zoning Board was misnamed in error and does not agree with the Towns' Zoning Ordinance, therefore it is necessary to dissolve this Board and create the Planning Board.

[25] From the June 1 2004 Red Cross Town Council Public Hearing/Meeting minutes and audio

Motion #154 - Councilman Smith made motion to dissolve the Zoning Board. Seconded by Councilman Hahn. Motion carried.

Motion #155 - Councilwoman Carpenter made motion to create the Planning Board. Seconded by Councilman Hahn. Motion carried.

The Mayor said he has comments and serious concerns that relate to the last Board. He is on every board by design [by default] and he wants to be sure the new Planning Board is aware of its responsibility to the Town, and that any action is handled in a legal manner. Mayor Quick said that some members of the Zoning Board had tried to circumvent the Town Council and get an official from the County to swear them in as the new Planning Board. There are three primary laws to conform to and they are as follows:

- NC General Statute 143 - Open Meeting Laws
- NC General Statute 160 - Cities and Towns governing zoning, etc.
- We have our own Zoning Ordinance and to be legal we have to comply with it. The Planning Board and other Boards appointed by the Town Council should be kept open and honest with the intent to serve the people, not to govern them.

At this point in the meeting, Michael Sandy, Planning Director for Stanly County, entered the meeting and the Mayor turned the meeting over to Mr. Sandy for a training session.

Mr. Sandy told the Council and Planning Board that the Board serves in an advisory capacity and makes recommendations to the Town Council. The Planning Board doesn't have the authority to make decisions on matters that come before it, only to advise the Town Council on how it believes such matters should be resolved and can also do land use studies. Mr. Sandy said the Planning Board might also serve as the Board of Adjustment if approved by the Town

Council. The Board of Adjustments makes quasi-judicial decisions and appeals are heard in local superior court. The Board of Adjustment can also hear special zoning permits, variances and special use permits. Mr. Sandy emphasized the importance of the Board not to contact any citizens concerning problems or issues; it is in violation of the law and could result in a civil lawsuit..."

"...C. J. Barbee requested that his name be removed from the Planning Board because they do not have any authority. Jerry Jordan also asked to be removed due to personal reasons." [26]

Unthinkingly, when we commissioned this Board in April 2003, we used the term "Zoning Committee". In January 2004 Council Member Speight requested the name change to "Zoning Board". Back in 2003 we should have use the term "Planning Board". It would appear that the use of the name "zoning" inferred to some that they were an all-encompassing board responsible for all aspects of zoning. As a result there were assumptions by some that the Zoning Board could assume responsibility of both the Board of Adjustment and Zoning Enforcement. However, at the time of their commission, the Town Council had charged them with the sole responsibility to redesign the zoning codes so that the codes would be specific to our town. The Town Council was to act as the Board of Adjustment. Anyone with a zoning conflict would need to file for a zoning change or come before the Board of Adjustment, not the Zoning Board.

It was important that it not appear that any of our areas of responsibility (Zoning Board, Board of Adjustment and Zoning Enforcement) were crossing over into the boundaries of the other.

There were two recent problems that had occurred which prompted this reorganization of the Zoning Board. Two of the Zoning Board members had gone to an individual's home to discuss his request to rezone a section of his property from residential to business. On the

[26] From the minutes of the June 2004 Council meeting

surface this doesn't seem like a problem but it creates potential legal problems in that if a Town official, including Zoning Board Members, makes a statement to the property owner concerning a zoning issue, and that zoning issue later goes to court, then any statements or comments made by them can then be used as evidence during the court hearing.

In the second and the most volatile issue, the owners had leased their building to a health club and were making changes to the building to accommodate the new business. Allegedly, a member of the Zoning Board had called the owners and told them that they would have to remove the modifications they had made to the exterior of the building because they were not zoned for it. The person that called them was a member of the Zoning Board "only" and not an appointed Zoning Enforcement Officer.

It appeared that the Board was losing focus on its mandate and migrating more towards functioning as an all-encompassing board - including zoning enforcement. By dissolving the Zoning Board and re-commissioning it as a Planning Board, it was my hope that this change would refocus the Board to the task that it had being charged to do.

It seemed to work because the problems went away. The new Planning Board soon became a very effective and impressive group of people. Under the leadership of Carolyn Morton they went on to hire a very competent planning consultant, Carol Rhea of Rhea Consulting, and create very impressive sets of codes. To me, the accumulation of these irregularities left me no other viable option but to do what I did by renaming. My actions were validated by the excellent performance of the newly created Planning Board.

2. June is the time for setting the budget for the next fiscal year (2004/2005). The Mayor (Ray Quick) and the Finance officer (Heath Hahn) made out the upcoming budget and Council Member Hahn presented it to the Council. This was the first budget to be voted by an elected Council for the Town of Red Cross.

The budget was challenged by Council Member Larry Wayne Smith. The minutes of this are as follows:

> "Councilman Smith still had questions on the first three items on the budget. He thinks that $1,000.00 is sufficient for Administrative Fees and $6,000.00 for Professional Fees. Mayor Quick said we can always amend the budget and funds not used can be rolled into the General Fund at the end of the year. Councilwoman Carpenter wants to put the money into a Building Fund for a Town Hall. After much discussion, Councilman Hahn made motion that we accept the budget. The Mayor took the option to call for a vote without a second to the motion. Vote was taken in alphabetical order. Councilwoman Carpenter voted no, Councilman Hahn voted yes, Councilman Smith voted no. The budget failed. Mayor Quick stated since the budget did not pass we will be unable to pay any bills after June 30, 2004."[27]

Council Member Chip Speight was not present.

As a result of the budget failing during a regular meeting of the Town Council it was necessary to schedule a special meeting for later in the month. We first scheduled a workshop to hash out our differences and then scheduled a special session of the Town Council to vote the budget.

I now believe, as a result of listening to the May and June 2004 audios together, that there may have been a problem in that some of the Council Members appeared not to understand how municipal budget's work. The following dialogue is taken from the audio of the May Town Council reading of the budget:

Larry Wayne Smith: "The first top items there, Heath (Finance Officer), would you explain those please sir."

[27] From the minutes of the June 2004 Red Cross Town Council Meeting

Heath Hahn: "Did he say explain?"

Larry Wayne Smith: "Yes!"

Heath Hahn: "Well, we all know what the word 'supplies' means. Is the question on the amount of dollars; is that what you're asking?"

Larry Wayne Smith: "With 'supplies', are we talking paper?"

Heath Hahn: "Anything we deem necessary."

Ray Quick: "Right now, I worked on Bobby Kay Thompson's computer and her software is obsolete. She does not have the updates to run the spreadsheets we need..."

Larry Wayne Smith: "A computer?"

Ray Quick: "Well, yea, we need that but we've got to have Microsoft Office right now. A computer would be good. She's running a Pentium and a Pentium has been obsolete since 97, I'd say..." "So it's seven years out of date."

[Author's Note: I had donated an old computer to the town for her to work on. I had an extra copy of Windows but didn't have an extra copy of Microsoft Office.]

C. J. Barbee (from audience): "So our town just buy one and let her use it. Let the town buy it and it'd be the town's - that's the way to go..."

Ray Quick: "That's a cost we've got up front now. That's going to be about $500 and it's not really an option, we're going to have to have it.

Mr. Barbee recommended a computer, that's really what we ought to do."

Larry Wayne Smith: "How much is a computer?"

Ray Quick: "Uh, one that serves our need will probably be about $1,500. You probably should have a scanner to go with it to scan documents - that would be another $150. Probably, $1,800 to get everything good."

Larry Wayne Smith: "I think that's something we ought to look into vs. paying $500 to redo that one."

Ray Quick: "No, that $500 is going to be an expense whether we buy another computer or not because the Microsoft Office will not come bundled with that computer.

Chip Speight: "That's an awful lot of money spent at one time, $500. Don't you think you can find it somewhere..."

Ray Quick: "Not if you stay legal and I would highly recommend not doing anything illegal as a town..."

(Interruption)

Ray Quick: "This is something we're not going to do tonight, but it explains part of supplies."

Larry Wayne Smith: "That just seems like a lot for supplies."

Ray Quick: "Well, the thing is, these are numbers that we will allocate. We have to end up with a zero budget at the end of the year. Now, going back to general fund, we've got $13,665 but we don't have to spend all that.

I'm stepping into Mr. Hahn's stuff and I apologize for that."

Larry Wayne Smith: "The 'Professional Fees', what does that include?"

Heath Hahn: "That includes all your legal work, your CPA,

auditors, and any legal expenses."

Larry Wayne Smith: "Lawyer?"

Heath Hahn: "Yes!"

Larry Wayne Smith: "How about 'Administrative'?"

Ray Quick: "The 'Administrative' would fall under the Mayor's Office and that's to handle anything that would come up - it's like a general fund for the Mayor. Like we had to host that dinner back in January, or February. That came out of that. Any contingencies, unexpected, it just gives us a little buffer to draw from - that's not really allocated."

Larry Wayne Smith: "Yea, I understand that. $8,000 is a pretty good buffer."

Ray Quick: "Well, what do you recommend?"

Larry Wayne Smith: "Um."

Ray Quick: "Well, what I'm saying is what's going to happen here is if we undercut ourselves we've got troubles."

Larry Wayne Smith: "Surely you won't spend $8,000?"

Ray Quick: "We didn't last year but we allocated. (addressing Finance Officer)" How much did we allocate last year?"

Heath Hahn: "On 'Administrative', $8,000."

Ray Quick: "Yea, well we didn't spend, maybe $500. That rolled back into the general fund, so there was no harm done.

I'm going to tell you what, Wayne, if you cut these back and you show a large surplus here, you better either have that money allocated to do something with or you'd better cut taxes, uh, the tax rate back. Which do you prefer to do?"

Larry Wayne Smith: "But you've got to spend this money..."

Ray Quick: "No, you do not. You cannot spend more than that. That is a ceiling."

Larry Wayne Smith: "Where does it roll to?"

Ray Quick: "The General Fund, at the end of the year."

Larry Wayne Smith: "Alright, uh, you've got $13,565 in general fund next year, right?"

Ray Quick: "Yea. That's unallocated moneys."

Larry Wayne Smith: "Town Hall would be good if we could do us a reserve fund."

Ray Quick: "A building fund?"

Larry Wayne Smith: "Uh Uh."

Ray Quick: "Now that can be done."

Larry Wayne Smith: "We're going to have some extra. I know these services are just going to go up on us. We're at the bottom of the budget on most of them any way."

Ray Quick: "Let me throw something up at you. I checked on this, I had said we needed a reserve fund and we need some way to protect it. Remember me bringing that up two meetings ago?"

Larry Wayne Smith: "Yea."

Ray Quick: "I went and checked with the Institute of Government, and I checked with Josh Morton [Town

Attorney]. There is no way we can do that because any ordinance or law we make now, the next Town Council, or this Town Council, can void it and do whatever they want to, so it doesn't, whatever is in the general fund is in the general fund. I would love to see a protected cash reserve that we had to maintain."

Larry Wayne Smith: "Right. I understand."

Ray Quick: "What we do now, another Town Council comes on, it might take a 180-degree turn and it could pull that money down to 8% - because you can't drop below 8%. That's from the Local Government Commission."[28]

From this point on the budget discussion went fairly uneventful. Unfortunately, when it came time for voting the budget, it was voted down in a two-to-one vote. I would not agree to defunding the Administrative line items and Smith would not support the budget with the administrative line items left in place. Council Member Speight was absent, Council Members Smith and Carpenter voted against the budget and Council Member Hahn voted in favor of the budget.

We did pass the budget in a special meeting called on June 29, 2004 and left administrative expenses at the previous year's level.

3. Discuss request from Locust to have joint meeting of Town Councils for exchange of views on zoning, ETJ's, and sphere of influence. Ray Quick presenting.

   This was great! All the Towns in western Stanly County would come together and work for the mutual interest of all (Locust, Oakboro, Red Cross, and Stanfield). Locust initiated this opportunity and it was a great idea.

[28] From Audio of the first reading of the 2004/2005 Red Cross budget, Red Cross Town Council Meeting of May 2004

Zoning, ETJ's, and spheres of influence are very important to any town. It is probably best to break each one out and describe them prior to stating what happened.

- Zoning - Every town controls zoning within its boundaries. Zoning is critical to organized growth, the health of the town, and the protection of its citizens. However, in this case the zoning issue being addressed at this time was not necessarily the creation of new zoning codes but for the creation of harmonic zoning between towns - where towns butt up against one another. This would create symmetry between towns so that anyone traveling from one town to the next would not recognize where one town ended and the other began. If it was business in one town then it would be business in the next.

  One additional aspect that Red Cross was prepared to discuss in an effort to establish a sort of regional zoning was that we recognized that Oakboro had an industrial park suitable for heavy industry and Locust had an industrial park suitable for light industry. Red Cross did not have an industrial park and we were not aware that Stanfield had a structured one. From our perspective we would be have been willing to entertain discussions on allowing Oakboro and Locust to have exclusivity on industrial parks. We would try to stay more professional, residential, and moderately retail. This could easily be envisioned as the start of an excellent master zoning plan for western Stanly County.

- Extra Territorial Jurisdiction - Many towns have established boundaries around their corporate limit where they extend their zoning enforcement out into the unincorporated areas. The people living in these areas are not a part of the town but do have to abide with the town's zoning codes. They do not pay the town taxes, do not vote in town elections, and seldom receive the services of the town - yet they have to comply with the zoning requirements established by the town. Often, but not always, one or more people from these outlying areas are elected to serve on the town's Planning Board.

- Sphere of Influence - This is more of a gentleman's agreement between towns. This is an agreement arrived at by town administrations where each town agrees that it will not extend its town boundaries any further towards another town than had been previously agreed upon. Nor would it annex/satellite properties past that previously agreed upon boundary. This would remove the potential of one town trying to grab property before the other town could. It would allow for a slower and more natural growth of the towns to occur.

Unfortunately, the sphere of influence agreement appeared to be the one that couldn't be agreed upon and caused the whole thing to fall apart. Although it has been a while, it seems it fell apart because Red Cross and Locust could not reach an agreement. Red Cross wanted to set the sphere of influence boundary at Barbee's Road and Locust wanted to set it at Brattain Road. Neither side was willing to compromise and the issue just faded away.

The towns in western Stanly County are kind of like four little ponds. As people move in the ponds will fill more, eventually the four ponds will become a single lake with four muddy spots where each town is. It would be better to see one pretty lake.

A master zoning overlay for western Stanly County would make a world of difference in the future of all four towns (Locust, Oakboro, Red Cross, and Stanfield). Each town would maintain its own identity and governing body but the average person, based on appearance, wouldn't know where one town ended and the next began. It would also allow each town to concentrate on its level of expertise, whether it is industrial, residential, commerce, etc., thus enhancing the whole of western Stanly County.

The residents of western Stanly County should encourage their elected officials to revisit this issue and make it work. Everyone (both the towns and the people) in western Stanly County would benefit if it happened.

Town Council Workshop Meeting (June 24, 2004):

A workshop was scheduled to resolve the impasse with the budget that occurred in the regular June Town Council meeting. Note: the budget was voted down in the June Council meeting and could not be brought back for a second vote in that same meeting.

Council Member Heath Hahn presented the following facts:

1. "Without a budget we will not be able to levy a tax for the Town (no tax collection).

2. We will not be able to pay bills.

3. If we do not have some form of a budget in place by July 1, 2004, we will be in violation of North Carolina law.

4. At that point the Local Government Commission could come in and take control of our finances.

    - They can set a budget of their own design for us to operate by.

    - They have the power to set our tax rate to whatever level they deem appropriate.

    - Do not underestimate the power of the Local Government Commission. They even have the power to pull a Town's charter.

5. With respect to the Stanly County Tax Office:

    - Talked to the Stanly County Tax Office and they can hold off issuing tax notices until sometime in mid July.

    - If we go past that point - I don't know - I'm not going to push the issue with them at this time? Based on previous instances of mid-term taxes, the tax was carried over and then added to the next years billing. In my opinion, it is possible that the Stanly County Tax Office will be willing to issue a special tax notice for an additional fee but it is equally possible that we will have to contract with an independent firm to collect taxes for us.

6. We can call a special meeting and vote the budget or an interim budget. If we do vote an interim budget we can prorate the finances for a given period of time - say 30 days. If we go this route it will satisfy the requirement of having a budget as of July 1, 2004, but will not allow us to levy a tax - only pay bills. We will still have the problem of issuing tax notices.

   Note: An interim budget is a special budget that shows, and allocates, expected cost for a given period of time but does not show revenues. Whatever money is spent under this interim budget will have to be reflected in the ordinance budget when one is finally adopted."

Please note that what Council Member Hahn told the Council is what could happen, not what would happen. It is highly unlikely that the Local Government Commission would step in unless the problem became so severe that we were unable to establish a budget at all.

The following is the minutes of that workshop meeting:

"Workshop Meeting
Red Cross Town Council
June 24, 2004
7:00 PM
Present: Mayor Quick, all Council Members, and twelve citizens

The Mayor called the meeting to order and welcomed the citizens. Prayer was by Councilman Hahn.

The mayor said it was necessary to hold this workshop meeting because the budget failed at the regular Town Council meeting. The meeting will be informal with a lot of discussion between the Council Members. Councilman Hahn said there are certain requirements the Town must meet and abide by or pay the consequences. The tax rate is $.016 per $100.00 valuation and total revenues is $145,680.00 for the year. Councilman Speight asked why we cannot have money going to a general fund. The mayor says revenues must equal expenses. Councilman Hahn said unless we do this we must reduce the tax rate. The Mayor said since we are a new town and not sure what expenses may accrue best to leave the tax rate at $0.16. This is our first full year in operation, and not sure what level of expenses we may have. The census update last fall generated an additional $25,000.00.

The Town cannot have a Building fund but instead can set up a Capital Reserve Fund, and must be adopted by the Council. Mayor Quick said once the money is put into this fund it is locked-in, and can only be used for Capital Expenditures. It cannot be designated for any specific expenditure, and can be designated as a line item on the budget. Need to check further with an accountant before setting up this type fund.

Mayor Quick says he is willing to help anyone with writing rules and procedures manuals for their job. Once these manuals are in place, Council Members can start working on goals. We, as a Town need to be in good position, because next couple years are going to be very important as far as growth and other issues we face. In regards to a Town Hall we are in good position, but will need to finance half of it. Can get grants of up to 35% or maybe higher.

The same laws apply regardless of the size of the Town. Red Cross has the same laws as Charlotte. General Statute 159 covers budget and finance control. David Lawrence at the Institute of Government would be a good person to call concerning budget questions. As expenses increase, building a Town Hall, employees, equipment, etc., we will not have a reserve. Therefore, we need to hire people to give guidance on the proper way to handle these issues.

The decision of a $250.00 cap on expenses any member of the Council spent without getting prior approval. The Mayor asked for one exception that is in the case of a "lock-down". He wants the authority to call in a conflict resolution team. If the Town Council reaches a point where they cannot work together' he wants 'a resolution team to come in and help solve the problem. Need consulting team to come in and train the Town Council on how to do their jobs. After much discussion the Mayor asked if any of the tax payers present would like to express their opinion.

Mrs. Barbara Huneycutt responded to the Mayors request and she said: She has attended three meetings and every time many issues have come up that have been hard to solve. She thinks it would be a good idea to call in a consultant team. As a taxpayer, she realizes that we are building a new town, and we want it to be perfect. She has just returned from Locust and they are having problems with their budget. Things are so bad people won't talk to each other and she wants no part of that. She is in Red Cross voluntarily, but doesn't want to be part of a town that cannot resolve issues. Being a new town, we may have legal issues that require professional assistance, whereas with older established towns this would not be a concern. She thinks the $250.00 cap is wonderful.

The Mayor said a mediator would come in, find out what the real issues are with each person, the real issues and not the emotional ones. Get everything on the table, talk, and reach a consensus.

Councilman Hahn asked each person on the Council if they would agree on the budget at the June 29, 2004 public hearing and each gave a verbal yes answer.

Mayor Quick called the meeting adjourned.
8:55 PM

Bobby Kay Thompson

Town Clerk"[29]

At the end of this workshop meeting the Council members said they would vote in favor of the budget. This was not a vote, only an agreement that a resolution had been reached. The actual vote would have to occur in a regular session of the Council.

Town Council Meeting (July 2004):

1. The Council voted to authorize payment to the County for putting the Town name on the water tower.

   In December 2003, we sent an email to Stanly County Manager Jerry Myers inquiring about the possibility of Red Cross being able to put the town name on the water tower.

   Fortunately, by June 2004, the County was preparing to do periodic maintenance on the water tower. This maintenance cycle included the repainting of the water tower.

   The County contacted us saying that they were agreeable to allow Red Cross to put our name on their tower provided we also allowed the County name to be included and paid the cost for the names application. Council Member Barbara Carpenter took the lead in this endeavor and we entered into contract with the County and the rest is history. It ended up costing us $2,950.

   Although we were glad to see our town's name on the water tower we were disappointed to see that the painters had messed up. They put our town name as "RED CROSS,NC" (the painters didn't put a space between the comma and the "NC"), so that at first glance it appeared to read "RED CROSSNG". We were very disappointed at the misspelling. In a way it's kind of ironic since in the early days Red Cross was called Red Crossing.

[29] Minutes of the June 2004 Town Council workshop

Public Hearing/Town Council Meeting (October 2004):

1. Edith Smith made a request to give the gravel road between the homes of Edith Smith and Blane Hathcock a name. In effect she was asking the town to recognize the mutual drive between the properties as a road. It seems that this drive was once a road going to various property owners located behind them. It is our understanding that the back property had once been prepared to be a housing development. However, today, and even though the roadbed still exist, those areas have grown up and reforested.

   Edith Smith said that, if a road name was approved, then they would like the road to either be called either "Smith Road" or "Hathcock Road". We contacted EMS and both the "Smith Road" and "Hathcock Road" names were already in use within the County and couldn't be used again. As a result the residents decided on the name "Morning Dove Lane".

   The Council saw no problem with this since at one time it was a road and, should development happen again, would probably again become a road. There was no cost associated with declaring it a road and giving it a name. All that was required was a public hearing (held November 8, 2004) and a vote of the Town Council. So Morning Dove Lane came into being.

   It may sound trivial to mention something like this but if no record of why things happen then within a couple generations no one will remember why a road came into being. It's a lot like the history of Running Creek Church Road. Mrs. Poplin told me at one of our town meetings that Running Creek Church Road came into being because her father had cut a path through the woods so that she could get out to the highway to go to school. More and more people began using the path and it eventually became a road.

   With respect to the school, I believe she was referring to Brattain School located on Pless Mill Road. Although the school is no longer there, the well that serviced the school is. If she walked to school it would have been about a mile.

2. During the comment segment of this meeting I stated that I had received a call from a developer wanting to buy approximately 200-acres of land within or near Red Cross to build a housing development. I didn't know of any tracks of land that size that would be up for sale and referred him to Stanly County Economic Development. I also stated that an individual (name withheld) in the Town had been approached by someone interested in buying his land for a business - I believe it was for a strip-mall.

   The general purpose of my telling this in the meeting was to increase both the Council's and Planning Board's awareness that the potential was there for development and that we needed to be preparing for growth. The Planning Board had not yet retained a consultant, and I was hoping this might increase the sense of urgency in getting our zoning codes set up.

3. "Request to speak to Council concerning subdivision Moratorium. Ronnie Williams presenting."

   "Motion #177 Council man Smith made motion to put a 120-day moratorium on subdivisions with exclusion on the Williams and Hill property for the transaction only concerning the Dollar General store. Seconded by Councilman Hahn. Motion carried."[30]

   The Planning Board was working on sub-division ordinances and commercial building codes for the Town of Red Cross and was requesting a moratorium be placed on both until they completed their work.

   It was also at this time that Dollar General was negotiating with co-owners Hill and Williams to purchase their property in Red Cross for the purpose of building a store. Dollar General wanted to purchase half of the five acre track that Hill and Williams had for sale. Apparently the property owner was afraid it would cause Dollar General to withdraw from negotiations if the town placed a

[30] From the minutes of the October 18, Red Cross Town Council meeting

moratorium affecting building codes and spoke in favor of exempting Dollar General from the moratorium/new building code requirements. (See Chapter on "Business Recruitment", "Dollar General").

Town Council Meeting (November 2004):

1. "Carolyn Morton [Zoning Board Chairman] has contacted Ms. Carol Rhea, Rhea Consulting in Shelby, NC, and thinks she would make an excellent Town Planner. Her fees are $85.00 an hour, and traveling time is half this amount. Carolyn believes that Ms. Rhea will be a great help in getting the town headed in the right direction. After much discussion, the Council and Planning Board think that a workshop meeting would be very beneficial to everyone. The Council voted, not as a motion, to get a contract for approval before making a legal agreement with Ms. Rhea. Carolyn will contact Ms. Rhea for setting up a date for the meeting."[31]

   I am not sure what the statement "The Council voted, "not as a motion" actually means? I believe that the Council voiced their approval but did not put it in the form of a motion to be voted on.

Town Council Meeting/Public Hearing (December 2004):

1. The Zoning Board agreed to retain a consultant to help them with setting up zoning codes specifically designed for our Town. They requested we retain Carol Rhea of Rhea Consulting. Voted and approved.

   Michael Sandy, Stanly County Planning and Zoning Director, had recommended her and subsequent follow-up indicated she would be an excellent person to serve as our consultant. She later went on to help us design our town's vision plan, land use plan, subdivision ordinances, growth plan and transportation plan.

   We couldn't have found a better person to fill this position. Her

[31] From the minutes of the November 8, 2004 Red Cross Town Council meeting

work was excellent and her ability to work through personality issues and reach core decisions was outstanding. There is no question that, with her assistance, we did achieve zoning codes representative of what our people wanted at the time of incorporation. Our Zoning Enforcement Officer, Robbie Foxx, summed it up best when he made the comment that "I still don't see how a small town like Red Cross could get someone of Carol Rhea's caliber to work with them?" Maybe we were just blessed?

We were also very fortunate in Carolyn Morton having assumed the position of Chairman of the Planning Board at this time. She helped make everything work. Morton had the ability to take charge of the Board, keep the Board organized and focused, and had the drive to keep it moving.

2. Council Member Barbara Carpenter requested a resolution of the Town Council that the speed limit on the section of Highway 24/27 running through Red Cross be reduced to 45 MPH. A letter of request was to be sent to DOT. The Council voted and approved the resolution.

   A resolution is non-enforceable; it is not a law or ordinance but is simply a statement of position or desire by the Town Council. A Town has no authority to set speed limits on State roads but may make request to the State to have those speed limits changed. Making a resolution and sending that resolution to DOT is as strong a request as a town can make.

3. Council Member Barbara Carpenter, along with the support of Lou Eubanks, requested a resolution by the Town Council that the Department of Transportation place landscaping medium along Highway 24/27 through Red Cross. They submitted a list of greenery that they wanted DOT to plant. The Council voted and approved the resolution.

   It fell to me to write the letter requesting this greenery. Because of the type of request and all the unpleasant confrontations we had already had with DOT, I was extremely embarrassed in having to send this letter. However, I was now obligated to write two letters; one requesting the speed limit on Highway 24/27 be reduced to 45 MPH and a second requesting DOT plant specific greenery along Highway 24/27. Both of which I was sure DOT would ignore.

Since the Council had voted resolutions on these, I had no choice but to follow through. Since the greenery letter was being driven by Council Member Barbara Carpenter and Lou Eubanks I requested that DOT contact them directly.

Town Council Meeting (January 2005):

Town officers were appointed:

Finance	Heath Hahn
Fire Protection	Barbara Carpenter
Police Protection	Larry Wayne Smith
Street Maintenance	Larry Wayne Smith
Town Improvement	Barbara Carpenter
Utilities	Heath Hahn
Waste Collection	Chip Speight
Zoning	Chip Speight

1. Discuss the need to contract with an engineer to do a sewer study of the Town. Ray Quick presenting

There was an excellent 90/10 sewer study grant available and I was asking the Council to allow me to apply for it.

A 90/10 grant means that the town provides 10% and the grant provider provides 90% of the cost. If the sewer study were to cost $60,000 then the town would provide $6,000 and the grant provider would provide $54,000 towards the cost of the study. If the town has to pay for a grant writer then the cost of that grant writer is usually folded into the $6,000 that the town is responsible for. Many times, if the grant does not go through, the grant writer does not charge for writing the grant. However, in this case, we could probably have gotten an engineering firm to write the grant application on the contingency that the firm would be allowed to do the study if the grant were awarded - much as Misenheimer had done.

By going ahead with the study at this time we would be accomplishing several things: (1) we would be able to take advantage of an excellent grant opportunity, (2) through the study, we would be obtaining needed information to guide us in planning for our future sewer needs, and (3) we would already have a required sewer study in our portfolio and be prepared when the time came.

The following are the minutes of that request:

> "Mayor Quick wanted to address the sewer study again and be sure that everyone understands. He stated that a sewer study is only the process of gathering information by an engineer. An engineer would do an analysis of what our needs will be in the future and where sewage is needed and the cost. With a 90/10 grant, which is available through the US Agricultural/Urban Development, on a $40.000 or $50,000 study our cost would be $4,000 or $5,000 (These estimates based on other towns our size.)
>
> Motion #204 Councilman Hahn made motion to pursue 90/10 grant and hire an engineer to a study of sewer needs for the Town. Since the motion was not seconded, the Mayor exercised privilege for a vote without a second to the motion. Councilman Hahn voted yes. Councilman Smith voted no and Councilwoman Carpenter voted no."[32]
>
> Council Member Speight was not present at this second meeting.

2. Contract with consultant Carol Rhea, Rhea Consulting, presented to the Council for approval. Approved with the addition of a hold-harmless clause. Contract was approved.

[32] From the January 2005, Red Cross Town Council minutes

Town Council Meeting (February 2005):

The following is in an excerpt from the Minutes of the February 14, 2005, Red Cross Town Council meeting.

"Mayor Quick asked for a motion to approve the agenda. The Council expressed their appreciation in getting the agenda on Wednesday prior to the meeting. They also did not want to approve the agenda, because of the following.

- No new item may be added to the agenda once it has been mailed out.
- No item may be inserted into the agenda for a vote unless that item has been listed as an agenda item prior to agenda's mailing.

The Mayor stated that any item can be discussed under comments from the Town Council at the end of the meeting, and any issue requiring a vote before the next meeting can be handled during a special call meeting.

After much discussion, the Council would not approve the agenda. Once citizen, C. J. Barbee continued to speak after being advised that the discussion was for the Council and was not open to the floor. After several warnings, Mr. Barbee, was asked to leave the meeting. When he did not leave as asked, Mayor Quick called the Stanly County Sheriff's Department for assistance. Before the deputy arrived, Mr. Barbee left the meeting. Shortly thereafter, three of the Council members Larry Wayne Smith, Chip Speight, and Barbara Carpenter, also left the meeting. Mayor Quick closed the meeting since only one member of the Council was present. Therefore no business was conducted in the February meeting."[33]

[33] From the minutes of February 14, 2014, Red Cross Town Council meeting

The reason for the problems with this meeting was that we had some very serious conflicts going on within the Council and I had great concerns. I wanted the problems aired and I wanted them on record.

It appeared that at times decisions were being made outside of and prior to formal Council meetings. Without involving full Council participation in these discussions, it meant there could be the ability to have controlling vote on issues brought before the full Council.

Council Member Larry Wayne Smith strongly objected to the agenda item of "No new item may be added to the agenda once it has been mailed out", stating that he felt the Council should be able to add items up to the time the Council voted final approval of the agenda in the Council meeting. He was equally strongly supported by Council Member Chip Speight.[34]

Council Member Heath Hahn interjected that it was his understanding that the request had been made in an earlier meeting that agendas should be distributed no later than Wednesday prior to thc meeting so that everyone would know and be prepared for what was on the agenda. Council Member Larry Wayne Smith responded "yes, but uh, but I think that there are things that would come up at the last minute that you would like to put on the agenda"[35] It should also be noted that in the May 2004, Council meeting I made a request/plea to the Council to submit items prior to mailing. At that meeting three items were added to the agenda after the opening of the Council meeting and prior to the approval of the agenda.[36]

The dialogue after the motion was made is as follows:

Ray Quick: "I have some concerns about this. I'm not sure where this Council is headed. I'm scared where it's headed. I don't

[34] From the audio of the February 2005, Red Cross Town Council Meeting (00:02:16)

[35] From the audio of the February 2005, Red Cross Town Council Meeting (00:07:02)

[36] From the audio of the May 2004 Red Cross Town Council Meeting (00:04:38)

know what to expect, and uh... I'll be honest with you; we haven't accomplished a thing this year. And you've done some good work on the signs [referencing Larry Wayne Smith's work on putting up the new street signs], but other than that we haven't gotten a thing done.

It's a shame..."

Larry Wayne Smith: "This isn't no big problem Ray, I think that.......

Ray Quick: "It is a problem because trust is not there anymore."

Larry Wayne Smith: "It isn't the trust..."

Ray Quick: "Yes it is."

Larry Wayne Smith: "It's just that we should have the right to add to the agenda should something come up. That's the way I feel about it."

Ray Quick: "I understand, but according to 'Robert's Rules of Order' until I yield I have the floor. I will accept comments, but that's all."

Chip Speight: "I thought we had a motion on the floor."

Ray Quick: "You do. This is perfectly legitimate"

"My reason for this is that I do not have confidence in the Town Council. I do not see the Council working in the interest of the Town. I am sorry to have to say that, but that is the reason I put this on here - I don't want to get blindsided by something I don't expect. Things that we have been voted to do we are not doing. We're not getting the Town set up, we're not working. We're not getting things done."

Larry Wayne Smith: "Ray, we're a new town."

Ray Quick: "We're a new town and we've got a lot of work to do. We need to get it done."

Larry Wayne Smith: "You're exactly right but we need to crawl before..."

Ray Quick: "We haven't got time to crawl because growth is coming and we've got to get things set up. We're one year into it, that's past time. We're in the fourteenth month of this Council and nothing substantive has been done other than getting the road signs up and the addresses changed."

Larry Wayne Smith: "That's a good start."

Ray Quick: "That is more grunt work than anything.

We should have our organization set up. We should have our rules and procedures set up. We should be gathering information on what we need to be doing five to ten years down the road.

We're turning down grants, turning down things that we ought to be doing."

Larry Wayne Smith: "I always vote against something when I don't know the price tag on it."

Ray Quick: "Ok, let's use last month for example. Last month I brought up a sewer study so that we would know what we would be facing five to ten years down the road. Do we need to be addressing sewer needs? If we do, what will we be facing?

Ok, there's grants out there, 90/10 grants, that, uh, if we go for them, their almost a given. It doesn't take a whole lot to get the grant. If it's a $30,000 grant, and we go for it, the State pays $26,000 and we pay $4,000. [Should have been the State pays $27,000 and we pay $3,000.] That is good money for an engineer to do a full study. And we voted it down. This is in violation of the trust the people have placed in us."

Larry Wayne Smith: "No it's not, no it's not."

Chip Speight: "People didn't want sewer out here. If they did, what was the one thing they said they wanted? They wanted to maintain..."

Ray Quick: "They wanted to, uh, absorb growth in as painless a manner as possible."

Chip Speight: "They wanted to, I heard one woman say she wanted us to stay just like we are."

Ray Quick: "Well, that's not going to happen and everybody knows it.

Chip Speight: "I know that."

Ray Quick: "Alright, we need to be informed because if we just hide our heads and do nothing it's just going to snowball on us. We're going to be behind and there is no way we're going to be able to handle it."

Chip Speight: "I think, well, we're working with the Town Planner. I still think you need to know where you're going to put the town before you start running the sewer.

Barbara Carpenter: "I do to, I think..."

Chip Speight: "I mean, I may be completely off base but, you want to spend that $5,000 and it's not where we're going to put the town."

Ray Quick: "Ok, so we've got a disagreement there. My concern is because I'm not seeing the good faith that I think ought to be shown by a Council where the interest of the community is being served. And I just don't see that."

Chip Speight: "Because, I won't vote for a 90/10 grant?"

Ray Quick: "Alright, that's one of em."

Chip Speight: "I just explained my reasons Ray."

Ray Quick: "Yea and I don't see your reason."

Chip Speight: "That's yours. Nobody's going to have the same..."

[Author's Note: Audio got a little garbled here so I was not able to finish out the last statement by Chip Speight or the sentence afterward. Both Chip Speight and Ray Quick were talking at the same time.]

Ray Quick: "...We were talking about getting the survey done for the waste [collection] and you were not going to invest the time. Anybody coming on this Council's got to be willing to invest the time."

Chip Speight: "I'll swap places with you any time, with the amount of time I've got and you've got, we'll see if you want to do it to."

Ray Quick: "I'm not going to back away from it."

Chip Speight: "you don't work the hours I work and you don't have the family responsibilities I have, and other outside interest. I explained to you that night why I wouldn't do it. I still stand on what I said."

Ray Quick: "Well..."

Barbara Carpenter: "I think that the Town Planner is similar to an architect and you've got to get your plan before you start building. The Town Planner's going to lay out a plan for us. I think we need to get her report before we start."

Ray Quick: "If we're going to go for a grant, it's going to take six

> months to a year to get the grant. If she can't get stuff put together by then, then we've got a problem."

Barbara Carpenter: "Well she just got started." Larry

Wayne Smith: "Let's get back to the agenda."[37]

Unfortunately, the meeting was disrupted and collapsed; however, I did formally close the meeting after three of the Council members left the meeting.

What the Council Members didn't realize was that by leaving, they had left their votes on the table. I did close the meeting after they had left, but unless they had been officially excused or the Council had officially closed the meeting then any item voted on from that point forward would automatically receive a yes vote from their vacant positions - regardless of whether they were physically there or not. Unless a Council Meeting is formally adjourned, or closed, then that Council Meeting remains open and any remaining Council Member(s) present can continue to conduct business. Any vote made would automatically receive a "yes" vote from their empty seat.

My intentions for that night were not to have the Council collapse, but to bring out into the open some of the problems we were having. I think the above dialogue brought out some problems, but not what I was hoping for. Once I had accomplished my objective I had every intention of yielding. However, once the former council member became involved, I lost control and the meeting fell apart.

The following is the article that ran in the Stanly News & Press on February 17, 2005 about this meeting:

[37] From Audio of the February 2005 Red Cross Town Council Meeting (00:02:10)

Red Cross Meeting Turns Hot
The Stanly News & Press
By Adrienne Williams, Staff Writer

In the first filibuster Stanly County has seen in years, Red Cross Mayor Ray Quick refused to yield the floor at Monday's meeting and called in the Sheriff's Department to eject a resident from the meeting.

The Council had blocked Quick's motion that no additions be placed on the agenda after it had been announced and mailed.

"There is a power struggle going on. You (should) go into a meeting knowing what is going on and nobody will try to slip things in," Quick said.

"I am repeatedly seeing things drift"

My confidence in the town council has deteriorated," Quick said.

"We haven't seen a single accomplishment since they were sworn in, as for as setting up the town and setting up the infrastructure. There is the feeling that we're not a town yet so we shouldn't be acting like one. But we should. We absolutely should for the people coming after us. Until we start acting like a town, we won't become one."

"The motion was made to be able to refuse (unannounced meeting agenda items) and seconded but no vote was taken," meeting attendee Lou Eubanks said. "The mayor was upset because it was his idea - he didn't want to be blindsided...then the mayor refused to relinquish the floor, said he was filibustering."

"The motion was made and blocked. The motion again was made and seconded, and my only option was to take the floor," Quick said.

"I did tell them I would accept comment, but I would not yield the floor," Quick said.

"The mayor was (making derogatory statements to) the council about items not approved in past meetings, like the sewer study, by the federal government in Red Cross," Eubanks said.

"Last month, I proposed a 90/10 grant for a sewer study," Quick said. "We'd only have to pay 10 percent and the federal government would pay 90 percent. We need to know where we'll be in terms of infrastructure and the sewers - and to just vote it down - I felt we had an obligation to the people to do what's best for the community."

"When a private citizen tried to speak, the mayor called the sheriff's department to evict the citizen," Eubank's said.

"I evicted C. J. Barbee from the meeting," Quick said. "The council was talking serous talk. I asked him to be quiet and he doesn't. I tell him to be quiet or leave. He still isn't quiet. So I asked him to leave. He still isn't quiet. I say to leave or be removed and he still isn't quiet. So I called the sheriff's department to have a deputy remove him. Then (council member) Larry Wayne Smith says, 'C. J. you better leave,' and he did but he isn't happy."

"Now it's bad to hurt people's feelings but sometimes they leave you no choice," Quick said. "It's really a shame. Mature people should be able to discuss things when they happen."

The council members walked out of the meeting after Barbee was ejected.

I did what I felt I had to do because I have an obligation to the people," Quick said.

"Red Cross sits in a very precarious position. If we don't do it right, we're not gonna make it as a town. We are a crossroads between existing municipalities. It would be easy for us to be absorbed, especially if we're not providing our own services and infrastructure," Quick said.

"Unless we establish ourselves and make wise decisions, we're not gonna make it as a town."

"We've got a clean slate, we have a chance to make a good community," Quick said. "I will do what I have to do within my power not to jeopardize that."

"I'm interested in quality of life as well as growing business," Quick said. "We don't have the infrastructure. Why vote down sewer if you want growth? I'm not saying put in sewer right now - where and when to put sewer is one of the strongest tools a town has to manage growth. What I am saying is that we should have taken advantage of federal funding to do the study.

"Sewer is just one thing I've been fighting for." Quick said. "We obtained an $8,000 grant to set the town up with computer internet. They had agreed to put the money in our hand. We were approved for the grant. They'd furnish web hosting for two years, but we'd have to agree to keep the site up for two extra years - and it was voted down. They refused the grant. We had to end up hiring out to buy a $2,000 computer instead of using the grant money. That's roughly $10,000 down the tube."

"Last June I proposed for a conflict resolution team to come in, and/or a team to give us training in how to function as a town and as a council through the Institute of Government," Quick said. "And this was shot down, too."

"I hate that all this has happened and I don't want to see it give Red Cross a bad name," Quick said.

"I hope that some good can come out of it. Maybe all this controversy will get the citizens of Red Cross to come out and attend the meetings, and be a part of creating this community.

"We urge all Red Cross citizens to come. We have the opportunity to do a lot of good here, and create a community we're all proud of and happy to live in. I hope people will come out and be a part of that."[38]

The Stanly News & Press referred to my actions as a filibuster, and technically they were correct. In the article Lou Eubanks is quoted as having said "then the mayor refused to relinquish the floor, said he was filibustering", however, I did not refer to it as "filibustering" in the meeting. In reality, it was probably not a filibuster because there was a great deal of dialogue going on between Council Members. It can be said that I was just keeping it from going forward to a vote.

As I stated earlier, my intent was to hold the floor until I got my piece said and got some things aired out - I didn't want it just forced through without discussion. I knew that the opposing group had control of the council through their majority votes and that there was no way I was going to win - but I was going to get some things brought out into the open and into the town record.

Town Council Meeting (March 2005):

1. In January I received a call, with followed-up letter, from the Mr. Norris Tolson, Secretary of Treasury for the State of North Carolina, concerning overpayment of Sales & Use Tax by the State to the Town of Red Cross totaling $73,565.72. They were asking for us to pay this money back. See the chapter on "Sales & Use Tax" for full explanation.

   "Mayor Quick said the Town has been overpaid in sales and use tax by $73,565.72. This amount was based on the Town having all four services in effect since the corporation date of 2002. Josh Morton Jr. was contacted for legal advice, but as of today he has not called. Mayor Quick said the State was very flexible in the way the money should be paid back. He wants to contact the other towns that have been overpaid and get legal support. Also will contact the League of Municipalities.

[38] Stanly News & Press, by Adrienne Williams, February 17, 2005

Motion #213, Councilman Smith made motion to give Mayor Quick the authority to seek legal and other options at a cost not to exceed $1,500.00 for means of not reimbursing the State tax money paid in errors. Motion was seconded by Councilman Speight which was approved by vote."[39]

2. Had short meeting with Council members after the Town Meeting covering:

"Waste Collection:

- Still need documented number of actual residents in town from Chip Speight.
- Letter not yet set up to send to people telling them how to handle waste – what days for pickup, what to do on holidays, what to do on bad weather, when the two annual pickups would be.

Establishing Rules and Procedures:
Action items on workshop were:

- Define the function of your office?
- Set the scope of your office?
- Establish you objectives?
- Set timetables for achieving these objectives?
- Review the material and insure it is clear and concise so that any other Council member can step in and cover your position should you be unavailable for a length of time. Also, this will allow other Council members to become more effective when asked to assist you in your specific area.

[39] From the Minutes of the March 2005, Town of Red Cross Council meeting

- List your primary contacts and what their relationship to your office is?"

I wanted to establish an Administrative Manual that would describe functions, rules and procedures, and methods of operation for the Town. Unfortunately, some of the Council continued to refuse to have rules and procedures.

Without the support of the Council majority I had no choice but give up on getting this done. It's unfortunate that some didn't seem to understand that, although we weren't a functional town yet, we needed to be preparing and getting things set up so that when we did start to grow we would be ready and have our controls in place. There is a lot more to being a town than appearance. It's a lot like a building, the facings and paint may look good but it is the foundation and framework that makes it structurally sound. Without a good structure a town, like a building, is nothing.

Public Hearing and Town Council Meeting (April 2005):

1. Held public hearing for commercial design presented by Planning Board. This was the first modification to building codes for commercial buildings in Red Cross. It defined types of structures, general appearance, setbacks, etc.

   "Motion #220 Councilman Hahn made motion to adopt the commercial design amendment which was seconded by Councilman Speight. Motion carried."

2. Lou Eubanks reported from the Planning Board. Made request that the town hire a part time enforcement officer with a cap of $20.00 per hour for about six hours per week. Recommended that this person not be a resident of Red Cross. She asked that $5,000 be added to the budget for this purpose. Item was not voted on.

   Note: This request should have originated with the town's Zoning Officer and not a member of the Planning Board since it was a request for expenditures for a different department.

3. Lou Eubanks, Planning Board, requested approvals for expenditures to the planning consultant in a five step process.

Item	Required Hours	Cost
Zoning Map	15 hours	$1,275.00
Commercial Designs assist	20 hours	$1,700.00
Zoning Amendment	100 hours	$8,500.00
Subdivision Amendment	50 hours	$4,250.00
Subdivision Workshop	10 hours	$ 850.00

"Motion #223 Councilman Hahn made motion to release $2,975.00 for the first two items recommended by the Planning Board. Councilwoman Carpenter seconded the motion which carried"[40]

Town Council Meeting (May 2005):

1. "Mayor Quick recognized Lou Eubanks who reported on behalf of the Planning Board. She recommended a zoning map workshop meeting on May 17th and May 23rd. These will be joint meetings with the Town Council and Planning Board at West Stanly high School Library. Councilman Speight has contacted Michael Sandy for his assistance in hiring a part time enforcement officer. One person has been contacted for this position at a salary of $20.00 an hour. Councilman Speight will discuss this at the next month's town meeting."[41]

2. "Council Member Chip Speight made recommendation to retain Mr. Milton Kern to teach a class on Robert's Rules of Order. Motion #228, Council Member Larry Wayne Smith made motion to retain Mr. Kern and send him a check for $50 to assist with his expenses. Motion seconded by Council Member Speight. Lou Eubanks will serve dinner to Mr. Kern and his guest at the Eubank's home."[42]

---

[40] From the minutes of the April 11, 2005, Red Cross Town Council meeting

[41] From minutes of the May 9, 2005, Red Cross Town Council meeting

[42] From minutes of the May 9, 2005, Red Cross Town Council meeting

The meeting did not materialize.

3. Discuss letter requesting de-annexation of property belonging to Jerry Jordan. Ray Quick presenting.

   "Mayor Quick said the Town has received a letter from Jerry Jordan's attorneys requesting that his property be de-annexed. His request has been referred to Josh Morton [town attorney]. Councilman Smith suggested that this matter be tabled until next month's meeting."[43]

   Upon investigation it was found that removal of property from corporate limits would be extremely difficult, if not impossible, without very unusual and mitigating circumstances. It would require a vote by the NC State Legislature to remove the property, which was very unlikely to be given considering the circumstances.

   Subject was tabled and not revisited.

Town Council Meeting (June 2005):

1. "Mayor Quick recognized Carolyn Morton, Chairman of the Planning Board. She said the Board will present Zoning Maps at the July meeting. She also recommends that the Council approve the contract to Rhea on the following three items.

Zoning amendment	100 hours	$8,500
Subdivision amendment	50 hours	$4,250
Subdivision workshop	10 hours	$ 850

   Motion #232 Councilman Smith made motion to approve the three items listed. Councilwoman Carpenter seconded the motion which carried."[44]

2. "Lou Eubanks will contact Mr. Kern for a date to meet with the

[43] From minutes of the May 9, 2005, Red Cross Town Council meeting

[44] From the minutes of the June 13, 2005, Red Cross Town Council meeting

Town Council and Planning Board. She will notify the town clerk with sufficient time to put and add in the paper."[45]

This was on the subject of having Mr. Kern teach a class on "Robert's Rules of Order" (May 2005). For some reason the class never materialized.

Town Council Public Hearing and Town Council meeting (August 2005):

1. Held public hearing to establish a central business district, primarily in the area of where the town hall property is today.

   The area being discussed was in the general area of the present town hall land. It did not cover the complete central intersection of Red Cross, only the south-east corner of the intersection of Highway 24/27/Highway 205.

2. Held public hearing to adopt a land-use plan as submitted by the Planning Board.

3. "Three residents expressed disapproval of the rezoning of their property and said they had not given permission for it to be rezoned. After much discussion and no one of the Council would make a motion to approve or reject the rezoning request, Carolyn Morton, Chairman of the Planning Board, withdrew the rezoning request."[46]

4. "Mayor Quick gave the Council and residents some very good news. He received letters from Rep. David Almond and Mr. Ed Strickland, Administration Officer NC Department of Revenue. Almond notified Mayor Quick that Senate Bill 420 passed the General Assembly and is now law. Under this bill, the Town of Red Cross is considered to have complied with the provisions of General Statute 136-41 for fiscal year 2002-2003 and the Town would not be responsible for repaying $73,565.72. Mr. Strickland stated in his

[45] From the minutes of the July, 2005, Red Cross Town Council meeting

[46] From the minutes of the August 8, 2005, Red Cross Town Council meeting

letter that with the passage of Session Law 2005-245, senate Bill 420, the Town of Red Cross is now in compliance with G.S. 136-41.2 for fiscal years 2002-03 and 2003-04. Therefore, the Town is entitled to receive all franchise tax on electricity, sales tax on telecommunications, and sales and use distributions previously paid during the above fiscal years and is not libel for reimbursing the amounts. Rep. Almond and Mayor Quick are due a lot of credit for their hard work in this matter. It not an easy task getting a bill passed through the General Assembly. Mayor Quick suggests that a resolution [of appreciation] be sent to Rep. Almond.

Motion #247 Council Member Hahn made motion to write a resolution concerning Senate Bill 420 and send a copy to Rep. Almond. Motion was seconded by Council Member Smith which was approved by vote."[47]

Public Hearing and Town Council Meeting (November 2005):

1. "Mayor Quick called the public hearing meeting to order. He read the tract numbers of the properties the Planning Board request be rezoned to CB. Council Member Smith requested to be excused because he has property that is being rezoned. The Council approved Council Member Smith's request. He left the meeting and did not vote. Ms. Rhea explained the Planning Board had been looking at the map of the Town and decided the best location for a Central Business district. As a result of their studies, the land they suggested would be the best. The Planning Board request the following properties having tax record numbers 56254, 9950, 36550, 22395, 11520, 11521, 11522 and 11523 rezoned from RA and R-20 to CB and Property Number 3578 from MR/RA to HB and Property number 14629 from RA to HB.

   Ms. Rhea answered questions for the concerned citizens."[48]

   Above rezoning request was approved by Council during regular

[47] From the minutes of the August 8, 2005, Red Cross Town Council meeting

[48] From the minutes of the November 1, 2005, Red Cross Town Council meeting

session.

Town Council Meeting (December 2005):

1. "Mayor Quick said looking back of the past two years three things were accomplished: name on water tank, discussion on building a town hall, and a lot of work on zoning. The Dollar Store will set a standard for future business in the Town. We were facing a debt of $74,000 to Dept. of Internal Revenue, but with proper research we did not have to repay. Mayor Quick also gave a report on his recent trip to Raleigh, NC. He said grants are still available but not as available as in the past. The grant we received but refused was valued at $50,000. One town received grants to give students in the fifth and sixth grades lap top computers. Another town received a grant that paid for all qualifying high school graduates their first year of that college."[49]

   The last couple sentences above sounds a little disjointed. I believe I was referring to the money from this grant having been used for the following purposes: according to the Mayor of Snow Hill, they used their $50,000 grant to install town wide wireless Internet for their residents. They were then able to use this initiative as a springboard to work out a deal with Dell Computers for laptops to be given to fifth and sixth grade students in the school(s) of their town. I don't remember saying anything about their town using the money to provide first year scholarships to their residents.

With respect to the minutes about Dollar General, it does not carry the meaning or intent of what I was saying. My reference to Dollar General was that they were the first to have to comply with our new building codes and we were well pleased with the outcome. My reference to a "standard", if that is the term I used, is that we have set a standard for our building codes, which was implemented with this first case and will be enforced with all future businesses.

[49] From the minutes of the December 13, 2005, Red Cross Town Council meeting

THE SECOND ELECTION (2006/2007)

Town Council Meeting (January 2006):

The Town Council consisted of:

Mayor	Ray Quick
Council Member	Heath Hahn
Council Member	Jerry Jordan
Council Member	Larry Wayne Smith
Council Member	Chip Speight
Town Clerk	Bobbie Kay Thompson

Officers Appointed:

Finance	Heath Hahn
Budget Control	Jerry Jordan
Fire Protection	Jerry Jordan
Police Protection	Larry Wayne Smith
Street Maintenance	Larry Wayne Smith
Tax Collection	Heath Hahn
Utilities	Heath Hahn
Waste Collection	Jerry Jordan
Zoning	Chip Speight

1. "Discuss having someone else outside of the Mayor generate the agenda - Larry Wayne Smith presenting."[50]

[50] From the January 2006, Red Cross Town Council agenda

"Motion #286 - Council Member Jordan made the following motion: (1) Agenda items to [be] submitted by the last Friday of the month. (2) Minutes of the previous meeting mailed with the agenda to Council Members on Wednesday prior to the Monday night meeting. (3) Town Clerk to prepare the agenda with the Mayor's approval before mailing. Motion was approved by vote. Council Member Hahn voted in opposition to the motion."[51]

2. Discuss establishment of Budget Officer - Larry Wayne Smith presenting.

   "Motion #285 - Council Member Smith made motion that we create the position of a Budget Officer for the Town and that Council Member Jordan be appointed to this position. Council Member Speight seconded the motion which was approved by vote. Council Member Hahn voted in opposition to the motion.[52]

   Budget control was moved from the Finance Officer, Council Member Heath Hahn, to Council Member Jerry Jordan.

3. Discuss scheduling training on "Robert's Rules of Order". Council Member Larry Wayne Smith presenting.

   Council Member Jordan made motion that we hold a workshop meeting for training on "Roberts' Rules of Order". Seconded by Council Member Speight.

   Training session did not materialize.

4. "Lou Eubanks asked about the zoning enforcement officer. Mayor Quick told Councilmember Speight to finalize the job description, advertise the position, and handle the interviews. He is to report his recommendations to the Council."[53]

---

[51] From the minutes of the January 2006, Red Cross Town Council Meeting

[52] From the minutes of the January 2006, Red Cross Town Council Meeting

[53] From the minutes of the January 9, 2006, Red Cross Town Council meeting

Town Council Meeting (March 2006):

1. "Motion #295 - Council Member Speight made motion to accept the contract for a zoning enforcement officer."

2. "Motion # 297 - Council Member Jordan made the following motion: (1) Mayor Quick be appointed to search for grants that apply to the Town of Red Cross and File documents necessary to secure such grants, (2) Keep the Town Council advised of progress being made on grants in progress, and (3) The Mayor serve as Red Cross liaison to work with other Stanly County Towns and cities in procurement of acceptable grants - to include all state and federal funding. Council Member Speight seconded the motion."[54]

   This was a carryover from a previous discussion in the February Council meeting where we had been talking about assigning responsibility for pursuing grants.

   In this meeting I had suggested Council Member Jerry Jordan to take the lead in pursuing grants. He declined, stating that he felt it was a mayoral function. I pointed out that I had not been successful in getting the Council to apply for grants and felt that he would have a better chance of getting support if he were the one presenting them.

   There were several factors for my wanting Council Member Jordan to take the lead in pursuing grants: (1) in the 2004/2005 term I had been unsuccessful in getting grant application request through Council, (2) there were strong signs that new grant opportunities were rapidly drying up due to declining economic conditions, (3) I felt that politically, based on past Council actions with respect to grant pursuit and with the disappearing grant opportunities, it would give my opposing group an additional tool for trying to force me off the Council, and (4) I felt that Council Member Jordan had the support of the opposing group.

   Please note that it is the responsibility of all Council Members to seek grant opportunities, present them to the Council and champion them

[54] From the minutes of the March 13, 2006, Red Cross Town Council meeting

through to completion.

3. "At last month's meeting, a citizen questions the position of Pro Tem Mayor. Mayor Quick researched and we do not have a provision stating we must renew this position at each election. He put the matter before the Council for their comments. Council Member Jordan suggested we continue as is. Larry Wayne Smith is the Town's Pro Tem Mayor."[55]

Town Council Meeting (April 2006):

1. Establish a method of assigning addresses for new residents and/or businesses in the Town. Ray Quick presenting.

   "Council Member Smith made motion to send a letter to EMS authorizing them to assign addresses for the Town. Council Member Speight seconded the motion. Motion was approved by vote. They will do this at no cost to the Town."[56]

   We had been contacted by Stanly County Emergency Services that since we were now a town, we were required to alter our address numbers to three digit numbers (as County residents we had been using five digit numbers). We had no choice but to agree and work with Stanly County Emergency Services to make the change.

   We put together the database of our people's addresses and wrote a cover letter (from the Mayor) and handed it off to EMS, which took care of the printing, mailing, and notifying entities like the power and utility companies.

   Unfortunately, and we're not sure why, a handful of the addresses got mismatched. As a result we had to go back and make corrections to those addresses. Fortunately, this was a minor glitch from the implementation standpoint. We apologize to those people that were affected. It should be noted that EMS did take care of notifying

[55] From the March 2006 Red Cross Town Council meeting minutes

[56] From the minutes of the April 2006, Red Cross town Council meeting

various agencies and the utility companies of the address changes because of this error.

The Post Office did honor both addresses for at least a year.

2. "Motion #305 Councilman Jordan made motion to pay the town clerk $200 a month starting now. Councilmember Hahn seconded the motion. Motion was approved by vote."

3. Councilmember Hahn made motion to give Mayor Quick the authority to obtain a website for the Town. Councilmember Jordan seconded the motion which was approved by vote.

Town Council Meeting (May 2006):

4. In the April comments from the Council, Council Member Jordan said the Town needs a website. Mayor Quick stated he can get a low cost two-year contract for about $600.

   I later reported back that I had found web hosting for $120 per year, including the cost of our URL, with our retaining the rights to the URL, and that I could create the website at no cost. I had made a generic pony website with a red/white/blue theme for review and the Council decided they wanted to use it.

   Motion #312 was voted and approved to proceed with establishment of website.

Town Council Meeting (August 2006):

1. "Mayor Quick recognized Mr. Crummy, who said the Department of Transportation is working with Oakboro and Red Cross on a Comprehensive Transportation Plan for the two Towns. Their purpose is to improve driving conditions and promote safety. They study future land use plans and develop roads to carry future traffic. These plans are updated every seven to ten years. He presented a slide presentation on the benefit of CTP.

2. Councilmember Smith gave a report on applying for Powell Fund money. This money would help upkeep certain streets and the State allows $23.00 per citizen for this purpose. At this time, the Councilmember Smith will check with Mr. Williams concerning this matter and will give more information at the September Council Meeting."[57]

Powell Bill funds come from tax moneys collected from the sale of road fuel. A portion of the collected tax is redistributed back to the counties and towns, provided they are participating in this program.

At this time Red Cross was not participating in the program, nor did the town have any adopted highway miles. With 768 people in Red Cross and the stated $23 per person this should result in approximately $17,764 in funds per year. Powell Bill Funds also allows $1,700 per linier mile of adopted highway.

It should be noted that once Red Cross did apply for and start receiving Powell Bill Funds the actual amount received per year was less than $15,000,

Town Council Meeting (September 2006):

1. "Zoning Council Member Speight, at the request of the Planning Board, asked that the $20,000 Planning Board budget for them be broken down into the following five categories:

Technical Assistance	$2,000
Workshop Meetings	$2,500
Zoning	$3,000
Subdivision	$4,000
Future Contracts	$8,250

Motion #331 Councilmember Speight made motion to amend the budget to breakdown the $20,000 designated to the Planning Board as the five categories listed above. Councilmember Jordan seconded the motion which was approved by vote.

[57] From the minutes of the August 14, Red Cross Town Council meeting

Councilmember Smith asked if the Zoning Officer has begun working for the Town. Councilmember Speight said he has only attended meetings. It was stated that he should check with Dollar General concerning the culvert and landscaping."[58]

2. Carolyn Morton, Planning Board Chairperson brought before the Council a request for amendments to the Subdivision Ordinance, and explained the recommended changes to the Council. Council Member Smith made motion to hold a public hearing at the October 9th Town Council meeting to hear these changes.

3. "Councilmember Smith discussed the Powell Fund money, which comes from the tax on gas, with Ms. Betsy Williams, Powell Fund Manager. According to Ms. Williams if the town adopts a dirt road that road can continue as a dirt road. This money can be used for sidewalks, bike trails, or stop signs. Powell Fund money can be collected for ten years before spending it. If not spent before the ten years are up the Town can be penalized on the amount of money received in the future. Only forty one towns out of five hundred in North Carolina do not apply for this money. If the Towns applies for and receives Powell Fund money a separate set of books will be required. After much discussion and the plans appear very good, the Council decided that more information is needed before a decision is made, therefore applying for Powell Fund money will be continued at the October Town Council meeting."[59]

Town Council Meeting (October 2006):

1. "Mayor Quick said that Steve Chambers [Chambers Engineering] recommended that Red Cross have a workshop meeting with Locust and Oakboro to discuss sewer issues. Councilmember Jordan suggested that Red Cross have a workshop meeting before meeting with Oakboro. It was decided that the Council will meet on October 19th at 6 PM at West Stanly Grill to discuss sewer needs and future

[58] From the minutes of the September 11, 2006, Red Cross Town Council meeting

[59] From the minutes of the September 11, 2006, Red Cross Town Council meeting

town hall.

2. Councilmember Smith recognized James Inman [City Manager, City of Locust], and he explained how they use Powell Fund money. He said Jim Kennedy Boulevard was built with this money. Mr. Inman stated money received from this fund is based on 75% on road mileage and 25% on population. The Town needs to do a cost analysis to determine how much money the Town would received visas cost to maintain adopt road(s). Questions were asked how would the Town decide which street to adopt? Mr. Inman said he will work with Councilmember Smith and the Council on this matter. After much discussion the Council decided to investigate the issue further before voting."[60]

   There are some questions about the mileage and population allocations as stated by Inman. In the August meeting Council Member Smith stated that we would receive $23 per capita and $1,700 per linear mile of adopted highway. The numbers stated by Smith are believed to be correct.

Town Council Meeting (November 2006):

1. Department Reports:

   - "Street Maintenance - one member of the Council asked about missing road signs. Mayor Quick has written a letter to DOT, but they have not replied. He and Council Member Smith are working on a cost analysis to check if it's feasible for the Town to apply for Powell Fund money.

     [The missing road signs appear to be due to the construction on the new four-lane highway. It was our belief that construction crews removed them to work but failed to replace them after the work was complete.]

   - Zoning - "Council Member Speight asked who should the

[60] From the minutes of the October 9, 2006, Red Cross Town Council meeting

Zoning Enforcement Officer, Cody Whitley, report. Mayor Quick stated Council Member Speight should be the liaison between the Zoning Enforcement Officer and the Town Council. Also a signed contract with Mr. Whitley should be filed with the Town Clerk."[61]

There was a problem in that some members of the Planning Board and Town Council appeared to want the Zoning Enforcement Officer to report directly to the Planning Board. These were two separate departments with each needing to report directly to the Red Cross Town Council member Responsible for Zoning. This was part of an on-going and long-term problem.

Town Council Meeting (December 2006):

1. Discuss contract for Zoning Enforcement Officer - Lou Eubanks presenting. Cody Whitley had been approved to serve in this position. The contract still needed approving by the Council.

   This appears to be an ongoing and frustrating problem. The contract for the Zoning Enforcement Officer should have been handled by Council Member Chip Speight, serving as the Council's Zoning Officer, and not a Planning Board Member. A town has to be careful not to create the appearance of allowing departmental responsibilities/influence to cross over into other areas of the town's administration.

   This concern is not unique, during the formation of the United States Government, there was considerable discussion where James Madison wrote: "but in which the powers of government should be so divided and balanced among several bodies of magistracy, as that no one could transcend their legal limits, without being effectually checked and restrained by the others. For this reason, that convention which passed the ordinance of government, laid its foundation on this basis, that the legislative, executive, and judiciary departments should be separate and distinct, so that no person should exercise the powers

[61] From the minutes of the November 13, 2006, Red Cross Town Council meeting

of more than one of them at the same time."[62]

Madison is addressing two concerns in forming the three branches of government; first he is arguing for separate and equal distribution of power so that no one branch may have disproportionate influence. Second, he is arguing that in doing so negates the effects of a powerful individual or group's influence on the overall function of the government. It is much the same argument with town government.

2. Larry Wayne Smith, with assistance of James Speight, took responsibility for changing the road name signs in Red Cross to make them compliant with the now required addressing system.

3. "Mr. Terry Hunneycutt complained about the loud music coming from the Colt Mini Storage. A band from Charlotte has been practicing there for several weeks. He has called the Sheriff's department two or three times. He is asking the Town council for their help in this matter. The Mayor and the Council told Mr. Huneycutt that they will try to help him with this problem."[63]

   The loud music was coming from a rental storage facility where renters (nonresidents) were using the facility to practice.

Town Council Meeting (January 2007):

1. "Mayor Quick gave a slide presentation of a basic draft for the Town's website and asked for suggestions and pictures. He also asked the Council for their pictures to put on the website. Because there is so much information that can be added, the Council decided to wait until next month before taking any action. The Mayor gave the Council a copy of the slide presentation to review."

   In the February meeting this will be approved. "Motion #361

[62]"The Federalist Papers" No. 48, "These Departments Should Not Be So Far Separated as to Have No Constitutional Control Over Each Other", From the "New York Packet", Friday, February 1. 1788

[63] From the minutes of the November 13, 2006, Red Cross Town Council meeting

Councilmember Hahn made motion to allow Mayor Quick $500 a year for the cost of a website for the Town. Councilmember Jordan seconded the motion. Motion was approved by vote."

Just for historical purposes, the first posting of the website for the Town of Red Cross to the Internet occurred in February 2007. Actual cost to the town was $120 per year.

Town Council Meeting (February 2007):

1. "After much discussion on the advantages and disadvantages, it was decided by the Council that it was for the best interest of the Town to pursue the purchasing of sewer capacity from the Town of Oakboro at a cost of $3.05 per gallon as previously quoted. Motion #362 Council Member Smith made motion to purchase 50,000 gallon sewer capacity from the Town of Oakboro. Councilmember Hahn seconded the motion. All members of the Council voted in favor of this motion."[64] (See Chapter on "Sewer" for details.)

   This action was precipitated from our workshop meeting on January 22, 2007 for discussing sewer issues. Present at that meeting were the five Red Cross Council Members and three representatives from Oakboro. At that meeting the Red Cross Council understood from the Oakboro representatives that they were encouraging Red Cross to consider buying sewer capacity from Oakboro (see Chapter on "Sewer Needs"). It was our understanding that they were recommending we consider purchasing 50,000 GPD at $3.05 per gallon. As a result, based off the understood recommendation, the Red Cross Council made the decision to go ahead and purchase a 50,000 GPD capacity block for future use.

Town Council Meeting/Public Hearing (March 2007):

1. "Mayor Quick recognized Carolyn Morton, Chairman of the Planning Board. She recommended that the Council adopt the Zoning Ordinance and turned the meeting over to Ms. Rhea who

[64] From the minutes of the February 12, 2007, Red Cross Town Council meeting

said in the new ordinance the language is more understandable, easier to locate items and the new ordinances has incorporated changes approved by legislation in 2005. Many items from what is a junk yard, distance to adult entertainment, pawn shops and gun shops were discussed before the Council voted on adopting a modified version of the ordinance.

Motion #364 Councilmember Speight made motion to accept the zoning ordinance dated March 12, 2007, taking out country clubs, to allow gun shops in CB, HB, and GB with a P (permitted with a certificate of zoning compliance from the zoning administrator) and shooting ranges with a S (S.U.P. [special use permit] from the board of adjustment). Councilmember Hahn seconded the motion. Due to the importance of this motion Mayor Quick asked for a roll call vote. Councilmember's Smith, Hahn and Speight voted yea, Councilmember Jordan voted nay. Motion was approved by vote.

Mayor Quick asked Carolyn Morton to introduce the members of the Planning Board, which she did and she also recognized Carol Rhea for all her help.

Before asking for a motion to close the public hearing meeting, the Mayor said zoning documents are the most important thing the Town will do."[65]

2. "Mayor Quick said someone has been discharging firearms on Sundays in the Town limits. Need to write an ordinance and submit to the Sheriff's Department for them to enforce.

   Motion #368 Councilmember Jordan made motion not discharging of firearms in the Town's limits on Sundays or 1/2 hour before sunrise or 1/2 hour after sunset on other days (these are the legal hours to shoot a gun [hunting hours]. Councilmember Hahn seconded the motion. Motion was approved by vote.

[65] From the minutes of the March 12, 2007, Red Cross Town Council meeting/public hearing

Councilmember Speight voted against the motion."[66]

Although not reflected in the minutes, there was considerable discussion on this issue during the public hearing segment. The Council recognized that the desires of two groups needing to be satisfied; (1) the people being annoyed by the excessive shooting and (2) the rights of hunters and large property owners within the town limits.

During the incorporation process there was a strong emphasis placed by a fairly large number of residents on not passing restrictive gun laws once we incorporated. However, some nonresidents were really abusing that right. It appeared that some renters at the mini-storage were using a large dirt pile at the back of the property for recreational shooting. They would shoot for two or three hours at night and, often, all day on Sunday. There was a housing development just a few hundred yards from where they were shooting and the residents began to complain.

3. "Councilmember Smith met with Terry Whitley and Larry Branch and they said they are working on new rates for sewer. Cost maybe $4.00, $5.00 or $6.00 a gallon. Motion #370 Councilmember Smith made motion to rescind motion #362 which requested that we purchase 50,000 gallon sewer capacity from Oakboro. Councilmember Jordan seconded the motion. Motion was approved by vote."[67]

In January the Town Council held a workshop meeting to address future sewer issues. At that meeting three Oakboro representatives unexpectedly showed up at our workshops and entered into discussion with the Council on sewer. It was the Red Cross Town Council's impression that they were encouraging Red Cross to purchase 50,000 gallon of capacity at $3.05 per gallon from Oakboro.

[66] From the minutes of the March 12, 2007, Red Cross Town Council meeting/Public Hearing

[67] From the minutes of the March 12, 2007, Red Cross Town Council meeting

In the February meeting of the Red Cross Town Council it was voted to respond to this understood offer and purchase a 50,000 gallon sewer capacity at $3.05 per gallon from Oakboro. Smith was authorized by the Council to approach the Town of Oakboro with the request.

In this meeting Smith reported back to the Council that he had talked with Whitley and Branch and was of the understanding that Oakboro was reviewing its pricing (interpreted as not selling capacity). It is not known if Whitley and Branch understood this was a formal offer to purchase capacity (see the Chapter on "Sewer").

4. "Mayor Quick said the Town's website is up and running. Log on at www.redcrossnc.com to access the website. Email has not been activated at this time. He still needs pictures."[68]

   Note: with the election of the 2012 Town Council the web address was changed to www.redcross-nc.com

Town Council Meeting (April 2007):

1. "Councilmember Jordan spoke with Ann Williams concerning the 28 acres of property. They are interested in seeing the Town purchase the property and use the house as the town hall. He told her contingent on four different items: appraisal, surveying of the property, approval by proper government bodies, and bring the house up to standard with the County's approval for a town hall. The building that is located on the property could be used by the County Sheriff's Department for their office. Councilmember Speight was not at the meeting but he is aware of the situation and is in agreement with purchasing the property. Before a vote was taken, each member of the council was asked to express their opinion. Councilmember Smith said it was a win-win situation for Red Cross. The house is an ideal building to convert to a town hall and the other building for a sheriff's office. Councilmember Hahn like to look at the situation,

[68] From the minutes of the March 12, 2007, Red Cross Town Council meeting

but doesn't see a problem, and asked about the square footage in the house. Mayor Quick said it would give the Town an identity, for the next fifty to a hundred years and make room for expansion. One citizen thought it was a great ideal.

Motion #376 Councilmember Jordan made motion to pursue with the Town's attorney to draw up a contract with the Williams to purchase the 28 acres for the Town of Red Cross at the price that has been circulated to the council, with the stipulation that (1) an appraisal be done, (2) the appropriate government bodies would approve and bless it (3) the house could be standard, within the budgeted guidelines, to be used as a town hall, and (4) this authorization is based on the signing of the contract. Councilmember Smith seconded the motion. All members of the Council voted in favor of the motion."[69] (See Chapter on "A Town Hall.")

Town Council Meeting (May 2007):

1. Lou Eubanks, as a part of the public hearing and representing the Planning Board, requested a 180-day moratorium on subdivision in order to give them time to complete their subdivision ordinance.

2. Richard Gregory requested the rezoning of his property, having tax record number 26681 be rezoned from RA to HB. His desire was to use to property for selling swimming pools and supplies.

3. Request by Mayor for Council to go into closed session. The following is the minutes of that closed session:

> "Motion #392 Councilmember Smith made motion to open the closed session. Councilmember Jordan seconded the motion. Motion was approved by vote.
>
> The Council reviewed the contract and under advisement of the

[69] From the minutes of the April 9, 2007, Red Cross Town Council meeting

Town Attorney voted to enter into contract to purchase the William's property. The agreement was to purchase the property at a value of $850,000 contingent on four conditions. These conditions being:

(1) The contract was signed.

(2) An appraisal from a North Carolina appraiser indicating that the fair market is not less than $850,000.

(3) Approval from the Local Government Commission of the State of North Carolina.

(4) The house located on the premises must be brought to Inspection Department Standards within the budget guidelines of the buyer.

Motion #393 Councilmember Jordan made motion to enter the contract with the Williams. Councilmember Hahn seconded the motion. All councilmember's voted in favor of the motion."[70]

It should be noted that Councils do have the right to call closed sessions when certain issues arise, the most common being contract/financial discussions and personnel issues. At that time the content of these meetings can be held private and the public does not have access to the content of the discussions within the meeting. However, once the matter has been resolved, with the exception of personnel issues, the information from those meetings becomes public record.

As referenced in the chapter on "A Town Hall", we discussed making an offer of $800,000 and being willing to go to $850,000. Had that information been made public prior to our making our initial offer to the Williams then there would have been no point in starting the negotiation at $800,000.

[70] From the May 2007, Red Cross Town Council minutes

Town Council Workshop (June 2007):

1. A workshop was called to discuss the upcoming meeting with the Local Government Commission pursuant to our efforts to purchase property for a town hall.

"Present - Mayor Ray Quick, Council Members; Larry Wayne Smith, Jerry Jordan, Heath Hahn, and Town Clerk Bobbie Kay Thompson. Absent was Council Member Chip Speight. Citizens present were Lou Eubanks and Dicky Hatley.

Mayor Quick called the meeting to order and stated the purpose of the meeting is to prepare for the upcoming meeting with the Local Government Commission. The primary objective being to determine what information will be needed, how to obtain that information and how we should structure it for the presentation to the Local Government Commission on June 27, 2007.

Actions determined in the meeting:

1. It was decided that Mayor quick, Council Member Jerry Jordan, Town Attorney Josh Morton, and, hopefully, the Town Auditor, Sam Turner be the ones to go to Raleigh on June 27, 2007, to meet with the LGC. Council Member Heath Hahn is to contact Sam Turner and see if he will be able to make the trip to Raleigh.

2. Discussed amount to be paid down. The Mayor stated that the previously discussed amount of $400,000 might be too much considering the need to modify the existing house. That we would probably be better off putting down no more than $300,000 since we would not want to see our general fund drop below $200,000 at any given point. Even at that level the financing would be well within our ability to handle. Council was in general agreement but left it open to somewhere between $300,000 and $350,000.

3. Council Member Heath Hahn is to contact Mr. Sam Turner and inquire if he can complete the 32-page financial form required by the LGC. If so, Mr. Turner is to contact the Town Attorney to coordinate this action.

4. Attorney Josh Morton stated that both parties, Ronnie and Anne Williams (seller) and the Town of Red Cross (buyer), has signed the purchase agreement. This agreement is contingent on several events as stated in the "Contract to Purchase". However, it appears there may be some difficulty completing the transaction by the September 30, 2007, deadline and Attorney Morton will contact the William's Attorney, Mr. Clegg Mabry, to see if it is possible to extend the contract an by additional 10-days. That if all goes well we should be able to close the deal by October 10, 2007.

5. Reviewed status with each of the three banks contacted; Sun Trust, First Bank, and Bank of Stanly. The Town has received favorable response from all three banks but still needs to follow up with Sun Trust for some hard numbers. Council Member Heath Hahn to contact Sun Trust. It was also suggested that we contact the Savings-and Loan in Locust.

6. In review of sewer needs. Council Member Jordan stated that we have a verbal commitment from the town of Oakboro to allow us to connect the Town Hall to the existing sewer lines belonging to Oakboro. However, there has been no [information] with respect to including the additional property in the hookup but he does not believe there will be enough volume difference to cause Oakboro to have a problem.

7. Mr. Morton advised us that a public hearing will have to be scheduled - the date for this will be set in the July Town Council Meeting.

8. Lou Eubanks will contact a local realtor for a listing of land price sales over the past 12-months for the area so that a comparison can be made between the price of the William's land and price of others sold and in the area.

9. I[t] was decided to take photos of the property to carry to Raleigh on the 27th. Mayor quick is to get photos of the house and property.

10. The Town Council committed to paper, through the use of a GIS map, both the present and future desires/usage for the land. Since the Town will use this land for 100 +/- years some of the projected expansions are possibly 20-years out.

11. The Town Council committed the following to paper:

    <u>Area A:</u>
    - Area to be reserved for present and future municipal purposes.
    - House to be converted to town hall. Cost to convert house to town hall estimated to be around $30,000 but will allocate $50,000.
    - Garage (one section finished inside) to be converted to a satellite Sheriff's Office.
    - Rest of land is open for future governmental growth.

    <u>Area B:</u>
    - Create park area
    - Make walking trails
    - Use existing ponds for recreational fishing
    - Set up picnic tables (preferably on concrete slabs with some covered)

    <u>Area C:</u>
    - Future ball fields
    - Future community center
    - Future library

- Future fire department

12. It was decided that the 0.78-acres at the northeastern corner of the William's property will serve as the entrance to the facility since the cross-over for the four-lane road is located in front of this property. It was decided that this area would have plantings, information signs, and flags.

13. Mayor Quick is to get the Stanly County GIS Department to draw up a map with the three different expansion areas drawn out and labeled for the trip to Raleigh.

14. Mayor Quick is also to do an Internet search for asking prices of land in the area."[71]

Town Council Meeting/Public Hearing (July 2007):

1. Lou Eubanks presented a rezoning request recommending that Council approve the request. Residents Harry and Gina Williams requested Bright Beginnings Day Car be rezoned from RA to HB (residential/agricultural to highway business). Rezoning was approved.

2. The Planning Board recommended that Colt Country Mini-Warehouses be rezoned from HB to GB, they were not aware that metal work was being performed on the premises. This did not qualify the property to be zoned GB. The owners were not present to answer questions concerning the metal works issue. The Planning Board requested the Council table the issue.

3. "Councilmember Jordan stated the Town has agreed on a contract with the Williams. He feels the meeting with the LGC was very good and they welcomed the project. The Town needs to schedule a public hearing as soon as possible and complete the formal application for the purchase of this property.

[71] From the minutes of the June 2007, Town of Red Cross workshop

Motion #404 Councilmember Jordan made motion to have a public hearing on July 24, 2007, at 6:30 PM at the West Stanly High School Library to discuss the acquisition of the Williams property for a town hall. Have the land surveyed, appraised, and a phase one environmental inspection completed and release funds for these expenses. Councilmember Speight seconded the motion. Motion was approved by vote."[72]

Town Council meeting/Public Hearing (July 24, 2007):

1. "Mayor Quick called the public hearing meeting to order, recognized Mr. Morton and welcomed everyone. Invocation was by Larry Wayne Smith.

   Mayor Quick said the Town of Red Cross is in the process of purchasing the Ronald J. and Ann M. Williams' property. After much consideration and thoughts about building a town hall, which would cost approximately $400,000, the Williams property became available. The decision was that it would be wiser to invest in this property. The house can be converted to a town hall [for] between $30,000 and $50,000. The other structure used for a satellite unit by the Stanly County Sheriff's Department, which will be an asset to the Town. Cost of the property is $850,000, with the part being financed at a low interest rate.

   Mayor Quick called for a public hearing [public comments] of the purchase of the land property of Ronald J. and Ann M. Williams.

   Dicky Hatley asked how much the town plans to pay down. The mayor said between $350,000 and $300,000.

   Bill Burris asked how long the Town would finance the property. Fifteen years was the answer. He also thought the purchasing of the property was a good idea.

[72] From the minutes of the July 9, 2007, Red Cross Town Council meeting

Mr. Morton [Town Attorney] has drawn up a resolution to be completed and mailed to the Local Government Commission in Raleigh and filed with the state of North Carolina."[73]

"Motion #407 Councilmember Hahn made a motion to make an application to Local Government Commission in Raleigh, NC for their approval to finance the purchase of 28.3 acres of property. Councilmember Jordan seconded the motion. Mayor asked for a roll call vote. The Council votes are as follows:

Councilmember Smith voted yes
Councilmember Jordan voted yes
Councilmember Hahn voted yes
Councilmember Speight voted yes"[74]

2. "Motion # 409 Councilmember Hahn made motion to hold a public hearing on August 13, 2007, at 6:30 PM in the West Stanly High School Library to consider, at the request of the Planning Board, a 180-day moratorium on sub-divisions in the Town. Councilmember Smith seconded the motion. Motion was approved by vote.

3. Councilmember Speight made motion to make an application to Local Government Commission for the $550,000 financing of the purchasing of 28.3 acres of property from Ronald J. and Ann M. Williams and proceed with the purchase. Motion was seconded by Councilmember Jordan. Motion was approved by vote."[75]

Town Council meeting (Closed Session) (July 31, 2007):

"During the closed session, Mr. Morton discussed the financing of the property. He has been negotiating with three different banks. Wachovia will charge a remittance fee of $1,000 and attorney's fee can be between $8,000 and $15,000.

---

[73] From the minutes of the July 24, 2007, Red Cross Town Council public hearing

[74] From the minutes of the July 24, 2007, Red Cross Town Council meetin

[75] From the minutes of the July 24, 2007 Red Cross Town Council meeting

Mr. Morton has also discussed this matter with Brian McDowell at Sun Trust and Brian McNeil at BBT. Mr. Morton will advise the Mayor of the best offer and he will contact the members of the Council.

Motion #415 Councilmember Jordan made motion to make a down payment of $300,000 on the property. Motion was seconded by Councilmember Hahn. Motion was approved by vote."[76]

Town Council emergency meeting (August 6, 2007):

"Present - Mayor Quick - the Council Larry Wayne Smith and Heath Hahn

Mayor Quick called the emergency meeting to order and stated [the] purpose of the meeting is to set a time and date for a public hearing on the financing and acquisition of the Ronald J. and Ann M. Williams' property. The Local Government Commission was not satisfied with the wording in the previous add Mr. Morton contacted the Local Government commission for the exact wording of the public hearing add

Motion #418 Councilmember Smith made motion to hold a public hearing meeting on August 21, 2007, at 6:30 PM at the West Stanly High School Library. The purpose of the public hearing is to allow citizen input on the application to the Local Government commission for the financing and acquisition of the Ronald J. and Ann M. Williams' property for a town hall at 176 East Red Cross Road. Councilmember Hahn seconded the motion. Motion was approved by vote."[77]

Unfortunately, both Council Members Jordan and Speight were absent from this meeting. However, both were fully aware of the business being conducted and conveyed their approval. Council meetings do not require all members to be present, only a quorum, or Council majority. Please note that there are procedures, ramifications, which can be enacted should a Council majority not notify a Council Member of a meeting.

---

[76] From the minutes of the July 31, 2007 special called Red Cross Town Council meeting

[77] From the minutes of the August 6, 2007, called Red Cross Town Council meeting.

Town Council Meeting (August 13, 2007):

1. The Council voted to rezone the Gregory property, having tax record number 26681, from RA to HB.

2. Council voted to apply a 180-day moratorium on subdivisions within the town limits. Motion by Council Member Speight and seconded by Council Member Jordan. Approved by vote.

3. "Council Member Jordan said the package the Council put together has been filed with the Local Government Commission. They did, however, advise Mr. Morton that the wording on the public hearing ad for the purchasing of the Williams' property did not meet their approval. They advised Mr. Morton how the ad should be worded. A new ad was placed in the SNAP and on July 31, 2007, an emergency Council Meeting was held and the date of August 21, 2007, was set to hold a public hearing on the purchasing and financing of the Williams' property" (see Chapter on "Red Cross works to get Town Hall").

   The reason for this emergency session was because we, the Town of Red Cross, had conveyed to the Williams our intent to commit to purchase by September 30, 2007. That date was almost upon us and we had to complete our commitment before the time ran out.

Town Council Public Hearing/Meeting (August 21, 2007):

A public hearing and subsequent Council meeting was held to present the community with the Council's plan to finance a portion of the purchase of the Williams' property.

The following are the minutes of both the public hearing and Town Council meeting:

"Mayor Quick called the meeting to Order at 6:30 PM and stated the purpose of the meeting was to discuss the acquisition and financing of the Ronald J. and Ann M. Williams property at 176 East Red Cross Road with a loan of $550,000 toward the purchase price of $850,000 and hold a public hearing to allow citizen the input on the application for financing and acquisition.

Mayor Quick called for a public hearing and opened the hearing for comments in favor of the application for the loan approval and purchase of the property and comments against the application and purchase. There being none Mayor Quick called for the public hearing to be closed for [at] the pleasure of the Town Council."[78]

"In Motion #427 Councilman Jerry Jordan made the motion that the Town of Red Cross pursues the application with the Local Government Commission for approval of the financing and acquisition of the Ronald J. and Ann M. Williams property at 176 East Red Cross Road with a loan of $550,000 toward the purchase price of $850,000. The motion was seconded by Councilman Speight and approved by vote.

Mayor Quick entertained a motion (#428) to go into closed session to consult with the town attorney.

The Town Council resumed the meeting in open session.

Motion #429 was made by Councilman Speight to accept the proposal of Branch Bank & Trust for a loan with a term of 15 years at 4.09% interest rate to finance the purchase of the Williams property. The motion was seconded by Councilman Jordan and approved by vote."[79]

I am a little uncomfortable with the wording of the second paragraph, but that is the way it was written. I believe it should have just read that I called for comments from the public, for both in favor and opposed, to the purchase.

[78] From the minutes of the August 21, 2007, Red Cross Town Public Hearing

[79] From the minutes of the August 21, 2007, Red Cross Town Council meeting

The following are the minutes of that closed session:

"During the closed session Mr. Morton discussed the proposal from Wachovia Bank, Sun Trust and Branch Bank and Trust to finance the purchase of the Williams' property. Quotes from the three banks were based on fifteen and twenty year loans. After much discussion the Council decided to go with Branch Bank and Trust at 4.09% for fifteen years."[80]

Town Council Meeting (October 2007):

1. "Lou Eubanks said that Tom Staples, who was unable to attend the meeting due to illness, had talked to someone in the Sheriff's Office about starting a neighborhood watch in the Town. Councilman Smith will check this out and report at the next council meeting.

2. Councilman Speight had a "word-of-mouth" contract with Mr. Ike Williams, which was continued after his death, with Ronnie and Ann Williams for use of the pastures. Councilman Speight was to maintain the fences, lime, fertilize, spray and bush hog the pastures. Mayor Quick and the Council agreed that they should continue this contract.

   Because Mr. Speight is on the Council, Councilman Jordan suggested asking the Town's attorney to write a simple contract concerning the use of the pastures. It was also discussed filling in the pond in front of the Town Hall, because the water level is so low..."

   [Periodically, there has been talk about filling in this pond in front of the town hall. Personally, I would hate to see that happen. The distance of the pond from the town hall, the shape of the slope leading to the pond, and the way the pond wraps around the corner of the town hall makes for a very picturesque view. If the town placed some benches and plantings near the pond it would make for a

[80] From the minutes of the August 21 2007, closed session of the Red Cross Town Council Meeting

very beautiful entrance to the town hall.]

3. "Motion #436 Councilman Jordan made motion that Councilman Smith be in charge of the renovation of the town hall. Councilman Speight seconded the motion which was approved by vote."[81]

Town Council Meeting (November 2007):

1. "Planning Board Report - Lou Eubanks reporting for the Planning Board said they have finished the revised subdivision plan. They requested tabling request from Councilman Smith for changing his commercial property from C/B to H/B to the December meeting.

At this meeting, a public hearing will be scheduled in January to consider the subdivision ordinance, the rezoning request by Larry Wayne Smith, and voluntary annexation record number 16815 located at 174 Bethel Church owned by Waller Edwin and Karen T. McDaniel.

2. Councilman Smith gave an update on the renovation of the Town Hall. Plumbing was roughed in with water and sewer pipes run to the bathroom, and the electrical wiring completed in a few days. Councilmember Hahn will be in charge of replacing the carpet and floor covering in the building..."

3. "Motion #440 Councilmember Smith made motion to move $60,000 to [from] the General Fund for the renovation cost of the town hall. Councilman Hahn seconded the motion. Motion was approved by vote...[82]

The Council originally allocated $50,000 for renovations to the town hall, however, the final cost of the conversion ended up being $72,000. There were a number of requirements for converting a home to a commercial building that we had not considered at the time of our purchase. Items such as installing additional joists under

[81] From the minutes of the October 8, 2007, Red Cross Town Council meeting

[82] From the minutes of the November 12, 2007, Red Cross Town Council meeting

the floor, extra railing and ramps for ACA compliance, work on the parking lot, etc.

4. "Mayor Quick talked to Robert Van Geons [Economic Development Commission] and he strongly suggested that the Town seek the help of a design civil engineer from Charlotte or Greensboro to do a commercial growth plan. The Council thought this was a very good idea and gave the mayor the approval to proceed with this idea."[83]

   Robert Van Geons, Stanly County Economic Development, advised us to seek a competent consultant for our commercial growth design. We made several attempts to address this issue but ended our pursuit of a consultant for the time being due to three primary reasons: (1) prices for a "competent" consultant was out of our price range, (2) we were no longer facing immediate threats from commercial development due to the crash of the economy and (3) we were still facing other pressing items that needed to be addressed by our Planning Board. It was still a balancing act of what needed to be addressed first and we felt the commercial growth design was something that could wait until a later date.

   A commercial growth design was still something our town did need to address once the other zoning design issues were completed. By the end of 2011 we did have both our growth and land-use plans in place, however, I am still not fully comfortable with the way the commercial growth design aspect is addressed. I would strongly encourage our Planning Board to revisit this issue.

5. "Lou Eubanks asked why the Town has not received any grants. The Mayor explained things the Town needs, grants are not available at this time."[84]

   This was a surprising question coming from Eubanks since she had been very actively involved in the town's activities. She knew there had been past battles over grants within the Town Council and she

[83] From the minutes of the November 12, 2007, Red Cross Town Council meeting
[84] From the minutes of the November 12, 2007, Red Cross Town Council meeting

should have been well aware of why we had not received any - especially the E-Government Utilization Project grant and the 90/10 sewer study grant. At the present time grant opportunities were rapidly drying up due to the declining economic conditions. Those that were still available were not applicable to us.

Town Council Meeting (December 2007):

1. "Councilmember Smith gave an update on the renovation of the Town Hall. He said things were going very well. Footings under the floors have been installed, which was a difficult task and some water lines and ducts move due to this process. Doors and trim have been installed and the sheetrock is almost completed, and the painting will be finished soon. Due to the holidays, the first town meeting will probably be in the new Town Hall in February 2008."[85]

2. There was a swearing-in and short meeting of the newly elected Town Council (2008/2009) after the close of the outgoing Council:

    a. The new Council Members were sworn in.

    b. Officers appointed.

    c. Motion #450 Councilman Smith made motion to affirm the contracts of the previous Town Council. Councilmember Hahn seconded the motion. Motion was approved by vote.

    d. Motion #451 Councilman Jordan made motion to approve the assignment of officers as submitted on the agenda with Councilman Greene replacing Chip Speight on Zoning. Councilman Smith seconded the motion. Motion approved by vote.

    e. Motion #452 Councilman Smith made motion that the Finance Officer and Town Clerk continue to be responsible for the post office box keys and the bank lock box keys.

[85] From the minutes of the December 10, 2007, Red Cross Town Council meeting

Councilman Jordan seconded the motion. Motion was approved by vote.

Motion #453 Councilman Hahn made motion that the Red Cross Town Council meet on the second Monday night in January 2008, at 6 PM, due to the Public Hearing meeting, at the West Stanly high School Library and beginning with the February meeting meet in the Red Cross Town Hall. Councilman Jordan seconded the motion. Motion was approved by vote. A public notice will be posted in the local paper concerning the new location of the February meeting and future meetings for the Red Cross Town Council.[86]

[86] From the minutes of the December 10, 2007, Red Cross Town Council meeting

THE THIRD ELECTION (2008/2009)

Town Council Public Hearing/Meeting (January 2008):

1. The Town Council consisted of:

Mayor	Ray Quick
Council Member	Darice Greene
Council Member	Heath Hahn
Council Member	Jerry Jordan
Council Member	Larry Wayne Smith
Town Clerk	Bobbie Kay Thompson

   Officers Appointed:

Finance	Heath Hahn
Fire Protection	Jerry Jordan
Police Protection	Larry Wayne Smith
Street Maintenance	Larry Wayne Smith
Utilities	Heath Hahn
Waste Collection	Jerry Jordan
Zoning	Darice Greene

2. Items discussed were zoning amendment changes, voluntary annexation request and property rezoning request. No notable actions were taken pending public hearings for the two annexation request and for the property rezoning request.

Town Council Public Hearing/Meeting (February 2008):

1. "Mayor Quick welcomed everyone to the new Town Hall. He said

we owe Larry Wayne Smith and Heath Hahn a great deal of gratitude for all their hard work. Larry Wayne was the project manager and did a fantastic job. He and Heath worked very well together on the project, and the Mayor personally thanked each of them. The renovation turned out better than anyone could have hoped for."

2. "Councilman Smith made motion to send a donation of $2,000 with a letter of appreciation for the use of the library for town council meetings with a copy to the Stanly County school superintendent and Stanly County Commissioners. Councilman Greene seconded the motion. Motion was approved by vote."

3. "Councilman Smith gave an update on the renovations of the town hall. He said he appreciated the help of Councilman Hahn and also Councilman Jordan. He said it had been a lot of fun but a lot of hard work with a few odds and ends to be completed. Councilman Hahn said he was proud of the way things turned out. He has ordered some custom made furniture which should be completed within the month. Councilman Jordan congratulated the men on a job well done and said we owe these men a lot. The cost came in at a very reasonable price. The men were recognized with a hand of applause."

4. Motion #473 Councilman Hahn made motion that the town names the meeting room The Hinson Room and the conference room The Williams Room. Councilman Smith seconded the motion. Motion was approved by vote. These rooms were named in honor of J. D. and Violet Hinson and memory of Ike and Helen Williams."

5. "The Mayor and Councilman Jordan met this morning with Doctors Wu and Langley with the Civil Engineering Department at UNC Charlotte to do a long range land use plan for the Town. They said both men were very professional and experienced. Part of the study will be done by graduate students which will help reduce the cost. They will look at the surrounding towns and what they are doing and use demographic information from the State. They will give the Town seven different approaches using a ten year period with the Council deciding which choice would best benefit the Town. By doing this study, it will take the burden off the Planning Board and

the Council to review and approve and sign before beginning the study."[86]

We, as a town, had reached the point where we needed to do a long-range land-use plan for the town. I looked around and it appeared the cost of consultants, at least the ones that I felt would be able to do the quality of work we were looking for, were just too expensive for us. However, the State of North Carolina had a division called the Division of Community Assistance, which provided towns this type of assistance. I contacted them; however, it would be some time before they would be able to start working with us. In talking with Darren Rhodes, Division of Community Assistance, he indicated that it would probably be the first of the next year before they would have an opening. From my perspective we were well behind where we should be in our plans development, six years into the incorporation. Still, I went ahead and got us put on their list.

During this time I continued to explore other options. I called Chapel Hill but they were booked several years out. I then approached Dr. Wu of UNC-Charlotte about the possibility of his school using our town as a project. One of the enticements was that they would be able to work with our town for a number of years as a long-term project, giving students some excellent hands-on experience. It would allow them to monitor the effects their design recommendations would have on our community.

Dr. Wu seemed interested and a meeting was set up with him. Council Member Jerry Jordan and I met with him and Dr. Langley at UNC-Charlotte. We were impressed with both of them and of their apparent understanding of what we were looking for. Unfortunately, after Dr. Wu reviewed our material and requirements, he contacted me and said that he did not feel that they could meet our needs.

By fall of 2008 the NC Division of Community Assistance was becoming available. I called and talked to Mr. Darren Rhodes and they agreed to meet with us. The Planning Board,

---

[86] From the minutes of the February 11, 2008, Red Cross Town Council meeting

Carol Rhea and I met with them. Based on this meeting we felt that, with the guidance of Carol Rhea, we could achieve what we wanted through them and the project was set up.

We had used Carol Rhea, Rhea Consulting, for our zoning code design but she was not able to take the lead in developing the land-use plan. It should be noted that she did agree to continue to serve as a liaison consultant representing the interest of the town on this upcoming project. The quality of her work on past projects and her knowledge and understanding of our desires for our community was something we, both the Council and Planning Board, felt needed to be retained, regardless of whom else we retained.

Town Council Meeting (April 2008):

1. "Zoning-Councilman Greene introduced the new zoning enforcement officer for the Town. He stated that Mr. Foxx is very experienced in this field and well qualified for the position. He recognized Mr. Foxx, who said that he and his family live in our neighboring town of Oakboro, and is employed by the Cabarrus County as a senior zoning inspector and is a certified zoning officer. He also serves the Town's of Midland in this capacity and also assists the towns of Harrisburg and Mt. Pleasant."

2. "Last Month the Mayor attended a meeting on the options of participating in the Recreation and Parks Trust Fund. The current study expires this year and study will be count under the point system. Last year the towns that participated paid about $50,000 and received $2,000,000 in grants. Cost is approximately $1.06 per capita. The Mayor is asking the Council for approval to send a letter of intent, not a commitment, to participate in this study. Councilmember Hahn suggested that the Mayor send a letter of intent. He asked if any Councilmember disagreed with no one saying no, with all being in agreement. The Mayor will send the letter."[87]

We, as a town, were interested in participating in this study because if

[87] From the minutes April 2008, Red Cross Town Council meeting

we ever did decide to develop some of the town's property into a park area, we would need the park study because a park study is required to be submitted as a part of the grant application.

10-years earlier Stanly County and all towns and the County had gone together and done a joint study, which covered the County and all municipalities in the County. Unfortunately, that study was expiring this year.

We were fortunate in that all the towns in the County were again getting together to commission the new study. We wanted to be included so that we could use it for obtaining a PARTF grant (Parks and Recreational Trust Fund). Basically, the PARTF grant would provide up to $300,000 matching funds towards park development.

We had acquired 28.3-acres of land for the town hall and had designated the back 12-acres as a future park area in our presentation to the Local Government Commission for approval of the land purchase. I think we were, at some point, willing to commit ourselves to the development of a park area for our town. We talked about putting in a gated child's play area, covered picnic tables on concrete slabs with grills, walking trails, a basketball court, restrooms, etc. We had three ponds on the property to complement the existing terrain and felt the picnic tables could be arranged around the ponds so that families would also be able to take their children fishing.

This was the major reason for our approaching Running Creek School and asking them to voluntary annex into our community, which they did. We were also talking with West Stanly High School about their using our park area for their cross country track team's practice area. We felt these two additional factors would greatly enhance our potential for acquiring a park grant once it again became available.

3. "Councilman Smith and Mayor Quick met with County Manager Jerry Myers and Sheriff Burris to discuss leasing the garage for ten years. A separate electrical meter will be installed at the garage but the Council discussed running a water line to the building. They also

discussed a need for a heat pump to be installed. The County will be responsible for their electrical and telephone service and the interior of the building. The Town will be responsible for the exterior of the building. Councilman Smith will check if the garage can be hooked to the Town Halls sewer system. The Town's attorney is reviewing the contract before it is approved and accepted.

Motion #485 Councilman Hahn made motion based on the approval of the contract with the Sheriff's Department that we commit to get the work completed on the garage for their use. Councilman Smith will be in charge of this work, and he stated that hopefully it can be accomplished for about $20,000, if not he will keep it as low as possible. Councilman Jordan seconded the motion. Motion was approved by vote."[88]

Town Council Meeting (June 2008):

1. "Motion #497 - Confirming contract with Stanly County Sheriff's Department. Council Member Smith presented the contract and covered changes requested by the Town of Red Cross. Council Member Jordan made motion to approve and Council Member Smith seconded. Motion was approved by vote."[89]

2. "Mayor Quick said that the study is dragging out and we may need to go ahead and start work on making the road into the Town hall a two-lane road. Council Member Smith will get some estimates on what it will cost to convert the road."[90]

   We were giving serious consideration to making the drive into the town hall a two-lane drive. We were already seeing some problems with bidirectional traffic during town meetings, and with the increased traffic from the new Sheriff's Office the problem would be further exacerbated. I had previously been told by the Board of Elections that the single-lane road was a major restriction for not

[88] From the minutes of the February 11, 2008, Red Cross Town Council meeting
[89] From the minutes of the June 9, 2008, Red Cross Town Council meeting
[90] From the minutes of the June 9, 2008, Red Cross Town Council meeting

being able to have a voting poll in our community.

With respect to a voting pole, in previous unofficial discussions with the Stanly County Board of Elections, I had been told that it was possible to establish a voting poll in Red Cross. However, there were two major concerns: (1) there was a question of having a room large enough to accommodate the polling booths and (2) there was a major concern with the single lane drive entering into the town hall.

It is my belief that, with the chairs removed from the meeting hall, there is sufficient room to set up polling booths and now that the drive into the town hall has been made two-way it is possible for Red Cross to establish its own voting poll. This is something the town now needs to pursue.

Unfortunately, at the time we were advised by two of our Planning Board Members that due to our zoning code requirements we would have to meet more stringent street construction requirements, which would substantially increase our cost. As a result we were forced to abandon our plans. We will find out later that information was incorrect.

3. "Mayor Quick stated that Oakboro was looking at putting bicycle lanes in their Comprehensive Transportation Plan and feels we need to look at doing so also. In doing so it would allow the Oakboro Bicycle lane to extend all the way to Red Cross. Council Member Smith expressed some concerns and asked for some time to review this before including it in our plan."[91]

   I never did find out what Smith's concerns were and, unfortunately, the bicycle lane was never included in our transportation plan. I would still encourage the town to pursue this at some future paving of Highway 205.

   Bicycle lanes are added to the side of the highway for non-motorized traffic to use. What I was asking for was that a bicycle lane be

[91] From the minutes of the June 9, 2008, Red Cross Town Council meeting

included in our Comprehensive Transportation Plan, which would extend along Highway 205 from Red Cross to Oakboro and connect to the Oakboro bicycle lane. There would not be a cost to the Town of Red Cross. If approved, at the next paving of Highway 205, a designated five-foot apron would be added to one side of Highway 205 for bicycles to use.

It may, at first glance, seem a little odd to want to do something like this for our community but as we grow there will be more people having an interest in riding their bicycles to Oakboro, especially if we do develop as a professional and residential community.

Another consideration on my part, and one that I spoke of during my presentation/request to the Council, was that Oakboro has a rail line going to Charlotte. They have a railway museum already established with their old train depot, and have the facilities already in place for establishing a passenger station. I can well envision that at some future point people may want use that rail line to commute to work in Charlotte. In my view we will eventually see the open space between Oakboro and Red Cross filling with residential developments. People moving from Charlotte will already have acceptance of rail travel through their prior use of the Charlotte Metro Rail System and will desire rail commuting. They will also be much more prone to use bicycles to get to the rail station.

Unfortunately, this was a (no cost to the town) community enhancement opportunity that the Red Cross Town Council failed to take advantage of.

Town Council Meeting/Public Hearing (September 2008):

1. A public hearing was called to hear the request of Jerry Jordan to annex three tracts of land into the Town of Red Cross. The properties having tax record numbers 22524, 36834, and 37731 are located at, or near, the intersections of Lakewood Road and Highway 24/27.

   In Council session: Council Member Jordan was excused from the

Council for the vote. Council Member Smith made motion to approve properties into the town. Voted and approved.

2. Council approved expenditures to the Division of Community Assistance for their assistance in the development of the Red Cross land-use plan.

Town Council Meeting (October 2008):

1. "Mayor Quick stated that the NC Department of transportation has given us two more years to prepare our land use plan [should be transportation plan]. Red Cross is a separate town and no longer a part of Oakboro in this study. Two hundred and fifty six transportation surveys were mailed to the residents.

2. Mayor Quick said he received an e-mail from the Council member Greene stating his resignation from the Council was effective immediately for personal reasons. The Mayor said he hated to see Greene leave. He has notified the Board of Elections and [contacted] the Institute of Government. The Mayor was advised that the Council can appoint someone to fill Greene's seat until the next election. At the 2009 election, there will be three seats on the Council to be filled.

3. Robbie Foxx [Zoning Enforcement Officer] suggested that the Town use Stanly Counties 2008-2009 zoning penalties with the exception on the second violation. The charge on the second violation would be $200 and not $250 that the County charges. The $200 charge would be in compliance with the Town's Zoning Ordinance.

   Motion #527 Council member Smith made motion that we accept the Counties penalties with the exception on the second violation to be $200 and not $250. Council member Hahn seconded the motion, which was approved by vote.

4. Mayor Quick said we need to start working on setting up land use and growth plans. Help is needed from the council, planning board

and citizens."[92]

Town Council Public Hearing/Meeting (November 2008):

1. Council Member Jordan was excused from the Council for this vote due to the rezoning of his property. Rezoning of both properties were approved (R/A to G/B).

2. Discussion on park study being conducted by the County of Stanly.

   "Mayor Quick said all towns in the County had agreed to participate in this funding. It is cheaper for the towns to combine than doing individual studies. The last study cost $80,000 and brought in three million dollars in grants. The cost for Red Cross is $1,160 ($1.50 per resident) for the Stanly County Comprehensive Recreational Plan.

   Motion #537 Council member Jordan made motion to approve funding for the Comprehensive Recreation Plan. Council member Hahn seconded the motion. Motion was approve by vote.

   [Since the town had 28-acres of land, and had presented its intent to reserve 12-acres as park land to the Local Government Commission during the loan procurement process, we wanted to be able to obtain grant funding from PARTF (Parks and Recreational Trust Fund).]

3. Mayor Quick stated that he and Council member Hahn met with the County [School] Finance Committee and asked for the[ir] consideration in the annexation of Running Creek Elementary School into the Town of Red Cross. This move would benefit the town in obtaining future grants and the school is bordered on three sides by the Town. The Mayor received a letter dated November 5, 2008, from Dr. Samuel DePaul... However the following evening, Mr. Mike Barbee, School Board member presented the matter to the School Board. The Board members unanimously approved the recommendation of the annexation.

---

[92] From the minutes of the October 13, 2008, Red Cross Town Council meeting

Motion #538 Council member Jordan made motion to set a public hearing on December 8, 2008, at 7:00 PM at the Town Hall, to discuss the voluntary annexation of Running Creek Elementary School into the Town of Red Cross. The motion was seconded by council member Hahn and was approved by vote." [93]

Town Council Public Hearing/Meeting (December 2008):

1. "Motion #543 Council member Smith made motion to appoint Kelly Brattain to serve on the Town Council until the next election. Council Member Jordan seconded the motion. All member of the council approved the motion.

   Mayor Quick gave the Oath of Office to Council Member Kelly Brattain, and welcomed him to the Council. Council member Hahn also welcomed him and presented him a name plate.

   Motion #544 Council Member Hahn made motion to recognize Kelly Brattain as a sitting member of the Red Cross Town Council. Council Member Smith seconded the motion which was approved by vote.[94]

   It should be noted that when a Council seat is vacated between election cycles a new public election is not called. The sitting Council may appoint a person to serve in the vacant position until the next public election. Darice Greene had served less than a year of his four-year term before resigning. Because Kelly Brattain was an appointed Council Member during the first half of a four year term, he would be required to run for office at the next public election. If elected at that election, he would again be required to run for office at the following election upon completion the existing four-year term. This may seem a little confusing and complicated but it provides a valid method for sustaining staggered terms (4-year terms) of public officials.

[93] From the minutes of the November 10, 2008, Red Cross Town Council meeting

[94] From the minutes of the December 8, 2008, Red Cross Town Council meeting

As to how Kelly Brattain was selected: Kelly went to the same church as I did and I asked him one Sunday morning before preaching if he would be willing to allow me to put his name in as a candidate for the vacant Council seat. He agreed and I presented his name to the Council Members during the workshop on November 17, 2008 called for addressing the replacement of former Council Member Darice Greene. All Council Members felt he would be a good candidate and gave their approval to proceed with the process.

2. "Motion #545 Council member Smith made motion that we accept Running creek Elementary School identified with Tax Record Number 14155 for voluntary annexation into the Town of Red Cross. Council member Hahn seconded the motion. Motion was approved by vote."[95]

Town Council Meeting (January 12, 2009):

1. "Ms. Eubanks asked again about staffing the town hall."[96]

   The Council had already responded to those expressed concerns by paying the Town Clerk $200 per month and assuring her that she could continue to work from home. Therefore, staffing the town hall was not a major concern at this time.

2. "Ms. Eubanks expressed concern for the Town to create a board of adjustments. Councilmember Brattain who replaced former council member Green will be responsible for this matter."[97]

3. "Ms. Eubanks also wanted to make the road into the town hall two lanes since the satellite office is completed. She was advised that this cannot be done at this time without raising taxes, which is not an option due to the present economic conditions. The Mayor and council member Jordan said that no member of the council would

[95] From the minutes of the December 8, 2008, Red Cross Town Council meeting

[96] From the minutes of the January 12, 2009, Red Cross Town Council meeting

[97] From the minutes of the January 12, 2009, Red Cross Town Council meeting

want to undertake any project that would increase taxes."[98]

It should be noted that the Council had previously discussed expanding the drive into the town hall into a two-lane drive; however, based on the town's zoning requirements, as stated by two Planning Board Members, the town didn't feel it could afford it. According to their statement, meeting our zoning requirements for the drive would probably force the cost to exceed $150,000.

4. "Ms. Eubanks suggested increasing the business in the Town to create more revenue. Council member Jordan stat[ed] that until the Town can supply water and sewer this would be difficult."[99]

Town Council Public Hearing/Meeting (January 27, 2009):

1. "Mayor Quick called the public hearing meeting to order and stated the purpose of this meeting is to rezone Tract Number 14155 listed as Running Creek Elementary School from County R/A to Town R/A.

   There were no comments concerning the rezoning of the school."[100]

   "Motion #552 Council member Hahn [made] motion that we rezone Running Creek Elementary School from County R/A to Town R/A. Council member Smith seconded the motion. Motion was approved by vote."[101]

   At first glance it may seem a little like a circular argument to have a public hearing for trying to convert property from its present zoning designation to the same zoning designation. The reason for this is that the County's R/A is different from Red Cross's R/A and we had to make the distinction by reassigning the property as being under Red Cross's zoning codes rather than the County zoning codes. Had we not done this then, by default, Running Creek School would be

[98] From the minutes of the January 12, 2009, Red Cross Town Council meeting

[99] From the Minutes of the January 12, 2009, Red Cross Town Council meeting

[100] From the minutes of the January 27, 2009, Red Cross Public Hearing

[101] From the minutes of the January 27, 2009, Red Cross Town Council meeting

under a zoning specification not supported by our town.

Town Council Meeting (March 2009):

2. "It was mentioned that a workshop meeting will be held on April 16, 2009, in the County Commissioners room by Bill Dustin of COG for the Board of Adjustment members. Because the Town has not appointed anyone to serve on this board no one will be attending.

   According to Robbie Foxx, Cabarrus County does not have a separate Board of Adjustments. Some of the people on the planning board also serve on the board of adjustments. Robbie Foxx recommended Board of Adjustment be at the discretion of the Council."[102]

   It appears there is still an ongoing push by some members of the Planning Board to have the Red Cross Planning Board assume the responsibilities of the Board of Adjustment. This issue had just been addressed in the January meeting?

   The statement that, "Because the Town has not appointed anyone to serve on this board no one will be attending", was an erroneous statement. It had been voted in 2003 that the Red Cross Town Council would serve as the Board of Adjustment until such time as the Planning Board completed its work on the zoning codes - so, the Red Cross's Board of Adjustment did exist even though it had never been called upon.

   There were two main reasons for having kept the two functions separate. The first, and probably most important, we were in urgent need of getting our codes completed and we didn't want anything to distract the Planning Board from that duty. The second was that the Board of Adjustment is a quasi-judicial board and has a lot of power. In some cases it can override the town's zoning codes and its decisions can only be challenged in local superior court, even the Town Council must challenge its decisions in court.

[102] From the minutes of the April 13, 2009, Red Cross Town Council meeting

Based on the above second reason, there was a great deal of concern in the early days that the powers of the Board of Adjustment could be misused by its members. A member could have an insatiable desire for growth - growth at any cost. Even to the possible point of making exceptions to the town's zoning codes for acceptance of businesses. With the Planning Board it could not be determined that the people had the needed qualities or wisdom to allow them the power that went with the Board of Adjustment. One of the most critical requirements of a Board of Adjustment Member is wisdom.

Town Council Meeting (April 2009):

1. Voted to return land that J. D. and Violet Hinson donated to the town. This was because the land was donated by the Hinson's for the purpose of building a town hall. Since the Town made the decision to purchase the Williams' property the donated property was no longer being used for its intended purpose and according to the contract the land was to revert back to the original owners in the event a town hall wasn't built on it.

   Normally, it is very difficult for a town to divest itself of land. However, in this case it was written into the original gift contract. We were just honoring an existing contract. The Town paid for all attorney fees and transfer cost. Cost was less than $1,000.

2. "Mayor Quick read a statement concerning various meetings and communication with the Town of Oakboro concerning purchasing sewer capacity from them. Before reading the statement, the mayor had discussed this with the council and received their approval."[103]

   This response was precipitated by our having been informed that an Oakboro Council Member, allegedly, had began lobbying against our exploratory talks with the County concerning some future extension of the proposed Endy sewer line to Red Cross (See Chapter on "Sewer Needs").

[103] From the minutes of the April 13, 2009, Red Cross Town Council meeting

Town Council Meeting (July 2009):

1. Discuss the town applying for Powell Bill Funds - Larry Wayne Smith presenting.

   "Council member Smith stated that the Town qualifies for Powell Bill Money, which is distributed based on population. Most all the towns in North Carolina, that qualify, have applied for this program. The Town of Red Cross would receive approximately $16,000 a year. The streets must be surveyed which will cost about a $1,000, if no changes cost the following years will be about $300 or $400 a year. The survey questionnaire must be mailed to Betsy Williams by July 21, 2009. Separate bank account and books must be set up for this money. A specific list states how this money can be used, and the Town can accumulate the money for ten years before using it.

   Motion #587 Council member Smith made motion to pursue for Powell Bill Money for the Town. Council member Jordan seconded the motion. Motion was approved by vote."[104]

2. "Council member Brattain discussed the enlargement of the Williams Meeting Room. He recommended the following changes be made which he estimates will cost about $6,500 to $7,000. He will get three sealed bids for this project. Following is a list of recommended changes."[105]

   It was brought before the Council in the June meeting that the present meeting room for the Planning Board was too small. It was proposed that two existing rooms could be combined (wall removal) to make a larger meeting room.

Town Council Meeting (August 2009):

1. "Council member Brattain recommended that Richard Baucom be given the contract to enlarge the William's Conference room for a

[104] From the minutes of the July 13, 2009, Red Cross Town Council meeting

[105] From the minutes of the July 13, 2009, Red Cross Town Council meeting

cost of $6,833 which will be paid at the time the work is completed. This contract includes all items listed in the minutes of last month's meeting.

Motion #592 Council member Brattain made motion that Mr. Baucom be given the contract to enlarge the Williams' conference room. Council member Hahn seconded the motion which was approved by vote.

2. Mayor Quick said that DSL lines have been installed, and recommended the Town purchase a laptop, answering service and phones.

   Motion #593 Council member Jordan made motion to purchase the above accessories for the town hall at a cost of $1,000. Council member Smith seconded the motion which was approved by vote.[106]

Town Council Meeting (September 2009):

1. "Council agreed to have Lou Eubanks represent Town of Red Cross on the CVB [Convention and Visitors Board] board. The council unanimously approved Ms. Eubanks serving on the Convention Visitors Bureau Board.

2. The Mayor has received a letter from the North Carolina Department of Commerce, Division of Community Assistance, stating that they will be happy to provide assistance to our staff with the development of a Town Land Use Plan. The only charge will be for reimbursement of cost incurred for travel, supplies, etc. directly related to this project. Plans are to meet every three months and with the next meeting being scheduled for October 19th, 2009, 6:00 PM at the town hall.

   Motion #600 Council member Smith made a motion that we work with Community Assistance in developing a Town Land Use Plan. Council member Jordan seconded the motion which was

[106] From the minutes of the July 2009, Red Cross Town Council meeting

unanimously approved by vote."[107]

Town Council Meeting (December 2009):

1. "Council member Brattain stated the need for a Board of Adjustments, because presently the Town Council is serving in this capacity, which is not the most desirable situation. One comment that other residents in the Town would be good to serve if there was some way to identify these people and get them to volunteer. The mayor suggested that [some] members of the planning board rotate to the board of suggestion [should be board of adjustment] and get new members for the planning board. After much discussion, the council decided to table this motion concerning this matter.

   Mayor Quick suggested that at the January 4, 2010, 6 PM meeting that the discussion of the Planning Board serving as the Board of Adjustment be continued. A public notice will be put in the paper concerning this meeting."[108]

[107] From the minutes of the September 14, 2009, Red Cross Town Council meeting

[108] From the minutes of the December 14, 2009, Red Cross Town Council meeting

THE FOURTH ELECTION (2010/2011)

Town Council Meeting (January 2010):

The Town Council consisted of:

Mayor	Ray Quick
Town Clerk	Bobbie Kay Thompson
Council Member	Kelly Brattain
Council Member	Heath Hahn
Council Member	Jerry Jordan
Council Member	Larry Wayne Smith

Officers Appointed:

Finance	Heath Hahn
Fire Protection	Jerry Jordan
Police Protection	Larry Wayne Smith
Street Maintenance	Larry Wayne Smith
Utilities	Heath Hahn
Waste Collection	Jerry Jordan
Zoning	Kelly Brattain

1. "Planning Board Report - Council member Brattain said they met last week, but hopefully will have some information on people willing to serve on the Board of Adjustment by the next Town Council meeting."[109]

[109] From the minutes of the January 11, 2010, Red Cross Town Council meeting

2. "Tom Staples addressed the Town Council with concerns and request that the town adopt Jet Drive and pave the road. He states there are seven houses on this road which is 2/10 of a mile long. Before any decision can be made more information will be required."[110]

3. "Mrs. Lavene asked why Red Cross did not join Locust, Stanfield and Oakboro when they discussed recycling in their towns. Mayor Quick stated we were not asked to meet with them; however, we have discussed with Waste Management a plan they are working on."[112]

   The present multi-municipal waste contract with Waste Management was coming to an end and it was now time for the four towns to start looking at establishing new contracts. We had heard that Locust was trying to negotiate a new contract independent of the other towns. It sounded plausible since their population was now above the 5,000 resident threshold, which would allow them a better price break.

   When we contacted Waste Management they offered to provide us services at the same rate as our present contract. This surprised us because under the old multi-municipal contract we were getting a discount and they were offering to continue with that discount. It didn't take a lot of logic to recognize a good deal. Waste Management has proven to be an excellent company to work with.

4. "Mayor has been discussing with Michael Sandy, County Zoning and Planning Director, to consider handling our subdivision ordinance since he is handling our permitting. The Council agreed for the Mayor to continue this discussion with Mr. Sandy. The Mayor will bring more information on this matter at the February meeting."[113]

Town Council Meeting (February 2010):

1. Established contract with the County of Stanly to administer the subdivision permitting for the Town of Red Cross. Approved by Council vote.

---

[110] From the minutes of the January 11, 2010, Red Cross Town Council meeting

[112] From the minutes of the January 11, 2010, Red Cross Town Council meeting

[113] From the minutes of the January 11, 2010, Red Cross Town Council meeting

"Mayor Quick spoke with Michael Sandy and since they are doing our permits they can also do our small sub divisions. Major sub divisions the planning board will review these and the Town will have the final sign off. The Mayor hopes to have a contract with the County by our next Town Council Meeting."[114]

2. Approve contract with Waste Management for recycle pickup

3. Approve $3000 contract with Rhea Consulting for implementation of the Land Development Plan.

4. "Council member Smith said Carol Rhea states Jet Drive does not have to be brought up to the new sub division ordinances, if the Town decides to adopt it. The residents have requested that the road just be gravel. Using gravel only does not qualify to use Powell Bill money, but would come out of the general funds. Ted Coble gave an estimate of widening the road to 18 feet and adding a cul-de-sac and put pipes at the driveways at the two houses at the end. The road will need to be surveyed which cost between $700 to $1,000. total cost for these changes would be $7,800. At Tom Staples house the road is 15 feet wide and other places it is smaller. There are two other roads in the Town that are in the same situation. Since only two council members are present, the council decided to hold a workshop meeting on February 22, 2010, at the town hall to discuss this issue."[115]

Town Council Meeting (April 2010):

1. Received request from consultant, Rhea Consulting, for an 80-hour contract increase resulting in an additional $5,000.00. After review the increase was approved.

1. "Planning Board Report - Mayor Quick gave the report for council member Brattain who was unable to attend the meeting due to

[114] From the minutes of the February 8, 2010, Red Cross Town Council meeting
[115] From the minutes of the February 8, 2010, Red Cross Town Council meeting

illness. The Mayor stated that the two VISA debit cards in the drawing were won by Harold Little and Blane Tucker. The mayor said the presentation was very good but the attendance wasn't well attended. The residents need to be involved when we have meetings of this importance."[116]

2. Announced to Council that the County had agreed (signed off) to handle our subdivision permitting. In lieu of a fee the County would retain any revenues received from permits.

3. "Council member Smith brought up the discussion of Jet Drive which had been tabled earlier. He said to prepare the 2/10 mile of road and add the cul de sac at the end of the street, add greave [gravel] and pave the street to meet the States approval would cost $80,000. He feels there are other issues in the Town that need priority over Jet Drive, one being the road into the Town Hall. With only a little over $14,000 in the Power [Powell] Bill Account, we need to wait several years for the account to accumulate before using it. The other members of the Council agreed with council member Smith. Therefore, the issue of Jet Drive was tabled to a much later date."[117]

Town Council Meeting/Public Hearing (November 2010):

1. A public hearing was scheduled to discuss some recommended changes to our zoning codes.

   I had asked our Zoning Enforcement Officer, Robbie Foxx, to review our zoning codes from the enforcement standpoint. As a result of his review there were a number of recommendations made for clarifying, streamlining, and reinforcing our ability to enforce our codes. In conjunction, the Planning Board had gone back and made the needed modifications. These modifications were being brought back to the Council for its vote. Changes were approved and voted acceptance.

[116] From the minutes of the April 12, 2010, Red Cross Town Council meeting
[117] From the minutes of the April 12, 2010, Red Cross Town Council meeting

Town Council Meeting/Public Hearing (December 2010):

1. "Mayor Quick called the Public Hearing meeting and welcomed everyone and had the invocation. He stated that the purpose of the public hearing is to discuss the Town of Red Cross Land Development Plan 2010-2030. Council member Brattain said the plan should answer any questions concerning land development. Mrs. Rhea stated that she has been working with the Planning Board for more than a year trying to plan every possible situation that may come before the Town. Council member Brattain and Planning Board member Dicky Hatley have worked faithfully with Mrs. Rhea and Mr. Darren [Rhodes] on this project."[118]

   Voted and approved in Council meeting.

Town Council Meeting (March 2011):

1. Voted to appropriate $2,097.88 for the purchase and installation of two signs "Welcome to Red Cross" at the east and west end of the town on Highway 24/27. Motion by Council Member Brattain and seconded by Council Member Hahn, approved by vote.

Town Council Meeting (May 2011):

1. "Motion made to approve purchase of 350-recycle carts for the mandatory recycle program. Ray Quick will write the grant request."

   This was to purchase the 96-gal carts at $55.75 each with required RFID tags at $1.50 each. Shipping will be $530.00. There will be a single flat fee of $300.00 to put the town's name on the carts.

Town Council Meeting (June 2011):

1. Town Clerk Bobbie Kay Thompson resigned/retired.

2. Voted to accept the DENR (Department of Environmental and

[118] From the minutes of the December 13, 2010, Red Cross Town Council meeting

Natural Resources) grant to help finance the purchase of recycle carts. Contract approvals will occur in the July Council meeting.

Town Council Meeting (July 2011):

1. Council voted to install Ms. Aloma Whitley as the new Town Clerk to fill the vacancy created by the retiring of Mrs. Bobbie Kay Thompson.

   When the present Town Clerk, Bobby Kay Thompson, announced that she was going to retire from the Town Clerk position we, the Town Council, started looking around for someone to fill the position. I was talking with my sister one night and she said that Aloma Whitley had just retired and would probably be an excellent person for the job.

   I talked with the Council and everyone agreed she would be an excellent person to fill the position. I then called Ms. Whitley and presented the idea to her. She said she was interested but wanted a couple days to think about it. Within a couple days she accepted the position.

2. Council approved $185 cost for a training session for new Town Clerk.

3. Received notification that our grant request for recycle carts had been approved. Vote to accept the grant passed.

4. Voted approval for contract with consultant for executive summary of land development plan.

   The executive summary is a condensed overview of the land-use plan, which is generally presented to the public. If a developer or business is interested in coming to Red Cross, one of the primary things they look at is the executive summary of the land-use plan. It will give them a good idea of the town's future direction and potential as relates to business/development.

Town Council Meeting (September 2011):

1. Held public hearing - "Mr. Ruben Crummey from DOT gave presentation with various maps and information on this "long-range (20-30 year)" plan. NC 24-27 is a Strategic Highway Corridor (SHC) and is designated as an expressway. Additional improvements are needed to upgrade to expressway standards from the Cabarrus County line eastward, which included access control measures and the removal of traffic signals."[119]

   There was a great deal of concern over this since it would eliminate stoplights and restrict access to Highway 24/27. An expressway is much like an interstate; it has limited access and requires overpasses and access roads. In our case we will see that the only proposed access within Red Cross, for accessing Highway 24/27, would be a half-cloverleaf overpass installed at the intersection of Highway 205/Highway 24/27.

   Based on our understanding of DOT's proposal it would have a tremendous adverse impact on all our plans: zoning codes, vision plan, growth plan, and land-use plan. It would also negatively impact property values and, in all probability, eventually lead to the loss of a number of homes within our community.

2. Workshop scheduled for Tuesday, September 13, so that Council members could discuss upcoming CTP hearing in Locust.

Town Council Public Hearing (September 2011):

A public hearing was held on September 26, 2011, concerning the reclassification of Highway 24/27 to that of an "expressway". (See Chapter "Making Highway 24/27 and Expressway" for full details.

From the minutes of the September 26, 2011, public hearing:

[119] From the September, 2011, Red Cross Town Council minutes

"Dana Stoogenke, Rocky River Rural Planning Organization had requested a public hearing for the Town of Red Cross, regarding North Carolina Department of Transportation Comprehensive Transportation Plan.

Mr. Ruben Crummey from the DOT office gave a presentation with various maps and information on this "long-rang (20-30 year)" plan. NC 24/27 is a Strategic Highway Corridor (SHC) and is designated as an expressway. Additional improvements are needed to upgrade to an expressway standards from the Cabarrus County line eastward, which include access control measures and the removal of traffic signals.

Andrew Galloway commented on what effects there would be to get rid of all stop lights.

Doris Brunette commented of the negative effect lack of access would have on the present and future businesses that may consider coming to the town.

Thelma Burris asked if the state would be taking any land and would make an offer for purchase.

Andrew Galloway asked if the town approved the CTP, would there be an opportunity to "re-visit" the plan at a future time.

Lou Eubanks asked if and when the town can look into pedestrian and/or bike plan. Dana Stoogenke told her the RPO could assist with that.

The general concern of the public and council at the meeting was questions of driveway and curb-cut access which would be either limited or not allowed, possibly replaced by service roads.

Council agreed to schedule a workshop for Monday, October 3 at 6:00 PM to further discuss the CTP to prepare for a vote at the October 10 town council meeting."

Town Council Meeting (October 2011):

1. The Town of Red Cross received a presentation from Raleigh DOT (Jamal Alavi and Ruben Crummey) with a request that the Town adopt a resolution endorsing Highway 24/27 being designated an "expressway". Motion made by Council Member Larry Wayne Smith and seconded by Council Member Jerry Jordan to reject the CTP plan. Plan rejected. (Please see the chapter on "Making Highway 24/27 an Expressway")

2. Received notification that the town would begin receiving Powell Bill Funds through June 20, 2012.

THE FIFTH ELECTION (2012-2013)

Town Council Meeting (December 2011) - First setting of newly elected 2012/2013 Council:

1. Elected officials

Mayor	Larry Wayne Smith
Council Member	Kelly Brattain
Council Member	Barbara Carpenter
Council Member	Heath Hahn
Council Member	Jerry Jordan
Town Clerk	Aloma Whitley

2. Assigned officers:

Clerk of Board	Aloma Whitley
Finance	Heath Hahn
Fire Protection	Jerry Jordan
Police Protection	Barbara Carpenter
Street Maintenance	Barbara Carpenter
Utilities	Heath Hahn
Waste Collection	Jerry Jordan
Zoning	Kelly Brattain

This was a short session of the newly elected Town Council that occurred immediately after the December session of the outgoing Council closed.

3. Newly elected Council Members took oath of office.

4. Council affirmation of contracts, establishment of fixed date and time of meetings, appointment of mayor pro-tempore, etc.

5. Council members assigned areas of responsibility.

Town Council Meeting (January 2012):

1. Funds requested and approved for getting website back online. Expected to cost between $250 and $500 with a hosting fee of $120 per year.

   With respect to getting the website back online: I was working on the website during the time of the 2011 elections and after the results of the election I never went back to it. I was not aware it had been corrupted and did not check the site again until I saw this comment on the agenda. I did offer to go back and repair the website but was told that the Town was going to go in another direction.

   I later found a possible explanation for this happening. In looking at Microsoft's update page I found the following:

   > "**Update for Windows 7 for x64-based Systems (KB2893519)**
   > Files or folders are removed unexpectedly when you perform a cut-and-paste operation on a Windows FTP client that is connected to an FTP site"[120]

   Since files are usually transferred to servers using FTP, and I did use FTP, this may be a possible cause? However, I think I did a copy command but really don't know what happened. This was the only related explanation I could find.

2. "Mayor Smith requested the council to consider (1) increasing the town clerk salary $200 per month because of the number of hours spent at town hall weekly; (2) an allowance of $.50 per mile for trips made for town business by the town clerk; and (3) change the title of office from Town Clerk to Town Administrator. Motion #746 was

---

[120] http://support.microsoft.com/kb/KbView/2891804

made by Jerry Jordan, seconded by Barbara Carpenter, voted and approved with no opposition for the three changes.

3. Dicky Hatley, chairman of the Planning Board stated that the final project for the Land Development Plan will now begin and requested the Council's approval of the contract with Carol Rhea for $5,000 for her services. She and Darren Rhodes from the Department of Community Assistance will present at a special meeting of the Planning Board scheduled for January 26, 2012 at Town Hall. Motion #747 was made by Jerry Jordan, seconded by Barbara Carpenter, voted and approved with no opposition to accept the contract with Ms. Rhea for the final project."

4. Comments from citizens: Lou Eubanks asked if someone who lived along the town's limits but was not a citizen could possibly pay a fee to get a recycle cart. Jerry Jordan said he would talk with Doug Barnette, Waste Management, about the possibility."[121]

   Council Member Jordan, at a later meeting, said this was not possible.

5. Heath Hahn submitted his resignation as a Council Member effective the close of the current meeting.

Town Council Meeting (February 2012):

1. "Mayor Smith presented Dicky Hatley to the council to fill the vacant council seat. Motion #752 was made, seconded and approved with no opposition."

2. Re-appointment of Department Positions

Finance and Budget:	Jerry Jordan
Fire Protection:	Kelly Brattain
Police Protection:	Barbara Carpenter
Street Maintenance:	Barbara Carpenter

[121] From the January 2012, Red Cross Town Council minutes

Waste Collection:	Kelly Brattain
Zoning:	Dicky Hatley

Town Council Meeting (May 2012):

1. "Mayor Larry Wayne Smith presented an estimate of approximately $1,619.99 from Southern States to spread 2-1/2 tons of Triple 17 fertilizer on the pasture areas. After brief discussion and agreement of the need, Motion #820 was made by Dicky Hatley, seconded by Kelly Brattain. Council members voted all in favor with no opposition."[122]

2. "Bids were received for the paving of the 50' entrance which was required by NC-DOT. C. K. Earnhardt & Son, Inc. presented the lowest bid. Motion #765 was made by Jerry Jordan, Seconded by Barbara Carpenter and voted by council all in favor with no opposing vote to accept the bid from C. K. Earnhardt & Son, Inc.

   [Although not reflected in the minutes it was reported that the total cost of paving the drive was $45,453.34, which was fully funded from the Powell Bill Fund.]

3. A bid was presented to the council from "Bulldog" Kluttz for bushogging the former pasture acres of $16.00 per acre for 25 acres ($400.00 per mow) three to four times a year. Motion #766 was made by Dicky Hatley, seconded by Jerry Jordan and voted by council to approve the bid with no opposing votes."[123]

Town Council Public Hearing/Meeting (June 2012):

1. Public hearing called for final reading of budget. Brought back into regular session and approved.

2. Council discussed and agreed on the use of the remaining Powell Bill funds for the asphalt paving expenses and the survey certification expenses.

[122] From the May 2012, Red Cross Town Council minutes

[123] From the minutes of the May 14, 2012, Red Cross Town Council meeting

Town Council Meeting (July 2012):

1. "Motion #781 was made by Dicky Hatley, seconded by Barbara Carpenter to pay off the debt with BB&T for the purchase of the Town Hall property. Council members vote all in favor with no opposition."[124]

2. "Council discussed a proposal for a 10-Year Anniversary Day of the Citizens of Red Cross. Motion #778 was made by Kelly Brattain, seconded by Dicky Hatley. Council members voted all in favor with no opposition. The date was set as August 4 from 5pm to 7pm. An amount of $1,200.00 was appropriated for the expenses of the event.

Town Council Meeting (August 2012):

1. Council Voted to pay one-fourth the cost of installing a fire hydrant on Hatley Burris Road.

Town Council Public Hearing/Meeting (September 2012):

1. Public hearing called for Comprehensive Transportation Plan for the Town of Red Cross and then voted to accept in regular session.

2. Voted to start charging people $0.25 per page for copies of agendas and minutes.

Town Council Meeting (October 2012):

1. Council Member Dicky Hatley proposed to council to have the current Planning and Zoning Board also serve as the Board of Adjustment for the Town of Red Cross. Motion #798 was made by Dicky Hatley, seconded by Kelly Brattain and voted in favor by council with no opposition."[125]

---

[124] From the minutes of the July 2012, Red Cross Town Council meeting

[125] From the minutes of the October 2012, Red Cross Town Council meeting

2. Comments from council - Mayor Smith told council that the District Manager/Lead Executive, Angela H Curtis, of the United States Postal Service denied the request for the Town of Red Cross to have its own ZIP CODE. However, the letter received states that "You will be allowed to use Red Cross, NC 28129 as an authorized last line address."[126]

Town Council Meeting (November 2012):

1. "Dana Stoogenke spoke regarding a resolution authorizing the Rocky River RPO's application to NC-DOT's Strategic Highway Corridor modification process to change the designation of Highway 24/27 "boulevard" as opposed to "expressway". After discussion of the matter presented Mrs. Stoogenke, Council voted in favor of the resolution to authorize Rocky River RPO application by Motion #804 which was made by Dicky Hatley and seconded by Kelly Brattain."[127]

Town Council Called Meeting (December 21, 2012):

1. "The purpose of the called "Special Meeting" was to discuss and vote on the new Comprehensive Transportation Plan before the end of the year 2012.

   After discussion by council, Motion #806 was made by Dicky Hatley, seconded by Jerry Jordan, and voted all in favor with n128 opposition to accepting the new comprehensive Transportation plan.[9]

Town Council Meeting (March 2013):

1. Council brought the final draft of the Town of Red Cross Transportation Plan for vote.

2. "Mayor Larry Wayne Smith presented an estimate of approximately

---

[126] From the minutes of the October 2012, Red Cross Town Council meeting

[127] From the minutes of the November 2012 Red Cross Town Council meeting

[128] From the minutes of the December 21, 2012, Special Meeting of the Town Council

$1,619.99 from Southern States to spread 2-1/2 tons of Triple 17 fertilizer on the pasture areas. After brief discussion and agreement of the need, Motion #820 was made by Dicky Hatley, seconded by Kelly Brattain. Council members voted all in favor with no opposition."[129]

Town Council Meeting (May 2013):

1. Resolution passed to join with other municipalities for support of the Parks & Recreation Trust Fund.

Town Council Public Hearing/Meeting (June 2013):

1. Public hearing for the final reading of the budget, passed in regular session.

Town Council Meeting (August 2013):

1. "Kelly Brattain reported that he had sent the application for establishing an Urban Bow Season" to Raleigh and would present to the mayor to sign when returned."

2. Adopted a "Resolution Authorizing the Application and Enforcement of the Stanly County Animal Control Ordinance in the Town of Red Cross."[130]

3. Motion made and seconded to reappoint Lou Eubanks to the Stanly County Convention and Visitors Bureau Board of Directors.

4. "Dana Stoogenke, Rocky River Rural Planning Organization, and Darren Rhodes, NC Dept. of Commerce, Div. of Community Assistance, were present to present the final draft of the Red Cross Transportation to council to review, with open floor for questions, comments or discussion. Council will have a Public Hearing on

[129] From the minutes of the March 2013, Red Cross Town Council meeting

[130] From the minutes of the October 2013, Red Cross Town Council meeting

September 20, 2012, to present the Plan publically."[131]

Town Council Meeting (September 2013):

1. "Reuben Crummy, Accompanied by Jamal Alvavi, of the NC Department of Transportation, and Marc Morgan, Stanly County DOT office, gave a power point presentation "update" on the CTP Amendment to include the City of Locust and the Town of Red Cross. Maps included were volume and capacity maps for current and future projections; a draft highway map showing possible alternative routes for future highway projects; public transportation and rail map; and two maps on the Stanly County CTP Amendment.

Town Council Meeting (October 2013):

1. "Council discussed a resolution stating that the Town of Red Cross would like to submit its Transportation Plan for the STAR Planning Award through the Small Town and Rural Plannin g Division of the American Planning Association. Motion #868 was made by Dicky Hatley, seconded by Kelly Brattain to submit the resolution; council voted all in favor with no opposition."[132]

[131] From the minutes of the August 2013, Red Cross Town Council meeting
[132] From the minutes of the October 2013, Red Cross Town Council meeting

THE SIXTH ELECTION (2014-2015)

Town Council Meeting (January 2014):

1. "Council discussed the plans for erecting a flagpole in the front area of town hall. Mayor Smith presented quotes to council from two companies for a 35' pole with a 6' X 10' United States flag and a 5' X 8' North Carolina flag. Motion #882 was made by Dicky Hatley, seconded by Barbara Carpenter to accept the quote from Condor Flag Company of Charlotte, NC at a cost of $3,801.63."[133]

Town Council Meeting (March 2014):

1. "An estimate was submitted to install the flag pole light. LED lights for the front of the building and a ditch for the wiring. Motion #892 was made by Jerry Jordan, seconded by Kelly Brattain, to accept the estimate of Wayne Brooks Electric for the work to be done. Council voted in favor with no opposition.

   [Although not reflected in the minutes, lighting was added at a cost of $825.00.]

2. An estimate was submitted for the removal of large tree stumps, removal of the large dead tree behind the parking lot, add an additional pipe at the driveway and spread a load of dirt over exposed rocks near the barn. Motion #893 was made by Kelly Brattain, second by Jerry Jordan, to accept the estimate of Ted A. Coble &

[133] From the minutes of the January 13, 2014, Red Cross Town Council meeting

Sons Grading Inc., for the tree and stump work, pipe instillation, and dirt over exposed rocks. Council voted in favor with noopposition." [134]

Town Council Meeting (April 2014):

1. Council appointed J. J. Curlee to the council.

Town Council Meeting (June 2014):

1. Budget approved by vote.

2. "Council discussed the Dear Urban Archery Season and voted to accept by Motion #911 made by Kelly Brattain, seconded by Barbara Carpenter. Council voted all in favor with no opposition."[135]

3. "Council discussed the size and color of the granite for the insert for the proposed new sign for the town and agreed on 4' by 8' black granite with frost lettering. After reviewing the quote from Locust Monument Plant for approximately $7,555.00 plus tax for this size of granite, Motion #916 was made by Jerry Jordan, seconded by Kelly Brattain, to allocate $15,000 total for the new sign for the town (this including the masonry quote of $6,000-$6,500 previously approved by council). Council voted all in favor with no opposition."[136]

Town Council Meeting (December 2014):

1. "Mayor Smith presented to the council a quote from Wayne Brooks Electric for the work to install lighting at the town's new masonry sign. Motion #942 was made by J. J. Curlee, second by Jerry Jordan to accept the quote for the lighting work; members voted all in favor with no opposition."[137]

   Although not reflected in the minutes, lighting was added at a cost of $2,900.00.

[134] From the minutes of the March 10, 2014, Red Cross Town Council meeting

[135] From the minutes of the June 9, 2014, Red Cross Town Council meeting

[136] From the minutes of the June 9, 2014, Red Cross Town Council meeting

[137] Form the minutes of the December 8, 2014, Red Cross Town Council meeting

Town Council Meeting (February 2015):

1. "Mayor Smith presented a citizen, Melvin Poole, who requested to address council on the current matters presented to the citizens of the county by the School Board regarding the closing of Norwood, Oakboro and East Albemarle schools, as printed in the Stanly News and Press on January 24, 2015. He commented on the hundreds of citizens attended the Board of Education meeting on February 3 to oppose the consolidation and redistricting, citing overcrowding and reassignment of so many students unacceptable. Mr. Poole stated that the Board of Education has not received transportation data related to the additional bussing of students, which could have a critical impact.

2. The letter of "Approval Pending Adoption" has been received from the U. S. Department of Homeland Security (FEMA) for the Cabarrus Stanly Union Regional Hazard Mitigation Plan. Representatives from each City/Town served on the Hazard Mitigation Task Force t identify the needs of all areas covered by the regional plan. All municipalities who represent this Regional Plan must adopt by Resolution in order to secure final approval from FEMA.

   Motion #956 was made by Kelly Brattain, seconded by Barbara Carpenter to approve the Resolution to adopt the Cabarrus Stanly Union regional Hazard Mitigation Plan. Council members voted all in favor with no opposition."

   There were no citizen comments.

3. Council Member Barbara Carpenter thanked Melvin Poole for his comments on the current matters impacting the county's schools.

4. "Council Member Jerry Jordan thanked Mayor Smith and his grandson, Andrew, for the work of removing and cleaning the old fence line along the highway, commenting on what an attractive impact it has made as motorist approach the new town sign from the

westerly direction."[138]

Town Council Meeting (May 2015):

1. Dana Stoogenke, RPO and Reuben Crummy, NC DOT office, updated council on current recommendations for each mode of transportation in the 2015 Stanly County CTP Amendment to include Locust and Red Cross. The CTP is based on projected growth for the planning areas. The modes of transportation includes Public Transportation, Pedestrian, Highway, and Bicycle, maps of each presented. Public meetings will be held probably in July and August in preparation for Adoption of the CTP plan. Mark Morgan of the Stanly County DOT office was present to provide additional information of affected areas, as he is logically more familiar with the roadways.

2. Landscaping expenses approved for new town sign.

3. Terms of office set for Board of Adjustment members.

Town Council Public Hearing/Meeting (June 2015):

1. Public hearing called for final reading of budget. Brought back into regular session and approved.

2. "Councilmember Barbara Carpenter stated the council needs to look into purchasing a lawn more for the purpose of keeping the walking trail mowed. Another suggestion by councilmember Jerry Jordan was to get a quote from Shaver's Lawn Service as they were already mowing the lawn of the town, to see what the increase would be for the walking trail. On another note, Mayor Smith mentioned that he had heard of possibly contracting with the state for the mowing around the ponds, using the extending arm of the tractor mowers the state uses, making the field area "much more attractive. All these suggestions to be reported on at the next or a later meeting."[139]

---

[138] From the minutes of the February 9, 2015, Red Cross Town Council meeting

[139] From the mintues of the June 8, 2015, Red Cross Town Council meeting

According to the "Weekly Post" the purchase of a tractor was approved in the July Town Council meeting at a cost of $14,300.

PLANNING & ZONING

The Zoning Committee:

The following are the people that have served on the Red Cross Planning Board through 2011:

2003
Barbara Carpenter
Lou Eubanks
Blane Hathcock
Marion Hubbard
Jerry Jordan

2004
C. J. Barbee
Ray Burleson
Lou Eubanks
Marion Hubbard
J. D. Hinson
Jerry Jordan
Carolyn Morton
Tom Staples

2005
Ray Burelson
Lou Eubanks
J. D. Hinson
Lou Eubanks
Carolyn Morton

2006
C. J. Barbee
Richard Baucom
Ray Burleson
Lou Eubanks
J. D. Hinson
Marion Hubbard
Jerry Jordan
Carolyn Morton
Tom Staples

2007
Richard Baucom
Kelly Brattain
Roger Haigler
Dickie Hatley
Marion Hubbard
Tom Staples

2008
Richard Baucom
Kelly Brattain
Lou Eubanks
Roger Haigler
Marion Hubbard
Tom Staples

2009	2010	2011
Richard Baucom	Richard Baucom	Richard Baucom
Lou Eubanks	Roger Haigler	Lou Eubanks
Roger Haigler	Dickie Hatley	Roger Haigler
Dickie Hatley	Marion Hubbard	Dickie Hatley
Marion Hubbard	Barbara Huneycutt	Barbara Huneycutt
Barbara Huneycutt	Rodney Plowman	Rodney Plowman
Tom Staples	Mark Tucker	Mark Tucker

Red Cross Takes Responsibility for Zoning:

In the first meeting of the Red Cross Town Council, the Council set up a public hearing for the transfer of ownership of zoning from the County to the Town. At the second meeting of the Town Council, after the public hearing, acceptance of ownership was voted and with all properties retaining the zoning that they had been assigned while under the jurisdiction of the County.

It should be noted that Michael Sandy, Director of Stanly County Planning & Zoning, did modify and adapt the County's zoning codes into a usable form for our town prior to our adoption. We owe him a debt of gratitude for this work.

We, the Interim Council, knew that Red Cross had to make changes to the zoning codes that we had inherited from the County. The dilemma was that we didn't know how to redesign, or convert, the County's zoning codes to codes that would serve our specific needs. Surprisingly, at this early stage we didn't even know what we wanted, other than we knew that the people had told us during the incorporation process that they wanted their lifestyle protected.

Figuring out how to get started was a problem. As the Interim Town Council we had to obtain more information. We set up a joint workshop with the Locust City Council for a get-acquainted meeting and to try and obtain information on how to get started forming our zoning codes. The results of that meeting were great. Locust offered us a lot of good advice and graciously offered to let us have a copy of their newly updated zoning codes to work from. They had just spent $18,000 to have theirs updated. Even Oakboro was extending an offertory hand.

In April 2003, the Town Council established a Zoning Committee for the Town of Red Cross. Appointed and sworn into that Board were Ray Von Burleson, Barbara Carpenter, Lou Eubanks, Blane Hathcock, Jerry Jordan, and Tom Staples.

It should be noted, for clarity, the Zoning Committee went through two additional name changes:

April 2003	The Zoning Committee commissioned.
January 2004	The Zoning Committee was renamed the Zoning Board.
June 2004	The Zoning Board was renamed the Planning Board.

It is doubtful anyone realized just how extensive and daunting the creation of our zoning codes would be. Our Planning Board spent its first twenty months trying to get established and organized. After the reorganization of the Planning Board in June 2004, Carolyn Morton took over as Chairman and the Board started moving forward. In December 2004 Carol Rhea, of Rhea Consulting, was officially brought on board to help them design zoning codes for the town. They went on to complete the following:

1. Zoning codes
2. Vision plan
3. Growth plan
4. Land-use plan
5. Transportation plan

It wasn't until 2012, with the completion of the Comprehensive Transportation Plan, that the Planning Board had all the above codes and plans in place. The time and labor requirements were extensive and the results these people achieved were outstanding.

All of Red Cross's codes were designed by the town's Planning Board; people from within the Red Cross community, under the guidance of competent a consultant. These people volunteered to serve on the Planning Board. They did not receive any money for their work and few received any recognition for their accomplishments. These were the people that defined our town and our future. They set the path for our future generations to follow. Anyone would be hard pressed to find another town that has zoning codes and plans as comprehensive and as closely tailored to their town's needs as those created by our Planning Board for our town.

I wish I could go into the same level of detail with the Planning Board as I did with the Town Council but I don't have that information. I did request information from the town but, unfortunately, the minutes of the Planning Board's meetings were just too cryptic, there just wasn't enough structured and usable documentation to allow me to put it to paper. I truly regret this because these people invested a tremendous amount of time and effort in developing our codes. They really deserve to be recognized for their work.

What is Zoning:

The simplistic answer is that it is the dividing land up within the town into zones and setting rules (by ordinance) on how land in each zone may be used. It allows a town to establish zones for business, residential, industrial, etc. so that each will not impinge on the other.

Under the law a town has the right to set standards of use for land within its corporate limits. If anyone questions the authority of a town to enact and enforce zoning codes then they must know a little history about land use regulations. It has been argued that the Fifth Amendment of the Constitution of the United States provides the individual protection from zoning using the section "nor be deprived of life, liberty, or property, without due process of law; nor shall private property be taken for public use, without just compensation." However, in 1926, the Supreme Court ruled that a town's right to establish and enforce zoning does not violate the Fifth Amendment.

Today, people accept this practice as a needed and valued tool for both creating organized growth and for the protection of the people from undesired use of adjacent properties.

For the individual there is an old saying about zoning: "zoning is good for everyone but me." Yes, zoning does restrict the unlimited right of the individual to do with their property as they wish; however, just as it protects the individual from their neighbors, it also protects the neighbors from the individual. Basically, it protects everyone from everyone else.

Proper zoning for a town consist of five basic parts, or needs: zoning codes, vision plan, growth plan, land-use plan and transportation plan. It should be noted that many towns combine their growth and land-use plans into a single plan. Each serves important functions in insuring the future health of the town and in the protection of its residents. The creation of these gives the town a comprehensive plan for its future development.

When we talk about zoning we usually think of allowed use. However, there is much more to proper planning for a town. A town must have some vision of how it wants to develop and of what it wants to become. It must have some plan to organize and separate dissimilar types of growth and it must have some plan for how land within its corporate limit is used.

It should be noted that, of the five parts, only the zoning codes are enforceable. However, the desires derived from the other four parts do influence the continued evolution of the zoning codes.

Zoning Codes:

As previously stated, it is the dividing up the town into land-use zones and setting rules (by ordinance) on how each zone may be used. Zoning codes are very extensive and specific and are enforceable by the town. The town's Planning Board and Town Council establishes guidelines, in the form of zoning ordinances, which protect all adjacent property owners, as well as the town's ability to manage organized growth.

With these codes a town can set standards for building construction, land-use, street connections, sewer extensions, signage, etc., even to the point of setting standards for something as esoteric as light trespass.

For example, Stanly County is fairly rocky and requires sewer line casings that are stronger, more resistant to cracking and puncture, than the standards set by the State of North Carolina. If a town, as in our case, does not have a more stringent standard built into its zoning codes then developers may only build to State standards. This would inevitably result in increased sewer maintenance cost. It is to the town's advantage to specify sewage requirements in its zoning codes

Some people may wonder why a town would want to set standards for light trespass. Consider a business that wants to light its parking lot. Rather than installing light poles that shine downward it decides to install more economical lights on the side of its building that shine outward into the parking lot. Depending on the intensity and focus of these lights, they may be able to shine with intensity for a half-mile or more. What if there was a housing development just a couple hundred yards from the business and they light up the houses as if it were daylight? Would the homeowners object to the bright lights? It is to the homeowner's advantage for the town's zoning codes to specify light trespass limits.

What if a developer has created a housing development in which no home is valued less than $500,000 and each home is on one acre of land. What if someone decides to buy two lots within that development and put in rental trailers, each of which may be able to hold multiple units? Do the property owners of the adjacent homes want some assurance that this will not happen in their development? It is to the homeowner's advantage for the town's zoning codes to specify types of use for the adjacent properties.

Or how about this one: what if someone wanted to put a farrowing house (raising hogs) on their property line directly adjacent to a housing development. Does the owner have the right to build the farrowing house, just a foot inside his property line, next to people's homes? It is to the homeowner's advantage for the zoning codes to specify setbacks from property lines.

Through the use of zoning, standards of use are established, as with the farrowing house where buildings must have setbacks, or buffers between properties boundaries, allowing for some protection between dissimilarly zoned properties. Basically, the purchasing homeowner can look at a town's zoning and have some assurance of how their property and adjacent properties can be used prior to purchasing their home.

For businesses the needs are just as great. Brick-and-mortar businesses have to have exposure so that people will see them and feel welcomed into their store. Businesses need an atmosphere conducive to their type of business. They also need transportation patterns that will allow easy access.

What about an owner who has invested heavily in his restaurant? He has a very nice brick building with an elaborate store front and a paved and well-landscaped parking lot with excellent lighting. Then an adjacent property owner decides to use his property for a junk yard. He installs a metal building near the entrance to his property with little setback so that the view of the restaurant is blocked. He does not fence in his inventory of cars, does not control weed growth and does not pave the front or provide street lighting. How will this affect the restaurant owner? Zoning works to prevent conflicts between dissimilar businesses.

Some businesses that frequently generate controversy are shooting ranges, bars, liquor stores, and adult entertainment. A town has the right to either allow or not allow shooting ranges, bars and/or liquor stores. All the aforementioned uses may be built into the zoning codes; however, a referendum is required before a town can allow alcohol to be sold within the town limits. Somewhat surprising, a town cannot completely ban adult entertainment. In North Carolina a town must, by State law, have at least one zoned area within its corporate limits where adult entertainment is allowed. What if someone wanted to open a bar, shooting range or adult establishment directly adjacent to a school, daycare or church? What would be the community's reaction?

I remember one such controversy occurring in Raleigh some years ago. I was doing some work there and had an apartment off Spring Forest Road in an area where there were a large number of apartments. It seemed someone wanted to build a topless/bottomless club in that area. Although the area was zoned to allow for that type of establishment, the people raised a great challenge and it became a major local political issue. My understanding is that the only thing that stopped construction was zoning. Raleigh's zoning required that an adult entertainment establishment must be located at least 1,000-feet from either a school or church. It turned out that the nearest edge of the proposed property was about 950-feet from nearest edge of an elementary school. As a result the developer was not allowed a building permit. This is a case where zoning protected the wishes of the people of that area. I don't know if it was done, but this was also a case where the people needed to follow through and petition the Raleigh City Administration to change their zoning so that they would not again be faced with the problem. The people only won their case by about 50-feet.

In any town the people have a responsibility to themselves, their families and their neighbors to understand the zoning that governs the use of their, and adjacent, property. If they don't stay informed then they may well become victims of undesirable zoning changes and allowed uses.

For towns, zoning offers a method of obtaining organized and harmonic growth. One of the major, and not often recognized, problems with inadequate zoning is control of traffic flow. If too many high volume businesses or high density housing developments are clustered together then it creates potential bottlenecks (traffic flow problems) that the town may not be able handle. It may well stress the town's ability to absorb and finance the requirements of supporting these businesses and developments.

An example of this that was dealt with during the creation of the Red Cross zoning codes was traffic flow between different housing developments. What if two developers were to build adjacent subdivisions independent of each other with each having only one entrance to main highway and no other way in or out of the subdivisions, would this not lead to traffic congestion. Red Cross's zoning codes requires that the developer's street system must allow street connections between adjacent developments so that traffic must be able to pass between developments without having to access the main highway.

The above are some examples of why zoning is necessary for both the people and the town. Each of the above examples can very well happen without proper zoning.

Again, zoning is good and necessary for everyone: the people, the town, and the businesses in the town.

Vision Plan:

A vision plan is just that, it is a vision, or hope of what the town will become. It includes all aspects, aesthetics, patterns of growth, perceptions of appearance, safety, functional use and perceived desirability by residents and potential residents. Basically, it is not only the hope of what the town will become but of how it will mature and be perceived by others. It can well be considered to be the master plan from which all other plans are derived.

A town's vision plan is not enforceable, it is only a stated desire by the town's administration that has been put to paper and agreed upon. The town council does vote on its acceptance/adoption, however, that vote is only in the form of a resolution, which is a statement of position and intent. As such, there are no binding requirements that any adopted vision plan must be followed.

As stated, the vision plan projects the town's needs and desires well into the future, possibly as much as 50-years. However, most town's base their plans on 20-year windows. As a result all other plans are affected by the vision plan in that they must be created and/or adjusted so that the town develops along that vision; even the zoning codes should reflect the values of the vision plan.

Surprisingly, over the long term a town's vision plan is considered to be fluid, in that it is constantly evolving. This evolutionary process is a very precarious balance of retaining those present desirable qualities against the need for making adjustments for the acceptance of future changes and needs as time progresses.

A town's Planning Board creates the vision plan and submits that plan to its town council for their approval. The Town Council usually votes acceptance of that plan, however, as previously stated, the vote of acceptance is in the form of a resolution and not that of an ordinance.

Just because a town has adopted a vision plan does not mean that the town's administration has to follow that plan. With each election the composition of council members will change, as well as their views, desires and beliefs on how the town should be ran and in which direction it should go. Like the town council, Planning Boards rotate old members off and new members on. These new people will often have a different perspective than the old members and may want changes made.

Growth Plan/Land-use Plan:

Although the Town of Red Cross created separate growth and land-use plans, many towns combine these into a single plan.

The primary reason for Red Cross's delineation between these two plans is because: (1) we recognized that that we basically had a clean slate from which to work and would be able to design our codes in greater detail than would have been possible had we been a more highly developed community and (2) we had the specific objective, or mandate, given by our people to protect the lifestyle we were currently enjoying and wanted to build as much safety into our plans as possible.

These two plans define the shape of the town, the location and separation of various businesses and residential properties, how developments will be shaped, the degree and amount of open space, etc.

Based on the town's vision, the growth plan literally defines the desired layout of the town as it grows. Think of the grooming of a banzai tree, the limbs are trimmed and shaped to allow the tree to grow into a unique design and desired appearance that eventually becomes aesthetically pleasing to look at. It is the same with a town's growth/land-use plan. By the astute management of growth patterns the town's administration is able to manage growth so that the town is able to achieve the appearance, functionality, and basic desirability that the residents want. It also greatly enhances the town's ability to keep its future financial obligations within reasonable constraint.

Transportation Plan:

A town's transportation plan is not only a map of the town's present street layout but the town's vision of how it wants future streets to be laid out and of how traffic needs flow within the town. It allows town's administration to preplan and have some level of foreknowledge of the impact that any given growth will have on the town's traffic flow. As such, the transportation plan provides the tools necessary for analyzing, projecting, and managing not only present but potential traffic growth demands.

The transportation plan is a nonbinding resolution that has been voted on by the town council. Although it is nonbinding it is recognized by NCDOT. As such NCDOT takes the town's transportation plan into consideration during its decision making process when planning for highway changes within the sphere of that town's transportation plan.

Big-box stores such as Wal-Mart and Target, both of which are traditionally viewed as high volume businesses, often generate localized traffic congestion. Through proper transportation planning, towns are able to anticipate required traffic flow changes for acceptance of these businesses and effect the required changes to the town's traffic structure.

Proper transportation planning addresses issues such as this and also allows towns to plan out potential future problems. The weakness is that most small towns do not have the financial resources to build and/ or modify streets. Still, they can plan and make recommendations to NCDOT for State owned roads.

Having a viable transportation plan is integral to a town's future. Regardless of the town's ability to finance actual road construction, it allows the town to view its transportation needs on a micro scale often not considered by NCDOT and make recommendations based on realistic and viable needs.

The following is an article taken from "Carolina Planning Journal" that was written by Carol Rhea, Darren Rhodes and Dana Stoogenke. It was well written and brings out a lot of good points about what we are trying to achieve for our community.

"Transportation Planning in a Growing Community

Carol Rhea, Darren Rhodes, Dana Stoogenke

The Town of Red Cross - Past and Present

Red Cross was founded in the late 1700s and for nearly two hundred years life changed very little. Originally called "Red Crossing," the Town owes its name to the rich red dirt of the Piedmont and the crossroads of what would eventually become N.C. 24/27 and N.C. 205. N.C. 24/27 remained unpaved until 1925, and N.C. 205 was not paved until 1941.

Rolling farmland dotted by farmhouses dominated the landscape. A few small-scale farming-related businesses and industries served the area, and by the early 1900s, several small stores operated at the crossroads. Life and land use remained fairly constant until the latter part of the Twentieth Century.

In 1962 Stanly County constructed a new high school in Red Cross. Housing developments began popping up in the 1990s as growth from Charlotte made the area more attractive as a bedroom community. More small businesses were established in response to the residential growth and more commercial development, pushing out of Charlotte and Albemarle, began creeping closer to town along NC 24/27. The quiet farming community was suddenly faced with being overtaken by unplanned, uncharacteristic growth. In an attempt to control this growth, adjacent municipalities began annexing new lands, coming closer to Red Cross. Their expansions threatened the Town's very existence as a separate and distinct place.

Incorporation was the first step Red Cross took to address these threats. On August 1, 2002, the North Carolina General Assembly approved the Town Charter. Shortly after incorporation, the Town's land area nearly doubled in size as many petitioned the Town for annexation. Years prior to incorporation, older town residents used to gather at Bill Hill's store at the crossing to dream of becoming a town. None of these residents lived long enough to see the importance of vision and long term planning for the citizens of Red Cross. Residents Ike and Helen Williams lived in a home near the crossing that today serves as the Town Hall and the nucleus of a future Town Center.

NC 24/27 (Old Red Cross Road) in the early 1900s (top image) and today (bottom image).
Images courtesy of the authors

The Growth and Impacts of N.C. 24/27

The rudiments of N.C. 24/27 were in place in Red Cross for more than a century before that stretch of road was designated N.C. 27 as part of North Carolina's original 1922 state highway system. It took years and lots of effort to develop this highway system and for most of that time the clear focus was on moving intrastate traffic with little or no thought to road impacts on the communities the traversed.

In the years since its designation as N.C. 27, the road has experienced many changes. It was paved in 1925 and co-designated N.C. 24 in 1963. In the mid 2000s, the road again "improved" through the town when it was reengineered as a four lane divided highway. It became clear to residents and Town staff that as a central road in divided Red Cross. The crossroads that was the center of the community for more than 200 years was no longer suitable as a town center. In 2010, in its first Land Development Code, the Town was forced to locate its planned town center in the southeastern quadrant of the crossroads to allow for density and pedestrian mobility.

NCDOT Plans for 24/27

In 2011, Red Cross staff worked with North Carolina Department of Transportation (NCDOT) staff on a draft Comprehensive Transportation Plan (CTP) for Stanly County. A key element of their plan was a continuation of refining access and intersections along the highway. This included implementation of NCDOT's Strategic Highway Corridor's Expressway designation. The Expressway design minimizes points of conflict. But in the eyes of the community, further separated the north and south parts of the town. The mention of a potential, but highly unlikely, grade separation at the crossroads alarmed Red Cross leaders. One of the many potential designs discussed in the plan included a cloverleaf interchange that would, in essence, completely wipe out their planned town center. Red Cross declined to approve the draft CTP. Instead, they contacted Carol Rhea, AICP, a partner with the Orion Planning Group (OPG), and asked for her help. Rhea had provided ongoing assistance to the town since 2002, leading efforts on code updates and the creation of the Land Development Plan, a project she shared with Darren Rhodes, chief planner for the Piedmont Office of the NC Division of Community Assistance.

The Red Cross Transportation Master Plan

After discussions with town leaders, the various stakeholders decided to move forward with a town-adopted, policy-based transportation master plan. With the Town's full support, Rhea and Rhodes pulled in Dana Stoogenke, AICP, Director of the Rocky River RPO, to help round out the consulting team. This team of public and private consultants not only provided a wealth of experience and knowledge, it helped to reduce costs and to make the plan affordable for the town.

For a town that owns and maintains less than one lane mile of road and has no sidewalk or bicycle amenities, a transportation master plan might seem unnecessary. The plan for Red Cross, though, communicated what the transportation network needs to be, in order to support their long range land development vision including the town center. While NCDOT made great strides in working with communities to address transportation needs within the context of planned land use, in the absence of a clear local vision of what the network needs to be and who it needs to serve, their plans may be at odds with a community's vision, as they were in Red Cross.

Working in concert, the consultant team took turns facilitating meetings, arranging speakers, researching plan elements and answering town questions. The Town's recently adopted Land Development Plan and the project's three consultants provided most of the guidance and information needed for the Transportation Plan; Tim Boland with Region 10 office of NCDOT also attended a meeting to discuss NCDOT's Superstreet approach in greater detail as well as state plans for N.C. 24/27. The Stanly County Planning Director and the Town's Zoning Administrator attended meetings as well, more to observe than serve as speakers. Both were very involved in the creation of the Land Development Plan.

In 2013, the Town met once again with NCDOT and shared their Transportation Master Plan, triggering potential changes to the CTP in Red Cross. Dicky Hatley, town councilmember and former planning board chair, summed up the effect their new plan had at this meeting saying "The plan gives Red Cross a lot more credibility with NCDOT. With our current Zoning Ordinance, Land Use Plan and Transportation Master Plan, I think we can grow and be happy with what we see."

Keys to Success

Despite the fact they were from separate agencies, Rhea, Rhodes and Stoogenke worked as a team to provide support to the Planning Board on the draft plan and to help the Board present the draft plan to the public and the Town Council. Although OPG took the lead on writing and compiling the plan, this, too, was a collaborative effort that reflects the work of the whole team as well as the Town. Good communication was key to the effective partnership among the consultants and between the consultants and Red Cross. As evinced in Red Cross, effective partnerships require relationship building and good planning requires the development of trust and honest discussion. This cannot be achieved through email or text messages; it requires a commitment to be on the ground in the community working with community leaders and citizens. Other key strategies that made this plan a success were:

- Help the community focus on the positive. Ask what does the community want instead of what do they NOT want.

- Understand roles and relationships within the community and between the community and other agencies such as NCDOT.

- Understand the purpose of the plan and how it will be used. Keep that in mind when structuring the planning effort and compiling the final document - don't over- or under-plan and don't use a one-size-fits-all plan because they rarely do fit.

- When the budget is limited get creative. There are often solutions, such as a 3-way consulting partnership used in Red Cross that can leverage resources.

Perhaps the most important take away from this project is that even the smallest town can create a transportation plan as long as there are dedicated citizens with a vision and partners willing to collaborate."[139]

Managing Zoning:

Most towns have three primary departments for managing and controlling zoning. They are the Planning Board, the Board of Adjustment, and Zoning Enforcement. Although they all work to manage zoning within a town, they are independent of each other, with each having specific and very important functions. In our towns case both boards and the zoning officer report directly to the town council member in charge of zoning.

The Planning Board creates and manages the zoning codes, the Board of Adjustment handles exceptions, or non-conforming issues, and zoning enforcement insures compliance to existing zoning codes. The town's council handles oversight. This delineation of power insures equitable and fair application of zoning to the towns inhabitants.

Of the three, only the Board of Adjustment is a quasi-judicial board, their rulings are enforceable and are not subject to town council approval or override. Any decision made by them is final and may only be overturned in local superior court.

It is important to note that the people serving on each of these boards must be sworn in respective to the board on which they will serve. However, it is not uncommon for the same people to serve on more than one board, especially in small towns.

Planning Board:

The Planning Board designs, maintains, and updates the towns zoning codes and reports to the Red Cross Council Member in charge of zoning. It may seem a little odd that, since the Planning Board creates and manages the towns zoning codes, it has no power to implement or

---

[139] "Carolina Planning Journal", "Transportation Planning in a Growing Community", by Carol Rhea, Darren Rhodes, Dana Stoogenke, Volume 39, pp 46-48

enforce those codes. That power resides solely with the town's council - with the exception of those powers granted to the Board of Adjustment.

It is the responsibility of the Planning Board to serve as an advisor to the Town Council when any zoning change request is heard or zoning modification are needed. It is rare that any zoning changes are voted by the Town Council without first consulting with the town's Planning Board.

Prior to 2009 it was not required that rezoning request be reviewed by planning boards, however, beginning in 2009 the State starting requiring a planning board review of all proposed zoning changes prior to presentation to the town's council. It should be noted that if the planning board does not render its recommendations to the town's council within 30-days of submission then the town council may act without the advice of the planning board.

Within the Town of Red Cross the Planning Board has not only the responsibility of managing the town's zoning codes, but also manages the vision plan, growth plan, land-use plan and transportation plan.

Board of Adjustment:

The Board of Adjustment is designed to handle nonconforming issues related to zoning compliance and reports to the Red Cross Council Member in charge of zoning. It is a separate Board independent of the Planning Board and zoning enforcement and its members are sworn in the same manner as the Planning Board. This Board is a quasi-judicial board and its rulings are binding. Both the Town Council and the complainant must abide by its decision. However, either may choose to challenge the Board of Adjustment's decision in local superior court.

It hears cases that do not conform to the town's zoning codes. These cases may range from a request for a zoning exemption to a temporary allowance for a use that is not allowed by the zoning codes.

Examples are: a resident wanted to put a fence in their front yard where that area had been zoned to not allow fences in the front yard. They wanted to do this to keep an early-stage Alzheimer parent from wandering off. Based on the condition and need, the Board of Adjustment allowed this nonconforming use for the duration of the illness. However, the allowance of the fence was only for the duration of the illness and was required to be removed afterward.

A second example was where a person wanted to place a mobile home on their property until they could sell it. The property was not zoned to allow mobile homes and an exemption was allowed for a reasonable period of time. Unfortunately, the owner was unable to sell the mobile home and it had to be removed after a few months.

It is even possible for an incoming business to request an exemption from some section of the town's zoning codes. However, as a cautionary note, Boards of Adjustment must be careful of the exemptions extended to incoming businesses. Depending on the exemption requested, future incoming businesses may have the potential for using that exemption as precedence for being able to obtain an exemption from that zoning requirement.

Zoning Enforcement:

Although Zoning Enforcement is independent of both the Planning Board and the Board of Adjustment, it is responsible for the enforcement of the town's zoning codes. It also reports directly to the Red Cross Council Member in charge of zoning. Its function is to insure compliance to the town's zoning codes. The zoning enforcement officer inspects new construction, renovations, etc, for zoning compliance and handles zoning complaints.

Zoning Enforcement has the ability to issue nonconformances, disapprove work, or even to halt work on a project. The issuance of nonconformance's may eventually result in the property owner being levied a fine by the town.

It should be noted that the Town of Red Cross does not have a fulltime zoning enforcement officer but does contract with a very competent individual having expertise in this area.

BUSINESS RECRUITMENT

Did we try to grow the Town? Nearly all of us wanted some growth. During the time I served as Mayor there were several attempts to recruit businesses into the town. It should be noted that these people acted as individuals and not as representing the official position of the town.

- Bobbie Kay Thompson contacted one of Dollar General's VP's about putting a store in Red Cross. After evaluating the possibility Dollar General did build a store - the store has proven to be one of the top stores in its district.

- Heath Hahn had discussions with an entity about putting a funeral home in Red Cross. It was considered but the entity finally decided on another location. It is not know if this was just a passing discussion or a serious consideration.

- Heath Hahn had discussions with an equipment retailer about putting an equipment sales business in Red Cross. There was an interest on the retailer's part but it is not known why it fell through.

- J. D. Hinson had discussions with a doctor about putting an office in Red Cross. There was an interest but it is believed to have fallen through due to lack of property availability/location and infrastructure.

- Jerry Jordan had discussions with a doctor about relocating to Red Cross. No information is available as to why this fell through.

- Ray Quick pursued the potential of recruiting a manufacturer into Red Cross. The Town had only one plot of land suitable/desirable and potentially available but the property owner eventually decided on developing the property differently.

All the above were forms of "trying to grow the town". However, when looking at each one individually, were these people justified in trying to recruit these businesses?

- Dollar General was a niche store that was needed in our community to serve our residents.

- The funeral home was a business that would fit in with our vision since it was a service business.

- The equipment retailer could be argued either way. However, it should probably be considered a growth driven desire.

- The doctor's offices were services that would serve our residents and fit well into our vision plan.

- The manufacturer did not fit in with our vision and there were some qualms about pursuing it. However, the potential for offering a fairly large number of jobs to our community off-set those reservations. This is one instance where the people will have to judge.

From my perspective I envision Red Cross developing more as a professional and/or services community. Due to our location in western Stanly County we are well positioned as a central location with the communities of Locust, Oakboro, Ridgecrest, Frog Pond and Stanfield, all being within a five miles radius of us, and we are on a main traffic artery. If a doctor, lawyer, bank, or other professional service wants to appeal to all these surrounding areas then there is no better location to put an office than in Red Cross. It may take 20-years, but I have no doubt that Red Cross will eventually develop as the central hub for western Stanly County.

Probably, there are four main reasons as to why growth hasn't started yet: (1) the economy is as bad, or worse, than it has been since the Great Depression, (2) lack of sewer availability, (3) population density within the immediate area, and (4) the lack of people in Red Cross willing to sell their property.

Dollar General:

Dollar General may never have considered putting a store in our community had it not been for Town Clerk Bobbie Kay Thompson. She called and talked to one of their executives in the corporate office and told him of her desire to see one of their stores in our community. Unfortunately, she no longer remembers his name - just that he was a VP. Evidently Dollar General did their research and found Red Cross would be a good place to put a store.

People might wonder why our people were so interested in seeing a Dollar General come to Red Cross. Well, we're a small community and it meets a niche that can't be filled by a convenience store or a large retailer. It is convenient, carries a lot of items that we use on a daily basis, and does so, normally, at a low cost. Going and getting what we need on the spur of the moment is a lot easier than going to a grocery store or a Walmart.

Most people usually consider Dollar General's stores as being of a generic type, however, the one they built in our community quiet different. The store is unique, their property is well maintained and they have proven themselves to be a good neighbor.

In the fall of 2004 Dollar General chose a piece of property just east of Gaddis Road on Highway 24/27. That land belonged to Reggie Hill and Ronnie Williams. It consisted of about five acres with a good rectangular layout facing Highway 24/27. Dollar General ended up purchasing the eastern half of the tract.

During the early phases of the property purchase some problems came up. The Red Cross Planning Board was working on building codes and subdivision ordinances and their presentation to the town Council just happened to occur during the time that Dollar General was negotiating with the property owners on purchase of the property.

The Planning Board was requesting the Town Council place a moratorium on subdivision and commercial building design until they completed their work on these two. Since these new codes would preclude the use of non-architectural metal buildings, there was some fear that Dollar General may back out of the deal should they be required to build according to the newly proposed Town codes. This created some unusual discussions and actions during our October 18, 2004, Town Council meeting.

Because of the Planning Board's request for moratorium on subdivisions and new building construction, a public hearing was held on Monday night, October 18, 2004. During the public hearing there was a fairly lengthy discussion on both subdivision ordinances and building codes.

Dollar General had not yet purchased the property and would be affected if changes were made to either of these. They would be affected by the subdivision moratorium because they were buying only half of the property tract, and as a commercial subdivision, would be required to submit plans of use.

During the public hearing the property owner spoke on behalf of allowing Dollar General a variance and/or an exemption to the moratorium.[140] Basically, it appeared that they were lobbying for Dollar General to be able to build using their standard building specs (standard metal frame building with probable brick front) with their main concern being that if Dollar General was required to build a more expensive building then they wouldn't follow through on the land purchase. They noted that Dollar General had over 7,000 stores in the United States with the majority having a basic design. They requested we exempt Dollar General from the moratorium or, in their opinion;

[140] From the Audio of the October 2004 Red Cross Town Public Hearing (00:45:44)

Dollar General might back out of the deal.

Council Member Larry Wayne Smith also expressed concerns in favor of Dollar General's standard design and noted that Dollar General would bring in valuable tax revenue and jobs.

Note: If calculated out, the tax benefit to Red Cross would result in $1,040 per year based on the stated $650,000 investment by Dollar General.

It should be noted that during this same public hearing three of the six Planning Board members and two Council Members expressed concerns with current commercial building codes and cautioned that we should enact controls (design standards) before allowing anyone to build a commercial building in Red Cross.

We left the public hearing and entered into the regular Council Meeting. As soon as we got to the section about implementing a moratorium on commercial building Council Member Larry Wayne Smith immediately made a motion to enact the moratorium with Dollar General being exempted from the moratorium, which was immediately seconded by Council Member Chip Speight.[141/142] When I tried to interject that we had not allowed for discussion, a previous council member (from the audience) started shouting that we had a motion on the floor and couldn't have a discussion until that had been settled.[143] Typically discussions on a topic occur with any motion; however, it did not happen in this instance. Larry Wayne Smith, Chip Speight, and Barbara Carpenter voted in favor of exempting Dollar General from the moratorium. Heath Hahn, who visibly did not agree, didn't cast a vote. Since there are only four voting Council Members the vote carried. None of the rest of the Council, Planning Board, or the people of the community had an opportunity to say anything during this stage. A

---

[141] From the Minutes of the October 18, 2004, meeting of the Red Cross Town Council

[142] From Audio of the October 18 2005, Red Cross Town Council Meeting (00:28:50)

[143] From Audio of the October 18 2005, Red Cross Town Council Meeting (00:29:20)

moratorium was placed with Dollar General being exempted from the moratorium.

It was my belief that if we didn't enforce our codes with this first commercial building then we would have little ability to enforce them in the future - that we may set precedence, allowing future businesses to bypass our building codes. This appears to be a case where the Town Council was more concerned with immediate growth than with long-term planning and the wellbeing of the community.

Fortunately, Dollar General didn't apply for their permit until after we had approved the new codes.

In Dollar General's defense, to my knowledge Dollar General never tried to influence the town on any decision and acted appropriately and cooperatively in everything they did. I doubt they were even aware of our internal political plays. Every indication I received from Dollar General was that they were being very cooperative and would be a good addition to our community. All the problems that occurred had been as result of actions from within the Red Cross Town Council.

As it turned out, some Council Members didn't realize, in a later meeting when they voted and approved the finalized codes that the Planning Board had submitted, was that they locked Dollar General into having to meet our new design codes. These same individuals appeared surprised when they realized what the vote had resulted in.

Dollar General went on to build according to our design codes and ended up with a really nice building that everyone was pleased to have in the community. I have compared it to other similar stores and believe its frontal appearance, with white columns and porch, and landscaping gives the impression of having improved curb appeal. The interior is spacious and pleasant to walk through.

After they started operation I heard comments from people in the community about how attractive, roomy, clean, and inviting the new Dollar General was. Some of the comments from people implied that the Red Cross Dollar General was even pulling customers from both the

Locust and Oakboro stores for these very reasons. Based on conversations with the store manager it has proven to be one of the more profitable stores in its district.

It should be noted that during construction of the store, during the placement of the rafters, the building collapsed. A crane was placing preassembled sections of rafters (roof sections) on the store and one of them toppled over causing a domino effect on all the others. One person was seriously hurt but did recover. Emergency services did an excellent job of handling the situation. Highway 24/27 was blocked off and traffic was rerouted around the area. It also brought news media in from surrounding areas - including choppers from Charlotte news stations. It appeared that the store had to be rebuilt almost from scratch since it also pushed the walls out. Other than that one incident everything went well.

The following is the news article from the Weekly Post about the Public Hearing and Town Council Meeting:

Red Cross places Moratorium on growth with one exception

The Weekly Post
By Beth McLain
Staff Writer

The Town of Red Cross has placed a moratorium on growth in the area but council members may have already taken actions that will make any future decisions on planned growth in the town invalid.

Members of Red Cross' town council met last week and placed a 180-day moratorium on any new subdivisions or commercial buildings according to Mayor Ray Quick. However, the board made an exception to the moratorium that may come back to haunt them in future request from those wanting to build commercial buildings in the town.

After a lengthy discussion on subdivision ordinances, the 180-day moratorium was enacted with the exception of the request to subdivide property for the purpose of having a Dollar General Store located in the town.

Ronnie Williams and Reggie Hill will be allowed to subdivide property on N.C. Hwy. 24-27 new Gaddis Road that they plan to sell to Dollar General. Williams told council that Dollar General would probably not build in Red Cross if the company had to invest the extra money that would be required to meet a more stringent building code.

The property at the corner of Gaddis Road will be subdivided and the portion that will house the dollar General will be approximately two acres. The store will be built on the eastern portion of the property. The other portion of the Williams and Hill property is to the west of the land in question, at the corner of Gaddis Road and N.C. Hwy. 24-27.

Quick said three of the town's six planning board members did express concerns with the current commercial building codes during the meeting and cautioned the board that controls should be put in place before allowing anyone to build a commercial building in the town.

However, Councilman Larry Wayne Smith made a motion to exempt Dollar General from the Moratorium and Councilman Chip Speight seconded the motion. Smith, Speight and Councilwoman Barbara Carpenter voted in favor of exempting Dollar General from the Moratorium while councilman Heath Hahn didn't cast a vote. The mayor votes only when there is a tied vote among other council members.

Smith said the planning board has been working diligently to get a zoning ordinance ready for council's approval and the 180-day moratorium will give them more time to work on the ordinance before further decisions have to be made.

"A moratorium was placed on commercial building with Dollar General being exempted from the moratorium," Quick said.

"In effect, it looks as if the council members sold the farm right out from under the people of Red Cross."

Now the mayor is concerned that, "in all probability, although we can set stringent building codes, the codes will not be enforceable since we have set a precedence of allowing Dollar General to build as they want to," the mayor said. He believes that an incoming business could now take the Town of Red Cross to court and very likely win a case against the new building code based on the town's past practice.

Smith, however, said he doesn't believe that decision made by council last week will have a detrimental effect on the future decisions made by town council. He said there are already some businesses in Red Cross that are similar to the structure that Dollar General will build. "I think it will be a benefit for the town. I don't think it's going to be junk," Smith said of the building Dollar General will build.

During the meeting Smith told council that Dollar General will generate additional tax revenue for the town. Based on the stated $650,000 investment by Dollar General, the extra revenue in property taxes for the town will amount to $1,040 per year, Quick said. The business is also expected to employ six people.

Smith said the tax revenue from the business will take some of the burden off the residential taxpayers in Red Cross. He said the county's top economic development official, Robert Van Geons, has made it clear to town officials that property taxes collected from residential properties won't pay all of the bills.

The Town of Red Cross currently operates on a yearly budget of $146,000 and Quick said the town is in "good financial shape" to continue operating. He said the extra tax revenue will not make a noticeable impact on the town's financial base.

"With this vote, I believe we have thrown all our hope for planning and growth of our community out the window and will, most likely, end up being just a section for strip businesses," Quick said. "If growth is left to its natural course, without regulation, then the section of Highway 24-27 between Locust and Albemarle will evolve almost exclusively as strip businesses without any real organization and will definitely not be in harmony with the community."

While Quick said he believes it is the responsibility of the town's council to look after the best interest of the people well into the future, he also said that the people of the community have a responsibility "to monitor the actions of the council and call council members to task if a council member violates his/her sworn oath to serve the people."

Quick said he wants members of the community to express their opinions concerning this issue to members of the town council "before the issue has time to go through." Red Cross council members are Barbara Carpenter, Heath Hahn, Ray Quick, Larry Wayne Smith and Chip Speight.[144]

Chicago Tube and Iron:

In 2008 Heath Hahn told me about Chicago Tube & Iron wanting to find some property along Highway 24/27 on which to build a plant. It is our understanding that Chicago Tube & Iron has added another 150 jobs to their new Locust plant.

Although Chicago Tube & Iron did not fit the general vision that we have established for our community, we felt the potential job creations it would provide to be a worthwhile tradeoff. For this reason we felt we should try to recruit them into our community.

Please note that we were not contacted by Chicago Tube and Iron, we just became aware of their desire to relocate. We felt that if we were able to put together and present a desirable package to them then there would be an excellent chance we could recruit them into Red Cross.

[144] The Weekly Post, by Beth McLain, October 27, 2004

At this point it should be noted that just letting a company know that we would welcome them into our community usually won't generate very much interest on the part of the company. The company still has to go out into the community and find property; evaluate property availability, provided services, workforce availability and skills level, etc. However, if the recruiting community puts together a package listing property where the property owner(s) will consider selling at some to-be-negotiated price and that there are sufficient services (sewer, transportation/access, workforce, etc.) to support the company then it will probably generate considerably interest on the part of the company.

Since this appeared to be an excellent opportunity to recruit a large scale employer into our town we felt that we definitely needed to try to recruit them. I pulled up Stanly County's GIS maps of our community and began looking around Red Cross for potential properties that would meet their requirements and where the owner(s) would consider selling. Although there were some excellent properties on Ridgecrest Road, we were limited in that it was our impression that Chicago Tube and Iron only wanted property along Highway 24/27.

In looking at GIS maps I had to eliminate most potential property owners because I felt the owners would be unwilling to sell. However, there was one undeveloped property facing Highway 24/27 that would meet Chicago Tube & Iron's needs and that I felt the owner would probably consider selling. It was the 50-acre track on the south side of Highway 24/27, just east of West Stanly High School. It had everything we were aware of that Chicago Tube & Iron was looking for. If we could obtain the owners willingness to sell then there was a high probability we would be successful in recruiting them.

Please note that all we were looking for from the land owner was a willingness to sell if a satisfactory selling price could be reached. The price negotiation would be totally between the buyer and seller; the town would in no way be involved in that negotiation. In addition, provided the land owner was willing to consider selling, we would then talk to DOT to make sure there were no problems with obtaining adequate access to Highway 24/27. It would also need to be determined if the County would be willing for them to hook into the existing sewer system.

This last item was probably the most critical since the present sewage trunk lines were not sized to handle any real volume.

With this information in hand we would have then brought it before the members of the Town Council and requested their support and permission to contact Chicago Tube & Iron with the proposal. There were several reasons for needing to bring it before the Town Council: (1) it was a large project, (2) it did not fit within the town's vision, (3) it would require rezoning of the property from residential/agricultural to manufacturing, and (4) it would have more impact and be more effective if the proposal were to be presented to Chicago Tube & Iron by the town.

I contacted the property owner, Jerry Jordan, and told him about this opportunity and he was interested. He and I went to see Robert Van Geons, Executive Director, of the Stanly County Economic Development Commission. In reviewing this opportunity with Van Geons, it was his opinion that this property would be suitable for that use but would be more valuable were it to be developed as a mix of business and townhomes. That it would yield a higher return on investment and, if developed that way, would be a greater asset to Red Cross as a new town than a manufacturing plant would.

Robert Van Geons pointed out that this property was within walking distance of the school and would probably receive a lot of pedestrian traffic. That it would be an excellent location for a series of shops with walking streets for people to gather, especially during high traffic times such as school related events. Parents would frequent the shops and students would walk over to the shops after school. Townhomes along the backside of the property would be attractive to young teachers in that they would be able to walk to both shopping and work (West Stanly High School).

As a result of this meeting Jerry Jordan decided that he would rather pursue this approach and develop the land as a mix of business and townhomes. I got to see some preliminary plans that Jerry Jordan had drawn up during a meeting he and I had with Dr. Wu at UNC-Charlotte (discussion on developing a land-use plan for Red Cross). Jordan's vision for the property was impressive and I had to agree that if this property were to be developed according his vision then it would be a real asset to Red Cross and the community as a whole. I think that if he were to create this development it would be one of the best things that could happen to our community in establishing our identity and in reinforcing our lifestyle.

Unfortunately, it was about this time that the economy took its bad downturn. It seemed no one was starting new developments. If, and when, the economy comes back I look forward to the realization of this development.

ANNEXATIONS

Since incorporating Red Cross has voluntarily annexed around 150 properties and has not involuntarily annexed any properties.

Although a number of single voluntary annexations into Red Cross have occurred, there are three events that are noteworthy because of the circumstances. They are as follow:

Red Cross Doubles in Size:

In the first Town Council meeting of the newly incorporated Town of Red Cross 120 individual petitions were received requesting voluntary annexation into the town. These petitions came from the 121 property owners that had been asked to wait until after the town became incorporated. Of the 121 property owners that were asked to wait, 120 still wanted to be voluntarily annexed into the Town. Once being declared a town we were able to accept them in using the rules of voluntary annexation. It is hoped that history will show these people as being charter members of the Town of Red Cross.

This unusual situation occurred, because during the incorporation process, we were required to be at least 40% developed and have a population density of at least 250 people per square mile. Had we tried to include these people at that time then the percent development and population density would have been below the required minimum and our petition would have been rejected by the Joint Legislative Commission on Municipal Incorporations. Any incorporation petition must clear the Joint Commission with a favorable recommendation before it can be addressed by the Legislature.

When the final town map for incorporation was drawn up we had to go around to each of these people and explain why we couldn't include them in the town. We wanted to become a town but we didn't want to hurt anyone's feelings. To our relief everyone seemed to understand the problem and was not offended at being asked to wait until after we were incorporated before trying to come into the town. They wanted to be a part of the Town and made it clear by requesting voluntary annexation at that first Town Council meeting. In my opinion they were already a part of the Town of Red Cross.

Since these were voluntary annexations it didn't require Legislative approval as would have been required of an involuntary annexation. All that was required was for the property owners to submit a request for voluntary annexation to the Town. The Town would then do a paper survey of the proposed properties and verify the acceptability/legality of the annexation. The person doing the verification would submit a letter to the town stating the properties had been verified as acceptable for annexation. The Town would then set a public hearing, hold the public hearing and, barring any problems, vote the properties into the Town. Of course the appropriate County and State agencies would then have to be notified and paperwork filed.

When these people came into Red Cross the town more than doubled in size geographically because the majority of these people were larger property owners

Barbee's Road Request:

In the November 2003 Town Council meeting we were approached by the people on Barbee's Road requesting annexation into the Town of Red Cross. They had heard that Locust was preparing to annex them. In response to this threat they came to us requesting voluntary annexation into Red Cross.

Our first assumption was that Locust was doing this in response to our incorporation. We felt that the people on Barbee's Road should have a choice as to whether they wanted to be annexed or not. After all, we had just been forced to incorporate ourselves in response to our perceived threat of annexation and these people had a right to choose which direction they wanted to go. If they wanted to come into Red Cross, then we should accept them.

We (Red Cross) gave the Barbee's Road committee a copy of the voluntary annexation request form and the requirements necessary to apply for voluntary annexation. From that point on the people living on Barbee's Road did all the work necessary to apply for annexation into Red Cross.

At the next month's Red Cross Town Council meeting the people on Barbee's Road presented their annexation request to the Red Cross Town Council. We were surprised to see how far the properties requesting annexation were extending down Barbee's Road. Were we to accept the annexation request it would have created a single long spur for several miles, almost the whole length of Barbee's Road - almost to the Town of Stanfield!

John Long, of the "West Stanly Weekly", was at our meeting that night and after the meeting I talked with him about the Barbee's Road annexation request. I'm glad I did because he gave me a lot to think about:

- This area would be well outside the Red Cross sphere and it would be difficult to provide services to the area.

- Traditionally, everyone (general County residents) considered Barbee Road to be a part of the Locust community.

- For Red Cross to annex Barbee Road, and create such a spur, would cause a destabilizing effect on western Stanly County.

- Although Red Cross could legally voluntarily annex Barbee Road, what we were considering was not what annexations were intended for.

There were other things he said but I don't remember them all. I do know that there was a lot of wisdom and sincerity in what he said.

Because this was such an extensive annexation, I knew I needed more information to understand if we were doing the right thing in accepting the Barbee's Road properties. It would take me at least a month to research and certify the boundaries of the Barbee's Road properties. I was the one that would do the verifications and submit the certification to the Town of Red Cross and I knew we couldn't do anything until I submitted my report. As far as Locust was concerned, they would have to go through the State Legislature to get approval. That alone would probably take several months, so we had time to do our research.

In my opinion, if Locust did intend to do an involuntary annexation, I felt we should help the people on Barbee Road. However, if Locust was not intending to annex them then we had no business annexing them.

I had to know if the threat to Barbee's Road was real and the only way to do that was to ask Locust. I called Wilson Barbee, Mayor of Locust, and met with him one-on-one. He assured me that there was no truth to the rumors nor were there any plans in the works to annex Barbee's Road. He pointed out that, under the current annexation laws; there was no way Locust could annex Barbee's Road even if it wanted to. Remember, this was just after the implementation/enforcement of new incorporation and annexation laws.

We (Red Cross) delayed the process giving Locust time to send out letters to the property owners on Barbee's Road assuring them that the rumors were false and that they (Locust) had no plans for annexing Barbee's Road property owners. As a result the people on Barbee's Road began withdrawing their annexation request. This ended up being the best outcome for everyone: Locust, Red Cross, the property owners on Barbee's Road, and western Stanly County as a whole. This was in 2003, and as of 2015, Barbee's Road residents continue to live outside of any town limits.

Although the Town of Red Cross could have legally annexed these properties into the town, it proved to be a wise decision that we did delay our acceptance. During my investigation it was found that Locust really didn't have any plans for annexing Barbee's Road.

There were some concerns that this "unfounded" rumor may have been started from within Red Cross with the intent of coercing the people on Barbee's Road to "voluntarily" annex into Red Cross. We also found that under the new State annexation laws, that were now being enforced, there was no way Locust could have involuntarily annexed these properties even if they had wanted to. The bottom line was that, as John Long of the Weekly Post put it, it would have been just plain wrong to have brought these people into Red Cross under these "false" conditions.

I have no regrets about going to Locust, talking with Mayor Wilson Barbee, and giving Locust time to respond. I may have not been politically correct in the eyes of some of our people by meeting with Mayor Barbee and delaying the annexation process, but what I did was the right thing to do.

As additional information: At the time we started our incorporation attempt, annexations were more political than technical. However, at the point in time in which this occurred, annexation laws were becoming much more technical. For a Town to involuntarily annex an area, that area must be adjacent (connected) to the Town and the annexed area cannot have an extended boundary that is greater than eight times the length of the boundary that is directly connected to the present town boundaries. An example of this is that if a Town annexes an area and the portion of that area that is directly connected to the present Town boundary is 1,000 feet then the length of the remaining boundary around the annexed area cannot exceed 8,000 feet.

Based on the above, the boundary ratio limitation alone would have been enough to have blocked Locust from annexing Barbee's Road.

In 2012 involuntary annexation laws changed to the point where a town must schedule a referendum and the people in a targeted area are able to vote on whether they want to be annexed into a town or not.

Running Creek School:

We didn't include Running Creek School during the incorporation process because we didn't want to extend the proposed town limits too far to the northwest and risk the potential of creating alarm for Locust. We would have liked to have included the school at that time but just felt it was too great a risk. These fears weren't unfounded because, apparently Locust did express some concerns about our incorporating.

Shortly after our incorporation we did send the School Board a letter inviting Running Creek School to join Red Cross but they declined.

In 2008 we decided to make another effort to encourage the School Board to voluntarily annex Running Creek School into the town. The major consideration for this attempt was due to the potential leverage it would provide when applying for grants - such as park grants and sewer grants.

I called and talked with Melvin Poole of the Stanly County School Board about Running Creek School joining the Red Cross Community through voluntarily annexation. He wouldn't express an opinion but did arrange to put us on the agenda for one of the School Board meetings.

The night of the School Board meeting came and Heath Hahn and I met with the Stanly County School Board and presented the ideal to them. We explained that there was no cost to the County by being in Red Cross and that there may be some minor benefits to the school. However, the greatest benefit would be to the Town of Red Cross. That it would allow us to demonstrate that we had two schools within our town limits, which should enhance our chances of obtaining grant money - especially in regards to our long-term plan of establishing a park.

No decision was made while we were there but we received word within a few days that they had decided to accept our invitation and voluntarily annex Running Creek School into Red Cross.

The following is a segment of the Stanly County School Board Facilities meeting minutes that resulted from that meeting:

"Facilities – Mike Barbee reported that the committee met on October 21. Agenda items included the following:"

- "Annexation of Running Creek School – Ray Quick, Mayor of the Town of Red Cross, addressed the committee to request the annexation of Running Creek School to Red Cross. The matter was referred to Dr. DePaul, who contacted County Manager Andy Lucas. Mr. Lucas indicated that the county had no role in approving or rejecting the annexation and the decision would be left to the Board of Education. On a motion by Mike Barbee and second by Chris Whitley, the Board approved to allow the voluntary annexation of Running Creek School to the Town of Red Cross. - November 4, 2008"[145]

[145] From minutes of Stanly County School Facilities Board meeting, November 4, 2008

THE WIDENING OF HIGHWAY 24/27

The major single item that led to the incorporation of the Town of Red Cross was the widening of Highway 24/27. This was going from the existing two-lane road to a four-lane road with divided medium. Within the Red Cross community there was a great deal of fear that it would invite an annexation attempt from either Locust and/or Oakboro. We had heard for years that both Locust and Oakboro wanted to annex us and with the completion of the four-lane we really believed there would be an annexation attempt.

For those having property along Highway 24/27 there was a great deal of trepidation in not knowing what was going to happen. Some people were afraid they would lose their houses, and some did. Some people were afraid it would increase their property taxes while others had dollar signs in their eyes thinking they would be able to sell their land for a small fortune. No one was expecting the economy to crash as it later did.

At the time the original plans were drawn up for the expansion of Highway 24/27 Red Cross was not incorporated. Red Cross was under the Oakboro transportation plan and no one had really given any consideration to Red Cross as an entity. Because of this the original plans were for a four-lane with grassy medium through Red Cross.

Once we became a town we felt that, as a town, we should have a four-lane with center turning lane (five-lane) through our town, much as was being done through Locust and Midland. The reason we were able to have this consideration was because actual construction on the four-lane didn't start until after Red Cross became incorporated. We eventually did get Red Cross broken out as having its own transportation plan but lost the battle for a five-lane.

The town's effort in trying to obtain a five-lane, instead of the originally proposed four-lane, began very early during the term of the Interim Council. The Interim Council voted a resolution in October 2002 to try to convince DOT to change the section of Highway 24/27 running through Red Cross to a five-lane highway.

We began actively pursuing a five-lane through Red Cross and I sent letters to our Legislatures; Representative Bobby Harold Barbee, Representative Wayne Goodwin and Senator William Purcell and to the respective DOT people; Highway Commissioner Larry Helms and Division-10 Chief Engineer Benton Payne requesting a meeting to discuss the issue.

The meeting was set up for February 7, 2003, at the Division-10 office with Benton Payne (and staff), Highway Commissioner Larry Helms, Representative Bobby Harold Barbee, Representative Wayne Goodwin, Senator William Purcell, Red Cross Mayor Raeford Quick and Red Cross Town Council Member Heath Hahn. There was also a surprising appearance by the Chamber of Commerce and Economic Development. These last two people were people we definitely did not want involved since we felt their interest would be focused almost exclusively on the desires of Albemarle the County.

I was to later find out in one of the Red Cross Town meetings that it was one of our own people that had called both the Chamber of Commerce and Economic Development. That person told me that they had called and asked them to attend the meeting because they thought that they could help us. We may, or may not, have been able to convince DOT to change the road - but bringing in these people opened our discussion up to the rest of the County and probably made our efforts for getting a five-lane substantially more difficult. I believe this meeting was one of the most decisive points in our efforts for obtaining a five-lane.

We did want our State Legislators involved since we felt many of DOT's decisions could be politically influenced. I am grateful to Representative Bobby Harold Barbee, Representative Wayne Goodwin and Senator William Purcell for attending this meeting. Unfortunately, Larry Helms could not be there in person but did attend through conference call - we could all hear him and he could hear all of us over the speakerphone.

In the meeting we stated our position and began discussions with DOT. The discussions were mostly between Red Cross and Commissioner Larry Helms. It was a good meeting. One of the most promising things that we left with was that of a statement by Commissioner Helms where he said to Benton Payne (Chief Engineer, Division-10) "Work with them and see if something can be worked out. If we have to make the change then we'll do it, but see if something can be worked out first". This may not be a direct quote but I believe it is close and the substance to be correct. We felt this was a clear indication that DOT was willing to consider converting from a four-lane with divided medium to a five-lane highway through Red Cross.

Over the rest of the year the issue continued to expand with others becoming involved. By late 2003 it was becoming an issue throughout the County with the County and the majority of municipalities within the County beginning to apply pressure to continue with the planned four-lane with divided medium.

The following is from the minutes of Stanly County, Local Government Liaison Committee, VFW Hut, Richfield, NC February 24, 2004:

"Stanly County
Local Government Liaison Committee
VFW Hut, Richfield, NC
February 24, 2004

Attendees:
Floyd Wilson, Jerry Myers, Gene McIntyre, Steve Morgan, Mary Ann Fisher, Raymond Allen, Roger Snyder, Bob Remsburg, Harold Green, Matt Brinkley, Tom Garrison, Calvin Gaddy, and Bill Peak.

Absent:
Representatives from Norwood, Oakboro, Red Cross, Stanfield and Misenheimer were not in attendance.

Guest:
Mrs. Rebecca Yarborough, CCOG...."

"Chairman McIntyre, Stanly County Commissioners, told..."

"...He then shared a request from Mr. Larry Helms, NCDOT Board Member for local support for the decision to construct a four lane divided highway through Red Cross as opposed to the five lane road as requested by some Red Cross residents.

Mrs. Yarborough and Jerry Myers shared with the group the background and rationale used by the Rocky River RPO is recommending a four lane divided highway for Red Cross. One of the first tasks of the newly formed RPO was to finance a study of the Red Cross area to determine a recommended design for the widening of Hwy. 24/27. The rationale for the recommended four-lane divided roadway with turn lanes is: a.) Traffic safety for students and staff near the entrance to West Stanly High School and the convenience store across the road from the School; b.) Overall traffic safety for the town; c.) Avoiding at least a year's delay for construction if the project had to be redesigned; and d.) Avoiding any future delays in completing the multi-lane connection to Charlotte and I-485 for the remainder of the County.

A number of representatives present indicated their support for the RPO recommendation and indicated that they would either adopt a resolution of support or write a letter to NCDOT supporting the the recommendation. Mayor Snyder, Albemarle, advised that any local controversy surrounding a DOT project could very easily send the money to support the project elsewhere."[146]

[146] From the minutes of the Stanly County Liaison meeting of February 24, 2004

The following is taken from the minutes of the City of Albemarle's web posting of the "Regular Meeting City Council" of March 1, 2004:

> "The City Council considered the adoption of a Resolution to endorse the Rocky River Rural Planning Organization study to retain the existing design for the widening of NC Highway 24/27. The City Manager reported that the Town of Red Cross would like a five-lane urban design through town instead of the proposed four-lane divided highway. He noted that the RPO has investigated this possibility and found that a five-lane urban design is more dangerous than the proposed design and this change to design would delay the project approximately one year. He noted the North Carolina Department of Transportation is proposing limited turn lanes in Red Cross as a compromise.
>
> Upon a motion by Councilmember Neel, seconded by Councilmember Hartley and unanimously carried, the following Resolution was duly adopted:
>
> (Resolution 04-12, To endorse the Rocky River Rural Planning Organization (RPO) study to retain the existing design on NC Highway 24/27.)"[147]

What Mayor Snyder is referencing is a previous implied statement from a member of DOT that DOT could abandon the road construction project through Red Cross and use the money that had been allocated for this stretch of highway to somewhere else along Highway 24/27.

We, Red Cross, had also heard that statement but discounted it based on the intensity of the statement and on the substance of our previous negotiations with DOT. What we had heard was implied but not stated as an actual option. It came across with the intensity of a bluff and not fact (not something under actual consideration). Also, in our February 7, 2003 meeting with DOT we understood definite

[147] From the March 2004, Albemarle City Council meeting minutes

indications that DOT was committed to the completion of the section of Highway 24/27 through Red Cross - even to the extent of putting a five-lane through Red Cross.

If DOT did agree to go with a five-lane through Red Cross then they would have to go back and redesign that section of Highway 24/27. Our understanding was that this redesign could take up to a year, thus delaying the completion of the highway by a year. It was highly improbable that either the County or the City of Albemarle were willing to wait.

As a part of DOT's efforts to convince us to concede to the four-lane highway DOT commissioned Centralina Council of Government to do a study of the highway through Red Cross. This was an effort on DOT's part to demonstrate the safety advantages of a four-lane over a five-lane highway. Centralina made their presentation in the May 2003 Town Council meeting. There was a large turnout of the public at this meeting.

Centralina made an impressive presentation; however, it did not appear to address our major concern, which was how five-lane vs. four-lane would directly affect our community. They talked about traffic flow and safety but did not appear to address our perceptions of what difference a five-lane vs. a four-lane would mean to us as a developing town, which was our major concern. If it was included in the presentation, it was not presented in a manner in which we could relate to.

DOT also expressed concerns with the entrance to West Stanly High School. They were using this as one of their major points against converting to a five-lane highway. In our continued effort to persuade DOT to revise their plans for the highway I called and got on the agenda for one of the school board meetings. J. D. Hinson and I went to the meeting along with a member of DOT's Division-10's staff. The problem was presented to the school board explaining why DOT considered the entrance to West Stanly High School to be one of the major reasons for not wanting to put a five-lane through Red Cross.

DOT offered some suggestions for modification to the entrance, and even presenting the option for a second entrance coming in off Lakewood Road. Unfortunately, the School Board continued to be firm. It seemed that they liked the entrance as it existed and wanted only that one entrance, the primary reason being that they could better maintain control of traffic coming into to the school by having only the one entrance.

It should be noted that it appears a group, independent of official Town Council efforts, began working towards obtaining a five-lane. A petition was circulated, the news media from Channel-9 News was called to Red Cross to do an interview, and a meeting was held with a Governor's aid in Raleigh.

Although I am expressing personal opinion only in the following statement, I believe the petition is what gave final closure to our five-lane efforts due to improprieties in the petition.

In another notable action, once it became apparent that the town was going to have a four-lane highway, Heath Hahn and I began working to try to get a crossover put in at Gaddis Road for the people living in the Rolling Hills subdivision.

We found that the Gaddis Road intersection to Highway 24/27 was too close to the intersection of Highway 24/27/Highway 205 for DOT to permit a cross-over to be placed at that entrance. However, if the Gaddis Road entrance were to be moved further away from the intersection of Highway 205/Highway 24/27 by at least a hundred yards then it would be possible to add a cross-over. Making this change would directly affect only two pieces of property. Those properties belonged to Ray Quick and Reggie Hill/Ronnie Williams.

Heath Hahn contacted Reggie Hill, who in turn contacted co-owner Ronnie Williams, to seek permission to allow the new Gaddis Road to cross their property since the new entrance to Gaddis Road would effectively split the Hill/Williams track of land in half. Even so, they agreed to allow Gaddis Road to cross their property. The change would put the new Gaddis Road entrance almost directly on the western side of where Dollar General now sits.

For my (Ray Quick) part I agreed to allow Gaddis Road to come across my property even though it would probably cut a couple acres off of one corner.

At this point we were all set with both affected property owners and DOT being agreeable to modify the highway design to allow a crossover at the new intersection of Gaddis Road and Highway 24/27. It was now time to let the rest of the Town Council know of our plan. To our surprise it upset one Council Member enough that we felt compelled to discontinue our plans for making the entrance change.

Please note that this did not come up as an item on the Council Agenda and no formal position was taken by the Council on the issue. The comments made were personal comments only.

MAKING HIGHWAY 24/27 AN EXPRESSWAY

Beginning in 2010, and coming to a head in 2011, the issue with Highway 24/27 was where the State wanted to reclassify Highway 24/27 as an expressway. DOT had sent letters to the towns along Highway 24/27 requesting each town adopt the new designation of "expressway".

The classification of expressway, as defined by DOT, is a major highway much like an interstate, having very limited access. Based on our understanding of the plans proposed by DOT, we did not see any projected access points to Highway 24/27 within Red Cross other than the single overpass proposed at the intersection of Highway 24/27/Highway 205. The homes and businesses already existing along Highway 24/27 would no longer have a direct entrance to Highway 24/27. Access roads would have to be built parallel to Highway 24/27 for allowing people to go to the overpass at Highway 205/Ridgecrest Road. This would again cause a major upheaval in our community.

Ten-years earlier our community suffered a major loss with the widening of Highway 24/27. People lost their homes and property to accommodate the four-lane. Now DOT again wanted to expand and upgrade Highway 24/27; an expansion that could potentially cause an even greater upheaval and loss of homes and property. What would happen to the center of our community if an overpass were to be installed? Would we lose the buildings and the church?

One of the early arguments (after 9/11) used for eliminating stoplights and restricting access (right turn only access/egress) was that Charlotte, as the second largest east coast financial center behind New York, is a potential terrorist target. As such, it is strategically important that the route from Fort Bragg to Charlotte be designed to allow for rapid access by the military.

As has been stated, there is a long range desire by the State to make Highway 24 a highway corridor from Charlotte to Morehead City. DOT has pointed out that this long range plan probably won't be realized for twenty or thirty years. The problem is that DOT is making those long range plans "now" to create that corridor and is acting "now" on those plans and is "now" requesting adoption of those plans by municipalities.

Even we in Red Cross have created long range plans that extend out to twenty years. We have acted on our long range plans by creating our growth plan, land use plan and vision plan, all of which extend twenty years into the future. At the end of 2011 Red Cross was actively addressing its transportation plan.

Inarguably there is some logic in DOT's long-range plan, Interstate-85 is to our north and Interstate-74 is to our south. It would be an asset for Charlotte to have another interstate between the two that leads to Charlotte - much as the Roman's set up their transportation system for "all roads lead to Rome". Using this analogy, it raises the question; is the "entity" Charlotte another Rome and is it so important that its enhancement and growth necessitates the negative impact and displacement of people many miles from Charlotte?

In September 2011, Mr. Ruben Crummey of DOT requested a public hearing be scheduled in Red Cross to encourage our adoption of the DOT plan to designate Highway 24/27 as an "expressway". Because of the importance of this to the community a letter was sent to each resident:

September 17, 2011

Dear Red Cross Citizen:

As you have been reading in "The Stanly News & Press" and "The

Weekly Post" the Department of Transportation has been holding public hearings with each municipality in our area. A public hearing has been scheduled to be held on September 26, 2011, at 7:00 PM in the Red Cross Town Hall.

The purpose of this public hearing is to allow DOT to present a 20-year plan for upgrading the status of Highway 24/27 to that of an expressway. Depending on the outcome of this presentation and input from the citizens of Red Cross the Town Council will be voting on acceptance of this proposal in the upcoming October Council meeting.

Since Highway 24/27 runs through the center of Red Cross, this plan will have a substantial effect on the long-term future of Red Cross. We feel everyone in our community should be fully informed and have input on any decisions that are made regarding acceptance of this plan by the Town of Red Cross. We strongly encourage you to attend this public hearing.

Please make plans to attend this meeting - it will have an effect on our Town's future.

Sincerely,

Raeford Quick
Mayor, Town of Red Cross

Although there were more people than normal at this meeting, the turnout was disappointing low considering the importance of this issue. Even today it is quite probable that a large percentage of our population still does not understand the issue, the implications, or of the effect it can and will have on our community.

Although we listened attentively to the presentation we withheld our support stating that we needed more time and information before making a decision. In reality, what we had heard disturbed us greatly. What DOT was proposing would be catastrophic to our town.

One of the main responsibilities of municipal government is to make long range plans. Plans that allow for controlled and planned growth and insuring the town's ability to provide services for that growth. It doesn't matter that events will happen twenty years in the future. The plans that are being made now will dictate and impact that future.

Were we to adopt DOT's request, then not only our long range plans but our short term plans would have to be completely redone. Effectively, any plans for placing a business or house along Highway 24/27 would have to take into consideration that at some future point there would no longer be direct access to Highway 24/27. If someone built near the highway then they would be faced with the possibility that service roads could be installed and any buildings/ homes in the way of those service roads might have to be demolished.

Should Highway 24/27 be reclassified as an expressway then access would be even more severely restricted. Service roads could, and probably would, be required for accessing Highway 24/27. Access to Highway 24/27 would require overpasses with ramps and/or clover-leafs. The design presented by DOT to the Red Cross Town Council in the October, 2011 Town Council meeting indicated that an overpass, with a half-clover-leaf, was the probable option for the intersection of Highway 24/27/Highway 205/Ridgecrest Road. This would be the only access to Highway 24/27 within Red Cross.

A half-clover-leaf means that the access loops are placed on only one side of the overpass. Any road accessing Highway 24/27, which could not qualify for an overpass, probably would not have to access Highway 24/27 directly and would become a dead end road or would have to use a service road to gain access to Highway 24/27.

The plans presented to us by DOT only showed the possibility of a service road on the north side of Highway 24/27. It was not stated that it would be installed, only that the possibility existed. It is not known what would be done on the south side of Highway 24/27 since there didn't appear to be anything in the plans for that side? Access to West Stanly High School would be off Lakewood Road or either, as discussed, another road could be created that would come off

Highway 205.

My personal assumption, based on the available information, is that there was no intent to put an access road on the south side of Highway 24/27. The people on the south side would have to redirect to Lakewood Road or, as had been hinted at, a possible new road would come in off Highway 205. It would probably come off Highway 205 somewhere along where Peachtree Road intersects with Highway 205 and parallel with Highway 24/27 somewhere behind the town hall property.

No citizen of Red Cross, based on the plan as proposed by DOT, would be in favor of having such restricted access. It would completely destabilize us as a town. All the money, time and hopes we had invested in our zoning, growth, land-use, vision plans and our future would be completely wasted.

As previously stated, the proposed DOT plan would require the creation of new access roads. Where would they be placed? How many would need to be installed? Who would pay for them? There were just too many unknowns. We definitely didn't have the funds to put access roads in ourselves nor had DOT indicated any commitment to installing them.

It had now come to the point where DOT was pushing us hard to pass a resolution endorsing their plans for an expressway.

Based on our understanding of the impact it would have on us, we didn't want Highway 24/27 declared an expressway under any condition. We felt it was a preposterous plan that would hurt not just us but a lot of other communities along Highway 24/27. We were never sure who would benefit from it - DOT was very vague on that part. However, we delayed giving a position statement in order to leave communication channels open.

With respect to leaving communications channels open, it was implied that if we didn't agree to the expressway designation then we may be excluded from future discussions on the highway, that it may even be years before we would be allowed to reenter into the discussions. They were delivering this with more intensity than normal.

Based on our perception of their commitment to the expressway and the intensity in which the implied "threat" was being delivered we could not determine if, or how much, they were bluffing.

I received an email from Reuben Crummy, DOT Transportation Engineer, requesting to come to our next Town Council meeting in November, 2011. In that email he said that Locust had told him that Red Cross was joining with Locust in opposing the expressway. I emailed him back and told him I would see that he was on the agenda for our next Council meeting. I also told him that Red Cross had taken no official position to-date and if someone told Locust this then they were doing so as an individual and not as a representative of the Town.

This was particularly concerning, if someone from our Council was creating Council policy and stating it to another town without the knowledge of the entire Council, then it meant we were developing a fracture within the Council, something we didn't need at this critical time. The expressway issue was so serious that our Council had to act as a single unified body.

In an effort to prepare for the upcoming November Town Meeting with DOT I called a workshop. I wanted to get everyone's input so that we would be working as a single entity. It was time we took an official position. I fully expected everyone would want to reject DOT's request for our adoption and I wanted us speaking with a single voice. For my part I just didn't see any way we could agree to DOT's request so, prior to the workshop, I prepared a statement declining our adoption of the expressway resolution request. I designed a "pony" statement to reflect what I believed would be consistent with the sentiments of the rest of the Council, something that would give us a template to work from for finalizing our position response. I wanted it so that we could turn down DOT's request while leaving an opening where we could continue discussing the issue with DOT.

This last part was important since DOT had implied that if we didn't agree to the resolution then we may be excluded from future discussions, and that it may be some time before we would again be allowed to participate.

Although not really applicable since we didn't use my position statement I still want a record of what my position was, because if I don't put it here I suspect it will be told quite differently in the future. For that reason I am inserting a copy of that "pony" position statement below:

Town of Red Cross

Position Statement

Designation of Highway 24/27 to "Expressway"

We have been asked by the Department of Transportation to vote on acceptance of applying the designation of "expressway" to the section of Highway 24/27 that runs through Red Cross.

As a Town Council our primary responsibility is to the wellbeing of our residents. Before making any vote we must have adequate information to make a qualified decision before making a change. We must know what the impact will be both short-term and long-term. Decisions we make today may affect our community twenty or thirty years in the future.

At this stage the information provided by DOT is in the concept stage. It gives no indication on what direction the design will take or of what impact it will have on our community once the changes start taking effect. Just by voting acceptance today our property values, the Towns zoning and growth plan, etc. will be altered.

By definition expressways have very limited access, are restricted to right-in/right-out access, interchanges are required at major intersections, and may also necessitate the instillation of access roads. Also, since the intersection of Highway 24/27 and Highway 205 has been "planned" to be a trucking access point, will an interchange be required? If it does will we lose Red Cross Baptist Church? At this point DOT is not able to supply any of this information.

When we vote for or against something it is because we have a reason. In this case there is simply not enough information provided for us to make an informed decision on something that will have such a tremendous impact on the future of our Town.

Please understand this distinction, we are not rejecting DOT's request - we simply can't vote to accept this request without more information. Since our only option in this vote is to accept or not to accept we have no choice but to vote not to apply our acceptance at this time.

It is our hope that DOT will remain open and willing to come back to us with more detailed information at a later date so that we will be more able to make a knowledgeable decision in applying our acceptance in designating Highway 24/24 as an "expressway".

Ray Quick
Mayor, Town of Red Cross

Again, this position statement was not used as part of the Red Cross Council's response to NCDOT's request for our adoption of the "expressway". It has been included only to illustrate my position on the issue.

As can be seen from the last three paragraphs of the position statement, the intent was to force DOT to continue to negotiate with us and to negate their implied "threat" of excluding us from further discussions. Although the semantics of my statement were subtle, they were substantive. The key was that I believed the highway plans were still too preliminary and DOT would be unable to supply adequate information for quite some time, giving us the ability to turn them down indefinitely without allowing them to play the exclusion card.

As previously stated, we held a workshop to discuss the issue prior to this meeting. Unfortunately, didn't everyone attend the meeting; Present were Kelly Brattain, Heath Hahn, and Ray Quick. Absent were Jerry Jordan and Larry Wayne Smith.

In this workshop we talked over our options. After much discussion it was decided to tentatively adopt the expressway designation due to fears that if we didn't then we would no longer have any voice or input into the process.

In the Council Meeting there were three voting members present (Heath Hahn, Jerry Jordan and Larry Wayne Smith). Absent was Kelly Brattain. We did reject DOT's request for adoption but not as politically correct as I would have liked.

All this occurred at the end of 2011. With the election of Larry Wayne Smith as Mayor, Red Cross did join with Locust in opposing the "expressway" designation and for encouraging DOT to consider a bypass around Locust and Red Cross.

The outcome, as it stands at the writing of this book, is that there are now two, but not agreed upon, potential options on the drawing board. The first is to bypass Red Cross and Locust to the north and the second is to bypass Red Cross and Locust to the south.

The disturbing thing is that DOT has still not made any formal commitment to installing a bypass, only presented the potential option for a bypass. Things have died down now that the economy has turned so bad and the old adage "out of sight, out of mind" is still applicable. It is not impossible that DOT can just pick up where they left off at some future point in time. If this happens then it may be possible to implement the "expressway" designation in its original form before anyone has time to react. Both Locust and Red Cross administrations must remain vigilant on this issue and ensure that doesn't happen.

SALES & USE TAX

A simplified explanation of Sales & Use tax is that it is tax money collected by the State of North Carolina anytime someone purchases something. A portion of the collected tax is redistributed back to counties and towns within the State on a monthly basis. Depending on how much people spend within the State, the return to the counties and towns is usually somewhere between $100 to $120 per person/per year. For Red Cross our receipt of Sales & Use tax is slightly more than the revenue from our town tax. Without it we could not keep our tax rate at 16-cents while still providing our current services.

There were two major issues that occurred with our receiving Sales & Use tax money. The first issue was when, in June 2003, we felt we were receiving less than our population count implied we should be receiving. The second issue was when, in February 2004, we were notified by the State that we needed to return $73,565.75 in funds that we weren't suppose to have received.

Sales & Use Tax Underpayment:

The major issue, outside of budget approval was the amount of Sales & Use Tax we were receiving.

In preparation for the 2003/2004 budget I noticed that our receipt of Sales & Use Tax was less than our population base indicated we should be receiving. I began looking into it and found that the State was only giving us credit for having 185 houses. Through our incorporation and annexations we were showing at least 235 houses. At a statistical 2.53

people per household, our population should be at least 594 people vs. the reported 468 people. Since Sales & Use Tax distribution is based on population, I believed we were receiving much less than we should have. We needed to address the issue.

In talking with the State Demographics I was informed that the only possibility we would have to change our population count would be for us to go through the US Census Bureau and obtain a revised census of our town.

I brought what I had learned before the Town Council in the June 2003 Council meeting and requested approval to commission this census. I felt it would cost us around $2,000 but it would mean that we would have the potential of receiving an additional $25,000 per year for the next seven years in additional Sales & Use Tax revenue. If we didn't get it corrected now then we would have to wait seven years until the 2010 census count was done. In short the total cumulative revenue loss to the Town would be about $175,000.

The actual cost of the new census ended up being $1,530.

As a result of that survey the US Census Bureau gave us a reported population of approximately 800 people. This meant that we would be receiving about $88,000 per year in Sales & Use tax instead of the $52,000 we were currently receiving - an increase of $36,000 per year. The projected cumulative revenue increase would amount to of $252,000 over the next seven years. This extra money would allow us to get on our feet much more quickly.

Unfortunately, but I guess understandable, during a later annual report the County reported our population at 768 people. My assumption as to why this happened is that the County used statistical numbers for their reporting rather than the actual numbers supplied by the US Census Bureau. Apparently, within our town limits, we must have had more than the statistical 2.53 people per household and/or a higher occupancy rate. This reduced our revenue in Sales & Use tax by $3,600 per year, resulting in an actualized increase in revenue of $32,400 per year.

Sales & Use Tax Overpayment:

On February 4, 2005, I got a call from the Mr. Norris Tolson, Secretary of Treasury for the State of North Carolina, concerning overpayment of Sales & Use Tax by the State of North Carolina to the Town of Red Cross totaling $73,565.72. Later that day I received an email with attached letter from James H. Cooke, Assistant Secretary of Revenue for Tax Administration, asking Red Cross to pay this money back.

Finance Officer/Council Member Heath Hahn presented the problem to the Council in the March 2005 Town Council meeting. Basically what had happened was that the State had started sending us Sales & Use Tax distributions shortly after we incorporated. According to the State Treasurer's office we were not suppose to receive this money until all of our services had been fully implemented. The last of our four specified service to be implemented was the contract with the Sheriff's Department for police protection, which took effect January 1, 2004. This meant that we had to return all the money received in Sales & Use tax distribution prior to January 1, 2004.

I asked the Council to allow me to investigate before we responded. By this time I had learned to not tell any more than was necessary. Just thinking of some of the things that had happened in the past, such as with the highway and zip code, I was afraid someone would do something to cause it to fail. I knew we couldn't afford to lose that much money; we were a new town and didn't have all that much money in the treasury. This amount represented half of our annual budget.

Fortunately the Council seemed fairly subdued on the issue and didn't ask many questions. It was voted to allow me to pursue this issue.

At each of the successive Town Council meeting I would inform the Council that Representative Almond was working on it and that the probability of our being able to keep the money was improving. Otherwise, I didn't give them any extra information.

Surprisingly, one individual kept pushing us to go ahead and pay the money back, or we would incur a lot of interest on it. I didn't think the

State would charge us any interest or set a time constraint since Secretary Tolson had indicated a willingness to work with us and the letter stated that we could pay it back in installments.

One of the first things I did was to contact our local State Representative, David Almond, to inform him of the problem and obtain any assistance he may be able to offer. He proved to be an invaluable source of information and assistance.

The following are the key points I initially provide to Representative Almond concerning the services we had declared in our incorporation petition:

Zoning:

- NCGS 120-163 did not require this service until January 1, of the third year of incorporation.
- Because Zoning is one of the most critical issues for incorporation it was a high priority and was addressed immediately. Once incorporated we worked as quickly a practical to assume control of our zoning – approximately 60-days to adoption from time of incorporation.
- Did have zoning as a line item but no money allocated because we were low on funds and did not have a good feel for what our expenses would be. So we drew our expenses for zoning from the administrative line item.
- Zoning was budgeted in fiscal year 2003-2004.
- A zoning committee was formed in early 2003 to rewrite our zoning ordinances.

Fire Protection:

- NCGS 120-163 did not require this service until January 1, of the third year of incorporation.
- Meetings were held with all the fire departments involved and verbal agreements for transition of coverage were reached prior to incorporation in 2002.
- Because we didn't incorporate until August 2002 the County of

Stanly had already levied a tax on fire protection preventing the Town of Red Cross from implementing protection in fiscal 2002-2003.

- Contracts were made in fiscal year 2003-2004 and Red Cross did assume responsibility beginning July 1, 2003

Waste Collection:

- NCGS 120-163 did not require this service until January 1, of the third year of incorporation.
- Because we didn't incorporate until August 2002 the County of Stanly had already levied a tax on waste collection preventing the Town of Red Cross from implementing waste collection in fiscal 2002-2003.
- Red Cross did actively pursue quotes and program implementation during the incorporation process.
- The Town of Red Cross negotiated a transitional agreement with the County of Stanly so that waste collection was covered for the entire fiscal year 2003-2004.
- Waste Collection was a line item in fiscal year 2002-2003 but no money budgeted.
- Waste Collection was budgeted in fiscal year 2003-2004 and was implemented.
- Red Cross was instrumental in setting up a multi-municipal contract for the Towns of Locust, Oakboro, Red Cross, and Stanfield with Waste Management where all Towns involved realized substantial cost savings. Red Cross is generally recognized as causing this to happen.

Note: Bob Remsburg, Locust City Manager, initiated and coordinated this contract. Mr. Paul Hamberis, Division Marketing Manager of Waste Management, contacted Bob Remsburg after the phone conversation I had with him.

Police Protection:

- NCGS 120-163 did not require this service until January 1, of the third year of incorporation.
- Red Cross did actively pursue quotes and program

implementation during the incorporation process.

- The Town of Red Cross negotiated an agreement in early 2003 with the County of Stanly for contract coverage to begin January 1, 2004.
- Police protection was a line item in fiscal year 2002-2003 but no money budgeted.
- Red Cross has worked from the time of incorporation to present to improve the Sheriff's Department coverage of the western end of Stanly County. We participated in the negotiation of a deal with the County Commissioners for a satellite Sheriff's station to be placed in Red Cross in 2002. This deal later collapsed due to territorial disputes between EMS and the Sheriff's Department.
- Red Cross is still committed to providing a satellite Sheriff's Office in our town hall once we get one built to serve the western end of Stanly County.

Representative Almond found that there were four municipalities affected. They were:

Town	Dollars Involved
Red Cross	$ 73,565.72
Mills River	$1,200,000.00 (round number)
Ossipee	$ 130,000.00 (round number)
Fairview	(Unknown)

According to Representative Almond:

"The whole situation originated with a disagreement between Mills River and Henderson County. In talking with Mayor Roger Snyder of Mills River this morning, he said that the Chairman of County Commissioners for Henderson County fought their incorporation "tooth-and-nail" and the Chairman of County Commissioners was the one that brought this issue up. He also said that they were looking at 1.2-million dollars in Sales & Use Tax. Mayor Snyder also said that Mills River has been having conversation with their Legislatures – I don't know the substance of these conversations. He

> said he would send me some documentation on what they have done to-date. One thing that seems odd is that Mills River had an extremely low tax rate with an operating budget of about $80,000.00 per year. This may not present well?"[148]

I called and talked to both the Mayors of Mills River and Ossipee. Ossipee already had their bill ready for presentation and felt they had an extremely good case for getting theirs through the Legislature. As such, they didn't want to make any changes or additions that might reduce their chances. I can appreciate their position and if the roles were reversed I would probably feel the same way.

In talking with Mayor Roger Snyder of Mills River, I didn't feel that we would want to attach our bill to theirs. I just didn't feel that they had a strong enough case to get theirs through the Legislature. Representative Almond had cautioned me that their petition may not present well and I had to agree. However, it should be noted that their bill did pass.

For our bill Representative Almond appears to have used the differences between two general statutes as the foundation for his argument that we should be forgiven our debt. In an email to me he said:

> "The key issue appears to be the difference between NCGS 120-163 and NCGS 136.41.2. NCGS 120-163 states all four services must be in place by January 1, of the third year of incorporation and NCGS 136.41.2 states that all four services must be in place before any Sales & Use disbursements can be received."[149]

There were two additional factors involved. Since we didn't incorporate until after the start of the fiscal year 2002/2003, the County of Stanly had already taxed and implemented both waste collection and fire protection for the fiscal year of 2002/2003. This prohibited Red Cross from being able to implement either of these. We did, however, include all services in our budget so I believe that, technically, we were in compliance with the letter of the requirement if not in the actual

[148] Email from Representative Almond, February 2004

[149] Email from Representative Almond, March 2004

application. These two factors, along with the conflicts between NCGS 120-163 and NCGS 136-41, were apparently enough to sway the Legislature into ruling us as having met the requirements.

We owe Representative David Almond a great deal for his work in getting this issue resolved. Although $73,565.72 doesn't sound like a lot of money for a municipality, it was a substantial amount for a new town such as us. It was almost the equivalent of half of our annual budget.

RED CROSS WORKS TO GET ZIP CODE

After incorporating we, as a Town, wanted to be able to use our own town name in our address. In early 2003 Council Member Larry Wayne Smith contacted the US Postal Service and made inquiries as to how we could obtain our own zip code. He reported back that we couldn't get a zip code at this time - we would have to have a population level of at least 4,000 people before the Postal Service would consider putting a post office in Red Cross.

In the May 2003 Town Council meeting the issue of street names came up about renaming Highway's 24/27, Highway 205, and Ridgecrest Road. It was suggested the names North Main, South Main, East Main, and West Main be used. At that time I interjected that this may create problems with EMS in having the same street names existing in both Oakboro and Red Cross but, if we chose to go this route, it may give us an opportunity to obtain our own zip code. That, like Albemarle, the Oakboro post office could have two zip codes being delivered from its office.[150] However, the Council did vote to change the names of Ridgecrest Road to North Main, Highway 205 to South Main, and Highway 24/27 to East and West Main.

An opportunity came in late January 2004, when I was contacted by Stanly County Emergency Services concerning a conflict in addresses between Oakboro and Red Cross. It seemed that there was a problem with having two North and/or South Main Streets in two different physical locations using the same zip code. If an emergency call came in

[150] May 2003 audio of Town Council meeting

to emergency services for a residence on North Main Street, Oakboro, NC, then how would emergency services know to respond to either North Main Street in Oakboro or to North Main Street in Red Cross, since both had the same zip code?

I met with Robbie Robinson, Director of Stanly County Emergency Services, and we discussed the problem. Our discussion led to the possibility that if we didn't change the names of our roads then we needed to see if we could designate Red Cross as an independent town through the assignment of a new zip code.

As a result of the 9/11 Twin Towers disaster, emergency services across the country had assumed a great deal of influence - especially in being able to meet emergency response needs. Using this as leverage we felt there was a real possibility we could convince the US Postal Service to grant us our own zip code. Robbie Robinson agreed to lend his influence in helping us.

I contacted the District Postmaster in Charlotte and began discussions with him. Although he made no commitment I got the impression he was amenable to the idea. It was my impression that if a letter was to be sent by Stanly County Emergency Services making the request then it would be granted. However, before sending the letter I had to get Council approval to take official action. Unfortunately, it would be March before I would be ready to bring the request before the Council.

Since Council Member Larry Wayne Smith was responsible for road maintenance I passed the information on to him for presentation to the Council. He presented it in the February 2004, Town Council meeting.

> "Councilman Smith stated that the three digit house numbers will be assigned to houses and business in the near future. However we do have a problem with EMS since Oakboro also has a North and South Main Street. Because of this maybe we can get a different zip code for Red Cross."[151]

[151] From the Minutes of the February 9, 2004 Red Cross Town Council Meeting

In this meeting I am confident the Council was made fully aware how the issue of conflicting street names would give us enough leverage to be able to get our own zip code - so that we could use a Red Cross address/zip code instead of the current Oakboro address/zip code for our mailing address.

Unfortunately, in the next Council meeting of March 2004, Lou Eubanks made a request to rename the roads. Below is an excerpt from the March 2004, Council Agenda:

> "Request for change of street names. Lou Eubanks presenting.
>
> Wants to change names of the following roads as was designated in Motion-62 by the Town Council:
>
> > Highway 205 from South Main to as yet unspecified name.
> >
> > Ridgecrest Road from North Main to as yet unspecified name.
> >
> > Highway 24/27 from East/West Main to as yet unspecified name(s).
>
> NOTE: With the passage of motion-62, it was agreed during the discussion that no road would/will be named after an individual. However, the Council does have the right to change both this and the road names."[152]

Lou Eubanks presented her request to the Council to rename South Main to "South Oakridge Road", North Main to "North Oakridge Road", East Main to "East Red Cross Road" and West Main to "West Red Cross Road".

According to Councilman Larry Wayne Smith, Lou Eubanks had come to him earlier with the proposal for changing the road names and he felt

[152] From the March 2004, Agenda of the Red Cross Town Council

it was a good idea.[153]

It was put into a motion by Council Member Chip Speight, seconded by Barbara Carpenter, and approved by vote. One dissenting vote by Heath Hahn.[154]

By changing the names of the roads in March 2004, it blocked us as a town from being able to get our own zip code. The roads didn't have to be renamed in this meeting; we could have renamed them at any later time. There was no time constraint imposed on us nor were there any cost associated with it. Emergency Services had communicated their willingness to work with us in getting our own zip code and my conversations with the District Post Master implied the Postal Service was willing to consider it.

Since this time Mayor Larry Wayne Smith appears to have made two additional attempts for obtaining a zip code for the Town of Red Cross.

1. "According to the October 2011 Town Council minutes "Council Member Larry Wayne Smith asked Mr. David Deese if he could look into the possibility of Red Cross having its own ZIP CODE; Mr. Deese said he would do so."[155]

2. According to the October 2012 Town Council Minutes "Comments from council - Mayor Smith told the Council that the District Manager/Lead Executive, Angela H Curtis, of the United States Postal Service denied the request for the Town of Red Cross to have its own ZIP CODE. However, the letter received states that you will be allowed to use Red Cross, NC 28129 as an authorized last line Address."[156]

---

[153] From the Audio of the March 2004, Red Cross Town Council Meeting (00:42:30)

[154] From the minutes and audio of the March 2004, Red Cross Town Council Meeting (00:53:15)

[155] From the October 2011, minutes of the Red Cross Town Council Meeting

[156] From the October 2012, minutes of the Red Cross Town Council Meeting

SEWER NEEDS

Providing sewer is, for any town, a major issue. Towns use water and sewer to encourage annexations and development that provide growth and increase the town's tax base. Businesses and developers are a lot more likely to come into a town that has established sewer and water services. It also allows towns to maintain control of growth patterns

It should be noted that much of what I am telling from this point forward is what I believe/understand from my perspective and involvement in studying the sewer needs of Red Cross and may not necessarily be fact.

It should also be noted that ownership of the sewer lines in Red Cross transferred from Oakboro to Stanly County in 2007 and Oakboro sold their treatment plant to Stanly County in 2014.

At the time of our incorporation the only sewer lines in Red Cross was the one installed to service West Stanly High School and the one still under construction to Ridgecrest School.

The following is a basic description of how the sewer lines are laid out in Red Cross today:

1. The main line going to the Oakboro treatment plant from Red Cross runs along Highway 205 from the intersection of Highway 24/27/Highway 205 to Oakboro. All other lines in Red Cross will join to this line main line.

2. The lines serving West Stanly High School runs west along

Highway 24/27 from the school to the intersection of Highway 205 where it connected to the main line going to Oakboro.

3. The new line that was being installed at the time of incorporation was from Ridgecrest School to Red Cross. It would run along Ridgecrest Road to the intersection of Highway 24/27/Ridgecrest Road, where it would then connected to the main line running along Highway 205 to Oakboro.

4. The newer Running Creek School line runs along Bethel Church Road to Highway 24/27 and then to the main Oakboro line at the intersection of Highway 24/27 and Highway 205.

5. During the highway widening construction there was discussion of adding an additional small spur line would run from the Running Creek School line, along Highway 24/27, to somewhere around Brattain Road. It is not known if this line was installed.

Since everyone in western Stanly County (Locust, Oakboro, Stanfield, and the western Stanly County Schools) was using the Oakboro treatment plant to process their sewer, it effectively made the Oakboro treatment plant a small regional plant for the western part of Stanly County. The rest of Stanly County, with the exception of Norwood, was using the Albemarle treatment plant to process their sewer.

Western Stanly County presented a unique problem for the County because its sewer system was not connected to the rest of the County's sewer system. One solution for the County was to transfer ownership of these school lines to Oakboro since these sewer lines were connected to the Oakboro treatment plant. After all, the Oakboro treatment plant was, in effect, serving as a regional treatment plant. This was apparently acceptable to both parties (The County of Stanly and Oakboro) because responsibility, and presumably ownership, was transferred to Oakboro by the County of Stanly.

At this point it may be good to insert some conjecture in that many believed that one of the main reasons for Oakboro being willing to take ownership of these lines was that they probably had long range plans for annexing the Red Cross community. Having these lines in our community would definitely have given them a much stronger case for annexation. We will find out later, after Red Cross became incorporated, that the ownership of these lines became less desirable to Oakboro. Especially since there were some undesirable technical issues with the Ridgecrest line that required both Oakboro and Stanly County to work together in keeping the Ridgecrest line functioning.

Sewer Study Grant:

In 2004, there was an opportunity for a 90/10 grant. A 90/10 grant meant that if Red Cross had a $100,000 project and obtained the 90/10 grant, then the grant would supply $90,000 and Red Cross would supply $10,000. This was an excellent opportunity for Red Cross to obtain a needed sewer study at a minimal cost.

The pursuit of this study was not for actual implementation but for gathering information that would allow the town to make more informed decisions on future needs. Should Red Cross ever decide to apply for any type of sewer grant, it would be required to have a completed sewer study in its portfolio as part of its grant submission request.

The best local advice I got came from Mayor Peter Edquist of Misenheimer. The following is the advice he gave me in an email on December 8, 2004:

"TO: Peter Edquest
FROM: Ray Quick

Peter:

At one of the meetings I believe you made the statement that Misenheimer had just completed a sewer study for the Town. Could you give me a short idea of what it entailed and how much it cost? I am thinking about recommending Red Cross do one.

Thanks,
Ray Quick"

"TO: Ray Quick
FROM: Peter Edquest

Ray,

What we actually have done so far is to apply for a Sewer Study Grant back in March, and then receive that grant award in August from the Rural Center. What I announced at the meeting was that we had received the grant award.

The cost of the study itself will be $41,000. With the grant, we have a 10% match requirement, so the Village will be responsible for paying $4,100.

Although we have been notified by letter that we were awarded the grant, we have yet to receive the official contract from the Rural Center. I just checked on this 2 days ago to see where we were, and was told that we would receive the official contract by year's end. As soon as we receive that, we can engage an engineering firm to actually perform the study. Study timing is 6-12 months.

Your costs for a study may vary a little from ours, but the 90/10 match will likely be the same, dependent upon available grant funds. We engaged an engineering firm to help us through the grant application process. There was no charge for this service as they are hopeful that their earlier help will give them a leg up when we choose who will do the actual study. (I am told that that the choice of who will do the work can be a simple election by the council, not necessarily an open bidding process.)

Our strategy is to first identify what the cost would be for a Village-wide sewer system (what cost burden would be placed on individual citizens?), then break up the system into component parts so that we can prioritize sections if necessary, and then to go for a grant as an unsewered community. (Be careful to remain an unsewered community if you have a choice. Grants are more likely if you have no service than if you have partial service already in place.) Finally, when we understand what the system would cost, in whole or in parts, we will judge whether not the community can bear the grant-discounted costs to get started on sewer.

Our best guess/hope today is that we would need about a $5-6 million system at a cost of only 10% to the Village. The big BUT is that this system would be tied to county lines leading to Albemarle's treatment plant, and the county's lines today may well not have the capacity to accommodate. Adding our own self-contained treatment facilities would likely make the project beyond our means.

Without sewer and water and transportation, no location is likely to attract industry, retail/restaurant/hotel businesses, or even multi-family housing. Tax base then remains stagnant and the growth of services to citizens can't happen despite the best of ideas and intentions. We already have the transportation and water. Sewer is the logical next thing for us to contemplate.

Let me know if we can help you.

With best regards,

Peter D. Edquist
Phone: 704-XXX-XXXX (USA)"

At this point some people may be thinking why should Red Cross be addressing sewer? My response is that, "no", we don't have to now; however, it is absurd to think that we will never have to address it. If there is a possibility that we will have to install sewer, whether it is in 10 or 50 years, then we need to plan for that contingency and be prepared. Consider the following:

- We are going to have to have a sewer study at some point in our future. Taking advantage of this grant would allow us to do a needed and required study at ten-cents on the dollar. My best guess is that a sewer study for Red Cross would cost somewhere around $50,000. Obtaining this grant would have reduced the town's cost to $5,000 and the grant would have funded $45,000.

- Anytime a municipality submits a grant request for sewer implementation, a completed sewer study must be included as a part of that grant request. A part of being prepared means already having a completed sewer study ready.

- In 2007 the County did take ownership of the sewer lines in Red Cross. Although many would consider these lines to be trunk lines they were not installed for that purpose, they were installed only for servicing the schools. As such, the County has no obligation to provide sewer service to Red Cross. It will be the responsibility of the Town of Red Cross to finance and install all sewer instillation within the town limits.

  As a qualifier to the above statement, the County has indicated a willingness to work with Red Cross; however, it has been made clear that it will be up to Red Cross to finance its own sewer instillations.

Since the grant was available, and I was sure we would qualify for it, I brought it before the Council in the December 2004 Town Council meeting requesting permission to apply for it. Unfortunately I was met with a lot of opposition by the Council majority and could not persuade them to allow me to apply for it. Because this was such an important issue for Red Cross I tried to force a vote of the Council. Council Member Smith made a motion to table it.[157]

Because I had such strong feelings about the issue I again approached the issue in the January 2005 Town Council meeting and did force a vote, which was voted down. The following are the minutes of that vote:

> "Mayor Quick wanted to address the sewer study again and be sure that everyone understands. He stated that a sewer study is only the process of gathering information by an engineer. An engineer would do an analysis of what our needs will be in the future and where sewage is needed and the cost. With a 90/10 grant, which is available

[157] From the audio of the December 2004 Red Cross Town Council meeting.

through the US Agricultural/Urban Development, on a $40.000 or $50,000 study our cost would be $4,000 or $5,000 (These estimates based on other towns our size.)

Motion #204 Councilman Hahn made motion to pursue 90/10 grant and hire an engineer to a study of sewer needs for the Town. Since the motion was not seconded, the Mayor exercised privilege for a vote without a second to the motion. Councilman Hahn voted yes. Councilman Smith voted no and Councilwoman Carpenter voted no."[158]

Council Member Speight was not present at this second meeting.

In reviewing the two audios (December 2004 and January 2005) there were concerns raised by Council Member Carpenter about the writing of the grant. However, writing the grant wasn't a problem, there were several people we could get to do it. Regardless, if a professional grant writer is used, the cost of writing a grant is often based on obtaining the grant; meaning that if the grant is not awarded then there is usually no charge for writing the grant. The grant writing cost is usually applied to the town's contribution to, or portion of, the 90/10 grant ratio. It should be noted that many engineering firms will write the grant request at no cost on the hope of being awarded the project. So, in effect, the cost of the grant writing is a wash.

The other objections to pursuing this grant appeared to be directed more towards concerns related to actual sewer instillation. Items such as needing to first see if Oakboro would allow us to hook into their system, cost of maintenance, needing to know where the actual instillation of lines should occur, etc. Based on these expressed concerns there is some question that the concerned Council Members may have been confusing a sewer study with actual sewer implementation?

However, the requested study wasn't for putting in or hooking up a sewer system; we just needed to do a survey of our town so that we would know

[158] From the January 2005, Red Cross Town Council minutes

what our options were and how we should plan for our future needs. It would give us a great deal of information for when the time came. Any actual sewer implementation would come later. Right now we just needed to understand what we would be facing if, and when, we did start considering putting in sewer lines. Also, if we were to submit a grant request at some future date to install sewer lines, a completed sewer study would be required to be submitted along with the grant request.

What if a business or developer came to Red Cross and wanted to bring in a substantial business or development, what would we be able to tell them about sewer? We couldn't send them to Oakboro because Oakboro was not responsible for Red Cross; they were only responsible for those lines that ran to the schools. Oakboro did not have the necessary information nor would they have paid for a Red Cross sewer study to gain that information. There was also a real question of how much additional capacity the school lines were capable of handling. We really needed the information the study would have provided.

It did not appear that the Council understood that incoming businesses and developments will want sewer and will look to the town to provide it. Any actual sewer instillation within the town limits will be the responsibility of the town to provide, not the County, not Oakboro, not anyone else.

Another aspect is that towns must be sensitive to absorbing cost - especially reoccurring cost. As a general rule developers will install a sewer infrastructure within the development they are building and after completion of the development turn everything over to the town, including ownership of the sewer lines. If the town doesn't understand the sewage needs based on topology and load demand, how will the town know it can handle the sewage requirements of that development? What will it cost the town in both short term and long term cost?

Again, it is unfortunate that we passed up on the sewer study grant because we are still going to have to do it at some point and now we will probably have to pay the total cost of the sewer study ourselves. The information this study would have provided would have been invaluable in helping us understand our future needs and in planning for our future.

Today, some will say that the County is now our sewer provider and they will take care of it. Yes, they do have some sewer lines in Red Cross but they are not our sewer provider. As it stands now, the County of Stanly has indicated a willingness to work with us, but it will be the responsibility of the Town of Red Cross to assume all cost for any instillation and/or expansion of sewer lines within the Town - including all cost of required studies.

Union County Sewer Plant:

In late 2004, Union County was looking at installing a regional sewer plant on the Rocky River in New Salem. This created a great deal of concern since there were strong indications that the State was starting to move to regional sewer plants over local sewer plants.

The potential of this plant raised some serious questions. If this happened would Oakboro still be able to apply for expansion grants as a regional sewer provider, especially if Union County were able to build a large regional plant in New Salem? If these conditions came together it could potentially reduce grant opportunities for any town(s) in the area for obtaining sewer processing facility grants.

To aid in understanding the issue it may be good to provide a little background. With the closing of Stanly Knitting Mills, the Oakboro treatment plant started feeling the stress from the lack of volume and had to start pumping fresh water into their sewage mix in order to maintain processing capability, which caused an increase in operating cost. To counter this problem Oakboro encouraged Locust and Stanfield to tap into the Oakboro facility.

Although this solved the problem, it transitioned the Oakboro plant from being a municipal treatment plant to being a regional plant. On the surface this transition may seem a minor issue, however, the cumulative effect and impact would become substantive.

Based on our observations, at the rate Oakboro was selling and promising capacity, coupled with the rapid growth we were observing in Locust, we felt that it would only be a matter of time before Oakboro reached its plant's capacity and would need to expand. If, and when, that happened would the new regional sewer plan in New Salem prevent Oakboro from being able to obtain grants for expansion? If the New Salem plant became a reality would western Stanly County have to start pumping sewage to the New Salem Plant?

There was one other point of concern and that was the endangered Carolina Heelsplitter, which populates the Rocky River. Their presence in the Rocky River limits the amount of discharge that sewer plants are allowed to direct into the river. It doesn't matter if one or twenty sewer plants are discharging into the Rocky River, the cumulative discharge cannot exceed a specific limit. The impact from the discharge of the proposed New Salem plant was an unknown that could threaten the Oakboro treatment plant.

We continued to monitor the issue until the plans for the New Salem plant fell through. Apparently, there was extremely strong resistance from the residents of New Salem.

Who Owns the Sewer Lines in Red Cross:

We never gave up trying to figure out a way to handle our future sewer issues. We had passed up on the grant opportunity for a sewer study but we still needed to develop some solution for understanding our future sewer needs. Not having a sewer study to draw from greatly handicapped our efforts in trying to determine those needs and of how to best address them.

In 2006 there started being some discussion as to who actually owns the sewer lines in the Red Cross area. We were hearing that Oakboro no longer wanted them and we were also hearing that the County had turned them over to Oakboro several years ago and that the lines did now belong to Oakboro. We also heard that Oakboro had discussed, and discarded, the option of turning the lines over to the Town of Red Cross. The question of ownership continued for the rest of the year.

In January 2007 we set up a meeting with the County Manager (Jerry

Myers) and the Stanly County Utilities Director (Donna Davis) to try and gather additional information on sewer. In preparation for that meeting we had a workshop. The following is a handout that I gave to the Council Members to work from.

Please understand there are some inaccuracies and assumptions included in this handout, but it was based on the best information we had been able to gather at the time. None of this information should be considered valid by the reader since much has changed over the years. Again, it is included only for providing the reader an understanding of our interpretation of the issue at that point in time and to provide some insight into the reasons for our actions.

"Sewer Issues

Items for consideration by the Town of Red Cross

1) **Sewer lines within the Town limits.**

   There are four main sewer lines running through the Town of Red Cross. All are presently under the management of the Town of Oakboro.

   a) The first line runs east/west along Highway 24/27 from Stony Run Subdivision to the intersection of Highway 24/27. Primary emphasis is to service West Stanly High School with ownership presently under contention between the Town of Oakboro and the County of Stanly.

   b) The second line runs north/south along Ridgecrest Road from Ridgecrest School to the intersection of Highway 24/27 and Ridgecrest Road. Primary emphasis is to service Ridgecrest School with ownership presently under contention between the Town of Oakboro and the County of Stanly.

   c) The third line runs east/west from the intersection of Highway 24/07 to Providence Church and to Running Creek School with ownership presently under contention between the Town of Oakboro and the County of Stanly. The section, or spur, from the intersection of Highway 24/27 and Bethel Church Road to Brattain Road is believed to be owned by the Town of Oakboro – status/condition is unknown.

d) The fourth line is the line running from Red Cross to Oakboro and is a six-inch pressure line. The condition, specs, and capacity are not known. Also, I am not sure of the actual ownership. It may be bundled into the package with the schools.

2) **Potential problems associated with the above stated lines:**

a) The line running to West Stanly High School and Stony Run are set up to handle existing capacity. Although I am not sure, I believe that a section of the six-inch line was replaced with dual three-inch lines during highway construction. I have no idea why this was done? However, this has proven to add unanticipated restrictions to flow capability. Also, any moderate-to-substantial increase in demand on this line will require the existing pumps be replaced with heavier pumps.

b) The lines running to Ridgecrest School seems to have major problems. Ridgecrest School is not pumping enough sewage through this line to keep the sludge from going anaerobic. This causes the formation of gas pockets that keep the pumps from working efficiently. As a result someone has to go out and bleed off the gas. I believe this has to be done more than once per week? There are six pumps along this line. Note: See "Questions" at the bottom of this section.

c) The lines running to Running Creek School are having some of the same problems as the Ridgecrest lines, but to a lesser degree. I do not have a feel for the frequency of this.

d) I do not know the condition of line extending from Bethel Church Road to Providence Church. It is my understanding that this line was put in by DOT and is servicing only one house?

e) It should be noted that pumps are sized to demand and not the size of the line. In short, the sewer load determines pump size.

Pumps cannot be too large or cavitations will result. If they are too small they will not be able to move the required sewage volume and/or will burn out prematurely. As additional users are hooked up it becomes necessary to upgrade pumps along the line.

Questions:

We still have considerable questions about flow rates, especially concerning those from Ridgecrest School?

a) What will happen to the lines during summer vacation for these schools?

b) At what frequency does the volume of the line need to be replaced to prevent gas buildup in the lines?

c) Is this a solvable problem or will it continue to be an expensive maintenance issue?

d) If the problem is solvable – how much will it cost to correct the problem?

e) Do we need to have a meeting with Chambers Engineering to discuss, or gain additional information?

3) Sewer capacity and allocations of Oakboro processing facility:

a) 900,000 GPD Total processing capacity by the Oakboro facility.

b) 123,400 GPD capacity purchased by the City of Locust with an option to purchase additional capacity up to 240,000 GPD.

c) 150,000 GPD purchased by the Town of Stanfield. There is presently no outstanding purchase options.

d) 15,000 GPD estimated for the Ridgecrest and Running Creek School lines. Actual capacity undetermined since this line is presently under contention between the Oakboro and the County of Stanly. No numbers are available for the spur that continues along Highway 24/27 to Providence Church but I believed this is folded in to the original 15,000 GPD allocated for Running Creek School. This is the permitted number but is believed to be embedded within the Oakboro usage.

e) 17,500 GPD permitted for the Stony Run Subdivision. This is the permitted number but is believed to be embedded within the Oakboro usage.

f) 8,500 GPD permitted for West Stanly High School. This is the permitted number but is believed to be embedded within the Oakboro usage.

g) The Oakboro facility typically processes between 250,000 and 350,000 GPD. During peak rains volume has spiked to 1,300,000 GPD – or 400,000 GPD over permitted usage.

h) Oakboro has, or is in the process of, increasing permitted processing capacity to 1,200,000 GPD.

i) Unofficial, and purely subjective, estimates of the next major plant expansion will be around 2012 with no future capacity estimates stated to-date.

4) Financials for Oakboro sewer plant:

a) Present rate to purchase capacity from Oakboro is $3.05 per day gallon usage.

b) Estimated cost for Oakboro to increase capacity from 900,000 GPD to 1,200,000.00 GPD is est. $3,500,000.00

c) Estimated cost for Oakboro to increase capacity to 3,000,000 GPD is est. $17,000,000.00

d) Do not know the cost per gallon of processing for the Oakboro facility?

5) Unanswered potential capacity problems:

Oakboro appears to be permitting on the assumption that sewer flow is a constant value. That is, with no allowance that a municipality may exceed its permitted capacity at any given time. This fall Oakboro has experienced short-term flow rates in excess of 1,300,000 GPD during rains – Note that Oakboro has a stated capacity of 900,000 GPD. Some of these occurrences appear to be directly attributable to one or two municipalities.

To-date Oakboro has reported four sewer spills with some in excess of 400,000 gallons (11-04-06 Weekly Post) or 230,000 gallons (SNAP 11-28-06). Part of this has been attributed to rains in Locust and Stanfield. North Carolina law requires any spill of 1,000 gallons or greater to be reported to the State.

This raises several questions:

a) Should Oakboro permit on a maximum flow rate much like power companies do to commercial customers for peak demand, or should they leave it at the present base rate?

b) If spills continue to be a problem can Oakboro be forced by the State to change its permitting standard to reflect permitting for a maximum flow rate?

c) Given the above problems, how close is Oakboro to being forced to stop selling capacity and/or forced to expand by the State?

d) If Oakboro decides to, or is forced to, expand. Will Oakboro assume all cost of the expansion or will it request some assistance/payment from its permitted clients?

e) It is my understanding that once 85% of capacity has been sold then no additional capacity can be let out. Also, at 90% capacity a plan must be submitted for intended expansion.

6) **Ownership of lines within Red Cross:**

a) The County of Stanly received permitting to install lines to schools in 2001 and, as I understand, entered into a verbal agreement with the Town of Oakboro to turn over the completed sewer lines to Oakboro in exchange for a waiver of tap/capacity fees.

b) Due to design problems it appears the Town of Oakboro is not presently happy with the level of maintenance required on these lines and may be challenging ownership of these lines with the County of Stanly – with the intent of turning these lines back over to the County. This issue may become clear within the next couple months?

c) In the October 10, 2006, meeting of the Oakboro Town Council the Oakboro Town Administrator made a recommendation to the Council (public record) that a three-party negotiation/agreement might be made between Oakboro, Stanly County and Red Cross. It is my understanding/interpretation that the Ridgecrest, Running Creek School, West Stanly High School, and Stony Run subdivision sewer lines could possibly be given to the Town of Red Cross. In so doing, enter into some negotiations with the County of Stanly to compensate Red Cross for the assumption of these lines (including purchase of sewre capacity for these lines from Oakboro). Red Cross would also be expected to purchase an additional 25,000 GPD. This would work out to Red Cross ending up with a total combined "purchased" capacity of 66,000 GPD.

15,000 GPD	for Ridgecrest and Running Creek Schools
26,000 GPD	for West Stanly High School and the Stony Run Subdivision
25,000 GPD	additional Capacity to be purchased by the Town of Red Cross
66,000 GPD	total to be assigned to the Town of Red Cross

7) **Questions about above proposal?**

a) The Oaboro Town Council rejected this proposal. Much will still depend on the outcome of the negotiations between the County and Oakboro. I would expect that before this is over there should be considerable "wiggle room" for negotiations?

b) Why did Oakbor reject this proposal? It would appear that this deal would have been a win-win situation for Oakboro. If Red Cross were to be brought into the equation Oakboro would still be able to divest themselves of the lines in Red Cross and would still receive payment for the capacities for each of the schools - the end result for Oakboro should be the same. Additionally, Oakboro would receive an additional $75,000 in purchased capacity from Red Cross as a part of this agreement deal. We need to gain a deeper understand of all the issues involved and what Oakboro's objectives and motivations are?

c) If some deal were to be worked out for Red Cross to assume ownership of these lines. What would the long-term maintenance cost be? Can these lines be put into good operational condition and what would it cost to do so if it were possible?

d) The Stony Run subdivision that is attached to the West Stanly School line poses a unique problem. It is a satellite of the Town of Oakboro. Would there be some adjustment, or allowance, for this Stony Run usage being included in the "purchased" capacity since Oakboro collects all property tax for this development?

e) Is it possible Oakboro is anticipating an increase in capacity from 900,000 to 1,200,000 GPD and hoping to bring Red Cross in at a higher GPD rate? If the expansion to 1,200,000 GPD does occur at the anticipated cost of $3,500,000 then the purchase rate for capacity should increase to $5.20 per gallon. This would alter the 66,000 GPD purchase from $201,300 at the $3.05 rate to $343,475 at the $5.20 rate.

f) Would it be to Red Cross's advantage to go ahead and purchase some capacity for future use while it is at the lower rate?

8) Upcoming meetings:

I'm planning to have a meeting with Ms. Donna Davis of Stanly County Utilities on January 10, 2007 at 4:00 PM. I believe this meeting will yield considerable more depth to our understanding of sewer issues, at least from the County's perspective.

This is a much more complex issue and with much deeper dynamics than it would first appear on the surface. Please give me your thoughts and feedback. Do we need to have another workshop to discuss these issues? If we do have a workshop do we need to bring in Chambers Engineering to discuss or gain additional information?

Ray Quick
12-30-06"

Again, the above information may or may not have been accurate but it was based on our best assumptions/understanding at the time. It should also be noted that this was before the economic collapse.

After going through the above outline in the workshop, there was little to be added and the Council felt we had a fairly good understanding of the issues.

On January 10, 2007 Heath Hahn and I met with the Stanly County Utilities Director. The following is a copy of the summary of that meeting that was passed out to all Council Members.

"Sewer Issues

Meeting with Stanly County Utilities
January 10, 2007

Heath Hahn and I (Ray Quick) met with Ms. Donna Davis and Mr. David Gill at the Stanly County's Utility Department office on Wednesday, January 10, 2007. We told them that we were anticipating that we would be under a great deal of pressure to provide sewer service for our Town within the next two-to-three years. At this point we are trying to collect information to help us make a quality decision on how to address the issue and which direction to go. We found them to be fairly open, but cautious, and very knowledgeable and informative.

The following is a mixture of information provided by Ms. Davis and Mr. Gill and of assumptions on our part that were gained from this meeting.

Specific items discussed were:

1) We left with the understanding that the sewer lines (servicing the schools) running through Red Cross do still belong to Oakboro. Although unspoken I got the impression that this issue is still not fully resolved.

2) It was also our interpretation that the sewer lines under discussion were designed to service the schools and not for carrying additional loads such as subdivisions. This means that there is still a question as to whether these lines can be used on any scale other than to service the schools. This question will probably have to be discussed/resolved with a civil engineer to obtain a qualified answer?

3) Stanly County requires sewer lines to be of higher specs (better metal and thicker walled) than the State standard due to the rocky conditions of our soil. It was also suggested that we might desire to fold some similar requirement into our Town codes - that is to develop specifications for sewer construction.

4) Oakboro's sewer processing capacity vs. current "actual" demands and near future capacity demands as well as Oakboro's plans to handle future demands appears to be an unknown. Although Oakboro's sold/obligated capacity is well below their maximum processing capacity there appears to be some disturbing imbalances with the actual volumes that are going into the processing plant vs. the planned/sold volumes. Our interpretation to this is that Oakboro may be closer to their maximum capacity than they realize and/or wish to admit. This leaves a serious question as to how Oakboro plans to handle/accommodate both near and long-term future demands.

5) Should we go into the sewer business we must give careful consideration as to the type of system we want to install? Each type has its own unique problems.

a) Vacuum system

b) Pressure system

c) Gravity system

d) Hybrid system

6) Contract vs. capital expenditure – If we do to get into the sewer business we will have to make a decision on how we want to manage it. Three basic options are:

a) Build the system, service it ourselves, and maintain it with our own people.

b) Build the system ourselves and contract the servicing of it. This method usually covers only routine maintenance. Any upgrades or major repairs will have to be contracted with another agency.

c) Obtain grants and/or financing and allow another municipality to take ownership of it.

7) When asked about engineering firms three names were offered:

a) [Name Omitted] – Based out of Pinehurst and with an office in Charlotte.

b) [Name Omitted] – Based out of Raleigh and with an office in Charlotte.

c) [Name Omitted] – Albemarle. Has done good work for the County and knows the area. There may be a conflict of interest since he is also doing work for both Oakboro and Locust.

8) Stanly County, through the Stanly County Sewer Authority, is hoping to run sewer lines to Endy within the next three-to-five

years. There is a possibility that we may be able to enter into some negotiation with the County for extending the line on to Red Cross. This will have to be explored further? If this approach is possible it may offer Red Cross and western Stanly County some valuable options. Not only will it give Red Cross a second option in its sewer considerations it also may be a way of providing some relieve to Oakboro and western Stanly with regard to sewer processing needs in the region.

9) Should Red Cross wish to participate in the Stanly County Sewer Authority there may be a possibility that we can obtain some representation on the Authority Board?

Based on the outcome of the above meeting Heath Hahn and I feel the Town of Red Cross needs to discuss some of these issues with the County of Stanly. We have set up a meeting with Mr. Jerry Myers (County Manager) for Thursday, January 18, 2007, for the purpose of gaining additional information from the County's perspective and with respect to the Stanly County Sewer Authority.

Ray Quick
01-10-07"

"Meeting with County Manager on 01-18-07

If it turns out that the County does have to take back the sewer lines going to the schools and they may wish to enter into some sort of agreement with us.

Suggested option was for the County to install sewer and control it. We would work with them in obtaining grants, etc. Any expansion would have to be paid for up front (by Red Cross).

Ray Quick
01-18-07"

Red Cross Seeks to Purchase Sewer Capacity from Oakboro:

In late January 2007 the Red Cross Town Council held a workshop to discuss our sewer needs. To our surprise three Oakboro representatives showed up at the start of this workshop. In this meeting the idea of Red Cross joining in with the other Towns in western Stanly County and purchase capacity from Oakboro was promoted. Basically, let Oakboro be the regional provider for western Stanly County. It was our understanding the Oakboro representatives were suggesting we consider purchasing somewhere around 50,000 GPD. They stated that they were charging a purchase price of $3.05 GPD. After the Oakboro representatives left we discussed what we perceived to be an offer and decided to show good faith by making a purchase. We didn't have any immediate need for this capacity but it would be good to have the reserve for future use as well as for building a "partnering" relationship with Oakboro.

In the February 2007 Red Cross Town Council meeting it was voted to purchase 50,000 GPD of sewer capacity from Oakboro at a cost of $152,500. Council Member Larry Wayne Smith was authorized to take the lead in this purchase.

There were two reasons for this: (1) it would convey to Oakboro that Red Cross was willing to take a vested involvement in western Stanly County sewer and (2) we were worried that Oakboro may run out of capacity before we were actually ready to start installing sewer. After all, Oakboro representatives had extended an offering hand and it was now up to us to respond.

In the March 2007, Red Cross Town Council meeting Council Member Larry Wayne Smith reported back to the Council that he had approached Terry Whitley and Larry Branch, of Oakboro, about purchasing capacity and was informed that Oakboro was in the process of reevaluating its pricing structure and the new pricing could exceed $5.00 per gallon.[159] It appeared Oakboro was not selling capacity. As a result of

[159]From the March 2007 Red Cross Town Council minutes and in the audio of the Council Meeting.

Smith's report we rescinded our offer to purchase capacity.

It is unknown as to why this change in position appears to have happened? Maybe they (Oakboro representatives) didn't realize that what we understood from them at our workshop meeting was that they were representing the Town of Oakboro and making offer to sell us 50,000 GPD at $3.05 per gallon. We felt that these three Oakboro representatives had come to our workshop to solicit and/or insure that we were looking to Oakboro for our sewer needs. It is also possible that when Smith approached Whitley and Branch, they didn't understand that Smith was approaching them with a formal offer to purchase capacity from Oakboro?

Although the proper method would have been for Smith to have made a formal request through the Oakboro Town Manager, he probably approached these two because they were the ones that came to our meeting with the suggestion. Still, from our perspective we felt that this response was reflective of the Oakboro Council's position and if they were opposed to our purchase of capacity (our interpretation at the time) then there was no point in continuing to pursue the purchase. Because of this we voted in the March 2007 meeting to withdraw our offer to purchase sewer capacity from Oakboro.

Red Cross Looks to the County for Sewer:

To our relief the County did end up taking formal ownership of the school sewer lines that ran through Red Cross.

Our discussions with the County indicated that they were willing to work with us; however, the people of Red Cross would be clients and, should Red Cross wish to install lines, it would be the responsibility of Red Cross to obtain funding for those lines. That included working with the County in obtaining grants. Of course any grant(s) obtained by the town would be turned over to the County for actual implementation - and that was agreeable with us. Remember, these were still all unofficial discussions and had no actionable or committable/contractual foundation at this point. We were also under the impression that 15,000 GPD of the 95,000 GPD that the County had purchased from Oakboro during the sewer ownership transfer was purchased to make allowances for the needs of Red Cross. This clearly indicated to us that the County was willing to work with Red Cross.

Because of the inconsistencies we incurred in trying to purchase capacity from Oakboro we started looking at other potential long range options that didn't require us to be dependent on the Oakboro processing facility.

Since the County was planning to install a sewer trunk line from the Albemarle treatment plant to Endy, Red Cross began to unofficially explore and promote the possibility of one day extending that line from Endy to Red Cross. Please understand that although we were serious about it, we were not looking at anything actuality happening for some time; we were just trying to get the groundwork laid so that we would have some viable future plan to work towards. In some respects it could be called "blue-sky-talking", much like the men sitting around Bill Hill's station and talking about Red Cross one day becoming a town - maybe a few degrees more serious.

There were several factors that made this seem a viable option.

1. The County of Stanly was planning to install a sewer line from the Albemarle sewer plant to Endy (half way to Red Cross).

2. The issue of ownership of the sewer lines in Red Cross was now settled and the County had accepted ownership of them. As such the County now owned, and was responsible for, a large geographical percentage of sewer coverage in western Stanly County and all of the lines in the Town of Red Cross.

3. Since the Red Cross lines were now a part of the Stanly County owned sewer system we felt there was a potentially legitimate reason for wanting to connect them to the rest of the County sewer system. After all, the Oakboro plant had, at least in our opinion, limited processing capability and growth would force something to happen in the not-too-distant future. We had our doubts about Oakboro's future ability to finance any substantial expansion of their processing facility.

4. We felt that Albemarle had tremendous excess capacity and that it would be more economical for the County to extend the Endy sewer line to western Stanly County than to contribute to an Oakboro sewer plant expansion.

Based on these unofficial discussions with one of the County Commissioners and the County Manager about the possibility, it started to look as if the possibility did exist. The three primary people from Red Cross involved in these discussions were Heath Hahn, Jerry Jordan and Ray Quick of Red Cross and, from the County's side, a County Commissioner and the County Manager.

In 2009, at one of the Mayor/Managers meetings the City Manager of Albemarle informed me that (allegedly) an Oakboro Council Member had phoned him expressing concerns about any extension of a sewer line from Endy to Red Cross. Later in a meeting with the County Manager I was told that (allegedly) the same Oakboro Council Member had also been to see him expressing concerns about any extension of the proposed Endy sewer line to Red Cross.

I must admit that I was surprised that Oakboro was even aware of our informal discussions, let alone thought them serious enough to need to lobby against. The only assumption I can make is that someone from the Red Cross Council had mentioned our talks with the County to someone on the Oakboro Council.

Since it appeared this was now becoming a premature political issue that may create friction between Red Cross, Oakboro and the County, we decided it would be more prudent to discontinue discussions. After all, we were only having exploratory talks. We had found out what we needed to know and if a viable opportunity did come up at some future date then we would have an idea of what we wanted to do and be ready to pursue it.

However, Oakboro's involvement in our exploratory discussions with the County didn't set well with the Red Cross Council. We had been greatly offended in 2007 by the events surrounding what we had perceived to be an offer by three Oakboro representatives to sell capacity to Red Cross and then having been turning down when we took them up on it. Now an Oakboro Council Member, based on statements from the Albemarle City Manager and the Stanly County Manager, (allegedly) had apparently become involved in our informal discussions, as previously stated, trying to dissuade the County from considering any future sewer line extension from Endy to Red Cross. We didn't know what Oakboro was trying to do but our assumption was that they just didn't want Red Cross to have sewer.

Call it just being frustrated, but we, the Red Cross Town Council, just didn't want to walk away without letting Oakboro know how we felt. At the suggestion of one of our Council Members I wrote up a statement and the whole Council agreed to it.[159]

In the April 2009 Red Cross Council meeting I read the statement as follows:

"Statement of position regarding sewer

The Town of Red Cross has set quietly and watched as events have unfolded regarding sewer needs in western Stanly County. Due to recent events we now feel compelled to speak out.

The Town of Oakboro's recent actions in attempting to block the County sewer line at Endy from extending to Red Cross has placed the future of Red Cross, as well as the rest of western Stanly County in jeopardy.

Red Cross has serious concerns over Oakboro being the sole sewer provider for western Stanly County.

- Oakboro once claimed ownership of the sewer lines in Red Cross but have now given those lines back to the County. Those lines serve West Stanly High School, Running Creek Elementary School, and Ridgecrest Elementary School.

[159] Minutes of the April 13, 2009, Red Cross Town Council meeting

- Oakboro turned down Red Cross's offer to buy sewer capacity from them: however, within a few months they sold additional capacity to Locust. To Red Cross this was a clear indication Oakboro has no intention of allowing Red Cross access to the services of the Oakboro sewer plant.

- Oakboro bypassed the towns in western Stanly County and went directly to Albemarle and the County in an effort to block the extension of the proposed sewer line from Endy to Red Cross. To our knowledge no effort was made on Oakboro's part to talk with any of the other three towns in western Stanly County. Oakboro's method of blocking this expansion implies that they have no idea of how they are going to meet future needs.

- Red Cross does not feel Oakboro has the ability to meet the long-term sewer needs of western Stanly County. We do not see Oakboro's tax base or tax rate sufficient to finance the level of expansion necessary to serve western Stanly County. Who does Oakboro expect to finance what could well be a twenty-million dollar sewer plant expansion?

The Town of Red Cross is willing to consider Oakboro's desire to be the sewer provider for western Stanly County. All that we ask is that they be willing to set down with us and show that they have a viable plan, a realistic means of achieving that plan, and a willingness to work fairly with everyone. If they can't, then we ask them to lend their support in getting a County sewer line ran to western Stanly County.

If Oakboro is not willing to talk with Red Cross then we will have no choice but to turn to the County for our sewer needs and encourage the extension of the proposed sewer line from Endy to western Stanly County. We encourage Locust and Stanfield to adopt a similar position.

Ray Quick
Mayor, Town of Red Cross"

Below is the article about our statement that ran in the "Stanly News & Press":

"Red Cross feels slighted by Oakboro on wastewater services

By Tiffany Thompson, News Editor

Tuesday, April 14, 2009 — As sewer services are a crucial resource for towns and cities looking to grow, the town of Red Cross took a stand Monday night that could determine its immediate future.

Currently, the only town in the western Stanly County area that has the ability to provide sewer services is Oakboro. Lines now extend from Oakboro into Locust and Stanfield to supply sewer services, but each town has to pay a fee to Oakboro for the treatment of the wastewater that flows through these lines.

Red Cross Mayor Ray Quick said the town has been observing actions taken by Oakboro in regards to the sewer services, and he believes it is time for the town to take a stand.

"The town of Red Cross has sat quietly and watched as events have unfolded regarding sewer needs in western Stanly County. Due to recent events we now feel compelled to speak out," Quick said in a statement of position regarding sewer during the Monday night town council meeting.

According to Quick, Red Cross approached Oakboro about buying sewer capacity nearly three years ago but was turned down. Instead, Oakboro issued the capacity to the city of Locust.

Councilman Jerry Jordan further explained that Oakboro's sewer lines extend to three local schools — West Stanly High, Running Creek Elementary and Ridgecrest Elementary, but these lines were abandoned.

As a result, the lines were not maintained until the county stepped in and began the maintenance.

The most recent action on Oakboro's part, according to Quick, is an attempt at prohibiting the county from extending sewer lines from Endy into Red Cross.

The statement of position continues with:

"The town of Oakboro's recent actions in attempting to block the county sewer line at Endy from extending to Red Cross has placed the future of Red Cross, as well as the rest of western Stanly County, in jeopardy.

"Red Cross has serious concerns over Oakboro being the sole sewer provider for western Stanly County.

"Oakboro once claimed ownership of the sewer lines in Red Cross but have now given those lines back to the county. Those lines serve West Stanly High School, Running Creek Elementary School and Ridgecrest Elementary School.

"Oakboro turned down Red Cross' offer to buy sewer capacity from them; however, within a few months they sold additional capacity to Locust. To Red Cross, this was a clear indication Oakboro has no intention of allowing Red Cross access to the services of the Oakboro sewer plant.

"Oakboro bypassed the towns in western Stanly County and went directly to Albemarle and the county in an effort to block the extension of the proposed sewer line from Endy to Red Cross. To our knowledge no effort was made on Oakboro's part to talk with any of the other three towns in western Stanly County. Oakboro's method of blocking this expansion implies that they have no idea of how they are going to meet future needs.

"Red Cross does not feel Oakboro has the ability to meet the long-term sewer needs of western Stanly County. We do not see Oakboro's tax base or tax rate sufficient to finance the level of expansion necessary to serve western Stanly County. Who does Oakboro expect to finance what could well be a $20 million sewer plant expansion?"

Quick said the town would be willing to work with Oakboro if a clear plan was explained, but if no attempt was made, the town would turn to the county for support.

"The town of Red Cross is willing to consider Oakboro's desire to be the sewer provider for western Stanly County. All that we ask is that they be willing to sit down with us and show that they have a viable plan, a realistic means of achieving that plan and a willingness to work fairly with everyone. If they can't, then we ask them to lend their support in getting a county sewer line ran to western Stanly County," the statement continues.

"If Oakboro is not willing to talk with Red Cross, then we will have no choice but to turn to the county for our sewer needs and encourage the extension of the proposed sewer line from Endy to western Stanly County. We encourage Locust and Stanfield to adopt a similar position."

Quick said it is important for all of the western Stanly County municipalities to work together instead of as separate entities for the betterment of the entire community."[160]

After our position statement was published in the local papers I was informed by one of the Oakboro Council Members that if Red Cross would present a request for sewer purchase to the whole of the Oakboro Town Council, it would be approved. This offer was brought back to the Red Cross Council, but it was decided not to continue pursuit of the purchase.

I appreciate the Oakboro Council Member contacting me; it restored my faith in Oakboro as being a good neighbor and indicated that this was not the official position of the Oakboro Council.

---

[160] From the "Stanly News & Press", April 14, 2009

The following are responses posted in the "Stanly News and Press" editorial section from both Terry Whitley and Larry Branch of Oakboro:

"Whitley responds to sewer issues

Sunday, April 19, 2009 — I am responding to the article written Tuesday, April 14th, 2009 in the Snap concerning the town of Red Cross' position regarding sewer, during the Monday night Town Council meeting.

It is unfortunate that much of the statement is based on inaccurate or insufficient information about Oakboro's ability to provide waste water treatment to Red Cross and other western areas of Stanly County.

I will not attempt to respond to details of the statement, however, as a Commissioner of the Town of Oakboro, I will refer only to the paragraph in the statement that said, "The town of Red Cross is willing to consider Oakboro's desire to be the sewer provider for western Stanly County.

All that we ask is that they be willing to sit down with us and show that they have a viable plan, a realistic means of achieving that plan and a willingness to work fairly with everyone…"

It is unfortunate that Oakboro has been made to appear as the bad party in this matter. This is not the case.

I assure you that Oakboro has the ability and willingness to provide this service, and I extend an invitation for a meeting between Red Cross and Oakboro, at the earliest possible date, to address these issues. The problem rest totally with poor communications, failure to plan and work together.

Terry Whitley
Town of Oakboro"[161]

[161] From "The Stanly News & Press", April 19, 2009

"Mayor makes false statements

By Larry Branch, Town Administrator for the Town of Oakboro

Thursday, April 16, 2009 — In regards to the article in April 14 Stanly News and Press, the town of Red Cross has made a public "statement of position regarding sewer."

The town of Oakboro wishes to correct the false statements made by Red Cross Mayor Ray Quick.

It's the town of Oakboro's position that Mr. Quick has made no effort to contact Oakboro prior to their public statement and in my opinion it is due to his lack of knowledge concerning the facts.

Therefore, the facts are as follows.

First, clearly at no time did Red Cross make a formal request for sewer capacity; however, there was some informal conversation concerning the possibility of them acquiring some sewer capacity.

At the time of our discussion, we informed them there was a moratorium on all future connections of said lines due to the system not operating properly.

We have not heard from them since that time. Quick has never visited my office to obtain any information concerning sewer.

Also, Quick stated "Oakboro turned down Red Cross' offer to buy capacity from them; however, within a few months they sold additional capacity to Locust." This is untrue.

Oakboro has complied and fulfilled its obligation to provide Locust 240,000 gal/day capacity in accordance with the Intra-Municipally Agreement, and have not sold any additional capacity above the amount agreed to per our Agreement of July 5, 1995.

Oakboro has entered into an agreement with Stanly County and it states in the agreement: "The parties of the Agreement wish to acknowledge that the County has, in an official and legal capacity, held ownership (Sewer Lines) and that the Town of Oakboro as maintained, controlled and collected revenue from certain sewer lines in Western Stanly County, said sewer lines servicing Running Creek and Ridgecrest Elementary School and that is also acknowledged that the Town and County, at various times, have discussed transfer of ownership of said Lines to Town with said transfer not occurring."

In the agreement it also states: "The Town and the County do hereby mutually acknowledge that County has full ownership of the Lines in question as well as pumps and other appurtenances incident to the operation of the Lines."

Oakboro agreed to sell Stanly County 50,000 gal/day capacity for the Red Cross area and at no time were these "lines" ever abandoned.

In response to the sewer needs for western Stanly County, Oakboro has taking the following actions to provide additional future sewer capacity for the Western Stanly County Regional Wastewater System.

In 1995, Oakboro entered into an intra-municipal agreement between Oakboro/Locust and Stanfield. This agreement is for a 20-year period from the commencement of said services and may renewed by up to four five-year options after termination between the parties. Again, let me state Red Cross was never a part of said agreement and at that time they were not incorporated.

In order for Oakboro to plan for future capacity we currently have two sewer projects in design or in the permitting phase and a third is the continuing "corrective action plans" for the rehabilitation of our in-town sanitary sewer collection system.

The projects are:

Installation of an 180,000-gallon equalization basin (EQ) to prevent future sanitary overflows at the McCoy Main Pump Station. Design is complete and has been submitted to DENR for permitting.

Construction is expected to be complete in approximately four months. This project will provide additional capacity for other future projects.

Oakboro is in design for our project entitled "McCoy's Creek Main Pump Station Upgrades and the installation of a 16" parallel Forced Main to the Wastewater Treatment Plant."

Completion of this project will also make available additional capacity.

Oakboro continues to do rehabilitation of our in-town sanitary sewer collection system and continues to budget and seek additional funding to correct the inflow and infiltration problem.

In response to the statement that Oakboro is attempting to block the county from installing a sewer line from Endy to Red Cross, this is incorrect.

Oakboro has never attempted to block the county from extending any sewer line; however, Red Cross due to our Agreement with Stanly County, will have to negotiate or work with Stanly County for their sewer needs. Not Oakboro.

We do not own or maintain the sewer lines in your town as stated above.

It is impossible for us to understand how Ray Quick could think Red Cross would purchase sewer capacity since they don't own even one sewer line to transport it in!

The only feasible method of sewer service to Red Cross would be through Stanly County's sewer lines per the Oakboro/Stanly County Agreement.

That is one of the primary reasons we allotted the county 50,000 GPD of sewer treatment to the Red Cross community.

> If anyone needs verification of any statement that I have made, please visit my office in Oakboro, Monday through Friday 8 a.m.-5 p.m.
>
> Larry Branch is town administrator for the Town of Oakboro."[162]

In this article Larry Branch said that "First, clearly at no time did Red Cross make a formal request for sewer capacity; however, there was some informal conversation concerning the possibility of them acquiring some sewer capacity." Technically, he is correct: (1) we perceived the presence of three Oakboro representatives and their suggestions to be formal representations of the Oakboro administration and (2) our representative, Council Member Larry Wayne Smith, should have made a formal request to the Oakboro Town Manager rather than approaching Branch and Whitley. Although the full content of that meeting is not known, it is understandable why Smith went to Branch and Whitley. They were the ones that came to our workshop on sewer issues in January 2007 with the perceived suggestion that we consider buying capacity from Oakboro - or at least we were of the understanding that they were encouraging us to purchase capacity from them.

With respect to the statement of having placed a moratorium on sewer, it is unfortunate that it was not picked up on by the members of the Red Cross Council during the workshop. Had we understood this we would not have voted to purchase capacity in the February 2007 meeting. Also, our understanding of the rejection, based on Smith's report in the March 2007 Council meeting, was that Oakboro was not selling capacity due to its review of its pricing structure. This only added to our confusion.

> "Councilmember Smith met with Terry Whitley and Larry Branch and they said they are working on new rates for sewer. Cost maybe $4.00, $5.00 or $6.00 a gallon. Motion #370 Councilmember Smith made motion to rescind motion #362 which requested that we purchase 50,000 gallon sewer capacity from Oakboro. Councilmember Jordan seconded the motion. Motion was approved

[162] From "The Stanly News & Press", April 16, 2009

by vote."[163]

It is unfortunate, but in verbal communication, the difference in the intent of what a person is saying is sometimes different from that which the listener understands. That is one of the reasons contracts are so verbose - to remove the potential of misinterpretation.

Unfortunately, the proposed sewer line from Albemarle to Endy eventually fell by the wayside, most likely as a result of the economic downturn. For the County to have installed the lines to Endy at that time, during the highway construction, would have been the most economical time to have done it. Now it looks as if it may never become a reality. It should be noted that the County did carry the line as far as the Agra-Civic Center.

There is one other consideration that probably needs to be put forth about this apparent conflict between Oakboro and Red Cross. Please understand that the following is purely speculation and everything in this section from this point on must be read as speculation only since there are no tangible facts to support it.

The question is how did Oakboro know that Red Cross was having unofficial talks with the County about the Endy sewer line?

1. From the Red Cross side all communications concerning the town's inquires about the proposed Endy sewer line were verbal communications internal to our Town Council and, to our knowledge, no one outside of the Red Cross Council was suppose to be aware of these discussions.

2. It is doubtful the County Manager or County Commissioner(s) told Oakboro of the discussions since it was an Oakboro representative that (allegedly) approached them and the City of Albemarle trying to dissuade talks about the Endy line. Even we had not talked to Albemarle about this issue.

[164] From the minutes of the March 12, 2007, Red Cross Town Council meeting

3. Talks between Red Cross and the County were so unofficial, preliminary and lacking in substance that Oakboro should not have been alarmed even if they did hear of them. The County had not yet even committed to installing the line to Endy. This raises a secondary question as to what Oakboro was actually hearing.

Based on the above assumptions, one or more Red Cross Council Members may have mentioned our discussions with the County to an Oakboro Council Member. If this assumption is correct, then the question arises of was this information accurate or of concern to the point where the Oakboro Council Member(s) felt compelled to respond?

It would be easy to assume that the majority of both the Red Cross and Oakboro Town Councils didn't know what was going on in the background and were drawn into this fray by "out of Council talk".

This is an example of what a town council needs to be aware of, because if information is communicated out of context, there is no telling what may happen.

Follow-up information:

On May 14, 2014 the County of Stanly did purchase the Oakboro sewer treatment plant and is now the owner of that plant.

As a little history, the idea of an Oakboro sewer plant was initially proposed to the town by Stanly Knitting Mills in 1977. The Town committed to the instillation in January 1978 when the Town Commissioners (Mayor Claude Teeter and Commissioners Seymore Whitley, Roy Hinson, Hugh Crowell, Ray Rogers and Keith Dry) passed a resolution to commission this plant. The resolution was introduced and motion made by Commissioner Roy Hinson and seconded by Commissioner Ray Rogers. All Commissioners voted in favor of the motion.

Initial plant capacity was 500,000 gallons per day, later expanded to handle 900,000 gallons per day, and again expanded to 1,200,000 gallons per day.

Until its closure, Stanly Knitting Mills consumed about 70% of the Oakboro plant's capacity. However, when the mill began scaling back operations the Oakboro plant began running into problems due to lack of volume flowing through the system - not enough volume to allow it to be economically operated. Fortunately, the towns of Locust and Stanfield were able to pick up the slack.

One interesting thing is that when the Oakboro Treatment Plant began processing for Locust and Stanfield the plant shifted from being a municipal system to being a small regional system. Oakboro had done an excellent job in building and managing the plant, however, it would appear the increased obligations may have caused Oakboro to reevaluate its role in operating the treatment plant. The decision was made in 2014 to sell the plant to the County. Details of the transfer are available at the County office.

As I was gathering information on the Oakboro treatment plant I couldn't help but be extremely impressed, even amazed, with what these Oakboro Commissioners had accomplished in building the Oakboro plant. They were doing this back in the 1970's, at a time when most small towns would be terrified of trying to do something on this scale. Especially since none of these people had experience in this area.

Who would have expected these local men to have had that level foresight in recognizing the future needs of Oakboro and in their willingness to take this level of action in addressing those needs? What they did improved the Oakboro residents living quality as well as its future potential; it eventually improved the potential for the whole of western Stanly County. Had it not been for this treatment plant, today's growth in western Stanly County would not be possible. Think of where Locust would be today if they had not had access to the Oakboro sewer treatment facility.

Not many people would have had the conviction to have committed their town to something of this scale. When Roy Hinson introduced this resolution in January 1978, it was introduced with a stated sum of not less than $1,675,000. That was in 1978 dollars, not today's dollars. Very few town commissioners would be willing to lend their name as having committed to something of this magnitude.

It is truly rare when a town is fortunate enough to have a group of leaders of this caliber come together at one time. All of western Stanly County should be appreciative of what these men have done because, without their foresight, western Stanly County would not have the potential it is currently enjoying today.

A Possible Consideration for Funding Future Sewer Needs:

Although Red Cross does not have sewer, there is no question but what it will be required to provide it at some point in its future. I would encourage our Town Council to consider preparing for such time as the town does have to start installing sewer within its town limits.

Although funds may become available through grants, there is little question that it will place a strain on the financial resources of the town to finance instillations of any scale. For this reason I would suggest Red Cross create a cash reserve of not less than $1,000,000, specifically for sewer instillation. Based on today's economy, a more realistic cash reserve for addressing sewer instillation would be about $3,000,000. I say this because I believe the town has enough flexibility in its expenses, now that the town hall is paid off, to allow it to build such a reserve. If the town programs it over an extended period of time it should be able to achieve the minimum $1,000,000 level.

As qualifications for this position, I will reiterate some of what has been previously stated in this chapter.

1. As Red Cross develops and new people and businesses come in there is no question that at some point in the future the pull need from our people will require the town to start providing sewer.

2. The County owns the trunk sewer lines that run through Red Cross. They are not the town's sewer provider; however, they have indicated a willingness to work with the town. It will be the

responsibility of the Town of Red Cross to fund all sewer instillation. Even if grants are obtained, it will still be the town's responsibility to fund all associated cost and matching funds.

3. The County owned sewer lines in Red Cross were installed for servicing the schools and may not be able to handle any substantial volume. The County is under no obligation to assume the cost of upgrading those lines for meeting the needs of Red Cross. In all probability, it will be Red Cross's responsibility to finance those upgrades.

4. Red Cross has not yet done a sewer study, which will be a $50,000+ upfront required cost should the town decide to apply for a grant and/or install sewer lines.

It would be irresponsible for any Red Cross Town Council to think that that Red Cross will never have to supply sewer to its residents and businesses. It would be equally irresponsible for any Red Cross Town Council not to prepare for such time as when sewer will be required. Sewer will be a pull need driven by businesses and residents, and if the town has not planned for and is not prepared for implementation, then it will not be able to handle it when the time comes.

Remember, if the town cannot serve its residents then the residents may need to look elsewhere. No person serving on our Town Council would want their legacy to be that of causing our town to fail. This issue is that serious.

GRANT OPPORTUNITIES

E-Government Utilization Project Grant:
In the September 2003, meeting of the Red Cross Town Council I proposed sending at least two people from Red Cross to the Rural Center Conference in Raleigh on November 3-4. This conference was to cover subjects on small town needs.

Unfortunately everyone seemed to be tied up and couldn't go. I felt there was a lot to be learned so I decided to go by myself. It proved to be worthwhile in that it gave me some ideas of things we needed to explore for the town and some additional contact names of people that might be able to help us. One of the most exciting and immediate things that I came out of the conference with was the opportunity to obtain a grant for electronic needs. Since we were in need of computer and communications equipment I felt this would be a great opportunity for us to get our electronic needs set up at virtually no cost to the town.

In the next town meeting after my return I gave the Council an update of what I had learned. One of the most interesting was of a grant that would pay for electronic needs for up to $50,000. It was a 100% grant, meaning that the town wouldn't have to contribute any matching funds. Still, I needed to gather information on it before I would know the full extent of the grant content.

Although I had informed Council Members earlier that this grant was available I had not, at that time, gone through the formal process of asking the Council for permission to apply for it. I was still in the process of gathering information. Unfortunately, based on the information I later received, the window from applying for the grant would be closing before I could again bring it before the Council for their approval. I asked Barbara Carpenter to complete the grant application and we mailed it in. However, we would still have time to withdraw our request should the Council not agree to the application. After all, it was a 100% grant and I couldn't see anyone having any objection to it.

I brought it to the Council at the next available meeting. Although very subdued, no one on the Council objected to the grant application. I explained that, due to the fact that the grant submittal window was going to close before the Council met again, it was necessary to go ahead and submit the application or we would have lost the opportunity.

I felt this was too good a grant to pass up. It would qualify us for any need up to $50,000. During my presentation to the Council I stated that I felt we had an immediate need of $8,000. This was primarily for our known computer and communications needs. The grant was a 100% grant, meaning we didn't have to contribute anything financially. The only stipulation was that the town would have to set up a town website and maintain that website for two years.

As an added benefit, in addition to the grants financial contribution, the E-Government Utilization Project was going to provide training to help towns get the most value out of the grant. I stated that I would be willing to go for that training and anyone else on the Council that wanted to could also go. I knew it would be excellent training because it would be at the Cisco Academy in RTP

We were informed within a couple months that we had been awarded the grant and I brought it back before the Council for a vote of approval to accept the money and enter into agreement with the E-Government Utilization Project organization. Council Member Larry Wayne Smith opposed our accepting the money.[165]

The only thing left to do was for me to force a vote on it in hopes that no one would be willing to go on record as voting it down. Council

[165] From the minutes and audio of the 12-13-04 Town Council meeting

Members Smith and Speight voted against accepting the grant and Council Members Carpenter and Hahn voted in favor of accepting it. Since it was a tie between Council Members it was up to me, as Mayor, to break the tie. I decided not to cast a vote and just let it die.

Why did I not cast the tie-breaking vote? Well, based on past experience I fully believed that without the support of the full Council I would not be able to do anything constructive with the grant were we to accept it. Were I to go ahead and sign the paperwork for this grant then we might end up in legal trouble if we didn't use the money for its intended purpose. As badly as I wanted this grant there was no way I was going to take the risk.

I was really embarrassed to have to call the E-Government Utilization Project Foundation and tell them that our Town Council had decided not to accept the grant. They were really nice about it and even offered to allow me to attend the training sessions at no cost.

We could have done a lot with $50,000. Snow Hill took the money they received and installed city wide wireless Internet in their town. They later used this initiative as a springboard to secure computers for students of their schools. I believe they worked out a deal with Dell Computers for either a no cost or low cost purchase. Would we have thought of that option, I don't know. I do believe that had we taken advantage of the Leg-Up training sessions (included in the grant in addition to the money) it would have given us a lot more insight and options for improving our town.

USDA-UD Grant (Sewer Study):

United Stated Department of Agriculture, Urban Development - There was an opportunity for a 90/10 grant - meaning that if we had a $100,000 project we would supply $10,000 and the grant would supply $90,000. I was asking to be allowed to apply for this grant.

As part of setting up the Town, we needed to have a sewer study of our Town on file. No, we were not preparing to start installing sewer but, as a town, we would eventually be faced with having to address the issue and needed to have an understanding of the issue and be prepared for it when the time came.

A sewer study wouldn't necessarily tell us exactly where to place sewer lines but it would tell us where the most advantageous places would be to put future lines, possible line capacity needs and how to plan for growth. Basically, it would be a template for future sewer implementation and a good tool in helping us develop our growth plan.

Misenheimer had gone through the process for obtaining this grant earlier in the year, so I contacted Mayor Peter Edquist for information. The information I received from him was very positive and I felt we definitely needed to pursue this grant opportunity. It should be noted that one of the key things he cautioned me on was that we needed to apply for the grant as an unsewered community.

Since the grant was available and I was sure we would qualify for it, I brought it before the Council in the December 2004 Town Council meeting asking to be allowed to apply for it. Unfortunately, I couldn't get support of the Council majority to apply for the grant and my request was tabled.

Because the issue was so important I again attempted to address the issue in January 2005 and brought it back before the Council. The window for applying for this grant was quickly coming to a close and I felt strongly enough about it that I had to make one last try. See below in the town record minutes.

> "Mayor Quick wanted to address the sewer study again and be sure that everyone understands. He stated that a sewer study is only the process of gathering information by an engineer. An engineer would do an analysis of what our needs will be in the future and where sewage is needed and the cost. With a 90/10 grant, whis [which] is available through the US [Department of] Agriculture/Urban Development, on a $40,000 to $50,000 study our cost would be $4,000 to $5,000.
>
> Motion #204 Councilman Hahn made motion to pursue a 90/10

> grant and hire an engineer to [do] a study of sewer needs for the town. Since the motion was not seconded, the Mayor exercised privilege for a vote without a second to the motion. Councilman Hahn voted yes. Councilman Smith voted no and Councilwoman [Carpenter] voted no."[166]
>
> Council Member Chip Speight was not present at this meeting.

Again, it is unfortunate that we passed up on this grant because the town is still going to have to do the study at some point. We will not be able to apply for any sewer construction grants without having a completed sewer study included as part of the grant application. Most importantly, it would have provided valuable information for our future planning.

This was an opportunity that the Council failed to take advantage of in planning for the future and in getting the town set up.

Blue Cross Blue Shield Grant:

In February 2006 Blue Cross Blue Shield was offering a grant for their Emergency Preparedness program. Since we were planning to build a town hall on the property that J. D. and Violet Hinson had donated I felt we might have an opportunity for this grant. We needed all the financial assistance we could get.

Based on the description of the grant requirements I felt we could make some modifications to our plans for the town hall (Hinson property) that would allow us to meet the requirements of this grant. My thoughts were that (1) we could install a generator to power the facility, providing somewhere for people to go if they didn't have power and heat, (2) the Stanly County Sheriff's Department could use our facility as a hub for western Stanly County and in the event of a major disaster would be able to use the resources of the facility since it would be central to western Stanly County, and (3) we could install cooking ovens in the basement to provide food relief to people in the community should we have an extended power outage, especially during winter months.

---

[166] From the minutes of the January 10, 2005 Red Cross Town Council meeting

I talked with both the Sheriff and EMS Director and both indicated their willingness to participate in this plan. I brought it before the Council for approval to apply for the grant. The Council agreed and I completed the grant application and submitted it to Blue Cross Blue Shield.

After about a month we were informed by Blue Cross Blue Shield that we had passed the first cut of their selection process. Unfortunately, within a few weeks EMS changed its position and decided not to participate. This effectively killed the grant. I called Blue Cross Blue Shield and informed them of our withdrawal from the grant program.

In hindsight it worked out best that we didn't get the grant because we later decided not to build on the Hinson property and ended up purchasing the William's property for our town hall. With the purchase of the Williams' property we were still able to provide the Sheriff's Department with a building so that they could have a satellite office for western Stanly County.

PARTF Grant:

During our land purchase (town hall) loan approval application that we submitted with Local Government Commission, we had indicated that a portion of the property was projected to be used as a park. Unfortunately, we were not in any financial position to start implementing anything like this so shortly after purchase.

We begin exploring our options and the best opportunity for us to create a park came from the Parks and Recreational Trust Fund. Lindsey Dunevant, also a Stanly County Commissioner, was the State Parks representative that we needed to contact. In the fall of 2007 we got him to come to one of the Council meetings and he laid out the plan. A parks study would be required; and grants were available for up to $300,000 (50/50 matching grant).

Unfortunately, it was time for the County to again do their 10-year parks study, so we would have to wait until the new study was completed. It was expected that it would take a year to complete. All the towns in the County would be participating and the cost of the study would be prorated based on population. We agreed to participate and paid our portion of the study cost.

During Red Cross's land purchase approval request from the Local Government Commission the initial vision was that the town would develop the back 12-acres as a park. There were three ponds on this portion and we could put concrete slabs with tables under shelters with grills so that people could have picnics and we could also install a gated child's play area. Another thing that we would have like to have seen was walking trails around the park and to the picnic areas. In discussion with West Stanly High School these walking trails could also serve as a practice track for the school's cross-country team - which would help in grant applications. These would all be low cost but would still allow us to get the park started.

There was also some hope that we could obtain a small piece of property or right-of-way adjacent to Highway 205 which would allow us access to Highway 205. It would be great to have a road coming down beside the park to the town hall creating a street loop through the town property.

Unfortunately, by the time the parks study was complete the economy began turning bad and grant money dried up, including PARTF grants. We still kept this in the back of our minds waiting for grant funds to again become available.

One of the more interesting considerations on the town's part was the potential of installing a loop street, coming off Highway 205 to the town hall and out the town hall drive to Highway 24/27. The loop street would divide the park area from future expansion areas and provide for a very picturesque view when driving by the park. I still encourage the town to continue consideration of an access point along Highway 205 for the purpose of creating a loop street through the town property.

Recycle Grant:

In 2009 the State of North Carolina passed a law requiring municipalities to begin recycling. Fortunately, this new law allowed for phased implementation and, as a new Town, Red Cross used the later timelines for implementing its recycling program.

Since Council Member Jerry Jordan was responsible for managing waste collection he took the lead in soliciting prices from potential suppliers and for establishing contract(s) for services.

Based on the information provided by the service providers the town decided to again go with Waste Management. They were the most cost effective and provided the best support for the town's entry into the recycling program. Another compelling factor was that Waste Management was already the provider for Red Cross's standard waste collection service. It should be noted that Waste Management worked closely with the Town of Red Cross and provided valuable assistance in the actual implementation of its recycle program.

With the town's entrance into the recycling program, it had to provide a second set of waste carts for each household, the original ones for regular waste and a second for recyclable waste. Waste Management had provided the carts when the town first went into waste collection, however, this time the town had to weigh the cost/benefit of allowing them to provide carts for recycle or for the town to purchase the carts outright. After studying the issue it was found it would be more economical for the town to purchase our own carts. This was because the town was eligible for the "Curbside Recycling Roll-Out Cart Grant Program" grant that allowed grant money for the purchase of the carts.

As a result of our findings Red Cross entered into a contract with Waste Management of Carolinas, Inc. in February 2011 to be the recycler and with the town furnishing the recycle carts. The town's initial intent was to begin collection service July 1, 2011. However, because of the timing of our application for grant funding, actual collection began January 1, 2012. In November 2011 the town sent out letters of notification to the people of Red Cross and in December 2011 distributed recycles carts to each household.

Still, the recycle contract cost with Waste Management was substantial, at a cost of $9.91 per month per household, and having 320 households in Red Cross the cost per year, it came out to $38,000. From this point on it would be an annual reoccurring cost that the town would realize each year going forward. There was no choice; it was mandated by the State.

To the State of North Carolina's credit, they realized this would add an additional expense to municipalities and offered a grant opportunity for municipalities entering into this program. This was done through the "Curbside Recycling Roll-Out Cart Grant Program" sponsored by DENR (Department of Environmental and Natural Resources). Red Cross chose to participate in this program - which would cover approximately 40% of the cost of cart purchases. As stated in the "Curbside Recycling Roll-Out Cart Grant Program", "DEAO will reimburse grantees for the direct purchase of carts, not to exceed a rate of $25.00 per roll-out cart, up to a maximum reimbursement of $75,000.00." It should be noted that Waste Management was the one that made us aware of this opportunity.

The Town agreed to apply for the cart grant program. Town Clerk, Bobbie Kay Thompson, located a cart supplier and negotiated price with them and I completed and submitted the grant application. In a couple weeks the town was notified that it had been awarded the grant. However, it would not be able to receive the grant money until it supplied documentation demonstrating that it had its recycle program fully implemented. Red Cross felt that it could supply that documentation no later than March 2012 and would then receive a check for approximately 40% of the cost of our cart purchase. In follow-up, the town did receive the grant money as expected.

A TOWN HALL

The incorporation process started out using the basement of Red Cross Baptist Church and continued being held there until shortly after the incorporation.

There was a feeling by some of the people that we shouldn't be meeting in a church basement. It was suggested that the town meetings should be moved to the library of West Stanly High School. A motion was made and voted making it effective. Fortunately, both the school and school board were willing to allow the town the use of the school library.

The Town Council was sensitive to the need for establishing a formal town hall and made a total of four attempts.

The first opportunity came in December 2002, when Doris Whitley's house became available. When Highway 24/27 was widened Mrs. Whitley's house was one that was going to have to be moved or destroyed. Mrs. Whitley made the decision to have her house moved. On the suggestion of C. J. Barbee the Council began looking at that property.

Although the price was right and the design of the house would allow it to be converted to a town hall, the modifications necessary to convert it to a commercial building were prohibitive. It would require an almost complete rewiring, new heating and air conditioning, extensive structural modifications, and there was insufficient room for a meeting hall. These modifications were not only to increase the structural integrity needed to meet commercial requirements but to make the building ADA

(American's with Disability Act) accessible. By the time we figured up the potential cost of modifications we believed we would be looking at over $70,000 in just the building upgrades. We will later learn, based on our experience with upgrading the Williams' house, that there will be other hidden upgrade requirements that we weren't aware of. Since we knew that this building would not meet the long-term needs of the town it was agreed by all members of the Council that it was not economically feasible to pursue purchase of this property.

The second opportunity for establishing a town hall came when the town had the opportunity to purchase a plot of land near Westway Drive on Highway 24/27. Although the location was excellent the land was low and wet. In walking the land, there were crayfish holes in several locations indicating long-term wet conditions. Although it would be possible to convert this land by hauling in fill dirt it was also considered uneconomical.

During this time I talked with Representative David Almond and he arranged for us to meet with Congressman Robin Hayes. Council Member Heath Hahn and I met with him in March 2003, and discussed our problem with finances. Congressman Hayes contacted the US Department of Agriculture - Rural Development and they in turn contacted us. Heath Hahn and I went over to the Agra-Civic Center and talked with Mr. Dale Poplin, U.S. Department of Agriculture - Rural Development, and received assurance that they would help us in obtaining a loan once we were ready to apply. We didn't get any free money but did get backing for when we did need to apply for a loan.

Our third opportunity came from Mr. and Mrs. J. D. Hinson when they donated a 0.78-acre plot at the corner of their property that was adjacent to Highway 24/27. The only stipulation was that if the Town of Red Cross should ever abandon the property (not use it for a town hall) then it would revert back to them or their estate. This was an ideal location since it was located in the center of the community and had direct access to Highway 24/27.

The Town accepted the property and began making plans to build a town hall. We got Ted Coble to check the layout of the land and try to figure the building placement and foundation requirements. This looked to be an excellent piece of property for building a town hall.

As we began making plans we knew that we wanted the town hall to be able to meet the town's needs for at least 30 years. This meant that we would need to over-build the facility.

Things that were considered in the "over-building" were the town's future needs for staff and the additional office spaces necessary to support that staff. We also wanted to provide space for a satellite sheriff's office, as former Council Member C. J. Barbee had championed. We had talked to the Sheriff and, if we were to furnish the space, they would like a fairly large single room with its own restroom. They also wanted a direct outside entrance so that the deputies would not have to go through the town hall.

After everything was figured up it was determined that the cost of the project would be approaching $400,000. Although expensive, we believed it to be a viable investment.

During this time a fourth opportunity arose. As we were leaving a Council meeting one night (March 2007) we begin talking about the land Ronnie and Ann Williams had for sale (formerly the Ike and Helen Williams farm). Council Member Jerry Jordan made the comment that he didn't see why the Town couldn't buy the property? It was 29-acres and in an excellent location near the center of town and along Highway 24/27.

We began discussing the possibility among ourselves and everyone seemed interested, but not without some trepidation. The land had been on the market for $950,000. There was 29 acres, so it came out to $34,000 per acre. This seemed a little high but Council Member Chip Speight pointed out that (allegedly) the property owner on the other side of Highway 205 had been offered $1,500,000 for their land just a few years ago for a grocery store, so the potential was there. If we understood correctly that would put that land somewhere around $100,000 per acre. That statement seemed to change the tone of the discussion on the Williams' property from being just idle speculation to being a real consideration.

A part of our rationalization was that if we did buy the William's property, then at some point in the future, we would have the option to sell off part of the property at a higher value. If we did this ten or fifteen year out, then property value should be much higher. It might even be enough to offset most of our initial purchase cost. Knowing that we had this potential option helped sooth some of our trepidation about making such a large expenditure. Little did we realize that the economy was already in the early stages of what would become a drastic recession?

We didn't know it at the time but the selling of municipal property is a much more complicated process than just putting the land up for sell and selling it. My personal opinion is that the Town of Red Cross should not consider selling this property at any time. Possibly leasing it on a term basis, but not selling it. The Town will never get another opportunity like this one.

As we continued the discussion I suggested that we should make an offer of $800,000 and see what the William's response would be. That we should be prepared to go to $850,000 for a final offer. That would still put the land at under $30,000 per acre. Everyone seemed to feel that was viable and quickly accepted the idea of perusing the option of purchasing the property. Every step had to be approved in a legitimate Council meeting before any action could be taken.

Another compelling consideration was that, although the house was not designed to be a town hall, we could easily modify it to accommodate our needs for at least the next 20 to 50 years. We estimated it would cost about $45,000 to renovate the house for use as a town hall. If, at some future point, when the Town needed a larger facility then the Town would already have debt free land in a prime location on which to build. After all we were already considering spending up to $400,000 to build a town hall on the 0.78-acre tract of land that J. D. and Violet Hinson had donated to the town. We viewed this option as a win-win decision.

We would be owners of 28.3-acres of land with existing structures. The house could easily be converted to a town hall and the detached garage, with a partially finished apartment, would be ideal for serving as an auxiliary sheriff's office to serve western Stanly County.

I ran projections of both the cost of building on the land J. D. and Violet Hinson had donated to the Town and on the purchase of the William's property against the Town's revenues/expenditures and both options were feasible and well within our ability to manage. As an added benefit, by buying the William's property we would be creating a much greater asset base for the Town than with that of that of the 0.78-acres donated by J. D. and Violet Hinson.

If we built on the 0.78-acre tract donated by J. D. Hinson we had the money to do it without borrowing. However, if we bought the William's property then we would probably need to finance at least half the purchase price.

There were many things that made the purchase of the William's property more attractive. It already had the nice house that could be converted to a town hall. It had a detached double garage with semi-finished apartment that could be used by the Sheriff's Department. And it had plenty of room for expansion - there was even enough land for a park should the town decide to create one at some future date.

Jerry Jordan was asked to lead the negotiations with the Williams because of his experience in land purchases and negotiations. This proved to be a good decision because everything went well.

After going through proper Council proceedings Jordan approached Ronnie and Ann Williams with an exploratory offer of $800,000 and began negotiations. After price negotiations were complete a price of $850,000 was settled upon.

The Town Council passed a resolution of intent to purchase the land at a price of $850,000. This conveyed to the Williams' that the Town was serious and was fully prepared to make an offer once final approvals were obtained. The four conditions listed in that resolution were: (1) a survey of the land, (2) governmental approval, (3) acceptability of the house/structure for conversion to a Town Hall, and (4) appraisal. This was communicated to the Williams' in a formal letter from the Town of Red Cross.

We knew we couldn't make an outright purchase and would have to finance more than half the agreed to price. However, financing would not be bad in that it would allow us to acquire some form of credit ratings. Having a credit rating would be good for future contract negotiations and purchases should we need it.

We contacted the United States Department of Agriculture - Urban Development and were able to obtain a loan support commitment from them to allow us to obtain a loan. We talked to three banks and found an interest rate of 4.09% with Branch Banking and Trust Company for a 15-year loan. At that time it was below the current market rate, which was at around 6.5%. So the problem of financing was solved.

The next problem was getting approval from the Local Government Commission to enter into a loan agreement with Branch Banking and Trust Company. The reason we were required to get the approval from them was because we were obtaining a loan rather than making cash purchase. Had we been able to buy the land outright then we would not have needed their approval.

No town should underestimate the power of the LGC. Among LGC duties is the monitoring of towns solvency and transactions. Basically, what they would do in our case was to review our purchase request and approve/disapprove our applying for a loan. They would also monitor our loan payments to insure we made payments in a timely manner and eventually paid off the loan.

Council Member Jerry Jordan and I met with our attorney, Josh Morton, to gather information and get his assistance in starting the process with the Local Government Commission. Our attorney had been highly skeptical about our ability to gain their approval for a land purchase of this size. This was probably based on the newness of our town, the size of the town, and the size of the proposed purchase. However, we were not to be deterred.

Once we had everything lined up we were ready to seek the Local

Government Commission's permission to purchase the property and a meeting with the LGC was set up. We had a workshop meeting to discuss our upcoming meeting with the LGC and figure out what our needs would be. The following are the minutes of this meeting:

"Red Cross Town Council Workshop

West Stanly High School Library
June 19, 2007
7:00 PM

Present – Mayor Ray Quick, Council Members; Larry Wayne Smith, Jerry Jordan, Heath Hahn, and Town Clerk Bobbie Kay Thompson. Absent was Council Member Chip Speight. Citizens present were Lou Eubanks and Dicky Hatley.

Mayor Quick called the meeting to order and stated the purpose of the meeting is to prepare for the upcoming meeting with the Local Government Commission. The primary objective being to determine what information will be needed, how to obtain that information, and how we should structure it for the presentation to the Local Government Commission on June 27, 2007.

Actions determined in the meeting:

1. It was decided that Mayor Quick, Council Member Jerry Jordan, Town Attorney Josh Morton, and, hopefully, the Town Auditor, Sam Turner be the ones to go to Raleigh on June 27, 2007, to meet with the LGC. Council Member Heath Hahn is to contact Sam Turner and see if he will be able to make the trip to Raleigh.

2. Discussed amount to be paid down. The Mayor stated that the previously discussed amount of $400,000.00 might be too much considering the need to modify the existing house. That we would probably be better off putting down no more than $300,000.00 since we would not want to see our general fund drop below $200,000.00 at any given point. Even at that level of financing we would be well within our ability to handle. Council was in general agreement but left it open to somewhere between

$300,000.00 and $350,000.00.

3. Council Member Heath Hahn is to contact Mr. Sam Turner and inquire if he can complete the 32-page financial form required by the LGC. If so, Mr. Turner is to contact the Town Attorney to coordinate this action.

4. Attorney Josh Morton stated that both parties, Ronnie and Anne Williams (seller) and the Town of Red Cross (buyer), has signed the purchase agreement. This agreement is contingent on several events as stated in the "Contract to Purchase". However, it appears there may be some difficulty completing the transaction by the September 30, 2007, deadline and Attorney Morton will contact the William's Attorney, Mr. Clegg Mabry, to see if it is possible to extend the contract an additional 10-days. That if all goes well we should be able to close the deal by October 10, 2007.

5. Reviewed status with each of the three banks contacted; Sun Trust, First Bank, and Bank of Stanly. The Town has received favorable response from all three banks but still needs to follow up with Sun Trust for some hard numbers. Council Member Heath Hahn to contact Sun Trust. It was also suggested that we contact the Savings-and-Loan in Locust.

6. In review of sewer needs. Council Member Jordan stated that we have a verbal commitment from the Town of Oakboro to allow us to connect the Town Hall to the existing sewer lines belonging to Oakboro. However, there has been no [decision] with respect to including the additional property in the hookup but he does not believe there will be enough volume difference to cause Oakboro to have a problem.

7. Mr. Morton advised us that a public hearing will have to be scheduled – the date for this will be set in the July Town Council Meeting.

8. Lou Eubanks will contact a local realtor for a listing of land price

sales over the past 12-months for the area so that a comparison can be made between the price of the William's land and price of other sold land in the area.

9. It was decided to take photos of the property to carry to Raleigh on the 27th. Mayor Quick is to get photos of the house and property.

10. The Town Council committed to paper, through the use of a GIS map, both the present and future desires/usage for the land. Since the Town will use this land for 100+-years some of the projected expansions are possibly 20-years out.

11. The Town Council committed the following to paper.

Area A

- Area to be reserved for present and future municipal purposes.
- House to be converted to Town Hall. Cost to covert house to Town Hall estimated to be around $30,000.00 but will allocate $50,000.00.
- Garage (one section finished inside) to be converted to a satellite Sheriff's Office.
- Rest of land is open for future governmental growth.

Area B

- Create park area
- Make walking trails.
- Use existing ponds for recreational fishing.
- Set up picnic tables (preferably on concrete slabs with some covered)

Area C

- Future ball fields.
- Future community center.
- Future library.
- Future fire department.

12. It was decided that the 0.78-acres at the northeastern corner of the William's property will serve as the entrance to the facility since the cross-over for the four-lane road is located in front of this property. It was decided that this area would have plantings, information signs, and flags.

13. Mayor Quick is to get the Stanly County GIS Department to draw up a map with the three different expansion areas drawn out and labeled for the trip to Raleigh.

14. Mayor Quick is also to do an Internet search for asking prices of land in the area."[167]

I began preparing our package for presentation to the LGC and our attorney, Josh Morton, scheduled our meeting with them. Based on past experience in pursuit of project funding, it was important that we demonstrate that we were fully prepared, had thought everything through, including contingencies, etc., and had our proposal fully documented. This should insure that our proposal would go through fairly smooth. It should also greatly reduce the number secondary questions asked.

I tried to anticipate any potential questions the LGC may put to us and began gathering the information that I thought we would need for our meeting with the LGC. I prepared several packages so that everyone would have copies to work from during the meeting. Hopefully, the LGC would see that we had a viable plan. I included the following:

- Executive Summary
- Town's financial statement
- Town's budget
- Financing loan information - quotes from bank and USDA-UD
- Loan payment projections
- Map of the Town

[167] From the minutes of the June 19, 2007, Red Cross Town Council Workshop

- Map of the William's property
- Map of projected/desired use of the William's property
- Survey of land prices in the Red Cross area

The day for us to sit down with the Local Government Commission came and our Attorney, Josh Morton, Council Member Jerry Jordan and I (Ray Quick) went to Raleigh to meet with them on June 27, 2007. We found them to be polite and open. They did ask a lot of questions but seemed very pleased with the package we had prepared. The only problem found was that I had used a straight formula for the loan payoff instead of a declining retirement. This did not seem to be a major issue and the rest of the meeting went well.

We did not hear anything from them for several days. Although this was probably a good sign, it was still very hard to wait. Not hearing anything was good because it meant that they weren't coming back with additional questions. Either it was going to be good enough to get approval or it was going to be an outright rejection.

Finally the Local Government Commission sent their approval that we were clear to pursue the purchase of the property. Our attorney, Josh Morton, arranged for the contract signings.

As a Town we were required to have three specified Town Representative signatures on the contracts; the Mayor (Raeford Quick), the Finance Officer (Heath Hahn) and the Town Clerk (Bobbie Kay Thompson). The lender had one representative. We had to sign both the land contract and the loan contract. This was a momentous occasion for the Town of Red Cross - we now had a town hall.

As additional information, the loan was to be a 15-year loan; however, the Town did decide to pay the loan off in 2013, so that the land and Town Hall is now town property free and clear.

In June 2008, we entered into a contract with the Stanly County Sheriff's Department to allow them the use of the detached apartment/garage to serve as a satellite Sheriff's Office for serving western Stanly County. In that contract the Sheriff's Department would be responsible for all interior maintenance and upgrades. The Town would be responsible for all exterior upkeep. The contract was to be for one dollar per year for ten years. Larry Wayne Smith took responsibility for insuring that both party's needs were met. To-date it has worked out well for both parties.

Another thing that we did was to establish a method of maintaining the 25-acres of pasture land. Since Chip Speight had been renting the pastures from Ronnie and Ann Williams the decision was made to allow him to continue using the pastures rent free on the terms that he would fertilize, lime, spray and mow the pastures on an as-needed basis. During the time Chip Speight had the pastures he did a good job maintaining them.

In 2012 the town widened and paved the drive going into the town hall. The town has now taken the fence down and is maintaining the grounds.

HOW WILL GROWTH AFFECT RED CROSS?

It seems that once Red Cross became incorporated our community split into two groups, those that wanted us to quickly start looking like a town and those that wanted us to wait and get ready.

It has been said that I held the town back from getting set up. I guess that depends on which group is doing the telling. My emphasis was not on having us look like a town but on preparing Red Cross for growth and for the protection of our people and lifestyle. I am proud of the work that was accomplished by our people in establishing Red Cross's zoning codes, vision plan, land-use plan, growth plan and transportation plan. Unfortunately, due to opposing objectives, it took 10-years to get them in place. My hope is that we will continue down the path of the people's desire for our town and not let a few independent people have their desires drive the only path.

During the election of 2011 it was circulated that "Red Cross is under investigation by the State; it hasn't done anything since incorporating and now may lose its charter." This was a false statement that was circulated based on what I believe to be the premise that if we aren't looking like a town then we haven't done anything, regardless of what else has been accomplished.

Some of our people appear to be under the "Field of Dreams" delusion that, by being declared a town, businesses will automatically come. In the real world, businesses will only come to a location when they see there is a profit to be made. Rooftop counts and supporting infrastructure are prime factors used by businesses in determining the desirability of an area. If they are not there then businesses will not come, no matter how much we may wish for them.

For this reason I have included this chapter so that our people will weigh the desire for growth against the need for retaining those qualities we stressed during the incorporation process. Please understand that growth is fine so long as it occurs within the confines of our established zoning codes, vision plan, land-use plan and growth plan. Under no condition should we sacrifice the protection provided by our codes and plans for the sake of trying to make ourselves look like a town.

As a disclaimer: This chapter is to be considered an opinion chapter based on my experiences while serving on the Red Cross Incorporation Committee, the Red Cross Town Council and as a resident of the Red Cross community. I will readily acknowledge that I am no expert and my only intent is to bring out key points for the people of Red Cross to consider when thinking about what they actually want for the future of the Red Cross community.

Red Cross has great potential for developing into a central hub for western Stanly County, however, it is not yet fully developed and, unless work continues on developing its infrastructure, it may someday end up being absorbed into a neighboring town.

What is a City?

Cities have existed for thousands of years with Uruk being on record as the earliest know city, believed to have existed nearly 10,000-years ago. Perhaps the best know city administration was that of the Roman Empire, where Rome developed extensive aqueduct and road systems.

A seldom asked question is "what is a city or town"? Probably the best answer is that it is a concentration of population for the purpose of trade. There are exceptions to the rule where governments have created cities by mandate. Some present day examples of this are Washington, DC, which was a district cut out of the Columbian Territory, hence, the District of Columbia, and Brasilia, which was cut from the jungles of

Brazil. Still, the historical overriding reason for the birth of a city is as a result of the concentration of trade.

Surprisingly, it seems the driving force for the creation of U.S. towns today has shifted from the historically traditional reasons to the need for protection from annexation by another town. This was the reason the people of Red Cross chose to form a town.

This creates a conundrum for many small communities that have incorporated for the sole purpose of staving off annexation threats. If towns are traditionally "born" from trade, or as governmental centers, then it is that foundation that gives sustenance and durability to those towns. The conundrum is, in the absence of that foundation, what will sustain those small communities that have incorporated into towns since they are neither trade nor governmental centers and few have the population base, financial resources or infrastructure to attract businesses and/or take on the mantel of a "traditional town".

Some will go on to create a functional system with a vision and codes designed to steer their community in the direction they wish to go, while others will do nothing since their only objective was to fend off an annexation attempt. In all probability those that have done nothing will end up failing and will eventually be absorbed by another encroaching town because of their people's desire for the services offered by the other town.

To qualify for incorporation a community must meet the requirements set forth by the Joint Commission on Municipal Incorporations in both substance and function. At the core of those requirements, the community must set up a municipal government, collect taxes and provide services. One very important and strong benefit of those requirements is that it does require the community to become cognitively self-aware and take responsibility for itself as a collective entity. As a result, the community has the potential of becoming much stronger by having incorporated.

One notable omission to those requirements is that it seems to be left up to the residents of the newly incorporated town to decide on how they want their town to develop. It may be surprising, but there are some very well established and successful incorporated communities that have very little outward appearance of being towns. Most people would visualize them as something like hamlets with their town being defined as more of a concentration of people rather than businesses. Still, they have an effective governmental structure, established services and they have designed their community around their lifestyle.

As stated earlier, this creates a conundrum, and as we know a conundrum is a problem that is only hypothetically solvable. Is it possible that the shift in the driving force for incorporations has created a new type of incorporated entity that, although called a town, will no longer fit the mold of the traditional concept of a town? Has this opened the door to the creation of incorporated communities and should we begin embracing incorporated communities as viable and needed entities?

When looked at objectively there are a number of arguments supporting this position.

1. A community becomes much stronger through incorporation because it becomes self-aware and takes active responsibility for itself and for its future. It is able to act as a corporation, protecting its people from individual liability while entering into contracts for services, etc.

2. The structure of a formal town and an incorporated community are vastly different. Formal towns have a town center, consisting of a business district, with surrounding suburban areas, whereas incorporated communities tend to be much less defined. There is seldom a defined business district and homes are usually on larger tracts of land, spaced further apart, and are often intermixed with farm land. Any business development is usually minimal, supporting only the needs of the community.

3. Priorities of a town and an incorporated community are very different. Although unflattering, there is no denying that the prioritized focus of structured towns is based first on their

business needs and development with secondary focus on that of their residential population, whereas, incorporated communities place their first priority on the support of their residents.

4. Resource management is substantially different. There is no denying the needs of an incorporated community are substantially different than that of a structured town. Although both have the need to supply the basics of water, sewer, waste collection, police protection and fire protection, incorporated communities are not faced with many of the other necessities, such as street construction and maintenance, which are almost always required of structured towns. With this in consideration, is it not more cost effective for each to concentrate expenditures on respective and needed services rather than having a structured town trying to provide a panacea of coverage?

5. One of the most glaring problems with towns annexing communities is the dichotomy of trying to impose the zoning codes of an existing town on that of an established community. The annexing town may even have antiquated zoning codes that have very little applicable relevance to the community that the town wishes to annex. Established communities should not be required or allow themselves to be annexed into a town in order to obtain needed services when they have the capacity to provide the same services for themselves.

It has been shown; as with Red Cross, that incorporated communities do have the ability to provide the necessary services for their residents. Red Cross has designed and implemented zoning codes and supportive plans that are probably among the best in the State with respect to the protection of its residents, its lifestyle and the future health of its community. Red Cross has provided services such as police protection, waste collection, zoning, and fire protection. At some point Red Cross will provide sewer service to its residents, and the path is clear for providing that service without a tax increase, assuming the town's administration continues to use wisdom in managing the town. This gives a clear indication that incorporated communities are functional, viable and are needed entities within our state.

The Business of Managing a Newly Incorporated Town:

What about managing an incorporated community or small town, should it be ran like a business? Practically everyone would say that it is an absolute necessity if it is going to be successful. However, the objectives of a business are to achieve a profitable return on investment for its stakeholders, whereas, a town should be a revenue neutral service to its residents.

It is strongly suggested that our people consider the following dissimilarities between traditional business objectives and small town/community objectives before encouraging growth for the sake of growth. Hopefully, this section will provide some aid in evaluating the qualities necessary for those that may serve on our Town Council.

In the business world it is very impressive for managers to be able to say I have grown the business by this much or I have increased revenues and/or net profit by this much. It is a measure of success and is a demonstration of having done a good job. For a new town following that model, that measure of success is probably most often initially expressed through a desire to make the town grow and to begin providing additional services.

One of the major problems for municipal managers is how to measure their success? What do they measure? Quantifiable items such as tax base, geographical area, population counts, growth rates, budgets, etc. are measures that are most often quoted and given the most emphasis. If the numbers have gone up then the town's administration is usually considered as having done a good job. But do these indicators measure quality of life within the town?

Unlike tax bases or geographical areas, which can be quantified, quality of life within a town cannot be as easily measured or appreciated. If a town's administration concentrates on quality of life over the traditional concept of growth, then how will the people know that the administration is doing a good job? Most town administrations will quote crime rates, education levels, income levels and income distributions, services provided, etc. All are great indicators, but is that all that is necessary for having a desirable quality of life? Is it possible for a town to meet these indicators and still suffer from a sterile social environment?

Quality of life within a town is very difficult to define. It is the bad things, or errors, which allow people to understand and appreciate the good things in life. Probably, the best explanation for quality of life is when a person reaches the point where they like what they have so much that they are not willing to risk losing it for the potential gain of something else. Based on people's comments during the Red Cross incorporation process, it would appear that the majority of the people in the Red Cross community like their relationship with their community to the point where they are not willing to risk losing it for the potential of gaining something else.

Business Recruitment and Revenue Generation:

In the business world the general saying is that "if you're not growing then you're dying". If a business is not expanding then it is not maximizing its profit potential or meeting market needs and, as a result, is inviting competition. This endangers its long term future because if it is not expanding then a competitor probably is. This is a truism that has been drilled into every business major and is one of the cornerstones of American business philosophy.

Town Administrators face a unique problem because towns are not traditional "for profit" businesses and can not conform to traditional business models. Many, if not most, past involuntary annexations were "for profit" driven by towns as is much of the business recruitment in which towns still engage. Unfortunately, most towns still cling to traditional business models. In all probability most town administrators feel that if their town is not growing then it is dying, or at least failing to keep up with anticipated budget increases. After all, most towns have a ceiling on their ability to raise prices (tax rates) and must grow (business recruitment and annexations) in order to satisfy increasing budgets (cost). They must recruit businesses and enlarge their geographical footprint (increase revenue).

The bottom line is that towns must have increases in revenue to support increases in budgets. The two major sources of revenue for Red Cross are its tax base and Sales & Use Tax. There are other minor revenue sources, but these are the ones that count. Sales & Use Tax is based on consumer spending and is a reallocation of that tax revenue back to the towns by the State of North Carolina, as such; it is a revenue source that is outside of the town's control. However, the town does have control over property tax rates. If the town increases its budget then it must obtain additional revenue. If the Red Cross Town Administration starts spending more and a budget increase is required, then the only reliable place to obtain the needed revenue is through a tax increase.

Herein lays the problem with annexations and business recruitment for supporting budget increases in lieu of a simple tax increase - they are almost never free. For small towns with equally small budgets, they may create a cash infusion that dilutes the impact of a budget increase; however, the overall effect may well be a wash unless expansion can be maintained. Financial planning for a business in a fixed market is different from that of a business in an expanding market; small towns do not have this luxury, they cannot plan and program for continued expansion. They lack that degree of flexibility in both their potential market base and in their financial management that private enterprise is able to enjoy. For small towns, relying on the recruitment of businesses and annexations to fund desired budget increases is about as dangerous as relying on anticipated lottery winnings to pay upcoming bills. Small towns must operate within existing budgets and within the constraints of known and durable revenue sources.

Think about this; assume a developer builds a development containing 20 houses. The average tax value for each of those houses is $300,000. When the town annexes those houses the town's tax base will increase by $6,000,000. At a tax rate of $0.16 per $100 valuation, the town's tax revenue will increase by $9,600 per year. This also increases the town's waste collection cost by about $3,500 per year and fire protection cost by about $3,600 per year. Just these two additional costs have wiped out most of the expected revenue gains from the annexation. This is not considering any other associated cost, such as sewer, water and street maintenance.

Consider the following philosophy; towns should be operated efficiently like a business weighing benefit against cost without consideration for profit. Towns should not be operated as profit centers - they should be operated as a revenue neutral service to their stakeholders - the residents. Growth should not be driven by the desires of town administrations and Councils but by pull.

Nearly everyone would argue that towns are revenue neutral since budgets must be balanced. Yes, budgets are balanced, but towns are not revenue neutral because there is a lot of emphasis placed on town administrations for increasing services, which in turn drives the need for a larger tax base. Without the ability to increase tax rates it then becomes necessary to recruit more businesses and annex more property to support budget increases. Regardless of how it is argued, the bottom line is that an increase in either business recruitment or geographical footprint is a form of profit for the entity "Town". If town administrations work to increase either of these then they are pursuing profit and are not revenue neutral.

All towns want to grow. Even within Red Cross most of us have the desire of wanting to see business's come into our town. There are even some on the extreme end that want to see business at any cost, as has been reflected by the repeated statements made by one Council Member of "I want to see businesses and sidewalks all the way up and down Highway 24/27, from one end of town to the other". Still others are under the false assumption that growth is an abstract financial necessity as was quoted in the "Weekly Post" on October 27, 2004, where "Smith said the tax revenue from the business will take some of the burden off the residential taxpayers in Red Cross. He said the county's top economic development official, Robert Van Geons, has made it clear to town officials that property taxes collected from residential properties won't pay all the bills."[168]

For our community, the questions that should be asked are: (1) will the business enhance the quality of life within the town, (2) will the business

[168] "The Weekly Post", "Red Cross places moratorium on growth with one exception", by Beth McLain, October 27, 2004

alter the lifestyle that is currently being enjoyed, and (3) will the business displace existing people? These are all valid questions that should be answered before our town administration tries to recruit new business.

Annexations:

The preferred method for achieving geographical growth is through voluntary annexation. It is often driven by the desire of external property owners to gain access to the services of the town. This is why the developments of Arbor Heights and Stony Run requested voluntary annexation into the Town of Oakboro prior to the incorporation of Red Cross. If a town is attractive enough then people will request to come into the town. That's probably a good indication the town is healthy.

Surprisingly, voluntary annexations may not necessarily be beneficial to the annexing town. The cost of providing services to newly annexed areas may stress the town's finances. It is even possible that the town may annex a population base that is large enough to change the future matrix of the town administration. In this case a town can put itself in the Huntersville/Lake Norman paradox where population distribution alters the town's future.

In Red Cross we've had people voluntarily request to come into the town for several reasons. Some just wanted to be a part of the town, as was done immediately after incorporation. Some wanted protection from potential annexation by another town. Some found it was cheaper to be in the town (balance of taxes vs. services) than to remain outside the Town. The reason for this third option is because the County has an add-on fire and waste collection tax whereas the Town of Red Cross includes both in its base tax rate. Please understand that people are not choosing to pay city taxes so that they don't have to pay County taxes. County taxes have to be paid even by city residents. In our case it is cheaper to pay the city tax than to pay the County's add-on taxes, and when people want to include curb-side waste pickup over the County's convenience centers. However, there are two caveats to this: (1) it is possible that the town may/will increase its tax rate at some future date and (2) there is an upper limit on the property value where this becomes uneconomically.

A second method is involuntary annexation, however, this method substantially changed in 2011 and again in 2012. Towns may pursue this approach but must make a request, through referendum, of the people in the affected area for permission to annex them. I would strongly encourage the Red Cross Administration to gain a very thorough understanding of the new law covering this type of annexation before considering any attempt to annex through this method.

Corrections to the System:

In 2011, and again in 2012, the North Carolina State Legislature made major changes to the annexation laws. Most notably, in June 2012, with the passage of Session Law 2011-11 the General Assembly gave the people living in targeted "involuntary" annexation areas a voice.

The following is an excerpt from that Session Law:

"**SECTION 1.** Part 7 of Article 4A of Chapter 160A of the General Statutes is amended by adding a new section to read:

§ 160A-58.64. Referendum prior to involuntary annexation ordinance.

a) After the adoption of the resolution of intent under this Part, the municipality shall place the question of annexation on the ballot. The municipal governing board shall notify the appropriate county board or boards of elections of the adoption of the resolution of intent and provide a legible map and clear written description of the proposed annexation area.
b) In accordance with G.S. 163-58.55, the municipal governing board shall adopt a resolution setting the date for the referendum and so notify the appropriate county board or boards of elections.
c) The county board or boards of elections shall cause legal notice of the election to be published. That notice shall include the general statement of the referendum. The referendum shall be conducted, returned, and the results declared as in other municipal elections in the municipality. Only registered voters of the proposed

annexation area shall be allowed to vote on the referendum.

d) The referendum of any number of proposed involuntary annexations may be submitted at the same election; but as to each proposed involuntary annexation, there shall be an entirely separate ballot question.

e) The ballots used in a referendum shall submit the following proposition:

[ ] FOR [ ] AGAINST

The annexation of (clear description of the proposed annexation area).

f) If less than a majority of the votes cast on the referendum are for annexation, the municipal governing body may not proceed with the adoption of the annexation ordinance or begin a separate involuntary annexation process with respect to that proposed annexation area for at least 36 months from the date of the referendum. If a majority of the votes cast on the referendum are for annexation, the municipal governing body may proceed with the adoption of the annexation ordinance under G.S. 160A-58.55."[169]

In the past, people in targeted involuntary annexation areas had no voice in the involuntary annexation process and could be taken in by the annexing town; provided the annexation was supported by the town's local Legislator and was successfully carried through the State Legislature. This is why the Town of Red Cross incorporated, to block a perceived annexation threat by a neighboring town. However, as can be seen from the above excerpt, a dramatic change has occurred with the introduction of Session Law 2011-11, in that the targeted people now have a voice and may choose, through referendum, to accept or reject the municipalities desired annexation attempt. As such, this Law can be considered a great victory for the rights of the individual.

[169] http://www.ncleg.net/Sessions/2011/Bills/House/PDF/H925v6.pdf

For Red Cross, some might say that this law came 12-years too late. However, had it not been for the fear of being annexed by one of our neighboring towns we may never have considered incorporating our community? Today we are much better off by having incorporated. Our community has become much stronger, we have been able to obtain services that we would not have otherwise been able to obtain, we have been able to define and establish a long-term vision for our community and we are able to speak with a single unified voice. Had we not incorporated we would not have had a voice in opposition to NCDOT's plans for the proposed "expressway" through our community.

After having been involved in the establishment of the Town of Red Cross and in getting our codes established I have come to understand that there is no simple right or wrong solution to this annexation problem. Individual rights are critical to us as individuals and as a Country; however, long-term planning and organized growth are critical to a municipality and to us as a civilization.

In my opinion this change in the law is but a pendulum swing that will probably yield additional corrections somewhere down the road. I say this because there are always two sides to every argument. From the people's side, in the past, involuntary annexation laws were weighed heavily in favor of the municipality with the people living in the targeted involuntary annexation areas having no voice in the process. Many, if not most, involuntary annexations were driven by the financial desires of the annexing town. Seldom was consideration given to the impact on the community being annexed. The annexing town gained a larger tax base but the community being annexed lost both its identity and lifestyle. It lost its identity because it was absorbed into the town and it lost its lifestyle because the annexing town's zoning codes and ordinances were imposed on it, forcing it to assume the personality of the annexing town. The glaring question was - is it ethical to sacrifice one group of people's quality of life for the financial gain of another group? This law addresses that question and gives the people a level of control over their destiny.

From the municipal side there is also a valid argument for needing to have a method of controlled and organized annexations. People will continue to congregate and develop property around municipalities and many will want the services offered by that municipality. As such, some people will continue to request to be annexed into the municipality in order to obtain those services. However, never is developmental growth uniform and there will always be people that don't want to be annexed into the municipality. Growth often occurs along arteries, or corridors, with outlying areas remaining undeveloped and outside the corporate limit. This creates the potential for pockets of intermixed, unplanned and dissimilar development in those outlying areas that are outside of the control of, and are inconsistent with, the municipality's vision and growth plan. Municipalities must have symmetry in order to control cost, provide services and maintain uniform zoning, etc. Non-uniform, or even haphazard, expansion jeopardizes a municipality's ability to effectively manage new and future growth.

This change in the law has eliminated the problem with "for profit" involuntary annexations by municipalities, but has introduces a previously unknown selective annexation process that may well destabilize organized and planed growth. The true impact of this change may not be known for many years.

Although I am not normally a proponent of ETJ's (Extra Territorial Jurisdiction), this may be a case where ETJ's become necessary?

Extra Territorial Jurisdiction:

Although not normally considered a form of growth, Extra Territorial Jurisdiction (ETJ) can be considered a form of growth preparation. All towns will invariably argue in favor of having ETJ's. There is no doubt that at some point a future the Red Cross Town Council will be faced with this issue.

When a town establishes an ETJ, it is able to project its zoning code enforcement out past the boundary of its corporate limit and into the unincorporated areas around the town. This does three things for the town: (1) it protects the town and its residents from undesired development adjacent to the town that may be potentially harmful to the town and/or its residents, (2) it allows the town to extend its zoning out past its corporate limits and to project it vision further in time with a greater degree of detail and, (3) it allows the town to stake a claim on those unincorporated properties.

Is this a good practice? There are valid arguments for both sides. Having ETJ's boils down to two basic and opposing lines of thought; (1) it is good for the town because it adds insurance value to the future health of the town but (2) it often has an adverse impact on the individual rights of the unincorporated property owners. To put it another way, it is a balancing act weighing the welfare of the entity "Town" against the rights of the individual.

Using Stanly County as an example; the County does not allow towns within the County to extend ETJ's outside of their corporate limits. It is the County's assertion that the people living outside the town did vote for the County Commissioners but did not vote for the town's council and, as such, it should be the County that controls the zoning for those people. Although many towns do not like this argument, it is a very valid argument based on the philosophy of "right to representation".

It will be interesting to see what develops with respect to ETJ's now that the annexation laws have changed.

Town Revitalization:

There is also a potentially dangerous area of what is called town revitalization, which is where the town tries to improve its condition through internal modifications and improvements. Although not a true growth process it often ends up becoming a business recruitment process.

Although most would say this doesn't apply to Red Cross because it is a new town. There is a valid argument that it does, because revitalization means to recharge or make like new again. Revitalization is not limited to changes in appearance but may well extend to changes in the town's zoning codes, vision, land-use and growth plans. Since revitalization is a powerful tool for business recruitment, can it not also be applied to Red Cross? Remember, a town's Board of Adjustment has the ability to grant incoming business exemptions to the town's zoning codes.

Existing vision plans and land-use patterns are often altered during the revitalization process. In effect, the town administration is trying to recreate the town into a more productive and desirable entity, often at the cost of existing businesses and residents. Town administrators must be sensitive to, and able to, distinguish between revitalizing the town using its current assets and vision and revitalizing the town by replacement.

Several years ago one town in North Carolina gave a very good presentation on how they revitalized their town. The presentation was impressive and was something for the town officials to be proud of. They had renovated their downtown and recruited a number of new businesses to populate their stores.

Their presentation also gave some insight as to what may have caused many of the original businesses on their main street to close. It seems that the Town had made critical changes to their transportation structure, their business model, and was trying to make their Town "more modern".

True, the original businesses probably weren't the most profitable or highest traffic businesses on Main Street; however, these business owners had been in business there for many years, if not for generations. Still, the town administration was able to recruit new businesses to fill those empty stores and to tout their success in being able to revitalize their Town. Their actions made the entity "Town" healthier, but at the cost of some of their older businesses.

The two key impressions received from this presentation were (1) it was through the actions of the town administration that the original businesses failed and (2) the original business owners were replaced with business owners from other areas, and even other states. No one seemed to be concerned or even notice that some of their own citizens had suffered. In fact, they were very proud of their success at being able to "revitalize" their town.

Is this an instance of where the town administration was more focused on the town as an entity than as a service focused on the welfare of the people already living in that town? There is no question but what they did upgraded and improved the appearance of their town, but were they supporting and revitalizing their original businesses?

Think about this one, the town is healthier from the business standpoint but are the people of the town healthier for the revitalization? The new "replacement" people are - but what happened to the original people? Were the original people considered part of the town or were they just living in the entity "Town" and when they were no longer an asset to the entity "Town", discarded?

There are a lot of people that would disagree with the above statement. They would say that unless a town continues to grow and evolve then it is not healthy and will not have a promising future. From their perspective they are correct; however, they are looking at the town as an entity unto itself and not as a service to its people. The question remains "are the needs of the entity "Town" greater than the needs of the people that live in that town?"

Back in the September 2003 Red Cross Town Council meeting I talked about this distinction with Planning Board Member Tom Staples, where I said "but there's a fine line there where it's the people or the town. It's the people running the town and the town takes on its own identity and it works for what makes the town grow regardless of what serves the people. It's a very fine line and that's one we don't ever want to cross. Maybe I'm being overly sensitive but I can see it happening some day and I don't want to see it happen anytime soon. So, that's where I'm coming from."[170]

Tom Staples' response was that he fully agreed with what I said. That if it was up to him he would have every person in Red Cross involved in the creation of our zoning codes, but he realizes that's not possible. I told him that I agreed, and this may sound callous, but probably 90% of people would not be interested. It's hard to give up a cold drink, a recliner, and a mindless TV show, even for a little while.

---

[170] From Audio of the September 2003, meeting of the Red Cross Town Council (00:31:08)

Basically, a town will be whatever the residents want it to be. If the residents lose interest and abandon the Town then the Town will probably lose interest in them and abandon them. It is easy for a town to replace people, especially when it is for the good of the entity "Town".

Remember, there are always people ready to step in with their own objectives and take control. Their agendas are usually financially driven, but they may also be ego driven. These people will implement their own agendas and, because the residents don't know (or care) what is going on, the town will assume a state of being to where it develops it own "identity" with different objectives and needs than those of its existing residents. It will end up where the town administration is working to serve the entity "Town". Once it crosses that line, there will be no turning back.

If residents want their town to evolve and remain a desirable place to live then they must remain involved in the town's activities. They must know what is going on. They must know that the people they are putting in office will represent them as they want to be represented and are managing the town as the residents want it managed. They must hold their elected officials accountable for their actions. The residents must do this for their own protection. If they don't then they may well be replaced by others that the entity "Town" feels will be of greater asset to it.

On August 18, 2002, in my speech during our first swearing in ceremony, I made the following statement:

> "Unfortunately, Red Cross' becoming a town is like a double-edged sword. It can cut both ways. The town can serve the people or the people can serve the town. This is an important distinction.
>
> The people can sit back doing nothing and let the town take control to the point where they start serving it..."
>
> "...I can't repeat too strongly, the town council is here to serve the people of the town and not to serve the town. Pay attention and stay involved in the town government. Make sure this town doesn't fall

into a trap and take on a life of its own and try to take control of the people."

It is unfortunate that people often become disengaged and disconnected; we have an excellent community that needs the protection of its residents.

Planning, Programming and Providing Services:

The major responsibility of a town is to provide services to its residents. Unless a town can do this, there is little reason for it to exist. A town is nothing more than a very specialized non-profit corporation that has been formed by its residents so that they can represent themselves as a collective and procure services while insulating themselves from individual liability. True, a town is endowed with certain rights and privileges, as a governmental entity, that traditional corporations don't possess, but it is still a type of corporation.

When a town first incorporates it is given till the third year of incorporation to start providing services, this allows it to build funds in its general fund so that it will have a financial base from which to work. Still, most new town administrations will want to see immediate growth and increased tax revenue. However, the reality is that it often takes years to build that financial base and the basic infrastructure necessary to support the demand requirements of incoming businesses and developments. New town administrations must be on guard not to fall into an enticing trap of trying to grow too early.

It is inevitable that over time more people will come into the town and will want basic services such as waste collection, police protection, fire protection, zoning, water and sewer. The town will have no choice but to provide these services at some point. If the town cannot, or will not, provide these services, the people will seek these services from whoever can provide them.

Town administrations for new towns must identify, plan for, and continue planning for those services that will be demanded by the residents at some point in the future. For example, when Red Cross first incorporated the most urgently identified need, or service, was to satisfy the mandate given by the people during the incorporation process of protecting the community's lifestyle. To do that the town immediately took ownership of zoning and designed zoning codes specifically to meet the needs of the town. It then projected its future zoning needs and went on to expand that service to include a vision plan, growth plan, land-use plan and transportation plan - all for the protection of the people.

Not only is it the responsibility of a town administration to address immediate needs, but to identify the town's future needs. Most towns use a 20-year window for this planning. They must plan and prepare for implementation of those services that will be required of the town prior to the time those services actually become needed by the residents of the town.

One of the most daunting services to plan for is sewer. It is expensive. It is extensive. It requires a tremendous investment in both time and planning. Most importantly, it cannot be evaded because both residents and businesses will eventually demand it of the town.

Red Cross has established its basic services, such as fire, police, waste collection and zoning, but has not yet addressed the more difficult issues of water and sewer. Fortunately, Red Cross's finances are in good condition and the town does have the ability to plan for and provide for both water and sewer, however, Red Cross must begin planning and preparing for both before it is too late.

Some within Red Cross will try to deflect this concern by saying that Red Cross became a town to block a perceived annexation threat. That is true, but Red Cross will not continue to exist as a town long-term unless it can provide needed services to its residents.

Red Cross does have three basic options for meeting its future obligations of providing water and sewer to its residents, but only the third option gives Red Cross any real hope of enduring as an independent town:

1. Red Cross can choose to do nothing and when the people demand water and sewer, the town can choose to dissolve so that the people can request annexation into either Locust or Oakboro

for obtaining sewer and water.

2. Red Cross can choose to do nothing and when the people demand water and sewer, the town can request to merge in with either Locust or Oakboro so that one of them can be responsible for providing sewer and water.

3. Red Cross can take responsibility, as a town, and start planning and preparing for when it does have to start providing sewer and water.

Growth within Red Cross is not a question of "if" but of "when". Growth will happen, and the people and businesses coming into Red Cross will be expecting the town to supply water and sewer. Red Cross has to be prepared for the day that happens. If it doesn't, it won't survive as an independent town.

As has been previously stated in the Chapter "Sewer Needs", no person serving on our Town Council, present or previous, would want their legacy to be that of causing Red Cross to fail as a town. Because town records exist, it will be easy for historians to look back and determine the true causes for the success or failure of the Town of Red Cross.

MY PERSONAL THOUGHTS

On Incorporating Red Cross:
I fully believe we did the right thing by incorporating Red Cross. At the time we began our incorporation process the "current practice" annexation laws were such that either Oakboro or Locust could have annexed parts of our community had our local State Legislators been willing to sponsor an effort.

Apparently there had been a desire by some Oakboro Council Members to annex Red Cross. Per our Legislative Representative, he had been approached by some members of the Oakboro Council asking him to support Oakboro's annexation of portions of Red Cross. I think it was in 1999 or 2000 that they approached him. He did not support their request and the issue died.

Allegedly, they approached him with the request of being able to annex up Highway 205, 250-feet on each side of the highway, to the intersection of Highway 24/27/Highway 205 and then turn east along Highway 24/27, again annexing 250-feet on each side of Highway 24/27 to West Stanly High School and annexing the school in.

Based on my understanding, under the old annexation laws all that would have been required for this annexation to succeed would have been for the local Legislative Representatives to support the annexation and champion it through the Legislature. However, by the time we completed our incorporation process in 2002, the new annexation laws were making it much more difficult, if not impossible, for either Oakboro or Locust to annex us.

Heath Hahn and I, at the urging of Robert Thompson, initiated our community's incorporation process due to our fears of being annexed. I don't know if we would have actually called that first meeting had it not been for Robert Thompson coming to me, saying that he had heard I had been talking about incorporating Red Cross, and wanting to know if we could, or would, do something. Heath Hahn took the right approach in making the decision to call the people of the community together and presenting the idea to them.

For historical purposes, it was Heath Hahn that made the call for the first meeting to present the idea of incorporation to the people of Red Cross.

Although we didn't realize the full impact at the time, by incorporating, we would able to do things as a community while keeping our people immune from individual liability. It would allow our community to go out and procure services and establish standards for our community. Fortunately, after incorporation, our Council and Planning Board were wise enough to design those standards, to not change our community but to give us the tools for maintaining self-determination and our quality of life.

The Incorporation Committee:

Surprisingly, at least to me, was how receptive everyone was to the ideal of pursuing incorporation. In the first meeting all 47 people present voted to start gathering information and by the end of the second meeting everyone was ready to go ahead and start the incorporation process. The level of community support throughout the whole process was fantastic.

The incorporation committee worked hard to get all the work done and kept an overall common objective. The overall positive approach and energy brought to the committee by the members was impressive. Everyone worked to make the incorporation happen. I think J. D. Hinson was one of the most stabilizing forces in our group. When we did have differences in opinions he seemed to have an unusual ability to negate those differences and keep things running smoothly. I will always consider him to be among the wisest and most moral of men. Although often appearing to be unassuming and reluctant to take the lead, he had those desirable qualities that were necessary for a good leader - wisdom, concern for neighbors and very high moral standards.

Another unique strength that made the incorporation committee work so well was Heath Hahn's attention to detail. As with the petition signatures, he would verify that each committee member had been to all the houses they were responsible for contacting, when he found one that had been missed, he would go and get that person's signature. Because of the volume of information the committee was required to put together, this was an invaluable contribution. Basically, he kept the loose ends tied up.

I was amazed at the willingness of State and County people to help us. It seemed to be the norm that when we went into an office the people were willing to help in any way possible, even offering advice and to do things we needed but hadn't thought of.

As has been previously stated, the amount of information and documentation we were required to put together was daunting. The data crunching for our statistical information and creation of our final town map were extremely time-consuming. A lot of people probably thought that becoming incorporated was more political than technical and all we had to do was make the request to our Legislature and get our incorporation request approved. However, those times were long gone. We either had to do our own work or we had to hire someone to do it for us. There was no State agency that was going to do it for us. We did it ourselves because we didn't have the $8,000-$10,000 needed to hire it out.

We did meet the minimum requirements for our petition to proceed through the Joint Commission on Municipal Incorporations and get their approval, however, I question whether our petition would have went as smoothly as it did had it not been for the efforts of our Representative, Bobby Harold Barbee. It is unfortunate that most of our people will neither realize nor appreciate just how much support he gave our community in Raleigh.

The Need to have a Post-incorporation Vision Plan:

I am including this because it is not something normally considered during an incorporation process. After having gone through our incorporation process and in setting up the town, I have come to the understanding that it is absolutely imperative that any community going into an incorporation process must have some sort of documented vision of what they want their community to become once they do become incorporated. If they don't, then they may lose sight of their original objective and will, in all probably, run into all kinds of problems.

Creating a vision documents not only the reason for incorporation but what the people expect after incorporating. Basically, it establishes a documented common objective, or vision, for which everyone agrees to follow after becoming incorporated. As such, once the community becomes incorporated all future plans, and even the zoning codes, will be designed to reflect and support the values defined in that vision. This gives the people a baseline for setting up their town and for judging their town council's adherence to their wishes.

Based on our town's experiences, it might be good if the Joint Commission on Municipal Incorporations were to require incorporating communities to supply some form of post-incorporation vision statement in their petition to incorporate requirements.

Unfortunately, the Red Cross Incorporation Committee did not include a formal vision of what we wanted for our community after incorporation. This created a division after incorporation, with some wanting to quickly develop along Highway 24/27 while others wanted us to stay much as we were, at least until we had our structure and protections in place. This created a great deal of conflict within our town council and delayed our getting our town structure set up for several years.

Some may say the five-lane issue was what initially split our council, and to some degree they are correct. However, there is no question that the issue for a five-lane vs. a four-lane was only a symptom driven by the desire to make us look more like a town and for encouraging growth along Highway 24/27.

We are still struggling with our future direction, there still appears to be two opposing visions for our future - protection of community values and lifestyle vs. developing into a business center. If we do want to protect our lifestyle then we must put the protection of our lifestyle as our first priority and view growth as a priority so long as it does not infringe on our first priority. However, if we want to take on the mantle of a "traditional town" then we must work to recreate ourselves in that image and place that as our only objective, setting all other concerns aside.

Regardless, it often takes years before small communities/ newly incorporated towns reach the level of development necessary to encourage or entice businesses. Businesses are drawn to a location by a need for their services and if that need, including population base, is not there then it is nearly impossible to recruit them. However, by having incorporated, small communities have been given the tools to enrich and enhance their community and to prepare for the eventual growth that will no doubt develop.

For Red Cross, how we grow is much more important than just growing.

The Interim Town Council (2002/2003):

The transition of the incorporation committee into the Interim Council went very well and I was well-pleased with the work done by the Interim Council during this term. Unfortunately, it appears that the five-lane issue eventually became the dominant issue, with the Council spending an inordinate amount of time trying to achieve a five-lane highway through Red Cross.

The highway issue was important enough that I sought information and guidance from other towns that had gone through similar problems and drew from their experiences. I also talked with some people in DOT that I knew, ones that were not involved in the Highway 24/27 project, and listened to what they had to say. I then formulated my own opinion - and it was that a five-lane would be harmful to our community if we really wanted to retain our lifestyle.

As Mayor, I had to fully support the position of the Town Council, and I did work diligently to obtain a five-lane highway. However, I did let the other members of the Council know about the information I had procured and of my opinion of the effect it would have on our community. Unfortunately, it would appear that my having a different opinion didn't set well with some members of the Council and created a division that continued throughout my time on the Council.

As stated earlier, the division within the council resulted in some individuals working on obtaining a five-lane independently and without full Council's support and knowledge. Probably, at least in my opinion, the greatest credit for the five-lane failure goes to the person that called the Chamber of Commerce and the Economic Development Commission, inviting them to attend the meeting we had with our Legislative Representatives and DOT. I consider that one meeting to have been the most critical of all our efforts for obtaining a five-lane and to be the pivotal point where we lost the issue. See the Chapter on "The Widening of Highway 24/27". There was a second focal point, which was that of a petition for a five-lane that was generated outside of official town council efforts. I consider the irregularities associated with that petition to be what gave final closure to the five-lane issue.

For my part, I never could understand the reasons for the hard feelings that had been created over the five-lane issue. Everyone involved worked hard to obtain a five-lane for Red Cross, yet the animosity generated over the failure to obtain it was substantial.

The lifestyle mandate from the people was the primary objective I used going into the interim council. When we first adopted our zoning codes from the County I didn't have a well formulated plan for protecting our lifestyle, but I did know that we needed to put some kind of infrastructure in place to manage and control growth so that our community would have some protection. Even in our first public disclosure to the local papers in September 2001, I alluded to that need in our talking notes.

> "Highway 24/27 is in the process of being expanded from two-lane to four-lane and we have observed tremendous growth in Mint Hill,

Midland, Locust, and Stanfield as sections of the project were completed out of Charlotte. Highway 24/27 bisects our community and is a crossroads for highways going to Ridgecrest in the north and Oakboro in the south. **We have to be organized, have our city infrastructure in place, and be ready for the growth once the highway expansion reaches us.**"[171]

Some of the most timely and applicable advice came from Oakboro Council Member Terry Whitley during a Red Cross Town Council meeting in February 2003 where he made special emphasis on us not dwelling on the daily activities but to start addressing our long-term needs such as or zoning, growth plan, and vision plan. It was at this point that I realized these were the tools we needed if we were going to protect our people. As a result of his advice, I started pushing for us to start working on our zoning codes and we did create our Zoning Committee in April 2003.

I will admit that I did have some preconceived ideas concerning the creation of our zoning codes. I wanted zoning code designed by people from our community and to be representative of our community's core values.

There was a little bit of a dichotomy in my desires for the design of our codes. Although I wanted the codes to be designed by Red Cross residents' independent of the Town Council, I was exerting influence to some degree in that I insisted on three specific things:

1. I wanted our Planning Board to design zoning codes that were specifically designed to protect our lifestyle.

2. Under no condition did I want to see us adopt the zoning codes of another town; I didn't want us to create ourselves in the image of another town.

---

[171] From the September 3, 2001, incorporation committee talking notes during the disclosure of Red Cross's incorporation to the Stanly News & Press and the Weekly Post.

3. Under no condition did I want our Planning Board to try and do it without knowledgeable assistance. I was determined that our Planning Board would retain a competent planning consultant to guide them through the process.

This insistence on the above three requirements created a great deal of friction within both the Town Council and the Planning Board. It seems that we were split into two groups, one group wanting us to adopt or create zoning codes from those of another town and the other group wanting us to design codes specific to our community. For the sake of the town, I was of the group that was determined that we would have zoning codes tailored specifically to our community and we would get those codes in place before growth started.

Other than the above mentioned items, I tried to stay "hands-off" on the actual code development. I will acknowledge that I did monitor and seek some code reviews for insuring our codes were sound and applicable to our community. An example of this is where I requested our Zoning Enforcement Officer review our codes from the zoning code enforcement perspective. It did prove to be a worthwhile investment.

Although the Zoning Committee was commissioned in April 2003, it wasn't until December 2004 that they retained a consultant and really started productive work on our zoning. After everyone saw the results that were being delivered through the use of a consultant, both the Planning Board and Town Council fully adopted the use of a consultant and understood the importance of this resource.

The First Elected Council (2004/2005):

During the Interim Council I was very optimistic about Red Cross being able to get the town set up. However, I was very surprised at the actions of the Council during the 2004/2005 session. Within the first few months it became apparent that there was a major division within the Council, with seemingly completely different objectives. I don't know if it was based on a desire for control or a form of ostracism for my having expressed a different opinion over the five-lane? Regardless, the feelings were strong.

It did appear that one of the main objectives of the majority of the Council was for us to quickly begin looking like a town. There was an absence of concept with respect to what kind of businesses desired or of how to recruit them; the focus was on having Red Cross look like a town.

My objective going into this session, based off the mandate of the people during the incorporation process, was to protect our lifestyle. To do this we absolutely had to get our zoning codes, land-use plan, growth plan, and vision plan put in place before growth started. Resistance was high, with us not retaining a planning consultant until December 2004.

With respect to the Council, it seemed as if everything being done towards getting the town set up was being blocked; grant acceptance turned down, motions tabled, grant application request voted down, alternate agenda items, etc. These were the actions that prevented the town from being set up in the first years.

With respect to the outward perception of our town, I had been told by outside sources there had been remarks/jokes about Red Cross's difficulties. Based on my observations, I felt we had lost a tremendous amount of credibility and were being viewed by others as being disorganized, suffering from internal conflicts, having unreasonable expectations and being abrasive in our dealings.

Unfortunately, very little was accomplished by the Town Council during this session. The only really good thing that did come out of this session was the Planning Board's retention of a professional consultant in December 2004 for aiding them in designing our zoning codes. Although there were other important things that needed to be done, there was nothing more important than getting our codes in place.

The Second Election (2006/2007):

By the start of this session both the Planning Board and Town Council had fully accepted the use of a planning consultant for creating our own zoning codes. They were working enthusiastically on our zoning codes. With the addition of the new Council Member, Jerry Jordan, in this election, I was able to start making inroads into getting our administrative policies (SOP's) established. There was some initial resistance but, with the support of Council Members Jordan and Hahn, I was able to get the first draft through the Council. Unfortunately, I let other things take precedent and failed to follow through on getting it voted into implementation. I will always regret not having put this in place during my term.

In 2007 the town was able to establish a town hall. The Ike and Helen Williams property was up for sale and the town was able to purchase it. The property consisted of 28.3-acres with house and outbuildings. We were able to successfully convert the house to a town hall and the detached apartment/garage to a satellite sheriff's office. From my perspective I don't think we could have made a better decision. It gave the town a central location for a town hall, plenty of room for expansion, the potential for creating a park, and the establishment of a satellite sheriff's office for western Stanly County. By 2014 the town had paid off the loan on the property and it was free-and-clear.

It should be noted that Council Member Larry Wayne Smith took the lead and Council Member Heath Hahn assisted in converting the Williams' home into a town hall and did an incredibly good job. The community owes them a great deal of thanks for the outstanding work they did.

Overall this was a fairly good Council session. Unfortunately, the economy was beginning to get unstable and we were no longer seeing grant opportunities. Those that were still available were not applicable to us, and even those were rapidly disappearing.

The Third Election (2008/2009):

I ran for Mayor a second time because we had not yet fully gotten our infrastructure in place. We had made good progress on our zoning codes but still had a lot of work to do on our land-use plan, vision plan and growth plan. These had to be done before our town could be considered as having a good foundation. There was a fifth item that I also wanted to get implemented; that was our administrative policies, or SOP's

(Standard Operating Procedures).

I felt I had to stay in order to insure the work was completed on these items and that they were in place for the protection of our people's lifestyle. It turned out that this would not be a problem. Our Planning Board had fully accepted the guidance of a consultant and had adopted the values I had hoped for. Our planning consultant, Carol Rhea, was doing an unbelievably good job of keeping our Planning Board focused and in being able to converting their wishes to paper.

It may seem to the reader that I am spending an inordinate amount of time writing about the creation of our zoning codes, vision, land-use, and growth plans. I cannot emphasize enough the importance of these codes, they are probably the most single important thing a town can do once it gets incorporated. They define the town, protect the people, and set the future growth patterns of the town. The incorporation committee may have created the town but it is the Planning Board that defines, or makes, the town.

With respect to Red Cross having issued its "Statement of Position Regarding Sewer" in 2009, as Mayor, there are two things that I now wish I had done differently. First, I wish I taken it upon myself to write a formal letter to Oakboro requesting the sewer capacity purchase rather than delegating that responsibility to someone else. Second, when I heard of the alleged lobbying against our discussions with the County, I wish I had first gone to Oakboro, talked with them and gotten the full story. Oakboro has always proven itself to be a good neighbor and we should have remembered that.

Based on the editorials/articles written by Whitley and Branch (see Chapter on "Sewer"), I must agree with their assessment that there were problems with communication. However, the communication problems were probably a great deal more complex than would appear at first glance.

The Fourth Election (2010/2011):

By 2008 the country was spiraling into a full-blown recession and everyone was bracing for hard times. Recognizing the recession, the Town Council had already made a cognitive decision to pull back and not spend any more than was necessary. We didn't know how bad it would get or how long it would last. We just knew that it was going to be rough. The whole Council had gotten together and agreed to operate conservatively until the recession was over.

The Planning Board was still actively addressing our land-use plan and by late 2011 was getting ready to start working on our transportation plan. If there was anything good about the bad economy, it was that it was giving us time to get our codes in place.

The quality of work we received from the Division of Community Assistance in the development of our land-use plan was excellent. I believe we couldn't have reached a better compromise solution for the development of this plan. The DCA took the lead, but we retained our planning consultant, Carol Rhea, to mediate between the Planning Board and the DCA. Between the three, a balance was reached that probably best reflected our desires.

The only real issue to arise during this term was a request by DOT wanting us to pass a resolution of acceptance for designating Highway 24/27 as an "expressway". This was a very volatile issue that threatened to irreparably damage our town.

An expressway, as per my understanding of DOT's description, has limited access, with access occurring only at overpasses, much as is required with interstates. As a result, access roads would have to be installed along Highway 24/27 so that people could reach one of these overpasses to gain access to Highway 24/27. This would be extremely disruptive, and destructive, to the people living in our town.

The Fifth Election (2012-2016):

The issue of the conversion of Highway 24/27 to an expressway continued to be the dominant issue going into this session. Locust and Red Cross did go on to form an alliance to fight the proposed expressway.

Although I was no longer Mayor, I continued to monitor the town's activities. It would appear that no firm decision has yet been reached on the expressway issue. The actions of Locust and Red Cross did force the introduction of discussions about the installation of a bypass around Locust and Red Cross. DOT is considering the possibility of a bypass either to the north or south of Locust and Red Cross; however, as it stands as of this writing I have no knowledge of DOT being willing to commit to either.

My personal opinion is that under no condition should Red Cross agree to the Highway 24/27 designation of "expressway" unless a bypass is built around Red Cross, and, in my opinion, it needs to be installed to the south so that it will benefit both Oakboro and Stanfield. I say this with some trepidation because, regardless of where it goes, it will harm landowners, even to the point of destroying homes.

It should be reiterated, that although a bypass around Locust and Red Cross has been discussed, there has been no agreement or commitment to do so. The issue has just died down and will be reintroduced at some later date, probably when the economy recovers. When the reintroduction does occur, there is a real danger that the "expressway" designation may be pushed through before there is time to mount a response. It is imperative that both Locust and Red Cross remain vigilant and not allow this issue to slip through.

Other noteworthy items were the resignation of Heath Hahn in January 2012, the appointment of Dicky Hatley to the Council as his replacement, the passing of Dicky Hatley, and the appointment of J. J. Curlee as his replacement.

On a personal note: With the resignation of Council Member Heath Hahn, the town lost a strong supporter of the people. Heath Hahn was the one that initiated the first incorporation meeting and he worked hard to get the town incorporated and set up. During that time I never found an instance where he put his personal interest above the good of the town. I did understand his not wanting to continue on the Council and do not fault him for resigning. It is unfortunate that very few people will fully realize his contributions to the community/town.

With the passing of Dicky Hatley: Dicky began serving on the Planning Board and then migrated to the Town Council. During the time I worked with him I found him to be an asset to the town. His knowledge and understanding of municipal government was refreshing, his insightfulness into cause-and-effect was a strong asset to the Planning Board, and his ability to objectively evaluate issues was a much needed asset.

It was good to see the drive into the town hall finally widened and paved; something that was badly needed. Considering the amount of work required, it is impressive that the town was able to come in at the cost level it did and use only Powell Bill Funds for the instillation of the drive. Mayor Smith is to be commended on procuring the Powell Bill Fund money for financing this project.

The Methods used for the Fifth Election (November 2011):

This election took an unusual turn in that a new mayor was elected through write-in votes. I (Ray Quick) was replaced as Mayor by Larry Wayne Smith and Barbara Carpenter was placed in as a Council Member, both through write-in votes.

It would appear that Smith planned his campaign to occur a few days before the election where he and Carpenter went to selected houses encouraging people to write in their name. The strategy appears to be that, since no one was running against anyone else, voter turnout would be extremely low so that a write-in candidate would have a good chance of winning the election.

During this election there was one specific false statement circulated that I do take strong issue with. The false statement I am referring to is that of "The Town of Red Cross is under investigation by the State; it hasn't done anything since incorporating and now may lose its charter." To me, that false statement is leaving me an implied legacy of having done nothing.

I feel that I worked hard to help get Red Cross incorporated and in getting the town set up. I don't want false tells told. I want to insure that there will be an accurate record of what went on during the incorporation process and in getting the town set up after incorporation.

I am not sure what the term "Red Cross is under investigation by the State; it hasn't done anything since incorporating and now may lose its charter" means, other than it sounds ominous. There was no notification to the town of any investigation by the "State" or Attorney General's Office. I would encourage our residents to look through the 2011 and 2012 Red Cross town records for any occurrence of an investigation - none can be found. Inquiries can also be made to the Stanly County District Attorney's Office and the North Carolina State Attorney General's Office.

It doesn't tell who is being investigated or what they are being investigated for. I can understand a town official being investigated, but what would a town be investigated for? The only real implication from this statement is that the town has been abandoned, but that can't be true because there has been a lot of work done in setting up the town and in getting it operational. There is now a town hall with 28.3-acres of land, a satellite Sheriff's Office; all services are in place and fully operational and our zoning codes, vision plan, growth plan, land-use plan and transportation plan are now in place for the protection of our people. The town is in good financial shape. Basically, Red Cross is well established and functional as a town. It is true that we don't cosmetically look like a "traditional town", however, the recent additions of a flag pole, welcome signs, a paved drive into the town hall and a large town hall sign might make us look more officious.

The only comments I can make to those people that were told this are: (1) remember who told you this, (2) consider how little respect the teller must have had for you as person to have tried to manipulate you with something like this and (3) consider how little respect the teller had for our community to have placed this dark cloud over it.

I'm sure there are questions of why I didn't take action after I heard the rumors. The answer is that I made a conscious decision not to respond and let events take their course. From a personal standpoint I was ready to bow out. I felt that by letting the people make their choice I would be doing three things; (1) I would not be quitting because the people would be voting me out, (2) it would create a lot of needed discussion within the community, and (3) I would be leaving the town on a good solid footing.

With the false rumors, I felt that the people's understanding that they had been manipulated would be the strongest tool I could use for making the people understand that their involvement in the town is important. It will have an effect on their future and they will have to stay informed and involved if they want Red Cross to be a community that serves the needs of its people.

Surprisingly, I have had a number of people come to me and tell me that if I will run again, I will be elected. Probably, but I don't intend to serve again. I have done what I set out to do in helping get Red Cross incorporated and in ensuring the town is now set up correctly (protecting our lifestyle). It was nine years of hard work seasoned with a lot of frustration and disappointment in human nature and I have no desire to go through it again.

Politics and Ethics:

One of the more applicable definitions of politics came from Wikipedia where politics is described as: "is the practice and theory of influencing other people. More narrowly, it refers to achieving and exercising positions of governance — organized control over a human community, particularly a state. Furthermore, politics is the study or practice of the distribution of power and resources within a given community (a usually hierarchically organized population) as well as the interrelationship(s) between communities.

A variety of methods are employed in politics, which include promoting or forcing one's own political views among people, negotiation with other political subjects, making laws, and exercising force, including warfare against adversaries. Politics is exercised on a wide range of social levels, from clans and tribes of traditional societies, through modern local governments, companies and institutions up to sovereign states, to the international level."[172]

In our small community, where everyone knows everyone else and considers everyone to be a neighbor, it would seem hard to believe that anyone would want to force one's own political views on others or exercise control over others, as has been implied in the above definition of politics. It would be a natural assumption that anyone volunteering to serve in our town's government would do so only for the benefit of the community.

Surprisingly, it would appear that people elected to public office sometimes lose sight of the real purpose for their being in office. Maybe they get caught up in the politics or just wanting to do something and don't know what to do. Maybe it is because most of the people just set back and keep quiet while only a select few with personal agendas shout the loudest, causing the elected officials to lose focus on the real reason for their being there - to look out for the overall interest of everyone and not just those few that are shouting the loudest.

The changing roles that people adopt, such as going into politics, are often guided by ethics, or standards of conduct. It is very common for people to act differently in different environments, even to the point of taking on different values. For those of us that do serve in our town's administration, we need to be sensitive to the effects of political ethics and protect ourselves from their influence. We should remember that those powers that have been granted to a town's administration are not a right; they are a privilege that have been conveyed on the town's administration by the people of the town.

Unfortunately, based on observations of people within our community, I have come to the conclusion that political ethics allows for maneuvering anywhere within the limits of the law - so long as the actual law is not broken.

In our society we have three standards of conduct by which we conduct ourselves: morals, ethics and the law. The general illustration for this is

[172] https://en.wikipedia.org/wiki/Politics

much like thinking of a car headed towards a cliff. The first barrier is morals, where the car should stop, the second barrier is ethics, where the driver has decided to stop the car and the third barrier is the law, where society says the car has to stop or it will go over the cliff.

In reality, ethics is the least defined because it is the standard of conduct we set for ourselves. Aldo Leopold, in "A Sand County Almanac" best described ethics as being a standard of conduct that a person sets for themselves even when no one else is around to see. Surprisingly, most of us don't always constrain ourselves to the limits of the law - so our ethics can be less restrictive than the law. Think about comfortably driving down the road at 60 mph when the posted speed limit is 55 mph... Also, as previously stated, we may alter our ethics depending on the environment in which we are participating.

It frequently appears that when people deal with political issues, even within as small a community as ours, they will suspend their moral values and substitute political ethics, or limits of the law, as their only behavioral guide. That they believe that if there is a legal way of circumventing something without actually breaking the law, regardless of whether it is moral or not, then it is perfectly acceptable and, to some degree, admirable to do so. It would seem the freedom from moral constraints, and from recrimination by peers, when dealing with political issues is extremely liberating and addictive.

I am not talking just about people holding political office, but residents as a whole. In reality there seems to be very little difference between the two, so long as both feel they are dealing with political issues.

I have seen people talk to someone as if they were their best friend and then turn around and talk negatively about that person after they were gone. I have seen people tell outright lies without showing any stress or discomfort of having told a lie. I have seen people try to manipulate others and/or impose their will on others. I have seen people work for their own gain even though it would harm others. I have seen what I once thought were the most moral of people doing these things.

What Kind of Leaders Do We Need:

I am including this section because I think the people of Red Cross really need to consider what kind of people they want to have on the town council.

Most people would say we need businessmen that know how to run a business.

Most people would say we need people that know how to make money - a demonstration of success.

Most people would say we need well educated people that know how to do things.

Many people would say we need people with ideas.

Many people would say we need people that will make us prosper - or grow.

All of these are expressions in the abstract, and without real meaning. These are preconceived ideas of those values that we think should make for good council members. If a person is successful in their personal life then they should be good on the town council and make the town successful.

The real question is what do we want from our town council? Do we want to grow into a formal town like Oakboro or Locust? If we do then we need people focused on infrastructure building and business recruitment.

Based on what I have been told by the majority of our community's residents, they like their community and want it preserved. During my involvement with the town I have found most property owners being unwilling to sell their property. Why are these people not willing to sell out and leave? Do our people really like our community that much?

If that is the case then it is important that it be preserved. If we do want to preserve our community then we must have good administrators that understand our needs and desires. The real, and difficult, question is what type of person makes a good council member?

Let's take a look at those people we previously said would make good town officials:

- Businessmen and people that know how to make money are good managers because they have demonstrated the ability to manage their business and make a profit. Invariably, they are profit oriented and measure their success by the profit they generate. It can be said that they are profit driven. However, the objective of the people of Red Cross is not the pursuit of profit, and as we know profit for a town is historically measured by annexations, business recruitment, and tax revenues. The primary objective for our town council is for it to serve and protect our people, not to make our town a profit center. I strongly suggest our people read and understand the Chapter on "How Will Growth Affect Red Cross?"

- Well educated people are always desirable because they have obtained the needed tools to do things. However, as Norman Cousins put it "wisdom consists of the anticipation of consequences." In other words, knowledge without wisdom is potentially a dangerous thing. Anyone placed on the council must be able to anticipate the long term effect their decisions will have on our community. Bad decisions by town administrations often are not just blips but set off irreversible chain reactions that eventually affect a lot of people. Town council members must be able to anticipate the effect that the decisions they make today will have in years to come.

- Generally people with ideas are dangerous people. Seldom do they have the broad-based understanding necessary to adequately serve on a council. Instead, they usually have only a few ideas they want to implement, often of their own interest. Although these ideas are usually appealing to the people, they often end up being implemented at a cost that threatens long-term tax rates. It is very rare these people make good council members. They are almost always advocates for change and for building monuments unto themselves.

Surprisingly, there is another type of person that goes around promoting ideas, that is the professional politician. They will use one or two popular ideas to rally people to get them to vote for them. It doesn't matter whether they personally support the idea or not. Equally surprising is that people seldom consider the overall qualifications of the promoter, only that they like the idea being promoted and will vote for that person based on that single idea.

- People advocating growth are probably the most dangerous of all, they are the ones wanting to recreate our community. These people don't seem to be concerned that business development and recruitment will replace our neighbors and change our lifestyle. For Red Cross, these are the least desirable people to have on our town council.

What do I consider the best type of person to serve on our council? Well, thinking in the abstract, I would have to say a dedicated farmer that possesses wisdom, has concern for neighbors and has very firm moral standards would be about as good as anyone. I am not concerned about his education level because if he has managed his farm and family well then he has demonstrated wisdom - and wisdom, concern for neighbors and morality are the key elements.

Please note that in the following, when I am referring to a businessman, I am referring to someone that operates a place of business such as a retail business. I know that farmers are also businessmen, but of a different type.

To me, having a farmer manage a town is more applicable than having a businessman manage the town. I say this because the farmer is more of a generalist, where as the businessman is more of a specialist focused only on only those aspects related to his business. A major difference between a farmer and a businessman is that the businessman measures his success based on the profit generated by his business whereas the farmer measures his success based on the overall health of his farm.

A farmer has to manage his crops, livestock, land usage, water distribution, equipment, etc. He has to astutely budget his operational finances because he invest in fertilizer and seeds for planting, yet does not realize a return on investment until the crop is harvested. He has to keep up with market prices and trends. He has to plan for both good and bad years. He has to plan crop rotations several years into the future in order to maintain the quality of his land. All are anticipatory qualities necessary for a good council member.

Although I have used the example of a farmer to illustrate those qualities I feel are important to being a good council member, I am not advocating that our council members need to be farmers. I am advocating that we look past the obvious and into the core qualities of the person and put people, men and/or women, into office that have qualities that will strengthen, enrich, nurture and protect our town.

I will qualify this with what I said earlier, regardless of who is elected to the council, they must possess three basic qualities: wisdom, concern for neighbors and very firm moral standards. I would also like to reemphasize that wisdom is the ability to understand the long-term consequences of decisions, the ability to seek council and the ability to draw from available resources.

What is the future of Red Cross?

This section is just my opinion of where we are headed as a town. I will admit that I am bias in my opinion, but not without substantial cause. I believe we could be in trouble if our residents don't have an interest in our town or its future. We very easily could have people serving in our town's administration with personal agendas, for financial reasons and/or for a desire to make us look like a town, which can do great harm to both our community's future and to our lifestyle. These people could sacrifice our vision and zoning codes for achieving their desires.

As far as growth, growth is going to occur regardless due to our strategic location. Our current limiting factors are the economy, lack of sewer infrastructure and lack of people willing to sell their land. The key is that businesses will come when they see a need for their services within our community. They may not come into our community as quickly as some would like, but the businesses that do come will probably complement our community. However, efforts to recruit businesses for making us look like a town will, in all probability, cause our town's administration to lose focus on our codes and sacrifice them for the gain of business growth.

I don't know about other people, but I like my neighbors and would hate to lose them for the sake of making us look like a town. I think it would do our people good to think back to the time where we first began the incorporation process and remember what we wanted when we first chose to pursue incorporation. The two major expressed concerns were a fear of the changes that growth would cause and a fear of losing our lifestyle.

Getting to where we are today was not easy. There was a lot of hard work and time invested by both the Town Council and Planning Board.

Our codes have been designed, not to discourage growth, but to accept growth in a manner that will have minimal impact on our lifestyle.

We have established a vision of what we hope our community will become. It was created based on those desires we had when we chose to become a town. This Vision Plan is a non-enforceable desire that can easily be changed by any future town administration. To change it, no public hearing is required and no notice to the people has to be given, all that has to be done is a vote of acceptance by a serving Town Council. In reality, they don't have to change it, they can simply ignore it.

We have developed very comprehensive zoning codes and supporting plans that define our town and protect both our people and our future. They are critically important to us as a community.

Still, regardless of all that has been accomplished, Red Cross's ability to exist long-term is both tenuous and highly questionable. As has been previously addressed, our infrastructure is not yet fully in place or planned for. Our Town Council must continue to recognize and address the town's future needs. A failure to acknowledge that water and sewer will be a future requirement of our town may well lead to its downfall. Viable plans and courses of action must be put into place to address those needs for the time when it becomes necessary to implement them.

We, as a community, have a responsibility not only to ourselves but to our neighbors and to our future generations to protect the work that has been done in setting up our town and in insuring work continues towards developing our town's infrastructure.

Our future is not already set. We can never start over, but we can always change our path. With each election we can choose to make good or bad decisions. We must have vision, proper planning and astute management if we want to insure the future of our town.

Epilogue

As the reader has gathered from having read this book, the three greatest concerns expressed throughout this book are:

1. Preparing Red Cross for enduring long-term as an independent town.

2. Promotion and defending the zoning plans that have been established for the people's protection against the threat of opposing desires.

3. Ensuring the town has good people on the council to wisely lead it into a promising and desirable future.

As was alluded to earlier in this book, after the incorporation of Red Cross there were two opposing groups that developed. Those who wanted the town to immediately start growing and to start looking like a town vs. those that wanted to wait and prepare so that when growth did come the town would be ready to accept growth in a manner that would not be damaging the community and the lifestyle the people had been enjoying.

On November 9, 2015 an initiative was put forth to rezone the western portion of Highway 24/27 running through Red Cross to commercial mixed use to a depth of 600-feet on each side of the highway. This action confirmed to the author that the above three expressed concerns were not unfounded. This issue also prompted the author to halt release of this book and add this chapter as a closing chapter. The following is how this issue relates to those expressed concerns:

1. Since the completion of the transportation plan in 2012, the author is not aware of Red Cross having started any new initiatives towards preparing the town for the future. Red Cross has not yet fully established itself and must continue work towards that objective if it wants to insure its long-term existence as an independent town.

2. The rezoning overlay proposed in the November 9, 2015 Red Cross Town Council Public Hearing and Meeting appear to be in direct opposition to the plans that had been previously designed for the protection of the community, and appears to be designed specifically for the promotion of business. It is the author's opinion that had this change been implemented, it would have significantly damaged, if not invalidated, the town's existing vision, land-use and growth plans.

3. As has been previously stated in this book, Red Cross's leaders must possess wisdom, concern for neighbors and morality. This applies to all officials, Town Council, Planning Board, Board of Adjustment, Etc. In this case a person requested rezoning for a single tract of land. Upon review of the request, the Planning Board brought before the Council a request to alter the zoning for much of the western Highway 24/27 corridor. A public hearing was called and the issue was brought before the Town Council for a vote.

It would appear the author's expressed concerns were not unfounded, however, it would also appear the author underestimated the people's awareness and willingness to respond to actions which they feel are not in the best interest of Red Cross.

Historical Background:

The people of Red Cross knew Red Cross would probably be experiencing growth after the completion of the four-lane because of Red

Cross's central location in western Stanly County and because the major four-lane connecting Stanly County to Charlotte ran through the middle of Red Cross. There was a great deal of trepidation during the incorporation process from not knowing how the expected growth would affect and change the Red Cross community. No one knew the economy would soon begin its downward spiral, beginning in 2006 and becoming fully apparent by 2008, thus delaying that anticipated growth.

In some respects it can be said that all roads in western Stanly County lead to Red Cross. The major intersection in Red Cross connects directly to the towns of Albemarle, Locust and Oakboro and the communities of Frog Pond and Ridgecrest. Highway 24/27, connecting Albemarle and the rest of Stanly County to Charlotte, runs through the middle of Red Cross. It should also be noted that the Town of Stanfield is located about 5-miles to the southwest of Red Cross, but does not directly access Red Cross. As such, Red Cross does have the potential of one day becoming the central hub for western Stanly County.

For at least the last 20 years most planners and knowledgeable people have been of the belief that eventually the stretch of Highway 24/27 between Albemarle and Charlotte will someday develop into a series of small businesses - as has often been stated: "Highway 24/27 between Albemarle and Charlotte will eventually become just one long strip of business". As such, it was easy for the people of Red Cross to see that Highway 24/27 could eventually strip out along the highway through their community, with small independent businesses, jeopardizing the long-term desirability of having homes located along that highway - and Red Cross presently has a lot of homes along Highway 24/27.

This fear was not unfounded because there are numerous examples of where most towns have areas of "old town" that were built before modern planning and/or before municipal planning really developed into a science. Even within Stanly County most towns still have numerous signs of this type of growth. Some excellent examples of this type of evolutionary development can be observed along Highway 52 between Albemarle and New London and the eastern portion of East Main in Albemarle.

During Red Cross's incorporation process the most stated fear by the people, aside from the threat of being annexed, was the fear of growth and the effect it would have on the Red Cross community - would it change their community in undesirable ways?

When Red Cross became a town, one of the first things its Council did was to take control of zoning. Although there was considerable dissention within the Council, the decision was to create zoning codes that would provide as much protection for the people as possible while still being acceptant of new businesses. To insure the town had the best codes possible it brought in a very knowledgeable and competent planning consultant to guide its Planning Board through the creation of those codes. Although the cost was high, the town ended up with zoning codes and supportive plans that are probably among the best that can be obtained for supporting those needs that were stated by the people of Red Cross during the incorporation process.

One unique aspect of Red Cross's codes is that the Red Cross community no longer has to worry about "stripping out" along highway 24/27. These codes are designed so that business will be clustered; giving room for both business and residential growth, with each having its own dedicated space along Highway 24/27. This has an added benefit in that, since businesses are clustered, they must also grow outward from the highway. Likewise, home development must also grow outward from Highway 24/27, thus giving depth to the town. This arrangement allows each to have proportional and dedicated space along Highway 24/27.

To further protect this arrangement, the Red Cross zoning codes do not allow for "big-box" businesses, such as Walmart and Target, which encourage substantial peripheral growth around their sites. The maximum allowed single store footprint within Red Cross is 80,000 square feet, anywhere within the town limits.

Consider the following: it is very common to see fast-food and other high-traffic businesses develop around these types of stores to a radius, along the traffic arteries, of anywhere from one-quarter to three-eighths of a mile. The total impact to this change along a traffic artery can be expected to be no less than one-half to three-quarters of a mile, and depending on the town's layout and relative position to population centers; it may well cause peripheral business growth to extend much further towards those population centers.

Several things will happen as a result of this growth; (1 nearly all existing homes within that radius, along the traffic arteries, will be displaced with peripheral businesses, (2 a small town will face immediate financial distress in trying to meet the infrastructure needs of the rapid short-term growth and (3 substantially increased traffic will be noted for more than a half-mile around those facilities, even on secondary roads, thus impacting residents privacy and sense of security.

Another long-term consideration for not allowing "big-box" stores in Red Cross is the inevitable obsolesce that occurs. Assuming a Walmart or Target occupies a store on an average of 25-years before moving to a new facility. When that happens, a percentage of the peripheral business that surrounded the old Walmart or Target location will also move. The old "big-box" store site often remains vacant for some time until a new renter can be found. Sometimes it becomes a flea market, etc. These were two of the factors that the Red Cross Planning Board took into consideration when designing the town's zoning codes, and for setting a maximum footprint size of 80,000 square feet.

Red Cross Receives Request for a Zoning Change:

The issue which prompted the inclusion of this chapter began when the town received a rezoning request for a tract of land to be rezoned from agricultural/residential to commercial to allow the owner "to establish and build a paint and body shop on a vacant piece of property located on hwy. 24/27 near Providence Church."[173] As per standard procedure, anytime such a request is received by the town, it is first reviewed by the Planning Board for impact, compliance and acceptability for rezoning.

[173] From the October 5, 2015 Red Cross Planning Board minutes

Upon review it was found that the property was located in a zone that did not allow for an individual property to be rezoned for another use. In an apparent attempt to accommodate the request the Red Cross Planning Board decided to propose "a text change to the Current Land Development Plan to create a 600 feet corridor on each side of Hwy 24/27 from existing or proposed Right of Way through the city limits of Red Cross to change currently planned AGR to CMU (Commercial Mixed Use)."[174]

The following minutes of the October 5, 2015 Planning Board meeting may shed some light on the Planning Boards creative thought process related to this issue:

Members of the Planning Board are as follows:

Town Council Liaison	J. J. Curlee
Chairman	Lou Eubanks
Vice Chairman	Tina Eudy
Secretary	Dale Burris
Planning Board Member	Melvin Poole
Planning Board Member	Thelma Tomberlin
Planning Board Member	Harry Williams

"<u>New Business:</u>

Review a requested plan presented by Matt Morrow to establish and build a paint and body shop on a vacant piece of property located on hwy. 24/27 near Providence Church. This property is currently zoned AGR (agricultural/residential). Robbie Foxx pointed out that this property does not fit in to current Land Development Plan. He suggested looking at revising Land Development Plan. After discussion among P&Z members a proposal was put on the table.

Board proposes a text change to the Current Land Development Plan to create a 600 feet corridor on each side of Hwy 24/27 from existing

[174] From the October 5, 2015 Red Cross Planning Board minutes

or proposed Right of Way through the city limits of Red Cross to change currently planned AGR to CMU (Commercial Mixed Use).

Melvin Poole made a motion to approve the proposal, Tina Eudy seconded the motion, all members voted in favor, none against.

After adopting this proposal-motion was made by Melvin Poole to present to city council for approval of a 2.59 acre tract currently owned by Oscar Irvin, Record #32550, Book 762, Pg. 187 to be rezoned from RA to GB.

Harry Williams-seconded the motion. Vote was taken-all present in favor, none against.

Next item on the agenda-study current Mobile Home Zoning Ordinance.

Issues that were raised is that the current taxation values do not cover the services provided for some of these homes. Values decline over time and service fees go up.

Questions raised were, "Do we want to allow replacement of existing mobile homes?".

Dale Burris made a motion to table the item until next meeting. Harry Williams seconded the motion."[175]

A zoning change sign was placed at the property. A letter was sent by the Town Administrator notifying the property owner and adjacent property owners of the requested zoning change and of the scheduled public hearing and a posting was placed in the local newspaper, which was to occur on November 9, 2015 at 7:00 PM at the town hall for the purpose of rezoning the Oscar M. Ervin property.

[175] From the October 5, 2015 Red Cross Planning Board minutes

The following is the content of that notification:

"Larry Wayne Smith
Mayor

Councilmembers:
Kelly Brattain
Jerry Jordan
Barbara Carpenter
J. J. Curlee

October 8, 2015

Dear Town of Red Cross Property Owner:

Notice is hereby given that the Town of Red Cross will, on November 9th, 2015 at 7:00 P.M. in the Hinson Room of the Red Cross Town Hall, located at 176 East Red Cross Road, Oakboro, North Carolina, hold a public hearing to consider rezoning request RZ2015-2"

At the request of Matt Morrow, on behalf of Oscar M. Ervin, 203 Carter Road, Monroe, North Carolina, 28110, the town council of the Town of Red will be holding a public hearing for the following property to be rezoned: 558504538902, 2.59 Acres Red Cross Road. This property rezoning request is from RA-Rural Agriculture to a GB-General Business zoning designation.

Any questions concerning this petition should be addressed to the Town of Red Cross Town Hall. Anyone wishing to speak regarding the proposed rezoning of this property is encouraged to attend this public hearing.

Sincerely,

Aloma Whitley
Town Administrator
Town of Red Cross"[176]

---

[176] From letter sent to resident owning property adjacent to above said property

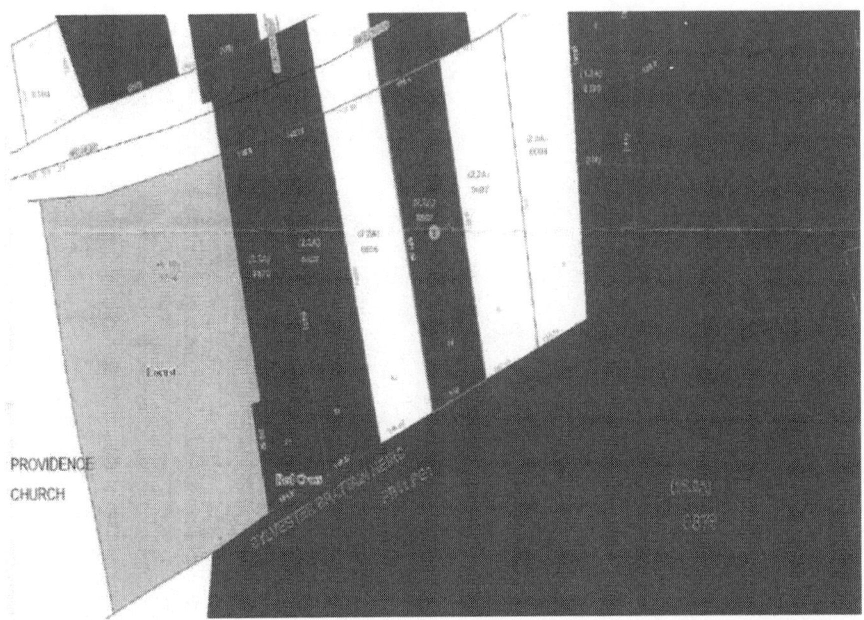

The above map[177] was included with the letter indicating the property to be rezoned.

Two public notices were placed in the Stanly News & Press (appears to be dated 10-25-2015) for public hearings. The postings are as follow:

> NOTICE OF PUBLIC HEARING Town of Red Cross Planning & Zoning Commission November 9th, 2015 7:00PM Red Cross Town Hall 176 E Red Cross Rd. Oakboro, NC 28129 ZONING TEXT AMENDMENT petition ZT01-15(ZT). Notice is hereby given that the Town of Red Cross will hold a public hearing to consider a text amendment of the current Land Development Plan. The proposed amendment would only modify the current Agriculture Residential overlay designation along the NC Hwy 24-27 corridor, to Commercial Mixed Use. 600' inward from the right-of-way. The balance of the Agriculture Residential overlay would remain the same. Any questions concerning this petition should be addressed to

[177] From letter sent to resident owning property adjacent to above said property

the Red Cross Town Hall. October 25 & November 1, 2015[178]

NOTICE OF PUBLIC HEARING Town of Red Cross Planning and Zoning Commission November 9th, 2015, 7:00PM Red Cross Town Hall 176 E Red Cross Rd. Oakboro, NC 28129 ZONING ATLAS AMENDMENT Petition RZ02-15 (R). Oscar M. Ervin, 203 Carter Road, Monroe, North Carolina, 28110 has made a request with the Town of Red Cross to Rezone Parcel #5585045389072, 2.59 Acres, Red Cross Road. This property rezoning request is from RA-Rural Agriculture to a GB-General Business zoning designation. Any questions concerning this petition should be addressed to the town of Red Cross Town Hall, October 25 & November 1, 2015[179]

Basically, the first public notice was to set a public hearing to modify the current zoning of those properties along Highway 24/27 to allow commercial mixed use at a depth of 600-feet on each side of the highway. It appears there were no notifications, other than the public notice placed in the newspaper, of the zoning text change for modifying the zoning overlay of those properties along Highway 24/27 (from about Smith Grove Road to Providence Church).

The second public hearing was to allow Mr. Ervin's property, near Providence Church, to be rezone from residential/agricultural to general business. Per standard procedure a zoning change sign was placed at the Oscar M. Ervin property, a public notice was placed in the local paper and first class letters were sent to all adjacent property owners.

Based on the understanding received during the presentation at the public hearing, in order to grant the property owner's rezoning request to convert his property from agricultural/residential to highway business, it would first be necessary to make a text change to Red Cross's zoning.

[178] From "marketplace.thesnaponline.com", Post Date 10-25-2015
[179] From "marketplace.thesnaponline.com", Post Date 10-25-2015

To accommodate this request the Planning Board developed a plan to add a zoning overlay through a zoning "text amendment" to the western part of Red Cross, along Highway 24/27, to alter its current use from residential/agricultural to that of commercial mixed use. Effectively, this change would alter a little over 40% of the portion of Highway 24/27 that is within the Red Cross town limits.

Red Cross Town Council Public Hearings (November 9, 2015):

Members of the Town Council are as follows:

Mayor	Larry Wayne Smith
Council Member	Kelly Brattain
Council Member	Barbara Carpenter
Council Member	J. J. Curlee
Council Member	Jerry Jordan

The night of the public hearing came and there were a number of residents present. The public hearing opened and immediately went to the rezoning of Highway 24/27.

All residents that spoke were against approving the zoning change with no one speaking in favor of the change. However, Planning Board Chairman Lou Eubanks did assure everyone that the change would not affect their property value or the usage of their land. From the people's side the primary concerns were a fear of losing the stability presently offered by the current zoning plan. As one resident put it, we've got a good plan in developing from the center outward. It was also pointed out that if this change is put in place then a business will be able to build right next door to them, and they didn't want that.

I also spoke at the hearing. I noted that I was aware of some of the administration's desire for growth but, during the incorporation process, the number one thing the people talked about, other than the fear of being annexed, was the fear of growth and the changes it would cause.

I then talked about how this proposed change to our zoning would undermine all we had worked for. The plans we have were designed to protect the people first and then to accept growth. Our plans were designed to cluster businesses so that both business and residential areas would each have space along Highway 24/27. That clustering was necessary if we wanted to develop the necessary depth to make the town sustainable. I gave examples of old growth, before modern planning, where businesses stripped out and told the Council that if they approved this, then that would be how we would develop. I also told the Council that if they approved this, then it would invalidate most of the plans we had invested so heavily in. That it would be like introducing a cancer into the town that would eat away at it until it wasted away.

I pointed out the lack of infrastructure and the difficulty in trying to create businesses along that stretch without having supporting sewer to support incoming businesses, that septic tanks alone would not be sufficient. That it was necessary for the town to develop its infrastructure first.

I went on to close out stating that all council members must possess three qualities: wisdom, concern for neighbors, and morality. They must be wise enough to know what the long-term effect will be from their decisions. They must care for their neighbors enough that they will place the best interest of their neighbors above their own and they must be moral and do what is right. Not because it is what they want, not because it is politically correct or because it is easy, but because it is the moral thing to do.

I know what I said may sound a little severe, however, I went into the meeting with the belief that the Council was prepared the pass the rezoning of Highway 24/27 on the recommendation of the Planning Board. It is still my belief that had it not been for the presence of a number of people in opposition to the proposed "text amendment", it would have passed it.

Before leaving the public hearing segment, the Council decided to delay the public hearing on the rezoning of Oscar M. Ervin's property until after the Council had voted on the text amendment. This was because the rezoning of the Oscar M. Ervin property would be irrelevant unless the text amendment passed. Had the text amendment passed, the Council had planned to go out of regular Council session and open a public hearing on the rezoning of this individual property. Once that was completed, the Council would return to regular session and vote on that rezoning request. However, it was unnecessary since the text amendment failed.

Red Cross Town Council Meeting (November 9, 2015):

1. "Matter of the Public Hearing for Zoning Text Amendment of the current Land Development Plan; discussion and vote by council on Resolution to Amend Zoning Text of Current Land Development Plan"[180]

   There were only two Council Members that spoke concerning the above text amendment prior to the call for a motion. Council Member Kelly Brattain stated that he didn't see how the Council could support it based on the feedback from the residents present. That it was the Council's responsibility to carry out the wishes of the people. Council Member J. J. Curlee, Zoning Officer, spoke of the general purpose of the ordinance, basically interpreted as a reiteration of the ordinance. However, when the call for a motion came, no Council Member would make a motion and the rezoning request died.

Author's Opinion:

Any time someone submits a zoning change request for a tract of land, the town is required to respond. The first step, after the town receives the request from the owner, is to submit that request to the town's planning board for their review on acceptability for rezoning. The planning board will have 30-days from the date the request was submitted to respond with their recommendation to the town's council. It will then be placed on the agenda for the next town council meeting and the council will vote to approve or disapprove the request. Although the council is not required to follow the recommendation of the planning board, it is very rare for them to rule otherwise.

---

[180] From the agenda of the November 9, 2015 Red Cross Town Council Meeting

If the ruling is not in favor of the property owner, the property owner does have one other potential recourse - a variance may be requested. Should a variance request be submitted, it will go before the town's board of adjustment requesting an exemption from that section of the land-use plan. Again, the potential for this approach is dependent on how the town's codes have been written. Many town's design their codes so that this cannot happen. Still, even if this approach is approved by the town's board of adjustment, it only means that the property owner may be excused from that limitation for that occurrence only. The property owner may then again request a rezoning for that property, however, notices must still be mailed to all adjacent property owners, a public hearing must be held and the town's council must vote on the acceptance of the zoning change. It should be made clear, however, that the town's board of adjustment does not have the authority to grant a zoning change - it is illegal under North Carolina law.

This case was highly unusual in that no notifications appear to have been issued for this "text amendment", for the rezoning of that section of Highway 24/27 from agricultural/residential to commercial mixed use, other than the public notice postings in the local paper. All affected property owners and adjacent property owners should have been notified by first class letter. Many towns will also publish a half-page advertisement in the local paper notifying the public of the intent, a map of the affected area and the date/time of the public hearing.

It should also be noted that the public does have the right to challenge the council's ruling. Within 60-days, from the date of the public hearing and vote, the town council's ruling may be challenged in court on procedural grounds. If it is found that proper procedures, including notifications, were not followed, the court will usually invalidate the town council's vote and order a new public hearing to be scheduled. However, if not challenged within that 60-day window, that right to challenge is lost and the council's ruling becomes a fixed town ordinance.

With this piece of property, it was located in an area that was designated residential/agricultural and the owner was requesting the property be rezoned to commercial use so that a body and paint shop could be built on the site. Usually, when a planning board reviews a zoning change request, it looks to see if the request is within compliance of existing zoning parameters and of what impact that change will have on the surrounding area. The planning board will then make a recommendation to the town's council based on those findings. However, this case was highly unusual in that this property was only the fourth parcel in from the edge of town, yet the Red Cross Planning Board made a proposal to change to the zoning along Highway 24/27 for much of the western part of the Highway24/27 corridor within Red Cross to accommodate that requested change.

It would appear from the turnout at this meeting that the residents of Red Cross understood what the long-term impact would be from making this change and responded. Those residents that spoke were in opposition to the change. Although a couple of the town's administration appeared to speak supportive of the plan, the Town Council heard the people. When it came time for a vote by the Council, no one on the Council would make a motion for the text amendment change and it just died.

Although this satisfied the wishes of those attending, in some respects it is not quite as good as having been voted down. It would have been more desirable, as per standard practice, for a motion to have been made, and seconded, to bring the text amendment to a vote and then to have voted it down. That way each Council Member would have gone on record with a stated a position on the issue. However, with the number of residents present, it is probable that the Council Members felt they would be perceived as being in favor of the proposal should they have made a motion.

In hindsight, it is the author's opinion that there appears to be several factors which may have lead up to this event, the two most prominent are, (1) all of the original people involved in the creation of the Red Cross codes, that really understood the objective and intent of those codes, have migrated off the Planning Board and (2) there still may be to be a strong desire by some to make Red Cross look like a town, as has been previously stated, for wanting to see businesses and sidewalks up and down Highway 24/27.

The following articles were written by the Stanly News & Press and the Weekly Post on this public hearing and town meeting:

"Red Cross citizens voice opposition to proposed LUP amendment

By Natalie Loyd
The Weekly Post

During a public hearing Monday evening, Red Cross Citizens spoke against a proposed zoning text amendment to the Land Use Development Plan. The proposed amendment involved the land along the NC Hwy 24-27 corridor which is currently designated for agriculture and residential use. The text amendment would modify the overlay map to allow for commercial use 600 feet inward from the right-of-way. The amendment would not change the current zoning designation, but would allow individual property owners to request re-zoning of their property for commercial use.

The proposed text amendment was prompted by a request to rezone a parcel of land along Hwy. 24-27 for a business. Because the current Land Use Plan does not allow for rezoning, the Planning and Zoning Board Recommended modifying the overlay map to allow for the possibility of rezoning for commercial use.

Red Cross citizens voiced opposition to the amendment.

"Growth has to be controlled growth," said Barbara Huneycutt, I don't want to disrupt what we have. We have such an amazing duty and ability to grow this area, but I don't think we should do a hodgepodge of things - something here, something there and something down the street."

Ray Quick urged council members to consider long-term effects on the community.

"If you do this, it's a cancer that is non-survivable." said Quick. "It [Red Cross] will not survive as a town."

"Growth will come because of our central location," he added, "it needs to be a slow and controlled growth."

After public comments were heard, Zoning Enforcement Officer Robbie Foxx further explained the amendment and answered questions from both citizens and council.

"I think the citizens have spoken on this. We're here to hear what everyone has to say," said council member Kelly Brattain.

The Council unanimously voted against the proposal."[181]

Opposition at public hearing leads to tabling of proposed amendment

By Joy Almond
for the SNAP

On Nov. 9 the people of Red Cross spoke, and their elected representatives listened.

A proposed amendment to modify the use of land along a portion of the N.C. Highway 24-27 corridor was struck down by the Town Council after Red Cross citizens voiced opposition during the public hearing.

Had Petition ZT01-15 passed, a 600-foot stretch of land inward from the right-of-way along the corridor would have been changed from Agricultural Residential overlay to Commercial Mixed Use. The balance of the Agricultural Residential overlay would have remained the same.

[181] The Weekly Post, by Natalie Loyd, November 18, 2015

The language of the amendment created confusion among some attending the hearing, and had to be clarified by the town Zoning Enforcement Officer Bobbie Foxx [Robbie Foxx].

"This is not rezoning the entire corridor at all," said Foxx. "it's called an overlay. The only thing that changes is the land use plan, which would potentially allow for any property owner along that corridor to request changes on their particular property only."

Barbara Huneycutt spoke in opposition to the zoning change, and expressed concerns of urban sprawl.

"Let me say, first of all, that I want to see growth in this community," said Huneycutt. "I think it's very important, I thing growth is good. But growth has to be controlled. I thing we have a land plan that brings us to the center of Red Cross and we grow that first."

Former Red Cross mayor Ray Quick voiced concerns of inadequate infrastructure for future development.

Specifically, Quick expressed concerns about the lack of sewer in the town, felling that septic tanks would be difficult to sustain businesses long-term. He referred to the potential passing of the amendment as "a cancer that is not survivable."

"It's a damaging thing to the community, and to the future development of Red Cross," Quick said of the proposed amendment.

As the Red Cross council took the amendment to a vote, none of the Town Council members made a motion to pass it.

"We're here to hear what everybody's got to say, and we've got to live in the community where it's at," Councilman Kelly Brattain said. "I think we're not ready for this now."

As none of the town commissioners made a motion to adopt the amendment. It was tabled.

> Failure to pass the zoning amendment also negated a request from Oscar M. Ervin to rezone a parcel of land on Red Cross Road from Rural Agricultural to General Business zoning."[182]

A Closing Note:

Red Cross's codes are well-crafted and, to some degree, interlinked. They are different from those of many towns in that they go into much greater detail in those areas defining the separation of business and residential. In some respects they can be viewed as being much like a well-made precision mechanical watch. All the gears are balanced with respect to each other and work well together, however, change or remove one gear without consideration for the overall watch, then it will no longer work or, at the least, is no longer a precision time piece.

Anytime the Red Cross Planning Board makes changes to Red Cross's codes, it needs to have a demonstrative need and an intricate understanding of the impact those changes will have on not only the community but the functionality of those interlinked codes.

On closing: it is satisfying to know, that when the Red Cross community faces a potential threat, the people are aware and are willing to respond and be heard.

[182] The Stanly News & Press, by Joy Almond, November 21, 2015

Appendix

APPENDIX-1

PETITION TO INCORPORATE THE TOWN OF RED CROSS

February 28, 2002

By Raeford Quick
Red Cross Incorporation Committee
16617 Hwy. 24/27, Oakboro. NC 28129
Phone: (704) 485-8065

PETITION TO INCORPORATE

THE

TOWN OF RED CROSS

Index

Executive Summary 3
Proposed Town Name 4
Location 4
Geographical Statistics 4
Population Statistics 5
Development 5
Form of Government 6
Interim Governing Board 7
Revenue 8
Proposed Services 8
Notifications 9
Petition of Voters 9

Petition to Incorporate the Town of Red Cross

Executive Summary

The people of the Red Cross Community are submitting this petition requesting the incorporation of the community into the Town of Red Cross. As indicated in this document, 92.1% of the voting population of the affected area has signed petitions in favor of this incorporation. This incorporation request is being driven by the community's need to absorb and manage the increasing growth that is now being further accelerated by an improving transportation infrastructure.

This community is located in the central-western part of Stanly County, North Carolina along the Hwy. 24/27 corridor connecting Albemarle (County Seat) to Charlotte. Red Cross assumed its identity in the late 1700's and has, over the years, evolved into a recognized and integral part of Stanly County. The January 2002 issue of "Our State" magazine wrote an article on Red Cross that helps capture the pride and ownership the people of Red Cross feel towards this community (see article-11).

Although listed as primarily residential and agricultural, Red Cross is a thriving community that is evolving into a town. With a statistical population of 536 people and a land area of 2.24 square miles, Red Cross's population density is 262.1 people per square mile yielding a development ratio of 50.2%. The community has more than a dozen businesses, two churches, a school, and 212 houses.

In pursuing the incorporation process the Incorporation Committee has followed and met the guidelines set by NCGS-120 with the one exception of certification of the total number of voters dwelling in the proposed town limits. This one item is outside the control of the people of the Red Cross community. The criteria for population density, percent development, town definitions (closeness to another town, boundaries, continuity of boundaries, etc), budget requirements, establishing of governing body, taxation, services, notifications, and petition of voters have all been met.

Unfortunately, the Stanly County Board of Elections has been tied up with the redistricting of Stanly County Voter Districts as a result of changes in North Carolina districting laws and has been unable to provide a certified count of total registered voters within the proposed town limits of Red Cross. The Incorporation Committee went house-to-house and did a documented census, using existing voter records provided by the Stanly County Board of Elections, to establish the total number of voters within the proposed town limits. This information is provided in this petition. It should be noted that the 385 petition signers were verified.

The people of Red Cross look with anticipation to becoming a town in Stanly County, North Carolina.

1. Proposed town name:
   The people of the Red Cross Community are presenting this petition to incorporate the community into the Town of Red Cross.

2. Location:

   The proposed town of Red Cross is located in the western part of Stanly County eleven miles west of Albemarle (County Seat), four miles east of Locust and, twenty-five miles east of Charlotte. NC 24/27 is the main east/west corridor connecting Albemarle to Charlotte. The intersection of three major highways, NC 24/27, NC 205, and Ridgecrest Road lies almost at the center of the proposed town of Red Cross. NC 205 connects the Town of Oakboro to Red Cross. Ridgecrest Road connects the community of Ridgecrest to Red Cross.

3. Geographical Statistics:

   The community of Red Cross came into existence in the late 1700's, deriving its name from the nearly impassable conditions of the crossroads during wet weather. The Red Cross community is an unincorporated community consisting of a mixture of farmland, residential development, and businesses.

   Population is primarily located along the three major highways with the exception of housing developments that are dispersed at various points within the community. The proposed town boundaries chosen/proposed for incorporation were selected based on the strong interest of the people within the affected areas, population distribution, population density, long-term economic considerations, and the general perception of the people within the community as being a part of the Red Cross community.

   Commercial development is primarily located on the major highways with some small businesses located on secondary roads. Residential development is scattered throughout the proposed town boundaries. Stanly County zoning within the proposed town limits is primarily low-density/agricultural with some specific areas being designated highway business and light manufacturing.

In defining the boundaries of the proposed Town of Red Cross, it should be noted that:

The proposed Town of Red Cross does not have any non-contiguous areas as is defined in "Boundary Description" of the Town Charter (see article-1) and Town Map (see article-4).

No part of the proposed Town of Red Cross is within the boundary of another town.

No part of the proposed Town of Red Cross is within five miles of a town with a population of 5,000 or more people.

Land area for the proposed Town of Red Cross is approximately 2.24 square miles or 1,435.61 acres (see article-5).

The land utilization of the proposed Town of Red Cross is:

Residential	594.90 acres[1]
Commercial/Industrial	51.39 acres
Agricultural/Open	713.99 acres
Institutional	75.33 acres[2]
Total	1,435.61 acres[3]

Using residential, commercial/industrial, and institutional acreage as a percent of the total acreage of the proposed town of Red Cross, the

[1] Allows a maximum of 6.48 acres per house – derived from NCGS § 120-167 requirements of 250 people/mi^2.

[2] 23.94 acres for church(s) and 51.39 acres for County school(s).

[3] Does not reflect roads, easements, or right of ways.

percent development is 50.2%.

4. Population Statistics:

The statistical population of the proposed Town of Red Cross is 536 people yielding an average of 262.1 people per square mile (see article-5). This was based on the 2000 U.S. Census indicated an average of 2.53 people per household in Stanly County and the Stanly County Tax Office 2001 records indicating 212 properties having houses within the proposed town boundaries. There are 2.045 square miles of residential and agricultural land area (Excluding commercial/industrial and institutional acreage) within the proposed town boundaries of Red Cross.

Red Cross has traditionally been a stable community with a low growth rate; however, in the past five years the community has noted a substantial increase in development/housing. This growth is now being accelerated by the improved access to the community from Charlotte as a result of widening of Highway 24/27. With the completion of the section of Highway 24/27 through the Red Cross Community population is expected to yield substantial growth over the next few years.

5. Development:

Using residential, commercial/industrial, and institutional acreage as a percent of the total acreage of the proposed town of Red Cross, the percent development is 50.2%.
An overview of the current state of development for the community of Red Cross is as follows:

5.1 Within the proposed town boundaries there are four "defined/evolved" developments that are referred to as "Rolling Hills". "Pecan Grove", "Hunter Ridge" and "Deerfield". Two other developments within the proposed town boundaries are "Stony Run" and "Arbor Heights". However, both of these are satellites of the town of Oakboro.

Two new residential developments directly adjacent to the proposed town boundaries are presently in start-up/planning, however, neither have residents at this time.

5.2 There is one high school within the proposed town boundaries and one K-8 school under construction directly adjacent to the proposed town boundaries.

5.3 There are two churches within the proposed town boundaries.

5.4 Land has been purchased within the proposed town boundaries for an Emergency Medical Center and a satellite Sheriff's Office. Construction is expected to start early in 2002.

5.5 A partial listing of commercial enterprises is as follows:

1 Daycare Center
1 State operated child development facility
1 Car sales and repair shop
1 Automotive service shop
1 Motorcycle repair shop
1 Antique/Collectibles store
1 Computer sales and repair store
1 Convenience store
1 Milk distribution company
1 Restaurant (will open as soon as sewer hookup is complete)
1 Mini-storage
1 Construction Company with offices and showroom

6. Form of Government:

The structure of the governing body of the town of Red Cross is a Town Council, which will have four (4) members and a Mayor. Until the first public election in 2003 (assuming incorporation prior to that date) an interim council consisting of five members of the community will function as town council (see chapter-3 of article-1 and article-6).

Town officers shall be elected on a nonpartisan basis and results determined by a plurality as provided in North Carolina Statute 163-292. In the initial election the two candidates receiving the highest number of votes will be elected to a four-year term and the two candidates receiving the next highest number of votes will be elected to a two-year term. The qualified voters of Red Cross shall elect the Mayor for a four-year term.

These elected officials will assume office with the first town meeting in the year after the election occurs.

7. Interim Governing Board:

In the event of incorporation before public elections have been held and to represent the town of Red Cross, the following residents have agreed to serve as the Red Cross Interim Council (see article-6). These people were selected by majority vote by the community during one of the incorporation meetings.

C.J. Barbee – C.J. Barbee is a life-long resident of Red Cross with family history dating back several generations in the Red Cross community. He served in the European Theater during WWII and is a retired elevator mechanic from Otis Elevator Company. He is active in community affairs. C.J. lives with his wife, Margie, at 16410 Pless Mill Road, Oakboro, NC 28129.

Heath Hahn – Heath Hahn is a life-long resident of Red Cross with a family history dating back several generations in the Red Cross community. He is a veteran of WWII and is active in community affairs. Charter member of Red Cross Baptist Church. Retired lineman for Union Electric. Worked for Flame Refractors for 15 years before retiring. Heath and Kathleen Hahn (married 56-years) have three children, six grandchildren, and two great-grandchildren. Heath and Kitty live at 16029 Hwy. 205 North, Oakboro, NC 28129.

J.D. Hinson – J.D Hinson is a life-long resident of Red Cross with a family history dating back several generations in the Red Cross community. Served in the US Marine Corp and is active in community affairs. Active member of Red Cross Baptist Church. Received Governor's Award for Community Service in 2001. Grew greenhouse vegetables at Red Cross for 25-years before retiring in 1991. He and his wife, Violet, live at 16588-A Hwy. 24/27, Oakboro, NC 28129.

Raeford Quick – Raeford "Ray" Quick moved to Red Cross in 1969. He graduated from West Stanly High School in 1970, UNCC with a BA in Business in 1976, and UNCC with a BS in Management Information Systems in 1999. He moved away in 1977 and returned to Red Cross in 1997. He is a member of Red Cross Baptist Church. He teaches computer information systems/computer engineering technology for Stanly Community College. Ray lives at 16617 Hwy. 24/27, Oakboro, NC 28129.

Larry Wayne Smith – Larry Wayne Smith is a life-long resident of Red Cross with a family history dating back several generations in the Red Cross community. He is a local businessman owning several investment/business properties in the Red Cross community. He and his wife, Larcenia, are members of Big Lick Baptist Church. Larry Wayne and Larcenia live at 16215 Hilltop Road, Oakboro, NC 28129.

8 Revenue:

8.1 Property Valuation – The combined property valuation (from the Stanly County Tax Office) is approximately $31,500,000.00. Of this, $28,350,000.00 is from real estate and $3,150,000.00 is from personal property.

8.2 Taxation – Based on a proposed operating budget of $76,749.74, it was determined the tax rate for the town of Red Cross should be set at $0.16 (sixteen cents) per $100.00 of valuation (see article-2). This would allow for $50,400.00 in tax collection that, combined with a realistic collection rate of 97%, would yield adjusted revenues from taxation to $48,888.00.

Sales and Use tax allocations (based on 2001 numbers and information from the State Tax Office) should yield and anticipated revenue of $53,600.00. Combined with taxation revenues total revenues should be $102,488.00 per year.

9 Proposed Services:

The town of Red Cross is proposing to offer four services with all services to be in effect by the first day of the third year after incorporation. These services are fire protection, waste collection, police protection, and zoning (see article-3).

9.1 Fire Protection – The Incorporation Committee has talked/held meetings with all agencies involved (fire departments, 911 Emergency Services, and the County Tax Collector) and all parties involved are agreeable to the proposed town of Red Cross assuming responsibilities for fire protection. Red Cross will be responsible for fire tax collection and disbursement of monies to contracted fire departments. The 911 Emergency services will not need re-mapping.

9.2 Waste Collection – The Incorporation Committee has talked with BFI, Inc. and Waste Management, Inc. and obtained quotes for trash pickup. Final quotes will not be given until the town of Red Cross is ready to enter into contract with the chosen company. However, it should be noted that a 20% buffer has been built into the waste collection budget to allow a more realistic estimate for cost of services at the time of contract.

9.3 Police Protection – The Incorporation Committee has talked with the Stanly County Sheriff and obtained an estimate of cost to contract police services through the Sheriff's Department. This contract will be very similar to contracts the Sheriff's

Department has with two other Stanly County towns (Richfield and New London) of comparable size to Red Cross. It should be noted that the Incorporation Committee was actively involved in the acquisition of a satellite Sheriff's Office at Red Cross for the purpose of serving Western Stanly County.

9.4 Zoning – Although the Incorporation Committee is prohibited from being involved in zoning, it did discuss potential cost associated with zoning with the Stanly County Zoning Office for the purpose of establishing a realistic and functional budget and has included this cost in the budget.

10. Notifications:

10.1. Notification to Towns – All towns and the County Commissioners in the County of Stanly have been notified in accordance with North Carolina General Statute 120-164. Acknowledgements have been received from all towns and the County Commissioners. It was not necessary to notify any towns outside of Stanly County since the county line is greater than five miles from the proposed town limits of Red Cross (see articles 8).

Town	Signer	Position	Date Acknowledged
Oakboro	Ms. Joyce Little	Mayor	November 16, 2001
Richfield	Mr. Floyd Wilson	Mayor	November 16, 2001
Albemarle	Mr. Roger Snyder	Mayor	November 16, 2001
Badin	Mr. John Garrison	Mayor	November 20, 2001
Locust	Mr. Wilson Barbee	Mayor	November 29, 2001
Norwood	Mr. Darrell Almond	Mayor	November 20, 2001
New London	Mr. Calvin Gaddy	Mayor	December 4, 2001
Stanfield	Mr. Mark Alberghini	Mayor	December 6, 2001

County Commissioners:

Mr. Kenneth Furr November 27, 2001

(Chairman of Stanly County Commissioners)

10.2. Public Notice – Public notice of Red Cross' intent to petition

the Legislature for incorporation was ran in the "Stanly News & Press" for three consecutive weeks starting with the third week of January in 2002 (see article-7).

11 Petition of Voters:

A petition was circulated (hand-carried to each house) among the population of the proposed town of Red Cross (see article-10). By a census of the Incorporation Committee there were 418 identified registered voters, of which, 385 signed (verified by Board of Elections and attached to this document) the petition in favor of incorporating the community of Red Cross. This yielded a 92.1% signing rate in favor of incorporating. Another 15 – 20 people signed the petition but refused to register and could not be counted.

It should be noted that the 418 registered voters are from a census of the Incorporation Committee doing a house-to-house survey and not from the Stanly County Board of Elections (see article-9). The Stanly County Board of Elections has indicated it would be some time before they could address the total registered voter count in the proposed town limits of Red Cross since they are presently trying to meet a deadline in re-mapping for the redistricting of Stanly County. Due to time constraints it was the decision of the Incorporation Committee to submit this proposal without formal verification from the Stanly County Board of Elections. Note, however, that the Stanly County Board of Elections did verify the 385 petition signatures obtained during the petition drive.

APPENDIX-2

TOWN OF RED CROSS, NORTH CAROLINA

BOUNDARY DESCRIPTION

(November 11, 2002)

Beginning at the northwest corner of the property having record number 17912, said point also being located on the boundary of the southern right-of-way of Lakewood Road, thence from said point of beginning with the southern right-of-way of Lakewood Road in a southwesterly direction to the northeastern corner of the property having record number 35434, said point also being located in on the boundary of the southern right-of-way of Lakewood Road, thence in a southerly direction with the eastern property line of above said property to the southeastern corner of the above said property, thence in a westerly direction with the southern property line of the above said property to the southwestern corner of the above said property, thence in a northerly direction with the western property line of the above said property to the northwestern corner of the above said property, said corner also being located on the boundary of the southern right-of-way of Lakewood Road, thence in a southwesterly direction with he southern boundary of Lakewood Road to the intersect of the boundary of the eastern right-of-way of NC 205 highway and the boundary of the southern right-of-way of Lakewood Road to a point, thence in a southerly direction with the eastern right-of-way of NC 205 Highway to the northwestern corner of the property having record number 33411, thence in a northeasterly direction with the northern property line of the above said property to the northeastern corner of the above said property, thence in a southerly direction with the eastern property lines of the properties having record numbers 33411 and 7078 to the southeastern corner of the property having record number 7078, thence in a southwesterly direction with the southeastern property line of the above said property to the northeastern corner of the property having record number 11124, thence in a southeasterly direction with the northeaster property line of the property having record number 11124 to the southeastern corner of the above said property, thence in a southwesterly direction with the southern property line of the above said property to the northeastern corner of the property having record number 914, thence in a southeasterly direction with the northeastern property lines of the properties having record numbers 914, 15245, and 10992 to the southeastern corner of the property having record number 10992, thence in a northeasterly direction with the northern property line of the property having record number 14219 to the northeastern corner of the above said property, thence in a southeasterly direction with the eastern property line of the above said property to the southeastern corner of the above said property, thence in an easterly direction with the northern property line of the property having record number 31144 to the northeastern corner of the above said property, thence in a southerly direction with the eastern property line of the above said property to the northeastern corner of the property having record number 31432, thence in a southwesterly direction with the southern property line of the above said property to the northeastern corner of the property having record number 31277, thence in a southeasterly direction with the property line of the above said property to the southeastern corner of the above said property, thence in a southwesterly direction with the southern property line of the above said property to a corner, said corner being the intersect of the southeastern property line of the above said property and the northeastern property line of the property having record number 24601, thence in a southeasterly direction with the northeastern property line of the property having record number 24601 to the easternmost corner of the above said property, thence in a southwesterly direction with the southeastern property line of the above said property to the southwestern corner of the above said property, said corner also being located on the boundary of the eastern right-of-way of Highway 205, thence in a southwesterly direction with the extended southern property line of the above said property to a point, said point being at the intersect of the southwesterly extended southern property line of the above said property and the boundary of the western right-of-way of Highway 205, thence in a northerly direction with the boundary of the western right-of-way of Highway 205 to a point, said point also being on the boundary of the intersect of the western right-of-way of Highway 205 and the boundary of the southern right-of-way of Bearclaw Road, thence in a southwesterly direction with the boundary of the southern right-of-way of Bearclaw Road to the northeastern corner of the property having record number 2714, thence in a southerly direction with the eastern property line of the above said property to the southeastern corner of the above said property, thence in a southwesterly direction with the southern property lines of the properties having record numbers 2714 and 7517 to the southwestern corner of the property having record number 7517, said corner also being located on the boundary of the eastern right-of-way of Bearclaw Road, thence in a southerly direction with the boundary of the eastern right-of-way of Bearclaw Road to the northwestern corner of the property having record number 8598, said corner also being located on the eastern right-of-way of Bearclaw Road, thence in a northeasterly direction with the northern property line of the above said property to the northeastern corner of the above said property, thence in a southeasterly direction with the eastern property line of the above said property to the southeastern corner of the above said property, said corner also being located on the boundary of the northern right-of-way of Big Lick Road, thence in a southwesterly direction with the southern property lines of the above said property to the southwestern corner of the above said property, said corner also being located at the intersect of the boundary of the northern right-of-way of Big Lick Road and the boundary of the eastern right-of-way of Bear Claw Road, thence in a westerly direction with the westerly extended southern property line of the above said property to the southeastern corner of the property having record number 14196, said corner also being located at the intersect of the boundary of the northern right-of-way of Big Lick Road and the boundary of the western right-of-way of Bear Claw Road, thence in a southwesterly direction to the southeastern corner of the property having record number 14196, thence in a southwesterly direction with the southern property line of the above said property to the southwestern corner of the above said property, said corner also being located on the boundary of the northern right-of-way of

Big Lick Road, thence in a northerly direction with the western property line of the above said property to the northwestern corner of the above said property, thence in a southwesterly direction with the southern property line of the property having record number 23991 to the southwestern corner of the above said property, thence in a northwesterly direction with the property lines of the properties having record numbers 23991, 23998, 18648, 21888, and 14189 to the northwestern corner of the property having record number 14189, thence in a northeasterly direction with the northern property line of the above said property to the northernmost corner of the above said property, thence in a southeasterly direction with the northeastern property line of the above said property to the easternmost corner of the above said property, said corner also being located on the boundary of the northern right-of-way of Bearclaw Road, thence northeasterly with the boundary of the northern right-of-way of Bearclaw Road to the southwestern corner of the property having record number 15172, thence in a northwesterly direction with the western property line of the above said property to the northwestern corner of the above said property, thence in a northeasterly direction with the northern property line of the above said property to the northeastern corner of the above said property, said corner also being located on the boundary of the western right-of-way of Highway 205, thence in a northerly direction with the boundary of the western right-of-way of Highway 205 to the southwestern corner of the property having record number 10415, thence in a westerly direction with the southern property line of the above said property to the southwestern corner of the above said property, thence in a northwesterly direction with the western property line of the above said property to the northwestern corner of the above said property, thence in a northwesterly, and then southwesterly, direction with the southern property line of the property having record number 22363 to the southwestern corner of the above said property, thence in a northwesterly direction with the western property lines of the properties having record numbers 22363 and 1280 to the northwestern-most corner of the property having record number 1280, thence in a northeasterly direction with the northern property line of the above said property to the southernmost corner of the property having record number 11487, thence in a northwesterly direction with the western property lines of the properties having record numbers 11487, 22353, 11676, and 11677 to the northwestern corner of the property having record number 11677, thence in a northeasterly with the northern property line of the above said property to the southwestern corner of the property having record number 15206, thence in a northwesterly direction with the southwestern property line of the above said property to the northwestern corner of the above said property, thence in a northeasterly direction with the northwestern property line of the above said property to the northeastern corner of the above said property, said corner also being located on the boundary of the western right-of-way of Highway 205, thence in a northerly direction with the boundary of the western right-of-way of Highway 205 to the southeastern corner of the property having record number 3501, said corner also being located on the boundary of the western right-of-way of Highway 205, thence in a westerly direction with the southern property line of the above said property to the southwestern corner of the above said property, thence in a southeasterly direction with the eastern property line of the property having record number 7419 to the southeastern corner of the above said property, thence in a southwesterly direction with the southern property lines of the properties having record numbers 7419, 21837, 29579, and 31471 to the southwestern corner of the property having record number 31471, thence in a northerly direction with the western property line of the above said property to the northwestern corner of the above said property, said corner also being located on the boundary of the southern right-of-way of Hatley Burris Road, thence in a northerly direction with the northerly extended western property line of the above said property to a point, said point being located at the intersect of the extended western property line and the northern boundary of Hatley Burris Road, said point also being located on the boundary of the northern right-of-way of Hatley Burris Road, thence in an easterly direction with the boundary of the northern right-of-way of Hatley Burris Road to the southwestern corner of the property having record number 30221, said point also being located on the boundary of the northern right-of-way of Hatley Burris Road, thence in a northwesterly direction with the western property line of the above said property to the northwestern corner of the above said property, thence in a northeasterly direction with the northeastern property lines of the properties having record numbers 30221, 26299, 7589, and 11055 to the northeastern corner of the property having record number 11055, thence in a northwesterly direction with the property line of the property having record number 27039 to the northwestern corner of the above said property, thence in a northerly direction with the western property lines of the properties having record numbers 35366, 34783, and 27039 to the southeastern corner of the property having record number 21028, thence in a westerly direction with the southern property line of the above said property to the southwestern corner of the above said property, thence in a northerly direction with the western property line of the above said property to the northwestern corner of the above said property, said corner also being located on the boundary of the southern right-of-way of Hilltop Road, thence in a westerly direction with the southern right-of-way of Hilltop Road to the northeastern corner of the property having record number 29654, said corner also being located on the boundary of the southern right-of-way of Hilltop Road, thence in a southerly, then southwesterly, direction with the eastern and southeastern property lines of the above said property to the most southeastern-most corner of the above said property, thence in a northwesterly direction with the southwestern property line of the above said property to the southwestern corner of the above said property, thence in a southwesterly direction following the southern property lines of the properties having record numbers 11059, 33667, and 16604 to the southernmost corner of the property having record number 16604, thence in a northwesterly direction with the western property lines of the properties having record numbers 16604, 16602, 16515, and 16447 to the northwestern corner of the property having record number 16447, said corner also being located on the boundary of the southern right-of-way of Hilltop Road, thence in a northerly direction with the northerly extended western property line of the property having record number 16447 to a point on the boundary of the northern right-of-way of Hilltop Road, thence in a northeasterly direction with the northern right-of-way of Hilltop Road to the southwestern corner of the property having record number 31187, said corner also being located on the boundary of the northern right-of-way of Hilltop Road, thence in a northerly direction with the western property lines of the properties having record numbers 31187 and 30099 to the northwestern corner of the property having record number 30099, thence in a westerly direction with the southern property lines of the properties having record numbers 31029, 22704, and 22166 to the southwestern corner of the property having record number 22166, thence in a southwesterly, and then southeasterly, direction with the property line of the property having record number 22702 to the southeastern corner of the property having record number 22702, thence in a southwesterly direction with the southeastern property lines of the properties having record numbers 22702, 20802, 22394, and 22392 to the southwestern corner of the property having record number 22392, said corner also being located on the boundary of the eastern right-of-way of Hilltop Road, thence in a southwesterly direction with the extended southeastern property line of the above said property to the intersect of the westerly extended southeastern property line of the above said property and the boundary of western right-of-way of Hilltop Road, thence in a northwesterly direction with the western right-of-way of Hilltop Road to a point where the westerly extended northwestern property line of the property having record number 13061 intersects on the boundary of the western right-of-way of Hilltop Road, thence in a northeasterly direction to the northeastern corner of the above said property, said corner also being located on the boundary of the eastern right-of-way of Hilltop Road, thence in a northerly direction with the northwestern property line of the above said property to the northernmost corner of the above said property, thence in a southerly direction with the property lines of the properties having record numbers 13061, 14576, and 14538 to the southeastern corner of the property having record number 14538, said corner also being located on the boundary of the northern right-of-way of Peachtree Road, thence in a northeasterly direction with the boundary of the northern right-of-way of Peachtree Road to the southwestern corner of the property having record number 3949, said corner also being located on the boundary of the northern right-of-way of Peachtree Road, thence in a northwesterly direction with the western property line of the above said property to the northwestern corner of the above said property, thence in a northeasterly direction with the northern property line of the above said property to the northeastern corner of the above said property, thence in a southeasterly direction with the eastern property line of the above said property to the southeastern corner of the above said property, said corner also being located on the boundary of the northern right-of-way of Peachtree Road, thence in an easterly direction with the boundary of the northern right-of-way of Peachtree Road to the southwestern corner of the property having record number 25708, said corner also being located on the boundary of the northern right-of-way of Peachtree Road, thence in a northwesterly direction with the western property line of the above said property to the northwest corner of the above said property, thence in a southeasterly direction with the northern property lines of the properties having record numbers 25708, 25709, and 2726 to the northwestern corner of the property having record number 22679, thence in a northeasterly direction with the northwestern property lines of the above said property and the property line of the property having record number 18120 to the northeastern corner of the property having record number 18120, thence in an easterly direction with the northeastern property line of the above said property to the eastern corner of the above said property, said corner also being located on the boundary of the northern right-of-way of Peachtree Road, thence in a northeasterly, then easterly, direction with the boundary of the northern right-of-way of Peachtree Road to the southwestern corner of the property having record number 22166, said corner also being located on the boundary of the northern right-of-way of Peachtree road, thence in a northeasterly direction with the northwestern property line of the above said property to the northwestern corner of the above said property, thence in an easterly direction with the northern property lines of the above said property and the property having record number 8335 to the intersect of the property having record number 10346, thence in a northerly direction with the western property lines of the properties having record numbers 10346 and 22200 to the northwestern corner of the property having record number 22200, thence in a westerly direction with the southern property line of the property having record number 9950 to the southwestern corner of the above said property, thence in a northeasterly direction, and then in a northwesterly direction, with the western property line of the above said property to the northwestern corner of the above said property, thence in a northeasterly direction with the northwestern property line of the property having record number 12578 to the northwestern corner of the above said property, thence in a northerly direction with the western property line of the property having record number 22941 to the northwestern corner of the above said property, thence in an easterly direction with the northern property line of the above said property to the northeastern corner of the above said property, thence in a westerly direction with the southern property line of the property having record number 26237 to the southwestern corner of the above said property, thence in a westerly, and then southerly, direction with the southeastern property line of the property having record number 4021 to the southeastern corner of the above said property, thence in a westerly direction with the southern property line of the above said property to the southwestern corner of the above said property, thence in an easterly, and then southerly direction with the southeastern property line of the property having record number 11420 to the southernmost corner of the above said property, thence in a northwesterly direction with the southwestern property lines of the properties having record numbers 11420 and 1325 to the southeastern corner of the property having record number 10753, thence in a westerly direction with the southern property lines of the properties having record numbers 10753, 4407, 24257, 4100, and 2092 to the southwestern corner of the property having record number 2092, said corner also being located on the boundary of the eastern right-of-way of Pless Mill Road, thence with the boundary of the eastern right-of-way of Pless Mill Road to the northwest corner of the property having record number 1139, said corner also being located on the boundary of the eastern right-of-way of Pless Mill Road, thence in a southeasterly direction with the northern property lines of the above said property and the property having record number 2559 to the southeastern corner of the property having record number 2559, thence in a southwesterly direction with the eastern property line of the above said property to the southern corner of the above said property, said corner also being located on the boundary of the eastern right-of-way of Pless Mill Road, thence in a southerly direction with the boundary of the eastern right-of-way of Pless Mill and then the boundary of the eastern right-of-way of Hilltop Road to the intersect of the easterly extended southern property line of the property having record number 12773 and the boundary of the eastern right-of-way of Hilltop Road, said point also being located on the boundary of the eastern right-of-way of Hilltop Road, thence in a northwesterly direction to the southeastern corner of the property having record number 12773, said corner also being located on the boundary of the western right-of-way of Hilltop Road, thence in a westerly direction with the southern property line of the above said property to the southwestern corner of the above said property, said corner also located on the boundary of the eastern right-of-way of Pless Mill Road, thence in a northwesterly direction with the westerly extended southern property line of the above said property to the southeastern corner of the property having record number 14376, said corner also being located on the boundary of the western right-of-way of Pless Mill Road, thence with the southwester, then western property line of the above said property to the southeastern corner of the property having record number 7891, thence in a westerly direction with the southern property lines of the properties having record numbers 7891 and 15523 to the northeastern corner of the property having record number 2557, thence in a southwesterly direction with the eastern property lines of the properties having record numbers 2557, 35571, and 2557 to the southeastern corner of the southernmost parcel having record number 2557, thence in a westerly direction with the southern property line of the above said property to the southwestern corner of the above said property, thence in a northerly direction with the western property line of the above said property to the northwestern corner of the above said property, thence in an easterly direction with the northern property line of the above said property to the southwestern corner of the property having record number 32551, thence in a northerly direction with the western property line of the above said property to the northwestern corner of the above said property, said corner also being located on the boundary of the southern right-of-way of Highway 24/27, thence in a northerly direction with the extended western property line of the above said property to the southwestern corner of the property having record number 18503, said corner also being located on the boundary of the northern right-of-way of Highway 24/27, thence in a northerly direction with the western property line of the above said property to the northwestern corner of the above said property, thence in an easterly, then southerly direction with the eastern property line of the property having record number 10666 to the southeastern corner of the above said property, said corner also being located on the boundary of the northern right-of-way of Highway 24/27, thence in a westerly direction with the southern property line of the above said property to the southwestern corner of the above said property, said corner also being located on the boundary of the northern right-of-way of Highway 24/27, thence in a northwesterly, then westerly, then northerly, then northwesterly, and then northeasterly direction with the western property line of the above said property to the northwestern corner of the above said property, thence in a westerly direction with the southern property line of the property having record number 10019 to the southwestern corner of the above said property, thence in a northerly direction with the western property line of the above said property to the northwestern corner of the above said property, thence in an easterly direction with the northern property line of the above said property to the northeastern corner of the above said property, said corner also being located on the boundary of the southern right-of-way of Bethel Church Road, thence in an easterly direction with the easterly extended northern property line of the above said property to the intersect of the easterly extended northern property line of the above said property and the boundary of the northern right-of-way of Bethel Church Road, thence in an easterly direction with the boundary of the eastern right-of-way of Bethel Church Road to the southwestern corner of the property having record number 11696, said corner also being located on the boundary of the northern right-of-way of Bethel Church Road, thence in a northerly direction with the western property line of the above said property to the northwestern corner of the above said property, thence in an easterly direction with the northern property line of the above said property to the southeastern corner of the property having record number 14316, thence in a northerly direction with the western property line of the above said property to the northwestern corner of the above said property, thence in an easterly direction with the northern property line of the above said property to the northeastern corner of the above said property, said corner also being located on the boundary of the western right-of-way of Running Creek Church Road, thence in a northerly direction with the boundary of the western right-of-way of Running Creek Church Road to a point where the westerly extended northern property line of the property having record number 18205 intersects with the boundary of the western right-of-way of Running Creek Church Road, thence in an easterly direction with the westerly extended property line of the above said property intersects with the boundary of the western right-of-way of Running Creek Church Road, thence in an easterly direction to the northwestern corner of the above said property, said corner also being located on the boundary of the eastern right-of-way of Running Creek Church Road, thence in an easterly direction with the northern property line of the above said property to the northeastern corner of the above said property, thence in a southerly direction with the eastern property line of the above said property to the southeastern corner of the above said property, thence in a westerly direction with the southern property line of the above said property to the southwestern corner of the above said property, said corner also being located on the boundary of the eastern right-of-way of Running Creek Church Road, thence in a southerly direction with the boundary of the eastern right-of-way of Running Creek Church Road to the northwestern corner of the property having record number 14315, said corner also being located on the boundary of the eastern right-of-way of Running Creek Church Road, thence in a southeasterly direction with the northeastern property line of the above said property to the southeastern corner of the above said property, thence in a southwesterly direction with the southeastern property line of the above said property to the southern corner of the above said property, said corner also being located on the boundary of the eastern right-of-way of Running Creek Church Road, thence in a southwesterly direction with the westerly extended southeasterly property line of the above said property to the intersect of the westerly extended southeasterly property line of the above said property and the boundary of the western right-of-way of Running Creek Church Road, thence in a northerly direction with the boundary of the western right-of-way of Running Creek Church Road to the southeastern corner of the property having record number 14315, said corner also being located on the boundary of the western right-of-way of Running Creek Church Road, thence in a northwesterly, then westerly, direction with the southern property lines of the properties having record numbers 14315 and 14316 to the northeastern corner of the property having record number 11696, thence in a southerly direction with the eastern property line of the above said property to the intersect eastern property line of the above said property and the northern property line of the property having record number 21581, thence in an easterly direction with the northern property line of the property having record number 21581 to the northeastern corner of the above said property, thence in a southerly direction with the eastern property line of the above said property to the southeastern corner of the above said property, said corner also being located on the boundary of the northern right-of-way of Bethel

Church Road, thence in a southerly direction with the southerly extended property line of the above said property to the intersect of the southerly extended property line of the above said property and the boundary of the southern right-of-way of Bethel Church Road, thence in a westerly direction with the boundary of the southern right-of-way of Bethel Church Road to the northeastern corner of the property having record number 11516, said corner also being located on the boundary of the southern right-of-way of Bethel Church Road, thence in a southerly, then easterly, then southerly direction with the eastern property line of the above said property to the southeastern corner of the above said property, thence in a westerly direction with the southern property line of the above said property to the northeastern corner of the property having record number 10666, thence in a southerly direction with the eastern property line of the above said property to the northwestern corner of the property having record number 15451, thence in a southeasterly direction with the northern property line of the above said property to the northeastern corner of the above said property, said corner also being located on the boundary of the western right-of-way of Brattain Road, thence in an southeasterly direction with the easterly extended northern property line of the above said property to the northwestern corner of the property having record number 15449, said corner also being located on the boundary of the eastern right-of-way of Brattain Raod, thence in a southeasterly direction with the northern property line of the property having record number 15449 to the northeastern corner of the above said property, thence in a southwesterly direction with the eastern property lines of the properties having record numbers 15449, 15448, and 1187 to the southeastern corner of the property having record number 1187, thence in an easterly direction with the northeastern property line of the property having record number 1186 to the northeastern corner of the above said property, thence in a southwesterly direction with the eastern property line of the above said property to the southeastern corner of the above said property, said corner also being located on the boundary of the eastern right-of-way of Brattain Road, thence in a southwesterly direction with the southerly extended eastern property line of the above said property to the intersect of the southerly extended eastern property line of the above said property and the boundary of the western right-of-way of Brattain Road, thence in a northerly direction with the boundary of the western right-of-way of Brattain Road to the southeastern corner of the property having record number 20477, said corner also being located on the boundary of the western right-of-way of Brattain Road, thence in a southwesterly direction with the southeastern property line of the above said property to the southeastern corner of the above said property, thence in a northwesterly direction with the southwestern property line of the above said property to the southwestern corner of the above said property, thence in a northeasterly direction with the northwestern property line of the above said property to the northwestern corner of the above said property, thence in a northwesterly direction with the southwestern property line of the property having record number 2558 to the southwestern corner of the above said property, thence in a northeasterly direction with the northwestern property line of the above said property to the northwestern corner of the above said property, thence in a northwesterly direction with the southern property lines of the properties having record numbers 15450 and 15451 to the southwestern corner of the property having record number 15451, thence in a southerly direction, then southeasterly direction, then southerly direction with the eastern property line of the property having record number 10666 to the northwestern corner of the property having record number 33403, thence in an easterly direction with the northern property line of the above said property to the northeastern corner of the above said property, thence in a southerly direction with the eastern property lines of the properties having record numbers 33403 and 18503 to the southeastern corner of the property having record number 18503, said corner also being located on the boundary of the northern right-of-way of Highway 24/27, thence in an easterly direction with the boundary of the northern right-of-way of Highway 24/27 to the intersect of the boundary of the northern right-of-way of Highway 24/27 and the northerly extended eastern property line of the property having record number 32552, thence in a southerly direction to the northeastern corner of the above said property, said corner also being located on the boundary of the southern right-of-way of Highway 24/27, thence in a southerly direction with the eastern property line of the above said property to the southeastern corner of the above said property, thence in an easterly direction with the northern property line of the property having record number 2557 to the southwestern corner of the property having record number 32550, thence in a northerly direction with the western property line of the above said property to the northwestern corner of the above said property, said corner also being located on the boundary of the southern right-of-way of Highway 24/27, thence in a northerly direction with the northerly extended western property line of the above said property to a point, said point being the intersect of the northerly extended western property line of the above said property and the boundary of the northern right-of-way of Highway 24/27, thence in an easterly direction with the boundary of the northern right-of-way of Highway 24/27 to the southeastern corner of the property having record number 7313, said corner also being located on the boundary of the northern right-of-way of Highway 24/27, thence in a northerly direction with the western property line of the above said property to the northwestern corner of the above said property, thence in an easterly direction with the northern property line of the above said property to the northeastern corner of the above said property, thence in a southerly direction with the eastern property line of the above said property to the southeastern corner of the above said property, said corner also being located on the boundary of the northern right-of-way of Highway 24/27, thence in a southerly direction with the southerly extended eastern property line of the above said property to a point, said point being where the southerly extended eastern property line of the above said property intersects with the boundary of the southern right-of-way of Highway 24/27, thence in a westerly direction with the southern right-of-way of Highway 24/27 to the northeastern corner of the property having record number 32550, said corner also being located on the boundary of the southern right-of-way of Highway 24/27, thence in a southerly direction with the eastern property line of the above said property to the southeastern corner of the above said property, thence in an easterly, then northerly, direction with the northwestern property lines of the properties having record number 35571 and 29938 to the southwestern corner of the property having record number 29938, thence in a northerly direction with the western property line of the above said property to the northwestern corner of the above said property, said corner also being located on the boundary of the southern right-of-way of Highway 24/27, thence in a northerly direction with the northerly extended western property line of the above said property to a point, said point being located at the intersect of the northerly extended western property line of the above said property and the boundary of the northern right-of-way of Highway 24/27, thence in an easterly direction with the boundary of the northern right-of-way of Highway 24/27 to the southwestern corner of the property having record number 2556, said corner also being located on the boundary of the northern right-of-way of Highway 24/27, , thence in a northerly direction with the western property lines of the properties having record numbers 2556 and 2554 to the northeastern corner of the property having record number 2556, said corner also being on the boundary of the western right-of-way of Brattain Road, thence in a northeasterly direction with the extended northern property line of the property having record number 2556 to a point, said point also being located at the intersect of the northerly extended northern property line of the above said property and the boundary of the eastern right-of-way of Brattain Road, thence in a southerly direction with the boundary of the eastern right-of-way of Brattain Road to a point, said point being the intersect of the boundary of the eastern right-of-way of Brattain Road and the boundary of the northern right-of-way of Highway 24/27, thence in an easterly direction with the northern right-of-way of NC 24/27 Highway to a point where the northern boundary of the right-of-way of NC 24/27 Highway intersects with the western boundary of Running Creek Church Road, thence in a northerly direction with the western right-of-way of Running Creek Church Road to the southeastern corner of the property having record number 12791, said corner also being located on the boundary of the western right-of-way of Running Creek Church Road, thence in a westerly direction with the southern property lines of the properties having record numbers 12791 and 14605 to the southwestern corner of the property having record number 14605, thence in a northwesterly direction with the western property line of the above said property to the northwestern corner of the above said property, thence in a northwesterly direction with the northerly extended western property line of the above said property to a point on the boundary of the northern right-of-way of Bethel Church Road where the northerly extended western property line of the above said property intersects with the boundary of the northern right-of-way of Bethel Church Road, thence in an easterly direction with the boundary of the northern right of way of Bethel Church Road to the intersect of the boundary of the northern right-of-way of Bethel Church Road and the boundary of the western right of way of Running Creek Church Road, thence in a northerly direction with the boundary of the western right-of-way of Running Creek Church Road to a point, said point also being the intersect of the westerly extended northwestern property line of the property having record number 24835 and the boundary of the western right-of-way of Running Creek Church Road, thence in an easterly direction to the western corner of the property having record number 24835, said corner also being located on the boundary of the eastern right-of-way of Running Creek Church Road, thence in a northeasterly direction with the northwestern property line of the above said property to the northwestern corner of the above said property, thence in a southeasterly direction with the northeastern property lines of the properties having record numbers 24835 and 14512 to the northeastern corner of the property having record number 14512, thence in a northeasterly direction with the western property lines of the properties having record numbers 22393, 6913, and 23153 to the northwestern corner of the property having record number 23153, said corner also being located on the boundary of the southern right-of-way of Smith Grove Road, thence in a northerly direction with the northerly extended property line of the above said property to a point, said point being the intersect of the northerly extended property line of the above said property and the boundary of the northern right-of-way of Smith Grove Road, thence in an easterly, then southerly, direction with the boundary of the northern, and then eastern, right-of-way of Smith Grove Road to a point where the boundary of the eastern right-of-way of Smith Grove Road intersects with the boundary of the northern right-of-way of Bethel Church Road, thence in a southerly direction with the southerly extended boundary of the eastern right-of-way of Smith Grove Road to the intersect of the southerly extended boundary of the eastern right-of-way of Smith Grove Road and the boundary of the southern right –of-way of Bethel Church Road, thence in a westerly direction with the boundary of the southern right-of-way of Bethel Church Road to the eastern corner of the property having record number 10751, said corner also being located on the boundary of the southern right-of-way of Bethel Church Road, thence in a westerly direction with the southern property line of the properties having record numbers 10751 and 14140 to the northeastern corner of the property having record number 24256, thence in a southerly direction with the eastern property line of the above said property to the southeastern corner of the above said property, said corner also being located on the boundary of the northern right-of-way of NC 24/27 Highway, thence in an easterly direction with the boundary of the northern right-of-way of NC 24/27 Highway to the southwestern corner of the property having record number 10709, thence in a northerly direction with the western property line of the above said property to the northwestern corner of the above said property, thence in an easterly direction with the northern property line of the above said property to the northeastern corner of the above said property, thence in a southerly direction with the eastern property lines of the properties having record numbers 10709 and 28571 to the southeastern corner of the property having record number 28571, said corner also being located on the boundary of the northern right-of-way of NC 24/27 Highway, thence in an easterly direction with the northern right-of-way of NC 24/27 Highway to a point where the boundary of the northern right-of-way of NC 24/27 Highway intersects with the boundary of the western right-of-way of Bethel Church Road, thence in a northwestern direction with the western right-of-way of Bethel Church Road to a point in the boundary of the western right-of-way of Bethel Church Road intersects with the westerly extended northern property line of the property having record number 2370, thence in a northeasterly direction with the extended northern property line of the above said property to the northwestern corner of the above said property, said point also being located on the boundary of the northeastern right-of-way of Bethel Church Road, thence in a northeasterly direction with the northern property line of the above said property to the northeastern corner of the above said property, thence in a southeasterly direction with the northeastern property lines of the above said property and the property having record number 24658 to the southeastern corner of the property having record number 24658, thence in a southwesterly direction to the southwestern corner of the property having record number 24658, said point also being located at the intersect of the boundary of the northern right-of-way of NC 24/27 Highway and the boundary of the northeastern right-of-way of Bethel Church Road, thence in an easterly direction with the northern right-of-way of NC 24/27 Highway to the southwestern corner of the property having record number 7456, said corner also being located on the boundary of the northern right-of-way of NC 24/27 Highway, thence in a northerly direction with the western property line of the above said property to the northwestern corner of the above said property, thence in a northeasterly direction with the northwestern property line of the above said property to the northeastern corner of the above said property, thence in a generally northerly direction with the western property line of the property having record number 22651 to the northwestern corner of the above said property, thence in a southeasterly direction with the northeastern property line of the above said property to the northeastern corner of the above said property, thence in a southeasterly direction with the northeastern property line of the above said property to the northern corner of the property having record number 26185, thence in a southeasterly direction with the northeastern property line of the above said property to the intersect of the property having record number 17165, thence in a northerly, then northeasterly, direction with the northern property line of the above said property to the northeastern corner of the above said property, said corner also being located on the boundary of the western right-of-way of Smith Grove Road, thence in a northerly direction with the boundary of the western right-of-way of Smith Grove Road to the northeastern corner of the property having record number 10659. Said corner also being located on the boundary of the western right-of-way of Smith Grove Road, thence in a southwesterly direction with the eastern property line of the above said property to the southeastern corner of the above said property, thence in a westerly direction with the southern property line of the above said property to the southwestern corner of the above said property, thence in a northerly direction with the western property line of the above said property to the southwestern corner of the property having record number 4481, thence in a northwesterly direction with the southern property line of the above said property to the southwestern corner of the above said property, thence in a northeasterly direction with the western property line of the above said property to the northwestern corner of the above said property, said corner also being located on the boundary of the southern right-of-way of Smith Grove Road, thence in a westerly direction with the southern right-of-way of Smith Grove Road to the northeastern corner of the property having record number 32435, said corner also being located on the boundary of the western right-of-way of Smith Grove Road, thence in a southerly direction with the eastern property line of the above said property to the southeastern corner of the above said property, thence in a northwesterly direction with the southern property line of the above said property to the southwestern corner of the above said property, thence in a northerly direction with the western property line of the above said property to the northwestern corner of the above said property, said corner also located on the boundary of the southern right-of-way of Smith Grove Road, thence in a northeasterly direction with the northerly extended western property line of the above said property to a point, said point being located on the boundary of the northern right-of-way of Smith Grove Road where the northerly extended western property line of the above said property intersects with the boundary of the northern right-of-way of Smith Grove Road, thence in an easterly direction with the northern right-of-way of Smith Grove Road to the northwestern corner of the property having record number 18489, said corner also being located on the boundary of the northern right-of-way of Smith Grove Road, thence in a northeasterly direction with the northwestern property lines of the above said property and the property having record number 30952 to the northwestern corner of the property having record number 30952, thence in an easterly direction with the northern property lines of the properties having record numbers 30952, 2540, 2479, 2446, and 2423 to the northeastern corner of the property having record number 2423, said corner also being located on the boundary of the western right-of-way of Jacob Road, thence in an easterly direction with the extended northern property line of the above said property to a point, said point being the intersect of the easterly extended northern property line of the above said property and the boundary of the eastern right-of-way of Jacob Road, thence in a southerly direction with the eastern right-of-way of Jacob Road to the northwestern corner of the property having record number 24746, thence in a generally northeasterly, and then easterly direction with the northern property line of the above said property to the northeastern corner of the above said property, said corner also being located on the boundary of the western right-of-way of Ridgecrest Road, thence in an easterly direction with the easterly extended northern property line of the above said property to the northeastern corner of the property having record number 3556, said corner also being located on the boundary of the eastern right-of-way of Ridgecrest Road, thence in a southerly direction with the eastern property line of the above said property to the southeastern corner of the above said property, thence in a southeasterly direction with the eastern property lines of the properties having record numbers 11281, 3347, and 25624 to the southeastern corner of the property having record number 25624, said corner also being located on the boundary of the northwestern right-of-way of Gaddis Road, thence in a northeasterly direction with the boundary of the northwestern right-of-way of Gaddis Road to a point, said point being where the northwesterly extended northern property line of the property having record number 28713 intersects with the boundary of the northwestern right-of-way of Gaddis Road, thence in a southeasterly direction with the westerly extended northern property line of the above said property to the northeastern corner of the above said property, said corner also being located on the boundary of the southeastern right-of-way of Gaddis Road, thence in a southeasterly direction with the northeastern property line of the above said property to the southeastern corner of the above said property, thence in an easterly direction with the northern property lines of the properties having record numbers 12921 and 1136 to the northeastern corner of the property having record number 1136, thence in a southerly direction with the eastern property line of the above said property to the northern corner of the property having record number 12922, thence in a southerly direction with the eastern property lines of the above said property and the property having record number 665 to the southeastern corner of the property having record number 665, said corner also being located on the boundary of the northern right-of-way of NC 24/27 Highway, thence in an easterly direction with the northern right-of-way of NC 24/27 Highway to the southwestern corner of the property having record number 20151, said corner also being located on the boundary of the northern right-of-way of NC 24/27 Highway, thence in a northerly direction with the western property lines of the properties having record numbers 20151 and 12653 to the northwestern corner of the property having record number 12653, thence in an easterly direction to the northeastern corner of the above said property, thence in a northerly direction with the western property line of the property having record number 20676 to the northwestern corner of the above said property, thence in an generally easterly direction with the northern property lines of the properties having record numbers 20676, 21255, 21915, 24584, 24586, 18565, 15504, 3429, and 19950 to the northeastern corner of the property having record number 19950, thence in a southerly direction with the eastern property line of the above said property to the southeastern corner of the above said property, thence in an easterly direction with the northern property line of the property having record number 3500 to the northeastern corner of the above said property, thence in a northerly direction with the western property line of the property having record number 33886 to the northwestern corner of the property having record number 33886, thence in an easterly direction with the northern property line of the above said property to the northeastern corner of the above said property, thence in a southerly direction with the eastern property line of the above said property to the southeastern corner of the above said property, said corner also being located on the boundary of the northern right-of-way of NC 24/27 Highway, thence in a southerly direction with the southerly extended eastern property line of the above said property to a point, said point being the intersect of the southerly extended eastern property line of the above said property and the boundary of the southern right-of-way of Highway 24/27, thence in a westerly direction with the southern right-of-way of NC 24/27 Highway to the northeastern corner of the property having record number 11320, said corner also being located on the boundary of the southern right-of-way of NC 24/27 Highway, thence in a southerly direction with the eastern property line of the above said property to the southeastern corner of the above said property, thence in a westerly direction with the southern property line of the above said property to the southwestern corner of the above said property, thence in a northerly direction with the western property line of the above said property to the northwestern corner of the above said property, said corner also being located on the boundary of the southern right-of-way of NC 24/27 Highway, thence in a westerly direction with the southern right-of-way of NC 24/27 Highway to the northeastern corner of the property having record number 3491, said corner also being located on the boundary of the southern right-of-way of NC 24/27 Highway, thence in a southerly direction with the eastern property line of the above said property to the southeastern corner of the above said property, thence in a westerly direction with the southern property line of the above said property to the southwestern corner of the above said property, thence in a northerly direction with the property line of the above said property to the southeastern corner of the property having record number 1861, thence in a westerly direction with the southern property line of the above said property to the southwestern corner of the above said property, thence in a northerly direction with the western property line of the above said property to the northwestern corner of the above said property, said corner also being located on the boundary of the southern right-of-way of Highway 24/27, thence in a westerly direction with the southern right-of-way of Highway 24/27 to the northeastern corner of the property having record number 12914, said corner also being located on the boundary of the southern right-of-way of NC 24/27 Highway, thence in a southerly direction with the eastern property line of the above said property to the southeastern corner of the above said property, thence in a westerly direction with the southern property lines of the properties having record numbers 12914, 12915, and 12634 to the point where the property having record number 12634 intersects with the boundary of the eastern right-of-way of Lakewood Road, thence in a southerly, and then southwesterly, direction with the eastern right-of-way of Lakewood Road to the intersect with the property having record number 12634, said point also being located on the boundary of the southern right-of-way of Lakewood Road, thence in a southerly direction with the eastern property line of the above said property to the southeastern corner of the above said property, thence in a westerly direction with the southern property lines of the above said property and the properties having record numbers 12920 and 9896 to the southwestern corner of the property having record number 9896, thence in a southerly direction with the eastern property lines of the properties having record numbers 12948 and 11523 to the southeastern corner of the property having record number 11523, said corner also being located on the boundary of the northern right-of-way of Lakewood Road, thence in a southerly direction with the southerly extended eastern property line of the above said property to a point, said point being where the southerly extended eastern property line of the above said property intersects with the boundary of the southern right-of-way of Lakewood Road, said point also being located on the boundary of the southern right-of-way of Lakewood Road, thence in a westerly direction with the boundary of the southern right of way of Lakewood Road to the northernmost corner of the property having record number 6510, said corner also being located on the boundary of the southern right-of-way of Lakewood Road, thence in a southeasterly direction with the northeastern property line of the above said property to the northeastern corner of the above said property, thence in a southerly direction with the eastern property lines of the above said property and the property having record number 3063 to the southeastern corner of the property having record number 3063, thence in a westerly direction with the southern property lines of the properties having record numbers 3063, 4027, 19740, 3093, 11040, and 17912 to the southwestern corner of the property having record number 17912, thence in a northerly direction with the western property line of the above said property to the northwestern corner of the above said property, said corner also being located on the boundary of the southern right-of-way of Lakewood Road, said corner also being the point of beginning.

Exceptions

Excepted from the above-described track are the following internal parcels:

1. Property having record number 11327.
2. Property having record number 11358.
3. Property having record number 17930.
4. Those parcels of land in Arbor Heights subdivision, and road right-of-ways of Redwood Drive and Birchwood Court recorded in Plat Book 17 Page 386 and previously annexed into the town of Oakboro, NC. By parcels, these properties being identified by the following pin numbers.
   - 4.1 That property having pin number 659503418442
   - 4.2 That property having pin number 559503418373
   - 4.3 That property having pin number 559503419204
   - 4.4 That property having pin number 559503349155
   - 4.5 That property having pin number 559504510006
   - 4.6 That property having pin number 559504500948
   - 4.7 That property having pin number 559504500889
   - 4.8 That property having pin number 559504501820

4.9 That property having pin number 559504501751
4.10 That property having pin number 559504502740
4.11 That property having pin number 559504504639
4.12 That property having pin number 559504505639
4.13 That property having pin number 559504506851
4.14 That property having pin number 559504505942
4.15 That property having pin number 559504503889
4.16 That property having pin number 559504514060
4.17 That property having pin number 559504502986
4.18 That property having pin number 559504515101
4.19 That property having pin number 559504514210
4.20 That property having pin number 559504512019
4.21 That property having pin number 559504513108
4.22 That property having pin number 559504511169
4.23 That property having pin number 559504511218
4.24 That property having pin number 559504511318
4.25 That property having pin number 559504503740
4.26 That drive by the name of Redwood
4.27 That drive by the name of Birchwood

APPENDIX-3

First Community Meeting
August 14, 2001

Heath Hahn

1. Let people be aware that there is a tablet on the table for them to list their names, addresses and phone numbers so that we can keep them informed of what is going on.

2. Also, If anyone has trouble hearing us – please let us know.

3. Introduce key people and ask people to hold questions until after the presentation.

Ray Quick

Why we are here:

2. Introduction and statement of why we are here.

    2.1. There's been a lot of talk about whether Oakboro or Locust is going to take us in as part of their town. This question is becoming more acute because of 24/27 being four-laned. Everyone knows Oakboro is headed out this way because it has annexed two areas in our community so far

    2.2. If we set back and do nothing we will eventually be taken in by Oakboro. It is my guess that this will happen in two to three years.

2.3. Just by meeting tonight to discuss what we want our future to be, we have eliminated one big problem. That is that three years from now we will not have to look back and ask ourselves what happened. We will have made a conscious decision on our future. If we choose to do nothing and become a part of Oakboro we will still know that we deliberately made that decision – to just let it happen.

2.4. We are here tonight to explore our options and, hopefully, make a pro-active decision on how we want our community to end up.

2.5. Whatever we decide tonight will be a major decision because it will, in all probability, set the course for the future of our community. Not only will it affect us for the rest of our lives but it will affect the future generations in Red Cross.

2.6. By having this meeting, it is our understanding that we have effectively halted, or blocked, any town from moving on us until we conclude our action.

Our problem:

3. One of the biggest constraints to growth in Stanly County has been the lack of a transportation infrastructure. That's why we have been able to enjoy our stable community as long as we have. But now that has changed with the four-laneing of 24/27. Long range expectations are that the 24/27 corridor between Charlotte and Albemarle will, in the next 25-years, become a major business corridor and we are going to be right in the middle of it and there is no way to stop it.

4. If we allow another town to incorporate us we will be subject to their ordinances, representation, and taxation. The most desirable thing would be for the people in this community to have self-determination. That is we would like to be able to chart our own course for the future. It will also keep all taxes local to our community.

5. Heath Hahn to tell the story about Big Lick

What options we have:

6. Like I said, we are not going to stop the growth – but we do have the opportunity to control it. We have four options:

    6.1. We can do nothing and let Oakboro absorb us and Red Cross will fade into oblivion like Big Lick.

    6.2. We can invite Oakboro to take us in and possibly gain some extra benefits.

    6.3. We can invite Locust to take us in and possibly gain some benefits from them.

    6.4. We can choose to make Red Cross a town and incorporate it.

5. This is what we have to make a decision on tonight. Do we want to:

    5.1 Set back and do nothing

    5.2 Invite Oakboro to take us

    5.3 Invite Locust to take us

    5.4 Incorporate Red Cross into a town

6 What those of us that called the meeting would like to see is Red Cross being incorporated into a town. To do this, we need to have a vote by the people on which of the four options to go with.

    6.1 Let things go on as is and do nothing

        6.2 Invite Oakboro to take us

        6.3 Invite Locust to take us

6.4 Incorporate Red Cross into a town

A brief outline of what can be done:

7 Before we do that there are some things you need to be aware of:

7.1 This is a first meeting and its main purpose is to find out if the people want to do anything.

7.2 We do not have many answers to questions yet because a committee has not been formed to explore the possibility.

7.3 If the people want to incorporate Red Cross then we will need to elect a committee tonight. Note that a committee is only a fact-finding and recommending body that can take no real legal action without the peoples approval. Before anything substantive can happen, it will require a vote of the people in the proposed town limits.

7.4 You have the part of General Statute 120-163 that deals with the incorporation of towns in North Carolina. It gives the basic requirements. We can meet these requirements.

7.5 This is a new law that was passed in 1999 and took effect January 1, 2000. Its primary purpose was to prevent communities from incorporating ad-hock townships just to block existing city expansions. It forces communities to assume the identity and functionality of a town

7.6 The general steps are to hold a first meeting, form a committee, decide on town boundaries, work out services, and propose budgets. Once that is done we can ask our state representative to present our request for incorporation to the state legislature and the county. We can then look at a possible vote. Again, Won't anything happen unless the majority of the voters approve it.

7.7 Because of the new law that took effect in 2000 we will have to do some of the following.

7.7.1 We will have to collect taxes – at least five cents per $100.00. There's no way around that. To save math – that is $50.00 on the $100,000. Realistically, it should be noted that there is no guarantee that we can hold it at five percent because we will also be required to provide at least four services in the third year following our incorporation. Look at the attached sheet on tax rates for Albemarle and Stanly County.

7.7.2 The services we will have to provide at least four of are:

7.7.2.1 Police Protection – We can contract with the Sheriff's Department

7.7.2.2 Fire protection – We can contract with Oakboro or Ridgecrest.

7.7.2.3 Water Distribution – We can contract with the county.

7.7.2.4 Waste collection – We can contract with the county.

7.7.2.5 Street maintenance – we can contract with the state.

7.7.2.6 Street Construction – We're not ready to even discuss that one.

7.7.2.7 Street Lighting – We'll have to investigate that one

7.7.2.8 Zoning – We should be able to do that one.

7.8 One additional thing, we've talked with Tom Garrison, the Mayor of Baden, and he is willing to set down with us this week and help us outline what we need to do. Before this meeting we need to have a committee appointed to meet with him.

8. We need to take a vote at this point. Do we want to peruse the opportunity to incorporate Red Cross?

9. Take questions and pole the people for any remarks they may have.

10. At this point we need to take a vote to see if the majority of the people here want to appoint a committee to peruse incorporating Red Cross. A hand count will be ok.

11. Take vote.

Heath Hahn

1. Ok, at this point we need to elect a committee to represent us. There are some suggestions that we should consider in picking these people.

    1.1. That they will represent the community's interest above their own.

    1.2. These people need to be willing and able to devote the necessary time to the committee for it to work. The process is going to about a year and a half.

    1.3. They will be able to effectively work with other committee members. That is that they will not just shoot someone down if they don't agree with the person's suggestion. That if the majority agrees to go one way and the individual wants to go another then the individual will continue to support the majority and work constructively to make the majority opinion work. I talked with one group of people that were in the process of incorporating and they were having a lot of problems because the group was trying to split in three different directions. We can't afford to let this happen to us.

1.4. As to committee size. It should be an odd number of people, no less than three people, and no more than nine. If a committee gets larger than nine people, it tends to fragment and loose its effectiveness.

1.5. We will also need to choose two alternates. These people will not have voting rights but will need to attend the meetings and stay current on all activities.

2. Get a hand count on the number of people that should be on the committee.

3. Get a list of suggested committee members from the audience and write it on the flip-board.

4. Give the people a slip of paper and have them write peoples names from the list on the paper.

5. Tally the papers and determine who the committee members will be.

6. Let the people know that once the committee has something to report they will notify the people and hold other meetings to keep them update.

APPENDIX-4

Community Meeting Agenda
August 28, 2001

C.J. Barbee
Introduction:

1. Let people know that there is a tablet on the table that they need to sign – put their name, address, and phone number on so that we can keep them updated.

2. Open the meeting with a prayer.

3. Introduce key people and ask the audience to hold questions until the core of the presentation is over.

4. Give an outline of the evenings agenda:

    4.1. Review what happened at the last meeting.

    4.2. Read minutes of last meeting.
    4.3. What has happened since the last meeting.

    4.4. Elect remaining two members of committee.

    4.5. What has happened since the last meeting.

    4.6. Actions that are to be taken over the next couple weeks

4.7. Take questions and/or suggestions from the floor

Linda Yow
Read minutes of last meeting.

Heath Hahn
Review of last meeting:

5. A meeting was held two weeks ago tonight by 47 people of the community to decide what they wanted to see happen to our community. The decision on the table was to select one of four options:

    5.1. Do nothing and let Oakboro annex us and let Red Cross fade into oblivion like Big Lick.

    5.2. Invite Oakboro to take us so that we could be sure we would be annexed into their town

    5.3. Invite Locust to take us so that we could be sure we would be annexed into their town.

    5.4. Choose to make Red Cross a town and incorporate it so that we can be self-governed.

6. The people at that meeting made four basic decisions:

    6.1. Pursue the incorporation process and try to make Red Cross a town.

    6.2. Chose to form a committee consisting of five people for that purpose.

    6.3. Elected three of the five-committee members so that those members could start preliminary work towards the incorporation process. The three people elected were C.J. Barbee, Heath Hahn, and Ray Quick.

6.4. Hold two of the positions on that committee open so that additional members of the community could have input on selecting the two remaining committee members.

7. These decisions were important decisions. What was decided at that meeting is going to have an effect on our community for a hundred years or more. It will affect the rest of our lives and the future generations of Red Cross.

8. The consensus at that meeting was that we do not have the choice of doing nothing. That we have to explore our options and try and take actions that will be the best for the people of our community. To that end the people at that meeting chose to form a committee and peruse incorporation of Red Cross.

9. Some people may, on first thought, consider this a little hasty. It's not, we are almost out of time in having any say on what happens to our community.

An overview of what we are looking at:

1. A new law was passed by the legislature in 1999 that took effect January 1, 2000 that was designed to prevent communities from doing ad-hock incorporations for the sole purpose of preventing towns from incorporating them. There are copies on the tables if anyone does not have a copy.

2. What is says is that if you are going to claim to be a town then you are going to have to act like a town. You're going to have to:

   2.1. Have a tax – a minimum of .05 on $100.00 – which equates to $50.00 per $100.000. In reality we expect the Red Cross taxes to be something less than .20 per $100.00.

   2.2. Have at least 250 people per square mile in the area you are incorporating.

   2.3. Provide a minimum of four of the following services.

2.3.1. Police protection.

2.3.2. Fire protection water distribution

2.3.3. Waste collection

2.3.4. Street maintenance

2.3.5. Street construction

2.3.6. Street lighting

2.3.7. Zoning

2.4. We feel we can meet these requirements.

Heath Hahn
Accept questions from the people:

Select the two remaining committee members:

> Author's Note: The two exploratory committee members selected at this meeting were J. D. Hinson and Larry Wayne Smith. The three selected in the first meeting were C. J. Barbee, Heath Hahn and Ray Quick.

Ray Quick
What we have done to-date:

1. We have gone to the County GIS office and obtained maps and a database of the Red Cross area. There is a copy of the map on the table for everyone to look at.

2. The map centers on Red Cross and shows all properties within a three-mile radius of Red Cross. This doesn't mean that we are looking at having a city limit of three miles. We may not be able to go but one mile. What we will have to do is:

2.1. Determine who wants to be a part of our town.

2.2. Determine the population density of those areas and insure we can meet the requirements.

2.3. In all probability we will have to take a census of the anticipated area to insure we can meet the 250 people per square mile requirement.

3. We have obtained some literature on procedures of incorporation.

4. Tom Garrison, the Mayor of Baden, has been in the hospital – so we have not yet been able to get the help we were hoping for from him.

5. We talked with Dan Short in Midland about their incorporation process. He is providing information on some additional funding as well as suggestions for incorporation.

6. We have met with Bobby Harold Barbee and obtained his support for our incorporation process.

7. We called David Lawrence with the Institute of Government and ran through what we have done to-date to be sure we were doing what needed doing. He said it sounded as if we were following the correct procedures.

C.J. Barbee

Things to do over the next couple weeks:

8. We want get a resolution from the Chairman of the Stanly County Board of County Commissioners, Locust, and Oakboro. Basically, this is just a letter from the city(s) stating that they will not object to our incorporation process.

8.1. We talked with Wilson Barbee, the mayor of Locust, and asked for a resolution from Locust on our incorporation process. He said that they would have no problem with it and if we would send them a letter they should be able to have us a response fairly quickly.

8.2. We have talked to Joyce Little, the Mayor of Oakboro, and she said they would have no problem with giving us one and that they wished us the best of luck in our efforts.

8.3. We will, at some point, need to get with the Stanly County Board of County Commissioners and get them on board.

8.4. Bobby Harold Barbee has given us a stack of outlining actions that need to be acted on. We will, over the next several weeks be addressing these items.

8.5. We will need to define a preliminary boundary for our town limits and start working out the details of the targeted area.

8.6. We fully expect that once we have established these boundaries we will need to take a census of our community to get an accurate count of the population. What will probably work best is for someone living on each of the roads in our area to go around to their neighbors and complete a sheet on each person. We will be printing these sheets out at a later date. If anyone is interested in doing this survey of their road – please let us know.

8.7. We need to identify an attorney to handle our legal needs.

8.8. We need to get committee incorporated as a non-profit organization so that all contributions to our incorporation process will be tax deductable.

8.9. We're going to need better than $5,000 to get this process through – We need to start taking pledges tonight!

Heath Hahn
Announce who the two newly elected committee members are.

Close out the meeting.
As follow-up to the above agenda - we later found out that we didn't have to have our committee incorporated as a nonprofit organization. Also, we never received resolutions from either Oakboro or Locust with respect to their approval of our incorporation process. With respect to obtaining an attorney for the incorporation committee we were fortunate in that Josh Morton agreed to serve in that capacity.

Committee Meeting (08-30-2001):
This was the first formal meeting of the newly appointed Incorporation Committee. I made out an agenda of items I felt we needed to cover:

1. Appointing a chairman of the committee.

2. Method of voting within the committee.

3. Our need for a secretary and treasurer.

4. Our need for an attorney.

5. Will we have to incorporate the committee?

6. Establish some form of outline for voting by the people on each action.

7. Standardizing our meeting outline.

8. How to respond to questions during public meetings.

APPENDIX-5

Community Meeting Agenda
September 25, 2001

C.J. Barbee
Introduction:

1. Welcome people.

2. Open meeting with a prayer.

3. Introduce Committee Members and point out Committee Chairman.
   Recognize John Long of the Weekly Post
   Recognize Michael Knox of the Stanly News & Press.

Linda Yow
Read minutes of last meeting.

C. J. Barbee
Pep-talk:

Everything is proceeding well and it looks as if Red Cross will be a town by this time next year. Everything seems to be falling in place and it looks as if we are going to meet all the requirements so that the legislature will approve our request for incorporation. It's been a lot of work and we have had to make some compromises, but we are going to do it.

Review of actions taken to-date:

1. We have identified an attorney to represent us during our incorporation process and to act as the town attorney for the interim town government. This is one of the required items we have to submit to Raleigh.

   It was the choice of the Incorporation Committee that we use Josh Morton. We have talked with him and he has agreed to let us submit his name as attorney on our request for incorporation.

2. Shortly after the last meeting C.J. Barbee (Incorporation Committee Treasurer) sent off the request for a tax number and should have it back at any time.

3. At the last meeting we asked for pledges and received $3,700.00 in pledges. This is a good start but we will need more than $5,000.00 (total) to complete this process. We will have three big expenses to pay for; the survey of the town limits, voting cost during the referendum, and the cost of Raleigh's survey verifying of our statistics.

   If you haven't yet pledged, I strongly urge you to do so tonight. You can give your pledge to C.J. Barbee. For those wanting to give money on existing pledges, again, see C.J. Barbee and he will take the money and give you a receipt. We are at the point were we are going to have to spend money. The expenses are going to start mounting this month – we are in the heart of the process.

4. At the last meeting we said we would have the town limits defined by this meeting, and we have! The need for this map has held up a lot of other work that we need to get done but could not start on until we had a valid town limit defined. Developing this map has been a lot of hard work requiring a lot of hours by everyone on the committee. It's not as easy a job as it appears to be on the surface.

Later on in the meeting we will go into an explanation of how, and why, we arrived at these boundaries. One nice thing is that we have been able to use the County's tax information and U.S. Census data to arrive at our figures without having to do an actual head count of the people in the area – and we have made the required numbers.

5. We have talked with our Representative, Bobby Harold Barbee, and he has promised us his full support in our incorporation process. This is a very important step since he and Arron Plyler will be the ones to present it to the legislature next spring and in getting the legislatures to pass it.

   Bobby Harold Barbee said he would get in touch with Arron Plyler and obtain his support for us. He also said that if we would have our petition to him before the next session of the General Assembly he and Arron Plyler would present it at the start of the next session.

   In fact, Bobby Harold Barbee is confident enough that we will succeed that he is petitioning to have the plans for the new highway 24/27 changed from a divided medium to a five-lane road starting at Bethel Church Road and going down past West Stanly High School. I hope he is successful in getting this done.

   It is important to note that we will have to get a positive recommendation from the Joint Commission on Municipal Incorporations before it is presented to the legislature. This is why we drew the town limits as we have – we have to meet the requirements as stated in GS 120-163.

   Most of you should have a copy of General Statute 120-163 from the last couple meetings. This statute defines those requirements. If you don't have a copy there is a stack on the table up front.

Ray Quick

Things we need to do tonight:

1. The first thing we need to do is make a formal decision on a town name. We, the Incorporation Committee, recommend the name of "Red Cross". If this not accepted by a majority of the people at this meeting then we will accept alternate names for our town.

   Take a vote on the town name!

2. We need to decide on an interim government to manage the town until we have the first public election. Public elections are held in odd years – meaning there will not be a public election until November 2003. For this reason the interim government will fill this roll from the date of incorporation until that election can be held.

   First we need to decide on what form of government we want to install. We suggest a mayor with a city council. The city council should consist of at least four people in addition to a mayor.

   Take a vote for acceptance of installing a mayor and city council.

3. Second we need to decide on who to put in this position. Standard practice is to install the incorporation committee as the interim council until formal elections can be held. This is because the Incorporation Committee is usually the most familiar with the mechanics and actions that have been taken in making the community a town. Remember, once Red Cross has been incorporated, the Incorporation Committee will have completed its task and be dissolved.

   The reason for this is because the Incorporation Committee will have completed it's incorporation responsibilities and will be dissolved the day Red Cross incorporates. At the time of incorporation it will become the responsibility of the Interim Government to take over as the town governing body.

It is required that we specify the form of government and the people that will serve on the interim council in our request to the legislature for incorporation.

We will now ask for a vote on acceptance of placing the Incorporation Committee in as the interim town government once Red Cross is incorporated.

Take a vote on acceptance of placing the Incorporation Committee in the position of town council once Red Cross has been incorporated

4. Third, we need to vote on acceptance of the proposed town limits – but first a little explanation of how the town limits were derived.

5. Assumptions:

   5.1. 2001 Census data indicates an average of 2.53 people per household in Stanly County.

   5.2. No specific numbers exist in incorporation requirements for land area requirements per house. Assumption made to use 250 people per square mile and 2.53 people per household as a baseline for calculating development per house.

   (640 acres per sq. mile / 250 people per sq. mile required = 2.56 acres per person)

   (2.56 acres per person X 2.53 people per household = 6.48 acres developed per house).

6. Land Area:

6.1. Non-commercial – 1312.21 acres or 2.05 square miles.

6.2. All Land (both commercial and non-commercial) – 1435.61 acres or 2.423 Square miles.

7. Land Utilization:

7.1. People per square mile – 261.64
Note: Does not include commercial property in calculations.

(1312.21 acres / 640 acres/square mile = 2.05 square miles)

(212 houses X 2.53 people per house = 536.36 people in town limit)

7.2. Percent development – .496

1.1.1.1. 711.69 total acres developed.

1.1.1.2. 594.92 total acres developed residentially. This allows 6.48 acres per house

1.1.1.3. 116.77 total acres developed commercially. This includes businesses, churches, and schools as well as other state property. It should be noted that, although power line right-of-ways and roads will be included in the town boundaries, we have not yet included them in these numbers.

Take vote on acceptance of town limits.

Heath Hahn
Things to be done:

We want to be ready to start the petitioning process by November 1, 2001. To do this we have a lot of work to complete. We will be:

1. Taking bids for potential services. As a town, we are required by GS 120-163 to provide at least four of eight specified services.

    1.1. Sheriff's Department

    1.2. Fire Department

    1.3. Waste Disposal

    1.4. Exploring road maintenance.

    1.5. Zoning – We will want to assume responsibility for these. By law, the Incorporation Committee can not act on zoning. However, the interim council will have 60-days from the date of incorporation to establish a zoning plan and submit it or loose the right to control zoning for the city of Red Cross.

2. Formulate a budget for the town – this includes establishing a tax rate. Remember, at the first meeting we stated that we are required to have a tax of no less than .05/100.00, however, in reality it will require more than that to have a functional town. And it was stated at our first meeting that it was our belief that we should be able to keep our tax rate below .20/100.00. We still firmly believe that.

   Now that we have a town boundary we can start work on that budget. Once we get bids for services we can start working up the numbers to see what our tax rate will be. All this will have to be completed before we can issue a signing petition to the people of Red Cross requesting incorporation.

3. Obtain resolutions from Oakboro, Locust, Stanfield, and Stanly County.

4. Draw up a town charter.

5. Have survey done. We have received the names of four people capable of doing this type work.

6. Draw up petition for signing. All the previously stated information will be included with the petition. So you will know what services are to be provided and the tax rate prior to signing the petition.

7. We hope to have all this work completed by November 1, 2001 and be ready to circulate the signing petition starting at the beginning of November. We will hold our next meeting on **Thursday, October 25, 2001**.

Close Meeting:

People, We are well on our way to becoming a town!
We thank you for your attendance and participation.

APPENDIX-6

Red Cross Community Meeting
October 25, 2001:

Introduction:

1. Welcome everyone to the Red Cross Town Incorporation meeting.

2. Open the meeting with a prayer.

3. Introduce key people.

   Incorporation Committee Members

   C.J. Barbee

   Heath Hahn

   J.D. Hinson

   Larry Wayne Smith

   Ray Quick

   Keeping Minutes

   Lynda Yow

Stanly County

Dan Baucom – Stanly County Tax Supervisor

Paul Reynolds – Stanly County GIS Office

Bobby Harold Barbee – Our representative for the 82nd district and the person that will be sponsoring our petition for incorporation to the Legislature next spring.

Ken Furr – Chairman of the Stanly County Commissioners

John Long of The Weekly Post

________________________ of the Stanly News and Press

4. Linda Yow to read minutes of last meeting.

5. C.J. Barbee to give financial report.

Pep-talk:

At the last meeting we said everything was going well and we're happy to report we that we feel it's going very well. All the parts are falling in place and we are well on our way to becoming a town.

Review of Last Month's Meeting:

1. We voted on and accepted the name "Red Cross" to be the town name.

2. We voted on and accepted having a Mayor and City Council as our form of government.

3. We voted on and accepted installing the Incorporation Committee as the Interim Council at incorporation to serve

as our city council until the first public election.

4. We voted on and accepted the proposed city limits of Red Cross as was shown on the map and presented by the Incorporation Committee.

   For the benefit of those that weren't present at the last meeting, the statistics we arrived at for our town are as follows:

   - Land area for the town is 2.423 square miles
   - Land utilization is 261.64 people per square mile.
   - Percent development is 0.496 percent.
     - ➢ 711.69 acres developed
     - ➢ 594.92 acres developed residentially
     - ➢ 116.77 acres developed commercially (businesses, churches, schools, and government property.

   These numbers are important because we are required to have at least 250 people per square mile and at least 40% development (Note: in addition to businesses, a home (including up to 6.48 acres) counts as developed land).

6. We also told you we would try to have resolutions from neighboring town and our have the town survey done. We have obtained verbal acceptance from both Locust and Oakboro. I regret to say that because we had so much work to do on the budget we didn't have time to follow up on them. That doesn't hurt anything because they only have to be completed in time to send to Raleigh.

Tonight's Business:

1. At the last meeting we said we would have a town charter, budget, and proposed tax rate ready for this meeting. We will be presenting it for your approval tonight. This is the last step we, as a community, will have to vote acceptance on before we start circulating a petition for incorporation. Red Cross as a town is becoming a reality.

2. Dan Baucom to present slide show from County prospective.

3. Show slide show of tax rate and list of services we plan to offer.

4. Ray Quick to sum up.

5. Take questions on budget.

6. We will take a vote on the acceptance of the budget as presented. We do ask however, that only those people that are to be in the city limits, as shown on the current map, vote on this budget. Does anyone need additional time to look at the map to see if they are going to be in the city limits?

Take Vote on Acceptance of Budget

1. Read proposed Charter out.

2. Take Questions on Town Charter.

3. Again, we will take a vote on the acceptance of the town charter as presented. We do ask however, that only those people that are to be in the city limits as shown on the current map vote on this budget. Does anyone need additional time to look at the map to see if they are going to be in the city limits?

Take Vote on Acceptance of Town Charter.

Last item of business:
We will need help from the community in circulating petitions for signing. We would like to have a couple people from each street (or road) volunteer to carry petitions around to houses. These petitions should be ready within a week and we sure could use the help. If you are willing to do this please let one of the committee members know.

Since petition signing is expected to take about six weeks and the holidays will be coming up we will have our next meeting on January 11, 2002. At this meeting we will give the results of the petition and have a copy of the package that we will send to Raleigh ready.

Thank everyone for their attendance and participation.
Close the Meeting.

The Fifth and Final Community Meeting (01-10-2001):
The fifth incorporation meeting was held on January 10, 2002, in the basement of Red Cross Baptist Church. The incorporation committee told the people that "This is the fifth, and probably the last, meeting of the Red Cross's community incorporation process. We do not plan to have another meeting until, and when, the results of the petition we send to Raleigh are known.

This meeting is to give an overview of everything done to date, the results of what we have learned, where we stand, and what actions are left to be taken."

We informed the people of the actions taken since the last meeting:

- That the petitions had been circulated and signed and we gave them the results of the petition.
- That we had started posting our notice of incorporation in the papers.
- That we had started sending letters of notification of our incorporation to

the County and other Towns within the County

- That we were crafting our petition that we would be sending to Raleigh.
- We tried to give them a full outline of the course our petition would probably take through the Legislature.

APPENDIX-7

Red Cross Incorporation Meeting
January 10, 2002

Introduction:

1. Welcome people.

2. Open meeting with a prayer.

3. Introduce Committee Members.

4. Recognize any officials/newspaper people present

   - 82nd District Representative - Bobby Harold Barbee

   - The Weekly Post – John Long

   - Stanly News & Press – ____________________

I guess everyone has heard about the article on Red Cross in "Our State" magazine? If you haven't read it we have placed a copy on each of the tables for people to read and pass around. It was a good article – it makes me proud of our community.

Reason for this meeting:

This is the fifth, and probably the last, meeting of the Red Cross's community incorporation process. We do not plan to have another meeting until, and when, the results of the petition we send to Raleigh are known.

This meeting is to give an overview of everything done to date, the results of what we have learned, where we stand, and what actions are left to take.

Where We Stand and What's next:
Since everyone is probably wondering how we're doing, we'll first give you an update on where we are at now and what is left to do.

1. We went from house to house in the petition signing and the results are as follows:

    - Estimated 402 potential petition signers in the community.
    - 366 people signed the petitions
    - 36 did not sign for various reasons.
    - This gave us an estimated signing ratio of 91% for our community.

2. The results from the Board of Elections are as follows: (It should be noted that we were surprised to find that quite a few people that signed the petition that thought they were registered but in fact were not).

    - We were not able to get a count of the actual number of people registered in our proposed town boundaries so we still have to go on our original estimate.
    - A breakdown of the Board of Elections results are as follows:
        - 310 people certified.

- 56 votes were rejected. A breakdown of this is as follows:
    - 42 people rejected for not being registered.
    - 9 people rejected for having an address other than that of Red Cross.
    - 4 people rejected for invalid signatures.
- Right now we are somewhere around 75% but hope to be able to pull it back up to the 90% mark by the time we are ready to send our petition off.
- What we plan to do is go back to these people with registration forms and try to get them eligible and then have our petition re-certified. This will probably take us a couple weeks.

3. We have started posting our intent to incorporate in the newspaper as required by NCGS-120. This posting will have to run for at least two weeks prior to our sending our petition to The Joint Committee on Municipal Incorporations. This means that it will be the end of this month before we can send the petition to Raleigh.

4. We are about half way through crafting our petition and will have it ready by the time the two weeks of our intent to incorporate public notice has run.

5. We will then send the petition to the Joint Committee on Municipal Incorporations for their review. They may have up to 60 days to review it before returning it to us. They will verify it for accuracy and for our having met the criteria for incorporation. Once completed they will return it to us with either a positive or negative recommendation. We can't see any reason at this point for a negative recommendation.

6. Once we get the petition back with the positive recommendation we

will hand it over to our State Representative, Bobby Harold Barbee, and he will take it to Raleigh and have a bill drafted. Mr. Barbee said he would need it by April 15, 2002.

7. Mr. Barbee said the Legislature would meet in mid May and he would present the bill during the first two or three days of the session.

8. Traditionally, if it is passed in the Legislature, it will come back to us and a referendum would be called for the people of Red Cross to vote on making Red Cross a town. Once the votes are counted and a 50+% majority is recognized we will then officially become a town.

9. The exception to this is that there is a fairly high probability that Red Cross will be declared a town in the Legislature and will not have to come back for a referendum because of the high percentage of our petition signing. Bottom line is that we will probably be a town by the end of May of this year.

Review of meetings and actions taken to date:

First meeting (August 14, 2001):

- This was an informal meeting of 47 people from the community to see if we, as a community, wanted to consider incorporating ourselves or allow the Red Cross Community to be annexed at a later date by another town.

- There was a unanimous vote that we should consider incorporating ourselves so that we could retain our identity as a community and to preserve our right to self-determination.

- It was decided that we would form a committee of five people to pursue the process and report back to the people our findings on the potential of incorporating.

- Three people were chosen that night. They were C. J. Barbee, Heath Hahn, and Ray Quick.

- It was decided to hold the other two positions open till the next meeting so that a better representation of the community could be present and have input on selecting the rest of the committee.

- A second, publicized meeting was set for August 28, 2001.

- The committee, prior to the second meeting did the following:

    - The committee of three later made contact with Bobby Harold Barbee and let him know of our intent to pursue an incorporation process for the community of Red Cross.

    - Obtained information on the incorporation process from the Institute of Government.

    - Talked to Mayors Tom Garrison of Badin and Dan Short of Midland.

    - Went to the GIS office and obtained maps and a database of the Red Cross area.

Second Meeting (August 28, 2001):

- There were 173 people present for this meeting.

- At this meeting all the information of the first meeting was reviewed and everyone brought up-to-date of the events that had taken place to-date.

- The remaining two committee members were elected – they were J. D. Hinson and Larry Wayne Smith.

- Some objection was raised that not all the community was involved in the first meeting and that the community might not want to incorporate itself. A vote was taken on continuing the incorporation process and 169 people voted in favor of incorporating, two voted against it, and two abstained.

- The committee, prior to the third meeting, did the following:

- Contacted and identified Josh Morton to represent us as needed.

- C. J. Barbee obtained a tax number for collecting pledges.

- Defined the proposed town boundaries.

- Reviewed the process with our State Representative, Bobby Harold Barbee.

Third Meeting (September 25, 2001):

- At this meeting the Red Cross Community voted on:

  - Voted on, and approved, naming the proposed town "Red Cross".

  - Voted on, and approved, having a mayor and town council (four council members) as the form of government.

  - Voted on, and approved, having the incorporation committee become the interim council when Red Cross becomes a town. This will be only until the first public election.

  - Voted on, and approved, the proposed town limits of Red Cross.

- All Statistical data was presented to the community:

  - The town is to be 2.24 square miles.

  - The statistical population of the town is 536 people.

  - Total number of dwellings is 212.

Fourth Meeting (October 25, 2001):

- The budget was presented, voted on, and passed.

- The town charter was presented and various components were voted on and passed.

APPENDIX-8

Note: This appendix is for illustration only, it has been several years since the information in this list has been used and it may no longer be valid.

THINGS-TO-DO TO INCORPORATE

1. Make sure the people are behind you. To file a petition you only have to have at least 15% of the registered voters sign the petition to incorporate to submit your petition. However, when it comes from the Legislature for referendum you must have a minimum of 51% of the voting people within the proposed town limits in favor of incorporation to be declared a town.

2. Although this might not seem all that important – it is imperative that you keep good minutes of all your public meetings. Record all vote counts – in favor, opposed, and those that abstain from voting. Appoint a secretary to keep records. It is not required that you make public notice of meetings during the incorporation process and prior to being sworn in on the town council, but once the town council is sworn in there cannot be a quorum of the council without public notice.

3. Communication is the most critical thing in getting incorporated. If you don't know – ask. Nearly everyone you seek advice from will be more than willing to help and often will offer additional useful information. This is the paid government employees - they know

what they are talking about. Be careful of elected officials - they often tell what they think as being fact without really knowing the fact.

4. Be sure you can meet the criteria of GS 120-163 and GS 120-164. If you can't then your petition will never clear the Joint Commission on Municipal Incorporations. These can be pulled up on the North Carolina Legislative web site.

   Need to check these out:

   NCGS 120-163 - Petition Requirements
   NCGS 120-164 - Notifications
   NCGS 120-166 - Proximity to Another Municipality
   NCGS 120-167 - Population Density
   NCGS 120-168 - Percent Development
   NCGS 120-169 - Boundary Requirements
   NCGS 120-169 - Required Services
   NCGS 120-170 - Tax Rates

Here is the outline we used:

- The Community requesting incorporation must have a petition signed by at least 15% of the registered voters in the incorporation area.
- The petition signatures must be verified by the county board of elections.
    - The petition must include:
    - The purposed name for the city.
    - A map of the city.
    - A paper survey of the city. (Check NCGS 120-163, may not have to do this?)
    - A list of services to be provided. Four of the following eight must be provided:
        i. Police protection
        ii. Fire protection
        iii. Solid waste collection or disposal
        iv. Water distribution

v. Street maintenance
vi. Street construction or right-of-way acquisition
vii. Street lighting
viii. Zoning

- A list of at least three people that will be serving on the interim government.
- A provisional charter for the town.
- The following statistical information must be included:
  i. estimated population
  ii. Assessed valuation
  iii. Degree of development
  iv. Population density
  v. Recommended form of government
  vi. Manner of elections
- A statement that the proposed municipality will have a budget ordinance with an ad valorem tax levy of at least five cents (5¢) on the one hundred dollar ($100.00) must be included.
- Include a statement of intent that the proposed municipality will offer four of the following services no later than the first day of the third fiscal year following the effective date of the incorporation:
  i. police protection
  ii. fire protection
  iii. solid waste collection or disposal
  iv. water distribution
  v. street maintenance
  vi. street construction or right-of-way acquisition
  vii. street lighting
  viii. zoning

5. There is a book, "Incorporation of a North Carolina Town" by Dr. David M. Lawrence, ISBN 1-56011-334-0 that is an excellent reference. Suggest getting a copy

6. Insure you have sufficient Legislative support. Although you will be dealing with the technical issues associated with the incorporation

process the final decision will be made on the floor of the Legislature. Bottom line is that this is a political decision – not technical. If you don't have the Legislative support then it will not pass, regardless of having met all the qualifications.

Suggest that you have a preliminary map of the desired area to be incorporated with some estimates of your ability to meet the criteria and the level of support within the community. This will help cognatize your local Legislator to your cause.

7. I would suggest keeping a low profile until you are well into the process. Hold a meeting of the people in your community to see if they support the effort. If they do then be prepared to make a public announcement to the local papers shortly afterwards. If you anticipate resistance, or special interest interference, then you may want to keep the public announcement low-key. It is possible that neighboring towns may have long-term plans of annexing you or have some reasons for not wanting to see you incorporate. If that is the case they can also address the local Legislators and try to persuade them not to support your efforts.

   Being involved in an incorporation process will not give you protection from annexation. However, if your Representative/Senator is behind you then they will probably not support an involuntary annexation attempt. Also, do not offend any official, City, County, or State – you are coming to them for their help! We found almost everyone to be very competent and helpful.

8. Go through NCGS 120.163 and NCGS 120.164 – break both of these statutes down into checklist and be sure to comply with all the criteria. Don't leave anything out or it will kick you out during the certification process in Raleigh – especially during the review done by the Joint Commission on Municipal Incorporations.

9. Get maps of the area (at least half-a-dozen) and determine the town boundaries. This has to be done before you can really do anything else. Use your County's GIS office.

- All land must be contiguous. Must not have any internal areas (completely encapsulated) that will not be included in the incorporation.
- Note requirements for distance from population centers. If you are too close to another town, depending on population, then you may not be allowed to incorporate. Verify this with the County GIS and the NCGS requirements that you have downloaded.
- Must have at least 250 people per square mile. This can be a statistical number based on the last US Census. Can get database from County GIS office.
- Must have at least 40% development. Count each house as 6.42 acres of developed land, regardless of the actual acres. Each house will count as 2.53 people and the occupancy rate for Stanly County is 92% for population numbers. Verify these numbers for your county - they may be different.
- See other required criteria as relates to proximity to other towns and county lines. This can be found in NCGS 120.163 and NCGS 120.164.

10. Determine the tax base of the proposed town. The County Tax Assessor can provide this information once you have defined your town boundaries. NCGS states that it must not be less than $0.05 per $100.00 valuation.

11. Determine the services to be offered. Get quotes from potential service providers. You will not be able to receive Sales & Use Tax until you start providing services. You must provide a minimum of 4 of the 8 listed services (see NCGS 163/164 for list).

12. Determine a budget. I would suggest projecting it out at least three years. You will not have to provide services until January 1, of the third year of incorporation. It should be noted that if you don't have expenses for at least four of the specified services stated in NCGS 120-163 you will not be eligible for sales and use tax. This tax is money sent to you on a per-capita basis and will probably be

somewhere around $110.00 per person per year. For example, if you have 1,000 people then this will amount to $110,000 additional income for the Town. Be sure to budget and incur expenses for four of these items in your budget. Must have a balanced budget!

13. Determine a tax rate. Suggest you plan for what it will cost when you get to full operation. You will be starting out with nothing in the bank and will need to build some working capital.

14. Identify a lawyer, for record, to be the town attorney. They should have municipal law experience. Most, if not all, this work does not require a lawyer – we didn't use one at all even though we had one listed as the attorney of record. Our incorporation cost was less than $500 – this was mostly for maps, postage, and supplies.

15. Determine the form of government (ex. town council with mayor).

16. Determine who will be serving on the interim council. The mayor does not have to be declared until incorporation. The mayor can be chosen at one of the incorporation meetings, by those serving on the incorporation committee. The mayor will have to be determined before the swearing-in ceremony.

    Some towns do not elect a mayor and choose to let the council appoint the mayor from within the elected council.

17. Draw up a town charter.

18. Something that we didn't do but I would highly recommend is get some sort of commitment from the people on how they want their town set up after incorporation. Put it in writing and get it voted by the community. Think of it as a post-incorporation vision statement. It will cut down on a lot of potential chaos after incorporation.

19. Get petition signatures (must have at least 15% of the voting population signing). Only registered voters can sign the petition. Get a copy of the voter registration database for the proposed

incorporation area from the board of Elections to verify that each person is in fact registered to vote. It is suggested you take voter registration forms with you. A lot of people will think they are registered but are not. Get them to fill the form out while you are there, get them back and personally take them to the Board of Elections. If you can get 80%+ you may be able to avoid referendum.

The petition must include the following:

- Reference to a tax rate for the proposed town.
- List of services to be offered. Must have minimum of four of eight specified services as pertains to NCGS 120.163.
- Map of proposed town.
- List of the people to serve on the interim town board – with a brief description of each person.
- Proposed town charter.
- Statement of statistics – population, assessed valuation, degree of development, population density, and form of government.

One item that we weren't aware of when we got our petition signed was that the date of birth of the person signing the petition must be included. We had to go back and get everyone's date of birth before we could submit the signatures.

20. Send letters (certified) to all towns within the County and to the County Commissioners notifying them of your intent to incorporate. Retain copies of all receipts pertaining to mailing these letters. Keep all returned letters. Would advise not doing this until well into the process and your intent is already public.

21. Send notice of intent to incorporate to paper – must run for two weeks prior to sending to Raleigh. Should be one of the last items before submitting petition.

22. With respect to the paper survey, I'm not sure what to tell you. We were told that we had to do one, however, NCGS 120-163 states that either by map or paper survey. You will need to check to see what the current requirement is. If you have to do one, it is not required that

it be done by a surveyor. It is not a physical survey. If required it will need to be included in petition to incorporate. We did our own.

23. Be prepared to submit you petition to your Legislator thirty days prior to the opening of the Legislative session. You will want your petition on the floor before any counter attempts can be mounted and you also want to be incorporated before the fiscal year begins on July 1 for tax purposes.

24. Give to your Legislator – he will give it to the Joint Commission on Incorporations for review. They will go through your information in detail.

25. The Joint Commission on Municipal Incorporations will review the criteria for your petition before it goes to the Legislature. They will give a positive or negative recommendation. If the recommendation is negative then it will not go to the Legislature. The contact person that we dealt with was (name omitted), North Carolina Division of Community Assistance, XXXX Mail Service Center, Raleigh, NC 27699-4313, phone (919) XXX-XXXX. He was very helpful.

26. Monitor bill progress through the Legislature. Be sure it doesn't stall anywhere – if it looks as if it is starting to stall then call your Legislator and get it moving again. If you expect any opposition be prepared to have someone in Raleigh to intercede on your behalf at any time you think the bill will be going before committee or for vote. If possible, keep everything low-key and professional and don't try to elaborate on items unless asked and then only respond to the actual question asked. Do not volunteer unnecessary information.

27. Be prepared to address zoning immediately after incorporation. At the time you incorporate the County zoning for the incorporated area will cease to exist and you will need to put something in place to fill the void. Misenheimer had a committee working on theirs during the incorporation process and was able to put their zoning in place almost immediately. Red Cross adopted the County zoning until such time as it could develop its own. Also, if anyone is outside of

compliance for their zoning you will need to have it read in at the zoning hearing so that the carryover can be enforced. If you don't then the people that are out of compliance will most likely be considered grandfathered and you will not be able to enforce it at a later date. If you don't adopt zoning within 60-days of incorporation then you will lose the right to set zoning!

28. Traditionally it takes a year and a half to two years from the time you start till you get incorporated. We did it in eleven and a half months. Don't let things go idle - keep it progressing. Also, don't let internal sub-groups split the incorporation process. If either of these happen then you will probably not make it.

Call me if you have any questions along the way. GOOD LUCK!

Ray Quick
(704) XXX-XXX